Social Studies in Elementary Education

Eleventh Edition

Walter C. Parker
University of Washington

Merrill
Prentice Hall

Upper Saddle River, New Jersey
Columbus, Ohio

Library of Congress Cataloging-in-Publication Data
Parker, Walter.
   Social studies in elementary education / Walter C. Parker.–11th ed.
      p. cm.
   Includes bibliographical references and index.
   ISBN 0-13-021337-3
      1. Social sciences–Study and teaching (Elementary)–United States. I. Title.

LB1584 .J3 2001
372.83'044'0973–dc21   00-028366

Vice President and Publisher: Jeffery W. Johnston
Editor: Bradley J. Potthoff and Linda Montgomery
Development Editor: Hope Madden
Production Editor: Mary M. Irvin
Design Coordinator: Karrie Converse-Jones
Photo Coordinator: Sandy Lenahan
Text Design: Books by Design
Cover Designer: Debra Rosario
Cover Art: Debra and Jeremy Rosario
Production Manager: Pamela D. Bennett
Director of Marketing: Kevin Flanagan
Marketing Manager: Amy June
Marketing Services Manager: Krista Groshong

This book was set in Minion by Carlisle Communications, Ltd. and was printed and bound by R. R. Donnelley & Sons Company. The cover was printed by Phoenix Color Corp.

Photo Credits: Silver Burdett Ginn: 2; Anthony Magnacca/Merrill: 9, 58, 144, 178, 195, 230, 254, 266, 284, 332, 340; David Young-Wolff/Tony Stone Images: 19; Laimute Druskis/PH College: 26; Barbara Schwartz/Merrill: 45, 235; Carol Hamilton Cobb: 75; Lynchburg Police Department: 79; Charles Gatewood/PH College: 96; Tom Watson/Merrill: 118; Courtesy of Southern Oregon Historical Society: 112, 354, 410; Anne Vega/Merrill: 154, 212, 380, 386; Richard Hutchings/Silver Burdett Ginn: 196; Scott Cunningham/ Merrill: 275, 320, 396; Susan Robichaud: 294; U.S. Fish and Wildlife Service: 434.

10 9 8 7 6 5 4 3
ISBN 0-13-021337-3

For Chalmerse A. Parker and Martha McClurg Parker

My father's civic commitment and good nature and my mother's unrestrained kindness and quiet passion for literacy have sustained me. I wish to honor them with this book.

ABOUT THE AUTHOR

Dr. Walter Parker teaches in the College of Education at the University of Washington in Seattle and chairs the Social Studies Education Program. His interests center on K–12 social studies curriculum and instruction generally and education for democracy specifically. His other books include *Renewing the Social Studies Curriculum, Educating the Democratic Mind,* and the elementary school social studies program *Adventures in Time and Place.* Also, he is the editor of the social studies research column for *Social Education,* the journal of the National Council for the Social Studies.

Walter was born and raised in Englewood, Colorado, and he taught in Northglenn, Colorado for ten years. He has a B.A. in Political Science (University of Colorado at Boulder), an M.A. in Social Foundations of Education (University of Colorado at Denver), and the Ph.D. in Curriculum and Instruction (University of Washington at Seattle). Walter resides with his wife in Seattle, where he enjoys their garden, the rain, the bookstores, the coffeehouses, and the movies.

PREFACE

The purpose of this book continues as it has always been: to introduce new teachers to the world of social studies teaching and learning in elementary and middle schools, and to help them unleash their intelligence and creativity on this vitally important subject area. The social studies curriculum is a great collection of tools, ideas, and stories—a veritable garden of delights—without which children would be ill-equipped for both private life and public life in a fast-changing world.

The rationale of this book continues as well: Without historical understanding, there can be no wisdom; without geographical understanding, no social or environmental intelligence; without economic understanding, no sane use of resources and, therefore, no future; and without civic understanding, no democratic citizens and, therefore, no democracy. This is why social studies matters. When children are empowered by knowledgeable and skillful teachers with the ideas, skills, values, questions, and attitudes that compose the social studies curriculum, their *judgment* is improved. Consequently, they can reason historically, help solve community problems, appreciate diversity, protect the environment, and, with deep understanding, empathize with the hopes, dreams, and struggles of people everywhere.

Instructors and readers of the prior edition urged me to retain the same organization of the book, which they found so straightforward and uncomplicated. There are three parts: the first orients readers to the mission of social studies education and to the diverse children we teach; the second concentrates on the curriculum—*what* we try to teach; the third on instruction—*how* we try to teach it. There are thirteen chapters overall, one more than the prior edition to allow for a new chapter (9) that focuses squarely on resources for teaching and learning social studies.

Instructors and readers also have appreciated the "Sampler" which accompanies the text as an ancillary. It contains core excerpts from *Curriculum Standards for Social Studies: Expectations of Excellence,* which is the acclaimed set of standards and instructional vignettes from the good people at the National Council for the Social Studies. The members of the committee who wrote these standards and vignettes are listed at the front of the Sampler. I know how hard these people worked, and I thank them for this unique and practical resource.

The central emphasis on citizenship education in a diverse society continues as well. The children in today's classrooms are even more culturally and racially diverse than in the past, which translates into new challenges for teachers. Teachers cannot continue to attend only to yesterday's familiar and comfortable categories of differences among children: development and ability. Educationally sound and loving responses are needed as well to ethnic, linguistic, gender, religious, and racial differences. Chapter 2 focuses squarely on diversity in the classroom, and this theme pervades the book. Children's story books, for example, are appreciated not only for the historical narratives they can convey, but also because different stories about the same event can help children understand that multiple perspectives are part-and-parcel of historical study. They are the norm, not the exception.

Citizenship education has a chapter of its own as well. At the same time that diversity is increasing in our society (*literally* increasing: there are more languages in the classroom each year, more religions, more cultures) and the quest to educate *all* our children intensifies as well, we teachers must also step up our efforts to nurture the common ground and the common good—the democratic ideals and institutions that stretch across our differences and bind us together in a civic community. Diversity is no threat to this civic unity. "We the people" created the government of the United States in part to protect this diversity. Educating children in such a way that they will not only exercise their freedom and celebrate their differences but take on the responsibilities of citizenship is the great mission of social studies education. There is much that teachers of even the youngest children can do, as readers will see in the pages that follow.

New to this edition

As there is continuity, so is there change. Much is new and renewed in this eleventh edition. It is more practical than ever, with more ready-to-use applications. You will find in chapter 3 a new idea-filled section on teaching about voting and elections, and in chapter 4 a new section on teaching historical reasoning to children—teaching them to "think like historians" rather than only absorbing history (though that is important, too). The chapter on lesson and unit planning (7) now comes before the chapter on teaching strategies. The teaching strategies chapter (8) concentrates on just three "classic" strategies for teaching social studies material at any grade level: concept formation, inquiry, and a time-honored procedure for teaching social studies skills. These are instructional methods or *scaffolds* that no beginning teacher would want to be without, and they are beloved by legions of award-winning social studies teachers. Of course, many additional strategies are detailed elsewhere in the text.

There are other changes as well. The following list gives the highlights:

- **Lesson Plans:** New model Lesson Plans are included that work well for beginning teachers. Now 19 model lesson plans pervade the text, including the four in the final chapter that make up the integrated unit called *Explore.* Each Lesson Plan features important social studies content, a sensible procedure, assessment, and ideas for curriculum integration. Additional lesson plans are available on the text's Companion Website.

- **Assessment:** There are scoring rubrics and portfolios for historical reasoning, map work, civic discussion, and literature, and chapter 10 lays the foundation.

- **Resources:** A separate resource chapter (9) has been added. From guest speakers to field trips, from the school multimedia center to the Internet, from textbooks to children's literature—knowledge of resources can make *the* difference to a new teacher.

- **Technology:** Technology/Internet applications run (should I say "speed"?) through the book. Ten "virtual field trips" are included for the first time in the new Resources chapter. Included in each chapter are a number of URLs to help readers expand their study of the content. These websites are conveniently linked to the text's Companion Website.

- **Integration:** The final chapter, *Social Studies as the Integrating Core,* has been revised to clarify the two most common and essential approaches to integrating social studies with other school subjects: infusion and fusion.

- **Considerate Text:** Each chapter opens with a "Chapter Snapshot" that captures the chapter contents in action, plus Main Idea, Key Concepts, and Chapter Outline. Also, there is a helpful introduction and conclusion to each chapter.

- **Cooperative Learning and Current Events.** These two topics continue as major chapters, but they have been pruned and sharpened so that they are directly relevant to new teachers of social studies.

Acknowledgments

I am grateful first and foremost to Professor John Jarolimek, for the invitation to assume responsibility for this book. John authored the first edition of this book in 1959. He was then on the faculty at San Diego State College (now San Diego State University); I was ten years old and a fifth-grader in Englewood, Colorado. John joined the faculty of the College of Education at the University of Washington in Seattle in 1962; I did likewise in 1985. With the 1993 revision of this text (the 9th edition), John invited me to join him as co-author with the understanding that I would gradually move into the driver's seat. With the present edition, the eleventh, John bids you farewell. He and I remain dear friends, and he is surely the book's closest reader. Perhaps no one has as many admiring friends in the worldwide social studies community as John Jarolimek.

I am indebted to a number of individuals who assisted in procuring photographs, artwork, and other materials. Sincere thanks go to Sharon Pray Muir, Oakland University; Michael Simpson, National Council for the Social Studies; Tom Condon, McGraw-Hill School Division; Kristin Palmquist, California Department of Education; Joseph A. Braun, Jr., Illinois State University; and my able assistant, Julie Rieg.

I want to express my gratitude and appreciation as well to a number of persons who gave generously of their time, whether reading drafts, offering suggestions, or otherwise challenging my thinking. These include Sheila Valencia, James A. Banks, Theodore Kaltsounis, Sam Wineburg, Geneva Gay, Allen Glenn, David Harris, Pam Grossman, Barbara McKean, Bob Howard, Akira Ninomiya, John Cogan, Roland Case, Ken Osborne, Carole Hahn, Somwung Pitiyanuwat, Diana Hess, Mary McFarland, Gloria Ladson-Billings, Barry Beyer, Jean Craven, Gloria Contreras, Valerie Ooka Pang, Bill Stanley, Paula Fraser, Doug Selwyn, Brad Coulter, Tarry Lindquist, Paulette Thompson, Bruce Larson, Terry Beck, Patricia Espiritu, Jonathan Miller-Lane, Carole Hahn, Nathaniel Jackson, Pat Avery, Pam and Gene Edgar, and Joe and Kathy Jenkins.

Heartfelt thanks also go to the reviewers who evaluated the previous edition of this book and offered such helpful suggestions for the current edition: Robert Agostino, Duquesne

University; Sally R. Beisser, Drake University; Kent Freeland, Morehead State University; Nancy P. Gallavan, University of Nevada, Las Vegas; Felipe V. Golez, California State University, Long Beach; Bruce E. Larson, Western Washington University; Barbara McKean, University of Arizona; Jay A. Monson, Utah State University; Tony Sanchez, Purdue University; and Wilson J. Warren, Indiana State University.

I was most fortunate, as well, to have the caring attention, commitment, and patience of my editors at Merrill: Brad Potthoff, Mary Irvin, and Hope Madden, and copyeditor Cindy Peck.

DISCOVER THE COMPANION WEBSITE ACCOMPANYING THIS BOOK

The Prentice Hall Companion Website: A Virtual Learning Environment

Technology is a constantly growing and changing aspect of our field that is creating a need for content and resources. To address this emerging need, Prentice Hall has developed an online learning environment for students and professors alike—Companion Websites—to support our textbooks.

In creating a Companion Website, our goal is to build on and enhance what the textbook already offers. For this reason, the content for each user-friendly website is organized by chapter and provides the professor and student with a variety of meaningful resources. Common features of a Companion Website include:

For the Professor

Every Companion Website integrates **Syllabus Manager**™, an online syllabus creation and management utility.

- **Syllabus Manager**™ provides you, the instructor, with an easy, step-by-step process to create and revise syllabi, with direct links into Companion Website and other online content without having to learn HTML.
- Students may logon to your syllabus during any study session. All they need to know is the web address for the Companion Website and the password you've assigned to your syllabus.
- After you have created a syllabus using **Syllabus Manager**™, students may enter the syllabus for their course section from any point in the Companion Website.
- Clicking on a date, the student is shown the list of activities for the assignment. The activities for each assignment are linked directly to actual content, saving time for students.
- Adding assignments consists of clicking on the desired due date, then filling in the details for the assignment—name of the assignment, instruction, and whether or not it it a one-time or repeating assignment.

- In addition, links to other activities can be created easily. If the activity is online, a URL can be entered in the space provided, and it will be linked automatically in the final syllabus.
- Your completed syllabus is hosted on our servers, allowing convenient updates from any computer on the Internet. Changes you make to your syllabus are immediately available to your students at their next logon.

For the Student

- **Chapter Objectives** – outline key concepts from the text
- **Interactive Self-quizzes** – complete with hints and automatic grading that provide immediate feedback for students

  After students submit their answers for the interactive self-quizzes, the Companion Website **Results Reporter** computes a percentage grade, provides a graphic representation of how many questions were answered correctly and incorrectly, and gives a question by question analysis of the quiz. Students are given the option to send their quiz to up to four email addresses (professor, teaching assistant, study partner, etc.).
- **Message Board** – serves as a virtual bulletin board to post—or respond to—questions or comments to/from a national audience
- **Chat** – real-time chat with anyone who is using the text anywhere in the country—ideal for discussion and study groups, class projects, etc.
- **Web Destinations** – links to www sites that relate to chapter content
- **Additional Resources** – access to chapter-specific or general content that enhances material found in the text

To take advantage of these and other resources, please visit the *Social Studies in Elementary Education* Companion Website at

www.prenhall.com/parker

CONTENTS

PART II   Social Studies Curriculum   57

PART III   Planning and Teaching Social Studies   211

12 The Literacy-Social Studies Connection 380

LESSON PLANS

On-line Lesson Plans

Please visit www.prenhall.com/parker to access the following lesson plans.

1 Writing an Autobiography

2 Becoming a Citizen

3 Multiple Perspectives

4 Comparing Communities: Geographic Themes

Orientation to Social Studies Education

CHAPTER 1

Social Studies Education: What and Why

Main Idea

The purpose of social studies education is to help students develop *social understanding* (e.g., knowledge of people and places near and far and of what happened in the past) and *civic efficacy* (e.g., the ability to think and act as a democratic citizen in a diverse society).

Key Concepts

social studies, social understanding, civic efficacy, curriculum goals, scope and sequence, grade and unit topics, conceptual themes

Chapter Outline

- Goals for the Social Studies: Social Understanding and Civic Efficacy
- Curriculum Scope and Sequence
- Trends
- Conclusion
- Discussion Questions and Suggested Activities
- Selected References
- Notes

Chapter Snapshot

As they come into class, the kindergarten children are excited to find a large strip of paper going down the middle of the classroom floor. Their teacher, Jacob Stern, tells them to hang up their coats and come sit beside the paper strip. The strip, he tells them, is a highway connecting two distant towns. Mr. Stern takes a toy car and starts driving it along the highway. "What might happen as someone drives along?" he asks. The children suggest a number of possibilities: running out of gas, getting tired, and being hungry. "What services might be necessary for people as they drive from town to town?" Tanisha suggests a gas station. A milk carton is placed along the highway and named "Tanisha's Gas Station."[1]

 A favorite website http://www.ncss.org/. This is the home page for the National Council for the Social Studies. It features teaching resources, discussion groups, conferences, summer workshops, and more.

Without historical understanding, there can be no wisdom. Without geographical understanding, there can be no social or environmental intelligence. And without civic understanding, there can be no democratic citizens and, therefore, no democracy. This is why social studies matters.

Seated in today's classrooms are children who, as senior citizens, will help this nation—the world's oldest constitutional democracy—celebrate its three hundredth anniversary in 2076. This, of course, assumes such an event will actually occur. Whether this nation survives that long depends in no small measure on how well today's school children are taught the ideas and information, the skills and habits, and the rights and responsibilities of democratic citizenship. When the public school movement developed momentum in the 1840s, the motivating vision was of a well-educated public that could meet the challenge of self-government, which is the defining attribute of democracy. In democracies, the people *themselves* are expected to be the rulers, solving problems and making policy, protecting diversity, and ensuring the liberty of people to express even unpopular views. With each new outbreak of "ethnic cleansing" (genocide) somewhere in the world, with each new hate crime committed in our own communities, with each such assault on the democratic ideal, we are reminded that democracy is a fragile social and political system. Many people in the United States take democracy for granted these days, but schoolteachers cannot afford to do so. In this respect, teachers must be civic leaders who understand that an ignorant or mis-educated public cannot maintain a democracy.

> Democracy is not a "machine that would go of itself," but must be consciously reproduced, one generation instructing the next in the knowledge and skills, as well as in the civic character and commitments required for its sustenance.[2]

Democracy is the only widely accepted path yet to have been invented for societies that are heterogeneous with respect to religion, race, ethnicity, social class, and national origin *and* that are committed to protecting and honoring this diversity. The democratic ideal celebrates government "of, by, and for the people," as President Lincoln said in his speech at Gettysburg, *and* it does not tolerate repression or discrimination. Democracy, then, is much more than a political system; *it is a way of life*—a way of being with one another, whether in the city hall, the shopping mall, or the classroom. It is certainly not a perfect path; in fact, it is frustrating, contentious, and often exasperating. The only thing worse than democracy, the saying goes, is all the alternatives. If democracy is to be the vision that holds this diverse society together, then the people must be educated for it. There can be no democracy without democratic citizens.

Goals for the Social Studies: Social Understanding and Civic Efficacy

According to the National Council for the Social Studies (NCSS), social studies education can be defined as follows:

> Social studies is the integrated study of the social sciences and humanities to promote civic competence. The primary purpose of social studies is to help young people develop the ability to make informed and reasoned decisions for the public good as citizens of a culturally diverse, democratic society in an interdependent world.[3]

This definition is like a two-sided coin. On one side is the subject matter that is studied. "Subject matter" is education jargon for the *what* of teaching and learning—the *curriculum*. It includes the facts, ideas, skills, issues, and methods of inquiry drawn from the array of fields called the social sciences: history, geography, civics and government (political science), economics, sociology, psychology, and anthropology. The humanities—philosophy, ethics, literature, religion, music and the visual and performing arts—are involved as well.[4] These fields of study or disciplines serve as *resources*: The social studies curriculum draws on them, blending and integrating them as needed to provide children with meaningful learning experiences. But to what ends? What are the goals?

On the other side of the coin is the purpose, which we introduced earlier as democratic citizenship: "the ability to make informed and reasoned decisions for the public good as citizens of a culturally diverse, democratic society in an interdependent world."

Another way to think about the two sides of this definitional coin is found in the vision statement of the NCSS: "Powerful social studies teaching helps students develop social understanding and civic efficacy."[5] *Social understanding* is knowledge of human beings' social worlds drawn from history, geography, the other social sciences, and the humanities. *Civic efficacy* is the readiness and willingness to assume citizenship responsibilities. These responsibilities include more than just voting. In a democracy, it is also one's responsibility to serve on juries and to be just and lawful; one is expected to be tolerant of political and cultural differences; it is one's duty to participate in creating and evaluating public policy; and it is one's duty to be civic-minded—that is, to think not only of oneself and one's rights and freedoms but also of the good of the whole community. In general, one must be both able and willing to walk the democratic path.

Schools typically approach these broad goals by way of three subgoals: knowledge, attitudes and values, and skills. More specific objectives are typically listed under each subgoal. When readers examine their state and local social studies curriculum guidelines, they will most likely find that the guidelines take this form or one that is similar.

KNOWLEDGE

Which social knowledge is most important? We can answer this question in three ways: disciplines, themes, and topics.

One way is to refer to the fields of study—the disciplines—where this knowledge is created. As we saw above, these are the fields of history, geography, civics and government (political science), economics, sociology, psychology, and anthropology.

But these are large fields containing huge numbers of ideas and information! Another way to answer which social knowledge is most important is to identify crucial themes drawn from these fields. Themes help teachers narrow the scope somewhat and give them a better idea of which social knowledge deserves the most attention. The *Curriculum Standards for Social Studies* created by the National Council for the Social Studies identifies 10 such themes. They are rapidly becoming the best-known knowledge themes for social studies instruction in the elementary and middle grades:

1. Culture
2. Time, Continuity, and Change

3. People, Places, and Environments
4. Individual Development and Identity
5. Individuals, Groups, and Institutions
6. Power, Authority, and Governance
7. Production, Distribution, and Consumption
8. Science, Technology, and Society
9. Global Connections and Interdependence
10. Civic Ideals and Practice

Take a minute now to read in the accompanying *Sampler* the brief descriptions of each of the 10 themes. The remainder of the *Sampler* spells out each theme and gives teaching examples for both early grades and middle grades. An NCSS website gives more details on each theme and provides links to teaching resources for each: *http://www.ncss.org/links/home.html*

A third way to answer the "Which knowledge?" question is to identify *topics*. For example, students should know about:

- The history, geography, and cultures of their neighborhood, community, and home state; how they are similar to and different from other places in the world; how people live and work there; how they depend on one another to meet their basic needs.
- The history and geography of the United States.
- The history and geography of the world.
- The foundations and principles of American constitutional democracy.
- The laws and government of the community, state, and nation.
- The world of work, of earning and saving, of production and consumption, in the local community, the state, the nation, and world.
- Basic human institutions (the family, education, religion, government, and the economy) and their variety across cultures.
- Human-environment interaction.
- Current events and enduring public issues.
- Men and women who have made a difference in their communities and beyond.

Looking back at the three ways of answering the question, "Which knowledge is most important?" we see 7 disciplines, 10 themes, and 10 topics. This should give readers a good, although very general, understanding of the goals of the social studies curriculum. Before we aim for a more detailed understanding, we should first get a similarly general understanding of the other social studies goals.

ATTITUDES AND VALUES

The second subgoal of social studies learning—attitudes and values—is directed less at rational knowledge and more at the affective domain, that is, the realm of emotion, feeling, loyalty, and commitment. Particular attitudes and values, also called dispositions or virtues, are essential to democratic citizenship. Without them, democratic government and civic life would be impossible. What are they? The following are typical examples of what readers will find listed in state and local curriculum guidelines in this category.

1. Developing a reasoned commitment to the public values of this society as suggested in its historical documents, laws, court decisions, and pledges (e.g., "liberty and justice for all").
2. Being able to deal justly and effectively with value conflicts that arise when making decisions about the common good.
3. Knowing the basic human rights guaranteed to all citizens and the role of constitutional democracy in protecting those rights.
4. Developing a reasoned loyalty to this nation and its form of government. Note that the "Pledge of Allegiance" is made not to a person but to a form of government: a republic (constitutional democracy).
5. Developing a feeling of kinship to human beings everywhere—to the human family.
6. Treating oneself and others with respect.
7. Taking responsibility for one's actions and fulfilling one's obligations to the political community.

SKILLS

The third subgoal—skills—identifies what students should be able to *do*. Of course, doing involves knowing; skillful behavior is skillful to a great extent because of the knowledge that supports it. A child is skillful at something because he or she *knows* how to do it well. Accordingly, the first and third subgoals, knowledge and skills, are closely related. This category often is subdivided as follows:

I. Democratic Participation Skills

   A. Listening to, expressing, and challenging opinions and reasons.
   B. Participating in classroom, school, and community decision making. Especially, participating in group discussions of public issues (classroom, community, international) with persons with whom one may disagree; leading such discussions; mediating, negotiating, and compromising.
   C. Working cooperatively to clarify a task and plan group work.
   D. Accessing, using, and planning community resources.

II. Study and Inquiry Skills (including reading and writing)

   A. Using and making time lines, maps, globes, charts, and graphs.
   B. Locating, gathering, organizing, and analyzing information from various resources such as books, electronic media, newspapers, and the library.
   C. Writing reports and giving oral reports.
   D. Distinguishing between primary and secondary sources.

E. Reading social studies materials for a variety of purposes—to get the main idea, to get information, to research all sides of a controversial issue, to detect author bias.

F. Forming and testing hypotheses.

III. Intellectual Skills

A. Identifying and clarifying problems and issues.

B. Drawing analogies from other times and places and inferring cause-effect relationships.

C. Drawing conclusions based on evidence.

D. Determining the strength of an argument or conclusion (critical thinking); distinguishing between fact and opinion; detecting propaganda.

E. Reasoning dialogically (arguing both for and against one's position on an issue).

Curriculum Scope and Sequence

Although most elementary and middle schools include history and the social science disciplines in their social studies programs, they do not ordinarily conduct separate courses in geography, history, political science, or the other social science disciplines. The usual organizational format combines components from more than a single field to form an interdisciplinary or integrated study around some theme or topic. For example, a sixth-grade class might study the topic "Crossroads of Three Continents—The Middle East." In such a study, geography would be essential, as would history, economics, and government. Doubtless, too, anthropology would be included because this area of the world was the birthplace of three of the world's major religions.

It is not the purpose of the elementary school to teach the social science disciplines apart from their relevance to children's lives. They should be taught in ways that will help children gain insight into the social and physical world in which they live. When children are making islands and mountains in the sandbox or learning to map the playground, they are dealing with geography in simple ways. When they learn about the need for agreed-upon rules in games, or when they compare the playground bully with the elected classroom president, they are beginning to understand basic ideas from political science (law, power, and legitimate and illegitimate authority). And when they dramatize the signing of the U.S. Constitution and are then helped to create a classroom constitution—a rulebook they agree to follow—they are having their first brush with history and self-government. In these ways, the subject matter is connected to what the children already know and do. But the curriculum should also broaden children's horizons, taking them to distant places and times—to the life of a scribe in Cleopatra's court, the boy crowned emperor in China, and village life in one of the first farming communities thousands of years ago. So, the social studies curriculum is connected to the child's life, *and* it enlarges that life outward to include the far away and the long ago. Thanks to children's vivid imaginations, this is often no great leap for them, but they need skillful adult guidance if the journeys are to be both enjoyable and productive.

Dramatizations with simple sets bring geography to life.

Study units and topics are consistent with the emphasis suggested by the district curriculum for that grade. Ordinarily, topics that have a concrete and familiar focus for children, such as homes, schools, families, neighborhoods, and communities, are placed in the primary grades. Topics that are more remote in space and time, such as the home state, the nation, and regions of the world, are focal points in the middle and upper grades. It must be emphasized, however, that this *does not* mean that first-graders spend a year studying *their* families, or that second-graders study only the local neighborhood or third-graders only the local community. Rather, a compare-and-contrast approach should be used. For example, children should learn how local houses and apartments are similar to and different from shelters long ago and far away. The same is true for families, neighborhoods, and communities. Contemporary social studies textbooks typically provide the necessary information for helping children make such comparisons: "Families and Friends in Canada and Mexico," "Island Homes and Desert Homes," and "America's First Communities" are typical of such units of study in the primary grades.

Teachers may begin a unit of study by focusing on aspects of topics familiar to the children, such as their own homes, schools, and families; then the study is expanded to include those same institutions long ago and far away. The movement from things that are close to those that are distant, either in time or place, helps to build a firm foundation for later learning. An NCSS position statement on early childhood social studies instruction makes this point clearly:

> One of the most important conclusions one can draw from the available research on early learning in social studies is the critical importance of the elementary years in laying the foundation for later and increasingly mature understanding. *There is reason to believe that teachers*

who miss these crucial opportunities to build interest, to introduce concepts from history and the social sciences, and to develop social perspectives and civic understanding may make it more difficult for citizens of the 21st Century to cope with their future.[6]

Building a firm foundation in an earlier grade to support learning that should occur in a later grade is the reason curriculum directors carefully plan the "scope and sequence" of a social studies program. The *scope* of the program refers to the subject matter—the information, ideas, skills, values, and attitudes—that the program is to include. The *sequence* is the order in which the various subject matters are to be presented. Below is a scope and sequence plan published by the National Council for the Social Studies.[7]

> Kindergarten—Awareness of Self in a Social Setting
>
> Grade 1—The Individual in Primary Social Groups: Understanding School and Family Life
>
> Grade 2—Meeting Basic Needs in Nearby Social Groups: Neighborhoods
>
> Grade 3—Sharing Earth-Space with Others: Communities
>
> Grade 4—Human Life in Varied Environments: Regions
>
> Grade 5—People of the Americas: The United States and Its Close Neighbors
>
> Grade 6—People and Cultures: The Eastern Hemisphere
>
> Grade 7—A Changing World of Many Nations: A Global View
>
> Grade 8—Building a Strong and Free Nation: The United States
>
> Grade 9—Systems That Make a Democratic Society Work: Law, Justice, and Economics
>
> Grade 10—Origins of Major Cultures: A World History
>
> Grade 11—The Maturing of America: United States History
>
> Grade 12—One-year course or courses required; selection(s) to be made from the following:
>
> Issues and Problems of Modern Society
>
> Introduction to the Social Sciences
>
> The Arts in Human Societies
>
> International Area Studies
>
> Supervised Experience in Community Affairs

Now, let's draw all this together. Please look again at the 10 themes identified in *Curriculum Standards for Social Studies* (see pages 5–6 and the accompanying *Sampler*). How might such themes be used with a scope and sequence plan of this kind? It is important to note that the 10 themes are ideas or, more precisely, concepts. Furthermore, as the *Curriculum Standards for Social Studies* make clear, these themes are recommended as the basis for instruction in *each* grade, kindergarten through 12th. What we can do, then, is select a grade level from the scope and sequence plan above (or the one provided by a local school district) and use the 10 themes to help plan units and lessons. For example, let us select the grade 3 emphasis, communities, and think of some focus questions that will engage children with each of the 10 themes.

GRADE 3, SHARING EARTH-SPACE WITH OTHERS: COMMUNITIES

1. Culture. How do the ways of life of people living in our community differ from those of people living in our sister cities in Japan and Russia?

2. Time, Continuity, and Change. What were the turning points in our community's history?

3. People, Places, and Environments. Why is our community located where it is, and how would our lives be different if it was located on the edge of the sea, in a desert, on an island, or high in the mountains?

4. Individual Development and Identity. How does learning in school differ from the learning that takes place elsewhere in our community—on the job, on the playing field, at home, at a city council meeting?

5. Individuals, Groups, and Institutions. What after-school clubs do young people belong to in our community, and how do they differ from those in our sister cities in China and Kenya?

6. Power, Authority, and Governance. What are the chief controversies people in our community face today over freedoms and rights, on the one hand, and responsibilities for the common good, on the other?

7. Production, Distribution, and Consumption. What things do people in our community want that they don't really need? How are these different from the wants and needs in our sister cities?

8. Science, Technology, and Society. How do our values influence the use of buses and cars in this community?

9. Global Connections and Interdependence. What three products are imported in the greatest quantities to our community? Are any products exported?

10. Civic Ideals and Practice. Who is eligible to vote in this community? Where can they register to vote? What percentage of them voted in the last presidential election? In the last local election? What can our class do to encourage eligible voters to vote?

What did we just do? In this example, we used two resources to create a powerful third-grade social studies curriculum. We took the topic "communities" from the NCSS scope-and-sequence recommendation, and then we elaborated the "scope" of that topic by using the 10 conceptual themes from the NCSS "curriculum standards."

Take some time now to draft a similar example for another grade level. This will give you experience in thinking conceptually about the social studies topical emphasis of a

GRADE 4, HUMAN LIFE IN VARIED ENVIRONMENTS: REGIONS

1. Culture.

   _____

   _____

2. Time, Continuity, and Change.

   _____

   _____

3. People, Places, and Environments.

   _____

   _____

4. Individual Development and Identity.

   _____

   _____

5. Individuals, Groups, and Institutions.

   _____

   _____

6. Power, Authority, and Governance.

   _____

   _____

7. Production, Distribution, and Consumption.

   _____

   _____

8. Science, Technology, and Society.

   _____

   _____

9. Global Connections and Interdependence.

   _____

   _____

10. Civic Ideals and Practice.

   _____

   _____

given grade level. Above, we applied the 10 conceptual themes to the topic of communities. The same can be repeated for the fourth-grade emphasis, geographic regions, or the fifth-grade emphasis, United States history, and so on. Let's try the fourth grade. You will probably need the accompanying *Sampler* to bolster your understanding of the 10 themes.

This is one of the most important curriculum-planning habits any teacher could develop. The gist of it, to review, is to apply the 10 social studies conceptual themes to the subject matter topical emphasis at a given grade level. In so doing, the *scope* of the topic is expanded and deepened so that a student's understanding is also expanded and deepened. Without this kind of planning, the teacher will be limited to skating across the thin surface of a topic, communicating facts about it, perhaps, but not helping students to organize the facts into powerful ideas that they can then apply to the *next* topic, and the *next*, and so on. With this kind of planning, students not only learn the *topic* that is currently emphasized, but they also learn *concepts* with which they can grasp more about subsequent topics. What results is a "snowball effect" that empowers students in each subsequent grade. Researchers call this the "Matthew Effect," named after the idea expressed in the Book of Matthew that the rich get richer and the poor get poorer. In modern terms, the rich get richer because they are able to invest their surplus, earning still more, which they can reinvest, and so on. The analogy to education is that the knowledgeable become more knowledgeable. The knowledge they already possess enables them to learn still more. Children become more knowledgeable as their *prior* knowledge serves as a fertile seedbed in which subsequent knowledge can take root.[8] A mind furnished with powerful concepts is indeed a fertile ground for the germination of new ideas.

UNIT TOPICS

We now provide examples of unit topics taught in grades K–8 in schools across the nation. These examples should not be construed as a model curriculum; they will not be precisely the same as those found in any specific school program. Rather, our intention is to help readers gain a better idea of what subject matter may actually be taught at different grade levels.

Kindergarten

Kindergarten programs ordinarily deal with topics that help to familiarize children with their immediate surroundings. The home and school provide the setting for these studies. With some kindergarten children it is possible to include, in a simple way, references to the world beyond their immediate environment:

Learning About Myself	Rules for Safe Living
Continents and the Globe	People Change the Earth
Working Together at School	Hooray for Holidays

Grade 1

Grade-1 studies are based in the local area, such as the school and neighborhood, but provision is made to associate the local area with the larger world. Basic work with history and geography begins. Units should provide for easy transition from the near-at-hand to the far away and back again at frequent intervals:

Who We Are and Where We Live	Diversity Now and Long Ago
Families at Work	Great Americans
Families Around the World	Farms, Cities, Islands, Jungles

Grade 2

The grade-2 program provides for frequent and systematic contact with the world beyond the neighborhood. By studying transportation, communication, food distribution, and travel, children begin to learn how their part of the world is connected to other places on earth:

Holidays in Other Countries	Transportation and Communication: Our Links to the World
Exploring Our Past	
People Work Together	Where and How We Get Our Food
We the People: Elections	How Neighborhoods Change

Grade 3

The grade-3 program often emphasizes the larger community concept: what a community is, types of communities, how communities provide for basic needs, how they are governed, their history, and their variety around the world. A comparative approach is recommended.

Rural and Urban Communities	Community Workers
Oldest and Newest Communities	Our City's Government
Washington, DC: Our Capital	Tokyo: Japan's Capital

Grade 4

In grade 4 the geographic regions of the United States are often stressed. Home-state history is also common (often by legislative requirement). A comparative approach is recommended: comparing the home state with other states and the home region with other regions.

History and Geography of the Home State

Regions of the US: the West, Southwest, Midwest, Northeast, and South

Deserts and Forests of the World (world regional comparisons)

Rivers of the World (world regional comparisons)

Grade 5

Almost all schools include the geography and history of the United States in the fifth-grade program. The program may focus on the United States alone, or on the United States plus Canada and Latin America. The fifth-grade emphasis should be coordinated with the eighth and eleventh grades in order to revisit difficult concepts (e.g., colony, constitutional democracy, slavery, civil war, culture, pluralism, justice, civil rights). Commonly, units coincide with historical eras. In some states students are introduced to all eras in the fifth grade, in others only through column one below.

The American Land	The Institution of Slavery
The Native Americans	The Civil War
European-American Encounters	The New Nation's Westward Expansion
The American Colonies	The Industrial Revolution
War for Independence	The World Wars
Creating a New Nation	The Civil Rights Movement

Grades 6 and 7

Sixth-grade programs may include the study of Latin America and Canada or the history and geography of the Eastern Hemisphere or Ancient Civilizations or World Geographic Regions. Each of these patterns is in common use. A major limitation of sixth-grade programs is that they attempt to deal with too many topics, which often results in a smattering of exposures without developing significant depth of understanding. The same criticism applies to the seventh grade. Stronger programs emerge if teachers carefully select a few units that are representative of basic concepts that have wide and broad applicability. For example, a class need not study each Third World nation to gain some understanding of the problems of developing countries.

The content of the seventh-grade program depends on that of grade 6. The Eastern Hemisphere or World Regions are popular choices for this grade. Some schools are developing exciting programs in anthropology in grade 7. World Geography is also included in some districts, as are studies of the home state. California schools shift from Ancient Civilizations in the sixth grade to Medieval and Early Modern Times in the seventh.

Western Hemisphere Emphasis

Cooperation and Conflict in the Americas	The Prairie Provinces
Three Incan Countries	The Saint Lawrence Seaway
The Organization of American States	The Amazon

Eastern Hemisphere Emphasis

The Birthplace of Three Religions	The World Wars
Ancient Civilizations	The Holocaust
The Dark Ages and Renaissance	Collapse of the USSR
Empires and Revolutions	Africa Today

Ancient Civilizations

Early Humans and Early Societies	India and China
Mesopotamia, Egypt, Cush	The Rise and Fall of Rome
Hebrews, Greeks, and Their Legacy	

World Geography (Comparative regional study)

The Five Themes of Geography	North America
Africa	South America
Asia	Oceana
Europe	

Grade 8

The study of the United States and of the American heritage is widespread in grade 8. The program usually stresses the development of American political institutions and consists of a series of units arranged chronologically. The fifth and eleventh grades also include elements of American history. Defining the emphasis for each of these grades and differentiating appropriately among them in terms of content and approach is necessary to ensure depth and breadth of understanding. A biographical approach effectively integrates social studies and language arts.

Mapping the Americas	Natives and Colonizers: Cultures in Conflict
Creating a Democracy	The Institution of Slavery
A Divided Nation	Birth of an Industrial Giant
Immigration	The U.S. and the World

Trends

Social forces matter. They shape our values and beliefs, our dress, our treatment of one another, and our thoughts. Social forces even shape our bodies, for physical beauty, too, is a cultural invention that changes from place to place. Unique social forces are shaping teachers who are beginning their careers now, at this juncture of time and place—at the beginning of a new millennium in North American society. Had you applied for a teaching position in the late 1950s, the successful launching of the Soviet satellite Sputnik would have loomed over the interview and been included in some of the questions you were asked. Had you applied in 1970, the war in Vietnam and anti-war protests might have shaped the interview. You may have been asked to take a "loyalty oath"—an oath swearing your loyalty to the United States and its laws.

Today the driving concerns are somewhat different: Teachers are being asked to take the vision of the public school more seriously than ever before, offering high-quality education to each child and raising the standards for student achievement (trends 1 and 5 below). They are being asked also to pay more attention to the teaching of civility and character (trend 2). They are expected to be not only computer users but also computer educators, capable both of using technology as an instructional resource and teaching children to use it wisely (trend 3). Moving comfortably among the school subjects, knowing when and when not to integrate them, and how, is another expectation (trend 4). During an interview for a teaching position, you most likely will be asked about one or more of these trends. Let us introduce them now, and we will revisit them throughout the following chapters.

TREND 1: ACCESS AND INCLUSION—TEACHING ALL OUR CHILDREN

The public school movement of the mid-1800s was geared to getting children *into* schools at public expense. That movement was quite successful, but once access to schools was extended to all children, access to good curriculum and instruction within them depended largely on the race, social class, and gender of the child. To varying degrees, it still does.

The U.S. Supreme Court ruled in 1954 that the segregated school system was failing to provide equal education for all children, and communities were forced to racially integrate their schools. Yet, the curriculum standards to which African-American children were held and the instructional support they were provided in the integrated schools sometimes were, and still are, lower than those for white children. Social-class status complicates the picture: Poor children are often held to lower standards, and minority children are disproportionately from poor families. Moreover, middle-class children do not have access to the same curriculum and instruction that generally are available to children from wealthy families who attend exclusive private schools.

Today's teachers are expected to work diligently to educate the diverse children of today's classrooms and to create more successful ways of doing so than have been developed thus far. Access to high standards—for everyone—are the goals. *Access* and *inclusion* are the watchwords. To this end, today's teachers are expected to acknowledge and root out their own prejudices and stereotypes and, thereby, recognize the intelligence and potential in each child. They are expected to set challenging expectations and provide a strong and supportive instructional environment for all students. As we shall see in the next chapter, this means not only examining one's own attitudes about racial, gender, and cultural differences, but also learning about the home cultures of their students, which in some cases may be markedly different from the culture of the school. In addition to gaining this knowledge, teachers must build bridges across the gaps—become multicultural. This in turn requires teachers to reflect on their own ethnic group membership and sex-role stereotypes and understand how these can shape their interactions with children and parents.

TREND 2: CHARACTER EDUCATION

Observers of this society have long been impressed by Americans' "habits of the heart." This was Alexis de Tocqueville's term over a century ago for the civic-mindedness he saw everywhere in the United States: people caring for neighbors, gathering food for the hungry, willingly limiting their own freedom for the good of the community (being "civic-minded"), and creating all manner of groups in which citizens step outside their families and preferences—outside their "private" lives—and associate with strangers to solve problems, undertake projects, and engage in hobbies. This is the leap into the public realm that makes democracies work. *This sort of activity, more than anything else, indicates the civic health of a society, which in turn makes democracy possible.*[9]

This civic activity still describes Americans, but there is evidence that it is in decline. The upsurge in violence committed by children, the cynicism of many adults toward social institutions, the uncontrolled influence of commercial media on children and the adults who teach them, the persistence of racism and ethnocentrism, and the general perception that manners, civilized dialogue, and public decency are on the wane—all this fuels the character education trend.

Schools across the nation are rapidly developing character education programs. At the heart of any character education program are the moral values that children are expected to develop and that teachers will be expected to encourage and model. Often these are drawn from the values that underpin the "rule book" of our society, the Constitution of the United States. Deriving the values from this source helps a planning committee focus on *public* values necessary for the common good in a pluralistic society, rather than private or personal values that might be meaningful only to members of a particular religion, ethnic group, or family. No broad agreement could ever be reached on private values, and, at any rate, none is needed in a democracy. (Totalitarian systems, on the other hand, reach deeply into the private values and family lives of citizens, banning all or some religions and, basically, punishing diversity.)

Public values are the citizenship values that bind us together as one people and regulate the ways we interact. Without them, we are a diverse array of individuals and cultures without a "glue"—a common identity—on which cooperation and civic life can be based. The following list of public values was identified by parents and teachers in the Baltimore County, Maryland, Schools:[10]

Compassion	Objectivity
Courtesy	Order
Critical Inquiry	Patriotism
Due Process	Rational Consent
Equality of Opportunity	Reasoned Argument
Freedom of Thought and Action	Respect for Others' Rights
Honesty	Responsibility
Human Worth and Dignity	Responsible Citizenship
Integrity	Rule of Law
Justice	Self-Respect
Knowledge	Tolerance
Loyalty	Truth

TREND 3: TECHNOLOGY

It is obvious to every reader that we live in an information-rich environment. New information is being produced more rapidly than ever before; the rate at which new information is generated has increased dramatically. Not only is there more of it, but its availability has increased, too. An "information superhighway"—the World Wide Web (WWW)—now runs directly through the middle of most schools and many of the homes of your students. New teachers now are expected to be computer users themselves and Internet guides for their students. New teachers can be reasonably expected to

- Load and use curriculum software
- Keep attendance and achievement records on spreadsheets
- Use word processing and digital image programs to send newsletters home
- Search the Internet for instructional resources and help children do the same.

Thanks to the Internet, students can take "virtual field trips" to places they have located on the globe.

You will find that computer resources are featured throughout this book. Chapter 9 describes a number of computer resources that are particularly helpful to new teachers. Among our favorites are computer-based simulations (e.g., *Where in the World Is Carmen Sandiego?)* and taking students on "virtual field trips"—to the White House, for example (at *http://www.whitehouse.gov/WH/kids/html/kidshome.html*) or historic Philadelphia, home of the Liberty Bell (at *http://www.libertynet.org/iha/index.html*), or to the Seven Wonders of the World (at *http://pharos.bu.edu/Egypt/Wonders*). Also, new teachers should know how to access the collections at great libraries and museums such as the Library of Congress (at *http://memory.loc.gov/ammem/ndlpedu/resource/socscirs.html*) and the Smithsonian Institution (at *http://educate.si.edu/*).

TREND 4: INTEGRATED CURRICULUM

Curriculum integration, also known as interdisciplinary education, comes and goes as a pressing concern of American educators and the public. It was trendy in the 1930s, faded out of the picture until the 1950s, and then faded out again until the late 1980s.[11] Each time it fades, the academic disciplines return to the forefront of the school curriculum with renewed vigor along with the suspicion that attempts to integrate the school subjects have, in spite of good intentions, produced mediocre results. There are signs today that the pendulum is swinging again: The latest flurry of interest in integrated education is moderating somewhat, and "disciplinary thinking" is once again being advanced as the best way to introduce children to the great questions, knowledge, and know-how of humankind—to the great human conversation. Howard Gardner, for example, the renowned psychologist whose popular theory of "multiple intelligences" (presented in next chapter) has revolutionized the way educators think about children's ability and potential, has titled a recent book *The Disciplined Mind.* In it he argues that the disciplines are indispensable in any quality education because they represent the highest achievements of talented human beings, toiling in concert across generations to explain issues of enduring importance. True, the best work of these talented individuals is interdisciplinary, but they are capable of this only because of their deep-reaching knowledge within the separate disciplines. Genuinely interdisciplinary education "is simply not feasible for most youngsters," Gardner concludes, because youngsters do not (and developmentally cannot) have the necessary foundation in the disciplines that would make such interdisciplinary work possible.[12]

Gardner does, however, favor what he calls "commonsense" integration in the elementary grades. The key to using curriculum integration in the classroom to increase the quality of education is to remember that integration is a strategy, not a goal. It must be aimed not at itself (that is, integrated education for its own sake) but rather at particular understandings and skills that we want children to build (that is, integrated education for the sake of helping children learn a high-standards curriculum). According to Gardner,

> The issues to consider are standards and accuracy . . . I call for educators to learn and propagate the best that is known and thought in the world. . . . I want all students to develop a sense of high standards; I want all students to strive for accuracy and to use evidence properly; I want all students to respect a range of groups and cultures . . . .[13]

These are goals; integrated curriculum is a sometimes-helpful tool.

Readers can evaluate how successful we have been in this text at providing models of "commonsense" integration. Each of the 19 lesson plans spread throughout this text contains integration suggestions, and two models of integration—infusion and fusion—are presented in detail in Chapter 13.

Social studies units, as we shall see, are often integrated units for three reasons. First, social studies learning almost always requires reading and writing. Children need to be taught to read maps, expository text material, primary documents, newspapers, reference books, and historical narratives. The social studies curriculum is the logical place to provide such instruction because this is where such material is encountered. Second, social studies itself is already an integrated school subject. The social studies curriculum integrates the disciplines of history, the social sciences, and the humanities. Third, many social studies units are animated by the same *way of knowing* that animates the science curriculum: inquiry, otherwise known as the scientific method of problem solving. When a unit centers on inquiry, the children are immersed in a problem or event that is put as a researchable question: Why did the *Titanic* tragedy occur? Why did the buffalo disappear in North America? Why did Rome fall? Does geographical setting determine the lifestyle of people who live there? Then, students formulate and test hypotheses, gather and weigh evidence, and, finally, draw conclusions. "Commonsense" integration, then, can find a good and logical home in the social studies curriculum.

TREND 5: CURRICULUM STANDARDS

There is concern today that children of all races, social classes, and cultures may not be sufficiently challenged by the school curriculum. This belief is coupled with the conviction that a more vigorous and substantive education is fully within our reach. A portion of this concern can be dismissed as the latest bout of social hysteria (these are uncertain times, and people search for scapegoats), part of it is due to political wrangling between Democrats and Republicans, and part of it is well-grounded in fact and theory.

In response, a number of national standards committees in a variety of subject areas were convened across the nation in the 1990s. Their task was to develop higher standards for K–12 schooling—standards that answer one of the great, controversial questions of all time: *What should our children know and be able to do?* Not surprisingly, people disagree over the answer to this question. New teachers wading for the first time into the cold waters of curriculum standards, and the political debates that swirl around them, should talk with colleagues and school administrators about the implications locally. "How," you might ask, "has the curriculum in this district been influenced by the various sets of voluntary national curriculum standards?" (This would be a good question to ask at the interview.) Anything is possible: There may have been no influence at all, or the district may have adopted a set of national standards verbatim. Something in between is more likely. Most important, find the social studies standards for the local school district and read them.[14]

There are five sets of national standards that are directly relevant to social studies. These are voluntary standards; no state or school district is required to implement them, yet most have drawn on them to some degree. They are most likely found in the curriculum library of school district offices or in your college or university library. You may find them on the Internet or write to the addresses given for a print copy. At the top of the following list is the best single set of standards for elementary and middle school teachers of social studies because it draws on and integrates the other four, which were developed for the separate disciplines of history, geography, civics/government, and economics. Each of the standards books can be ordered from the NCSS Bookstore online at *http://www.ncss.org/bookstore/standards.html*, or by telephone at 800-683-0812.

Social Studies (Integrated)

Curriculum Standards for Social Studies. Developed by the National Council for the Social Studies, c/o Whitehurst & Clark, 100 Newfield Ave., Edison, NY 08837. Call toll free 800-683-0812. Website: *http://www.ncss.org/standards/stitle.html. Note: Your textbook came with a* Sampler *of these standards. Please take time now to familiarize yourself with this booklet and read several of the teaching examples.*

History

National Standards for History.[15] Developed by the National Center for History in the Schools, University of California, Los Angeles. See especially the history standards for grades K–4 (one book, or see website below) and the standards for grades 5–12 (another book, or see website). There is also a basic "revised" version, but it contains less useful information for classroom teachers. Call toll free 800-421-4246. Website: *http://www.sscnet.ucla.edu/nchs/standards.html.*

Geography

Geography for Life: National Geography Standards. Developed by the National Council for Geographic Education, 16A Leonard Hall, Indiana University of Pennsylvania, Indiana, Pennsylvania 15705-1087. Call 412-357-6290. Website: *http://www.nationalgeographic.com/education/standards.html.*

Civics/Government

National Standards for Civics and Government. Developed by the Center for Civic Education, 5146 Douglas Fir Rd., Calabasas, CA 91302-1467. Call toll-free 800-350-4223. Website: *http://www.civiced.org/stds.html.*

Economics

Voluntary National Standards in Economics. Developed by the National Council on Economic Education, 1140 Avenue of the Americas, New York, NY 10036. Call toll free 800-338-1192. Website: *http://www.economicsamerica.org/standards.html.*

In the chapters that follow, especially in Chapters 3 through 5, we highlight each of these sets of standards. And, remember, a *Sampler* of the first set listed, the integrated social studies standards developed by the National Council for the Social Studies, accompanies this text.

State and Local Standards

In addition to these voluntary national standards, each of the 50 states has curriculum framework development projects. Most states view the national standards documents as *resources,* with teachers reading and pondering them, perhaps, but not adopting them wholesale. According to most reports, "few states feel any obligation to use them."[16] One Texas official put in bluntly: "If there is a conflict between the Texas standards and the national standards, this is Texas. And, by God, we would choose Texas standards."[17]

You can search online for state curriculum frameworks of interest to you. Below are a few states and their social studies curriculum websites:

- California: *http://www.cde.ca.gov/board/historya.html*
- Florida: *http://www.firn.edu/doe/curric/prek12/frame2.htm*
- Michigan: *http://cdp.mde.state.mi.us/mcf/ContentStandards/SocialStudies/default.html*
- Texas: *http://www.tea.state.tx.us/rules/tac/ch113toc.html*
- Washington: *http://csl.wednet.edu/Web%20page/2%20Academic%20Standards/standards/socialstudiesintro.html*
- Wisconsin: *www.dpi.state.wi.us/dpi/standards/ssintro.html*

In the following blank, write in your state and the www address for its social studies curriculum framework: _____

Conclusion

Why is there a social studies curriculum in the schools? Because without historical understanding, there can be no wisdom; without geographical understanding, no social or environmental intelligence; and without civic understanding, no democratic citizens and, therefore, no democracy. The goals of the social studies curriculum are social understanding and civic efficacy. Social understanding is knowledge of human beings' social worlds drawn from history, geography, the other social sciences, and the humanities. Civic efficacy is the readiness and willingness to assume citizenship responsibilities. The purpose of this introductory chapter was to examine these goals and various scope-and-sequence plans for achieving them. We showed how to use the 10 themes from the NCSS curriculum standards to elaborate the scope of the social studies curriculum emphasis for any grade (we demonstrated at the third grade the theme of communities). We concluded the chapter by considering five trends that will shape at least the beginning years of your teaching career: access and inclusion, character education, technology, curriculum integration, and the curriculum standards movement.

Of course, teachers don't only teach curriculum; they teach *children*. The children themselves are the concern of the next chapter. While a science textbook might take a biological approach to such a chapter, it is appropriate that a social studies textbook take a demographic approach, as readers shall see.

Discussion Questions and Suggested Activities

1. What are your memories of social studies curriculum and instruction from your elementary school years? Middle school years? Share these memories with classmates.

2. Interview two or three teachers in the school where you are student teaching. Find out what they regard as the most important themes and topics in the social studies curriculum for their grade levels. Also, share with them the list of 10 themes in the accompanying *Sampler* of the *Curriculum Standards for Social Studies*. Do they believe such themes are relevant to any grade level or only to certain grades and topics?

3. Determine where you can borrow the curriculum standards documents listed in this chapter under Trend 5. Are they in your university's curriculum library or in the school district where you are teaching? Also, locate them on the Internet. Skim each of them to see how you might use them as resources—going to them for both subject matter ideas and examples of classroom activities.

4. Locate a copy of the state social studies curriculum framework for the state in which you reside or to which you plan to move. (You probably can find it online.) Examine the organization of the framework. Is the goal statement divided into knowledge, attitudes and values, and skills, as predicted in this chapter? Is the curriculum scope and sequence similar to what was presented in this chapter? If not, in what ways do they differ?

5. With a partner, reread the definition of social studies education given near the beginning of the chapter and the explanation that follows it. In your own words, distinguish between *social understanding* and *civic efficacy* and try to quickly sketch a lesson plan that targets one or both of these.

Selected References

Brophy, Jere, & VanSledright, Bruce. (1997). *Teaching and learning history in elementary schools.* New York: Teachers College Record.

de Tocqueville, Alexis. (1969). *Democracy in America.* (J. P. Mayer, Ed.; George Lawrence, Trans.). New York: Doubleday. (Original work published 1848).

Haas, Mary E., & Laughlin, Margaret A. (Eds.). (1997). *Meeting the standards: Social studies readings for K–6 educators.* Washington, DC: National Council for the Social Studies.

Lickona, Thomas. (1991). *Educating for character: How our schools can teach respect and responsibility.* New York: Bantam.

Lindquist, Tarry. (1997). *Ways that work: Putting social studies standards into practice.* Portsmouth, NH: Heinemann.

Parker, Walter C. (1991). *Renewing the social studies curriculum.* Alexandria, VA: Association for Supervision and Curriculum Development.

Ravitch, Diane. (1995). *National standards in American education: A citizen's guide.* Washington, DC: The Brookings Institution.

Notes

1. National Council for the Social Studies, *Curriculum standards for social studies* (Washington, DC: Author, 1994), 54, 105.

2. *Report of the task force on civic education, The second annual White House conference on character building for a democratic, civic society* (May 1995), 3.

3. National Council for the Social Studies, *Curriculum standards for social studies,* p. 3.

4. Some scholars classify history along with the humanities rather than the social sciences because it has so much in common with literature. This makes good sense. Nevertheless, we prefer to place it with the social sciences for two reasons: (a) because its method of inquiry emphasizes evidence, and (b) because historians search for the truth of the matter as opposed to a good story.

5. Task Force on Standards for Teaching and Learning in the Social Studies, *A vision of powerful teaching and learning in the social studies: Building social understanding and civic efficacy* (Washington, DC: National Council for the Social Studies, 1992). Reprinted as a supplement to *Curriculum standards for social studies,* p. 157.

6. National Council for the Social Studies, *Position statement on social studies for early childhood and elementary school children preparing for the 21st century* (Alexandria, VA: Author, 1989), 19–20.

7. National Council for the Social Studies, *Social studies curriculum planning resources* (Dubuque, IA: Kendall/Hunt, 1990), 25–29.

8. H. J. Walberg & S. L. Tsai. (1983). Matthew effects in education. *Educational Research Quarterly, 20*(1983), 359–373.

9. Francis Fukuyama, *Trust: The social virtues and the creation of prosperity* (New York: Free Press, 1995), and Robert D. Putnam, *Making democracy work: Civic traditions in modern Italy* (Princeton: Princeton University Press, 1994).

10. Henry A. Huffman, *Developing a character education program: One school district's experience* (Alexandria, VA: Association for Supervision and Curriculum Development, 1994), 6.

11. For the earlier eras see Charles W. Knudsen, What do educators mean by "integration?" *Harvard Educational Review,* 7 (1937): 15–26; and *The integration of educational experiences,* The 57th Yearbook of the National Society for the Study of Education, ed. Nelson B. Henry (Chicago: University of Chicago Press, 1958).

12. Howard Gardner, *The disciplined mind* (New York: Simon & Schuster, 1999), 219.

13. Ibid., 58.

14. See William T. Owens very helpful advice for new teachers: Help for new teachers confronting the conundrum of content standards, *Social Studies Review, 38* (Spring/Summer 1999): 39–44.

15. In 1995, the curriculum standards for the field of history were met with criticism by talk show hosts and politicians, who charged they were written by a "secret group" of "liberal" and "ultra-feminist" historians. These accusations are silly. The history standards are politically middle-of-the-road, and they are charged with being overly conservative by an equal number of critics. For a conservative criticism of these standards, see John Fonte's The Naive Romanticism of the History Standards, *The chronicle of higher education* (June 9, 1995): A48. For a liberal defense, see Gary B. Nash and Ross E. Dunn, History standards and culture wars, *Social Education, 59* (January 1995): 5–7.

16. Lynn Olson, Standards times 50, *Education Week,* special report (April 12, 1995): 15.

17. Ibid.

Websites

http://www.ncss.org/links/home/html

http://www.whitehouse.gov/wh/kids/html/kidshome.html

http://www.libertynet.org/iha/index.html

http://pharos.bu.edu/Egypt/Wonders

http://memory.loc.gov/ammem/ndlpedu/resourse/socscirs.html

http://educate.si.edu/

http://www.ncss.org/standards/stitle.html

http://www.sscnet.ucla.edu/nchs/standards.html

http://www.nationalgeographic.com/education/standards.html

http://www.civiced.org/stds.html

http://www.economicsamerica.org/standards.html

http://www.cde.ca.gov/board/historya.html

http://www.firn.edu/doe/curric/prek12/frame2.html

http://www.cdp.mde.state.mi.us/mcf/ContentStandards/SocialStudies/default.html

http://www.tea.state.tx.us/rules/tac/ch113toc.html

http://csl.wednet.edu/Web%20page/2%20Academic%20Standards/standards/socialstudiesintro.html

www.dpi.state.wi.us/dpi/standards/ssintro.html

CHAPTER 2

Knowing the Children We Teach

Main Idea

Good teachers have always tailored social studies instruction to individual children. Today, however, the diversity within a single classroom is of a different kind, number, and range than in the past. The *demographics* of the classroom have changed. Today's teachers need to understand the changes and teach in ways that ensure equal opportunity to learn.

Key Concepts

diversity, demography, individualized instruction, culturally responsive instruction

Chapter Outline

- Guidelines and Teaching Examples
- Understanding Changing Demographics
- Conclusion
- Discussion Questions and Suggested Activities
- Selected References
- Notes

Chapter Snapshot

Each spring, the students in Ginny Moran's fourth-grade class conduct the "Citizenship Simulation." They simulate the ceremony at which people who have immigrated to the United States become citizens of this country. One child, playing the mayor, gives a welcome speech. Another, playing a federal judge, asks everyone a few questions from the "citizenship test": "What is the Bill of Rights? Who is eligible to vote?" Then the citizens-to-be take the Oath of Allegiance, followed by the Pledge of Allegiance. Afterward, there is a party with congratulatory speeches and songs.

 A favorite website http://www.census.gov/. This is the website of the U.S. Census Bureau where all sorts of demographic data can be found. Click first on state and county facts and then on "minority links."

Thinking back on the new class of children she greeted today—the first day of school—Ginny Moran could hardly believe the diversity: There were boys and girls, of course, and tall and short, outgoing and shy, doll players and ball players. They were born in Mexico, Yugoslavia, Ethiopia, Korea, and the United States. Four languages other than English, and even more dialects, were spoken at home. There were blacks, whites, Asians, and Hispanics. There were Muslims, Christians, Jews, and Buddhists. How did she know these things? She observed and she asked some questions, beginning with "Let's find out who we are and where we are from, what we like to do at recess, and how we spend our time on the weekends." One little boy was physically challenged, and the principal had identified two children who were intellectually gifted.

The children in today's classrooms are similar in many ways, too. They like to play and pretend, and they will sit transfixed for a good story. Cartoons enchant them, and they are hurt when teased or excluded from other children's play. They keenly observe the subtlest details in other children. They scribble before printing and print phrases before paragraphs, and they will not master the five-paragraph essay or the written report for many years— maybe never. Anyone who has spent time with young children knows they often talk to themselves while at play, and as they grow a little older this speech shifts to the "inside." Their physical, personal, social, and cognitive development progresses in fairly orderly ways.

As recently as a generation or two ago, Ms. Moran probably faced a classroom in which the children were remarkably similar in *appearance,* too. Children were required to attend their neighborhood school, and because neighborhoods were not racially integrated, neither were schools. Children with learning disabilities, physical challenges, and mental retardation often were not a part of the regular classroom.

All of this has changed dramatically in recent years for five key reasons: federally mandated racial desegregation of schools, immigration, changing birth rates, increased integration of housing, and inclusion of students with disabilities. Together these reflect the changing demographic pattern in the nation's schools, which can be summarized as *rapidly increasing diversity.* By the year 2026, demographers predict that we will have the inverse of the student population that we had in 1990, when white students made up 70 percent of the K–12 student body.[1] (Read that sentence again!) So completely have these changes already transformed our classrooms that today it would be difficult to find a classroom anywhere in America that is homogeneous with respect to the ethnic, racial, cultural, linguistic, and religious backgrounds of its students. Today's classrooms are lively aggregates of children that are increasingly diverse, and this diversity translates into new challenges for teachers.

New teachers need to be aware of and plan for this diversity even though there are so many other things to worry about. Three reasons stand out: effective teaching, knowledge of powerful ideas, and modeling the democratic way of life.

First, as we shall see in this chapter, teachers need to teach social studies subject matter to every one of their students. Without understanding the changing demographics of the classroom, without knowing their students, teachers can fall into the habit of teaching well only those students who are culturally similar to themselves. Quoting a native Alaskan teacher: "If there's someone who doesn't understand what I'm teaching, I try to understand who they are." Notice she does not change her curriculum; rather, she works to increase her knowledge of the child. Similarly, an African-American teacher remembered: "My instructors knew what you knew because they talked to you . . . . Teaching is all about telling a story. You have to get to know kids so you'll know *how* to tell the story."[2]

Second, *demography* and *diversity* are key social studies concepts that teachers need to understand in order to teach. Demography, a subfield of geography, is the study of human populations, especially their size, growth, migrations, living conditions, and birth and death rates. Diversity is variability—differences—within populations, especially with reference to ethnicity, race, culture, language, religion, and social class.

Third, schoolteachers are expected to be stewards of democracy. Democracy means that the people rule themselves (*popular sovereignty*), which requires the peaceful and respectful living together of groups and individuals who are different from one another. In a highly pluralistic nation like the United States, these differences exist in all their glory and difficulty right there in the classroom! Teachers must demonstrate that they understand the differences and respect them. In so doing, they are showing students how to behave in public places as democratic citizens should.

In one sense, the challenges posed by changing demographics and increasing diversity are not new. Good teachers have always tailored instruction to individual children, not ignoring differences but recognizing them and helping all children learn the curriculum. But the diversity in the classroom today is of a different kind and magnitude. Today's teachers cannot get by on yesterday's teachers' knowledge and skills.

Guidelines and Teaching Examples

Because children are different, they cannot possibly benefit equally from identical educational experiences. If everyone is treated the same, we simply institutionalize and perpetuate inequality. How? A school typically has a *culture*—a way of doing things, of speaking and thinking, and of relating to others. This school culture may or may not match the children's home cultures. For some children the cultural match between home and school will be a good one: The language matches, the dialect matches, and the customs match those already practiced at home. The school doesn't seem a strange or foreign place—*new* perhaps, but basically a continuation of the same ways of thinking and behaving. For these children the match gives them a head start, enabling them both to learn more and learn it more quickly. The effect is similar to having a red carpet rolled out to welcome them; they are "advantaged" by the match of home and school culture. Children for whom the home-school match is not so good are likewise "disadvantaged" somewhat. The teacher's style and instructional strategies are not as comprehensible, nor are the curriculum materials or guest speakers. The classroom customs may be "foreign" and sometimes unfathomable. Identical instruction for unidentical children, then, is not the best course. Gloria Ladson-Billings puts it this way in her book *The Dreamkeepers,* which details the work of successful teachers of African-American children: "Different children have different needs and addressing those different needs is the best way to deal with them equitably."[3]

TWO EXTREMES AND A MIDDLE WAY

Well-intentioned teachers have disagreed on how to teach children from diverse backgrounds. At one extreme is the belief that it is best to ignore differences among children. "I don't see color, I just see children," we have often heard. Or, "I don't care if they're red, green, or polka dot, I just treat them all like children."[4] Teachers holding this belief may sincerely understand that children are, after all, children, and alike in so many ways. But these teachers often are members of the majority culture, and they may be uncomfortable talking about cultural differences or race and may have little or no knowledge of the concepts of demography, diversity, ethnicity, culture, and second-language acquisition. On the other side are teachers who are so knowledgeable about and sensitive to individual and cultural differences that they are nearly paralyzed in their role as teacher. They shy away from teaching core subject matter to the whole class, partly due to anxiety about choosing which content and skills all children should learn and partly due to anxiety about selecting appropriate instructional strategies. "Who am I to choose?" we have heard such teachers say. "I just let the children choose. That seems the safest route."[5]

A middle way is needed. Good teachers walk a sensible path between ignoring diversity and being paralyzed by it. They see both similarities and differences among the children in their classroom, and they hold high learning standards for *all* of them—both boys and girls, native born and immigrant, rich and poor, gifted and challenged, Asian American, black, Latino, and white.

DIFFERENT OR DEPRIVED?

This middle way is *individualized instruction.* Individualized instruction means that children are provided with personally meaningful learning experiences that will help them to achieve curriculum goals. Traditionally this has meant that learning experiences should be tailored to each child's *capabilities.* This definition emerged in an era when educators were concerned mainly with ability, development, and intelligence differences among white, European-American children of the majority language and culture. The contemporary definition of individualized instruction encompasses not only children's capabilities but also the array of *cultural* differences they bring to class because of their diverse group memberships—ethnic, racial, social class, gender, religious, and linguistic.

Accompanying this definitional change is a shift in how educators view cultural differences. There are two distinct views of cultural diversity. One is the cultural *deprivation* (or cultural deficit) model; the other is the cultural *differences* (or pluralistic) model. According to the cultural deprivation view, children who are culturally different are thought to be culturally deprived. Their diverse languages, values, behaviors, and beliefs are viewed as less developed, less important, and less attractive when compared to the cultural attributes of the majority culture. Teachers holding this view might make comments such as, "If only we did not have to send the children home at night" and "What can we expect of kids with parents like that?" This is not a helpful attitude, Christine Bennett observes, "because it focuses on where our students *aren't* and blinds us to where our students *are.*"[6]

The cultural differences model, by contrast, assumes that schools need to be ready and able to teach children of all groups. This is part of the "American dream" that has attracted people to the United States from all over the world. It means that people of all cultures and creeds are free to be themselves while getting the best education possible. *Rather than arguing that culturally diverse children are unready for school, the cultural differences model argues that schools too often are unready for children*—that it is the schools' responsibility to teach, and teach effectively, all children. Teachers need to view cultural differences as strengths and be always on the lookout for ways to incorporate and build on those strengths. One way to begin learning about the demographic characteristics of the classroom *with* your students is to conduct a class census (see Lesson Plan 1).

Lesson Plan 1   WHO ARE WE? TAKING A CLASS CENSUS

Grade 3–8

Time One class period

Objectives This is a useful activity to lead at the beginning of the year to help you and the students know one another, to help the class build a sense of community, and to introduce a basic concept of social studies: demographic information about people (characteristics of populations).

Interest building Ask the students, "How many of us are in our classroom population?" Then, "How are we alike? Different?"

Lesson Development

1. *Assessment.* Ask students what they know about the U.S. Census.

2. *Build Background Knowledge.* Provide information about the U.S. Census as needed. (A census is required by the U.S. Constitution. It is taken every 10 years to provide information that helps us know who "we"—the people of the United States—are.) If possible, take students to the U.S. Census Bureau's website at *http://www.census.gov/*. There, students will see the U.S. population updated every five minutes, and they can click on their state and get a state census profile. They will find all sorts of demographic data at this site: the state population, predictions for population growth or decline in the future, the percentages of young and older people in the state, birth and death rates, and the number of doctors, schools, etc.

3. *Activity.* Ask students to complete the Census Survey. Then, select two or three surveys each day and ask the respondent to read it aloud. Keep a running tally of responses on the chalkboard. After everyone has shared aloud, the class can post the information on a bulletin board display, "Our Class Census," such as the following sample. This is a good opportunity to apply math skills.

OUR CLASS CENSUS, SEPTEMBER 20.

Population	Gender	Average Age	Avg. Number of Pets at Home	Avg. Family Size	Cookie Preference
27	Girls: 14 Boys: 13	9	1.5	3.5	Chocolate chip

CENSUS SURVEY: MR. ALBRIGHT'S CLASS

1. What is your name? _____

2. What is your age? _____

3. Check one: male _____ female _____

4. Do you have pets at home? If so, how many? _____

5. How many people are in your family? _____

6. What is your favorite kind of cookie? _____

Assessment/
Follow Up

Ask students what a census is. Ask students to guess (hypothesize) how other classrooms in the same school building will differ in census results from their own class. Then select and survey two additional classes, and compare and contrast the results. Help children display these data on a graph (see Chapter 5).

Materials

Copy of "census survey" for each student. U.S. Census Bureau website.

Integration

Mathematics: The class cannot tally at step 3 or develop the graph during the Follow-up without mathematical reasoning. The concept of "average" (i.e., the mean) is challenging. And rounding is an issue with averages. Should "1.5" pets be rounded up to 2?

■ ■ ■ ■ ■

SIX GUIDELINES FOR TEACHING IN DIVERSE CLASSROOMS

We now present six specific guidelines for teaching in ways that respect all the children in the class and help all of them learn the social studies curriculum. Each of the following chapters will expand on these guidelines; accordingly, we will not attempt to say everything now. Our purpose at this point is to just sketch these guidelines for teaching in America's increasingly diverse classrooms. Each guideline is followed by a number of examples and applications. The guidelines in brief:

1. Bridge the cultural gap.
2. Know thyself.
3. Vary the medium.
4. Expect much.
5. Vary the viewpoint.
6. Group and regroup.

GUIDELINE 1. CULTURALLY RESPONSIVE INSTRUCTION

Learn about the cultural and linguistic characteristics of the children in your class and adapt instruction accordingly. Teach in ways that bridge the gap between children's home cultures and the school culture.

The purpose of culturally responsive instruction is to help children maintain their cultural identities while learning the school curriculum. Doing so helps them learn what you want them to learn because they are not required to hide or feel bad about who they are. Teacher and researcher Kathryn Au, who worked many years with Native Hawaiian children at the Kamehameha Elementary Education Program (KEEP), writes that the "approaches teachers use to work with students of diverse backgrounds should allow students to retain and feel pride in their own ethnic and cultural identity. . . . Too often, students of diverse backgrounds find themselves in the position of having to choose between school success and their cultural identity."[7] This is an unfair choice for any child in a diverse, democratic society, and it systematically stunts the academic development of nonwhite and Hispanic students. One of the reasons many children from the majority ethnic and racial groups do better in school than many children from minority groups is that they do not face this choice. The school, typically, is already culturally responsive to majority children.

Teaching Examples

- A fifth-grade teacher begins her unit on the U.S. Constitution by asking students what they know about the bylaws and articles of incorporation of groups to which they belong in the community. Members of scouting groups and 4-H often are familiar with the rulebooks of these organizations. Students who are involved in religious organizations might know a little about their bylaws as well. African-American children, who may be the most deeply involved in church activities of all the children in class, "learn the significance of such documents in forming institutions and shaping ideals while they also learn that their own people are institution-builders."[8]

- Native Hawaiian students often are raised in families that practice sibling caretaking. At school, they might feel just as comfortable learning from peers as from an adult teacher. Accordingly, their teachers often pair them for practice and for teaching one another the meaning of what they are reading in their social studies books.

- The teacher learns to say "please," "thank you," "good morning," and "see you tomorrow" in the home languages of each of her language-minority children. She often uses these phrases when working individually with the children. She publicly praises these children for already being at work on a second language.

- A fourth-grade class is planning their classroom newspaper, which will be sent home to parents and to a fourth-grade "partner classroom" in another school. Their teacher brought in copies of weekly newspapers from local ethnic minority communities to serve as newspaper models.

- Noticing that the rural children in her class are picked on and called names by the town children, Ms. Brem (herself a "townie") goes to the county fair and rodeo each year, learns about farm life, and praises these activities publicly in the classroom.

- The teachers at Evergreen Heights Elementary School near Seattle decided at a faculty meeting that they would learn about their students' communities. Based on their experiences, they recommend the following activities:

  1. Collaborate with the ethnic minority communities in your area. Volunteer at youth centers and adult literacy programs.

  2. Ask the parents of immigrant children if their children are attending a Saturday language and culture school. Volunteer to share maps, globes, and other social studies materials.

  3. Find out what churches, mosques, and temples your children attend. Ask them about this. Go to an open house, choir concert, or picnic.

GUIDELINE 2. KNOWLEDGE OF YOUR OWN FAMILY HISTORY

History begins at home. Teachers need to study their own family history—its cultural and ethnic characteristics, language, migrations, dialects, religion, social values, gifts, and disabilities.

As leading multicultural education scholar James A. Banks said,

Teachers are human beings who bring their cultural perspectives, values, hopes, and dreams to the classroom. They also bring their prejudices, stereotypes, and misconceptions. Teachers' values and perspectives mediate and interact with what they teach and influence the ways that messages are communicated and perceived by their students. A teacher who believes that Christopher Columbus "discovered" America and one who believes that Columbus came to America when it was peopled by groups with rich and diverse cultures will send different messages to their students when they study European exploration of America.[9]

Teaching Examples

- Research and make your family tree and then narrate a family history. Share this with other teachers who have done the same. Think about how your own ethnicity shapes your interaction with your students. There's lots of help on the Internet. (A popular commercial website is *http://www.familytreemaker.com/allsearch.html*.)

- Examine one or two first-grade social studies textbooks published since 1995. "Families around the world" is a common theme. Search for representations of your family. Do you see yourself there? Are others there? Who is not?

- Visit culturally different neighborhoods in your own town or city and, if you can, in other nations. Such experiences provide a reflective mirror in which you can better "see" your own customs and values. (Self-knowledge is difficult for all of us without comparisons.)

- Read the histories of different American ethnic groups and compare them to your own.[10]

GUIDELINE 3. MULTIMEDIA

Provide variation in the ways children acquire social studies information, think about it, and express what they are learning.

The intake of new information is an essential requirement of social studies education. The conventional information sources have been the textbook, primary documents, children's tradebooks, other literature, videotapes, and the teacher. It is important to broaden the array of information sources with computer software, slides, films, recorded songs and speeches, paintings and photographs projected on the overhead projector, interviews, class discussions, and so forth. Psychologist Howard Gardner calls these "entry points." Different students will prefer and profit from different entry points.[11] Similarly, the ways in which children are asked to manipulate and *express* the information they have gathered need to be expanded: Children can translate information heard in a film to a bar graph or time line. They can organize information on charts, write plays and songs about it, compose narratives, and draw and reason mathematically about it.

Teaching Examples

- Teach children how to read and make charts and graphs depicting geographic or economic data they have gathered about their community.
- Teach children to re-tell a historical narrative as a play or song (e.g., dramatize the events of the Boston Tea Party or the Underground Railroad).
- Create self-contained learning centers that feature multimedia presentations on an important topic: hospitals in our community, our state capital, goods and services in our community, regions of the United States, or the U.S. Constitution, for example.

GUIDELINE 4. HIGH EXPECTATIONS FOR LEARNING

Expect, assist, and cajole all students to learn the social studies curriculum.

Children tend to perform according to their teachers' expectations. Teachers in the past often have expected less achievement from girls, students whose home language is other than English, African-American and Hispanic children, children with learning disabilities, and poor children. Sometimes teachers have lowered curriculum standards for these children or created an altogether different curriculum for them, thereby teaching them less important subject matter. In her wonderful book, *Other People's Children: Cultural Conflict in the Classroom,* Lisa Delpit calls this, simply, "teaching less."

Attached to low expectations are behaviors. A teacher who expects boys but not girls to develop sharp intellects may praise girls for *neat* work while praising boys for *thoughtful* work, or drill limited-English students on skills while helping language-majority children learn the powerful ideas of geography, civics, and history. Based on unconsciously held stereotypes, a teacher may expect Asian-American children to do well in math while expecting African-American children to misbehave.

Teaching Examples

- Call on girls as often as boys. Praise them for intellectual work—their reasoning and understanding—and provide constructive criticism. Be attentive to the misbehavior of both boys and girls. Use a checklist to help keep track of your feedback patterns. Ask a colleague to videotape your interaction and then return the favor.
- Make every effort to teach limited-English-speaking children the social studies curriculum, not merely language skills. Place the language instruction in the context of the social studies curriculum. Expect students to learn it. Use drama, art, construction, and music activities to lighten some of the language burden. For limited-English-speaking students, especially poor urban children, there is too often a "heavy dependence on the remedial drilling of basic skills to the virtual exclusion of more engaging, significant content," such as history, geography, and civics.[12]
- Monitor carefully your nonverbal behavior. Be careful not to shy away from culturally different children; they *will* feel it. Children notice if their teacher genuinely cares that they learn and the extent to which their teacher requires and helps them learn; and, like you, they remember it long enough to talk about it when they are grown.

GUIDELINE 5. MULTICULTURAL CURRICULUM

Help children understand key concepts, events, issues, and historical figures from diverse viewpoints.

Paying attention to *how* we teach is an important dimension of teaching in diverse classrooms. Paying attention to *what* we teach is another. Teachers should enrich students' learning of social studies topics by including multiple viewpoints or perspectives. Multicultural education is good education because it is more comprehensive. It lays one perspective on an historical event or character alongside others so that students can compare them and try to draw defensible conclusions.

Teaching Examples

- Children in the fifth grade should examine the American Revolution from the perspectives of loyalists as well as rebels, men and women, and slaves and free persons. They should study the westward movement of European immigrants from the viewpoints of native groups as well as pioneer families. When setting up a classroom store, help third-grade children plan for employees and customers who have disabilities and religious and language differences.

- Take care not to teach only the Anglo-American perspective on United States history. European conquerors came from Spain as well as England, and their history involves the American southwest more than the northeast. Asian immigrants came through San Francisco while European immigrants were lining up on Ellis Island in New York City. The popular term *westward expansion* refers to the Anglo-American immigrant movement from the northeast toward the already occupied lands (by natives) to the west. *Northward migration* would capture the movement of Spanish-speaking immigrants from the south.

- When teaching any social studies concept, include multiple viewpoints. For example, the teaching plan in the box on *immigration* that we present on page 405 in Chapter 12 contrasts Chinese immigration to America (using Laurence Yep's book, *Dragonwings*) with Russian immigration (using Ann Morris's *Dancing to America*). Another example: In the third-grade textbook program called *Adventures in Time and Place: Communities*,[13] European immigration to the United States through Ellis Island is contrasted with Asian and Mexican immigration through San Diego, and these are contrasted with the migration of African-Americans from southern to northern states.

- When teaching about the children's neighborhoods, emphasize both cultural diversity *and* the laws, values, and customs that bind us together as one people. We may be culturally many, but we are politically one (our constitutional democracy). Talk with children about the classroom rules, such as listening carefully to one another and respecting diversity, that "make us all one people."

- Teach directly about prejudice, racism, discrimination, and stereotyping. These are central social science concepts that children need to understand as social studies students and as citizens. In Chapter 8 we present a time-honored strategy for teaching any concept; *prejudice, discrimination,* and *stereotype* are no different. Learning any concept requires three or four vivid examples and a teacher who helps students do the necessary intellectual work of comparing, summarizing, and classifying. The U.S. Department of Justice maintains a glossary of such terms at one of its "kids' page" Internet websites: *http://www.usdoj.gov/kidspage/words.htm.*

- Many teachers and students visit the U.S. Department of Justice website at *http://www.usdoj.gov/kidspage/bias-k-5/index.htm.* Called "Hateful Acts Hurt Kids," this site is intended for children in kindergarten through fifth grade. It has four objectives: to promote discussion among children, parents, and teachers about prejudice, discrimination, and related issues; to sensitize elementary school-age children to the unfairness and hurt of prejudice; to give children who may be victims of prejudice problem-solving skills; and to show children what they can do as bystanders to help prevent or de-escalate hurtful acts based on prejudice. There are also numerous, brief stories about discrimination and prejudice which your students can read, and they are prompted to decide how they might act in a similar circumstance. See the sample at the bottom of this page.

- Have children write biographies about people who have courageously displayed toleration and insisted on the rights not just of themselves but of others. Hold them high as heroes. (See Chapter 13 for biography writing strategies.)

- Post the Voltaire quote, "I disapprove of what you say, but I will defend to the death your right to say it."

- Invite to the classroom historians, geographers, political scientists, economists, anthropologists, and sociologists—both men and women, disabled, and members of racial or ethnic minority groups. This helps break stereotypes while teaching social studies content.

" Nobody sits with me at lunch. They make fun of what I eat. They say it looks and smells funny. It's not peanut butter and jelly so they don't understand the food I bring from home. It's lonely at lunch."

What would you do?

Click on one of the following choices:

A. Ignore the other kid's teasing.
B. Talk to one of your close friends and suggest that she try your food.
C. Speak to your teacher about the problem.

Screen: From website called "Hateful Acts Hurt Kids."
Source: www.usdoj.gov/kidspage/bias-k-5/lunch.htm

GUIDELINE 6. FLEXIBLE GROUPING

Group children in various ways, and change the groups often.

During social studies instruction, groupings of children should be temporary and task-oriented. Often these groups are formed on the basis of a common interest—for example, working together on a display, construction project, play, or report. Other groups are formed on the basis of a common need. For instance, a teacher may work with a small group on reading their text, discussing a controversial issue, developing a map skill, or showing them how to use the materials in a learning center while other children are working independently. Avoid fixed groups in which children are separated permanently for whatever reason, such as reading ability, prior knowledge, or behavior.[14]

Teaching Examples

- Use whole-class grouping when children should have a shared experience—a discussion of a classroom problem, for example, or dramatizing a story about Abraham Lincoln or being introduced to time lines or different kinds of maps, charts, and graphs.
- Needs-based groups should be used sometimes to remediate students who need this kind of assistance but generally to help students achieve *beyond* what they normally do. This applies both to children with specific disabilities as well as to gifted children. This kind of assistance is called *scaffolding* because, like an actual scaffold erected next to a building, it lifts children up to where they can reach a higher level of competence than otherwise would be possible.[15]
- Use cooperative pairs when you want children to practice with information they have heard, give one another explanations, share responses to a reading, or test one another over material that has been studied. Pairs also can be used to coach one another if they are taught to ask good questions: questions that seek clarification, elaboration, a summary, or a prediction. Pairs are easier to form and disband than small groups.
- Use peer-tutoring pairs when a student who is more knowledgeable can help a student who is less so.
- Use cooperative learning in small groups of three to five children for tasks that are complex and require division of labor and group planning. Examples include making different kinds of maps (political, land form, vegetation, highway) of the same area, writing a multichapter "book" on Mexico or Canada, or creating a model of a Pueblo village. These groups should mix children of different abilities, social status, and ethnicity. (See Chapter 11 for details for making cooperative learning effective.)

Summary

These guidelines and examples should help readers explore some of the issues of teaching in diverse classrooms. We have sometimes heard (thankfully, not often) teachers in mainly white suburbs say, "We don't need multicultural education here." This is wrong for two reasons. First, even in the relatively homogeneous classrooms of mainly white, mainly black, mainly Hispanic, or mainly Native American children, teachers and students *still* will have to come to grips with racial, ethnic, and cultural diversity. This will be required particularly in social studies where the subject matter children encounter—the peoples and places, the races and religions, the customs and beliefs—can just as easily be interpreted through prejudiced and ethnocentric eyes as through curious and respectful eyes.

Second, even when racial and ethnic diversity is relatively minimal—say, in a white upper-middle-class suburb—teachers and students *still* have to think about gender and language differences. Children with gifts and disabilities are surely present as well. Teachers cannot ignore the differences for, as we saw earlier, doing so will cause unfair disadvantages for some children. While the red carpet is rolled out for some, it is not extended to all. If our goal is to teach all the children in our classrooms, to provide them with equal opportunities to learn, we need to roll out the red carpet for each of them and help each of them construct the big ideas and the powerful skills in the curriculum. This requires individual-centered education. When we individualize, we do not ignore differences among children; we pay attention to them and, therefore, we learn and we respond.

Understanding Changing Demographics

Let's look more closely at some of the characteristics of children in classrooms. Why? Because key social studies concepts are involved, and because it is not enough only to "celebrate diversity." Teachers need to *understand* diversity and understand it more deeply than professionals in just about any other field. The variables in brief:

1. Ethnicity
2. Culture
3. Race
4. Gender
5. Language and Dialect
6. Giftedness, Disability
7. Multiple Intelligences

ETHNICITY, RACE, AND CULTURE

A child's ethnic group membership and identity matter to the child and to others. Ethnic groups have different values and ways of seeing the world. Children from different ethnic groups do not behave in the same ways and do not necessarily learn in the same ways. Have you thought about the difference your own ethnicity makes in the ways you act, perceive, and believe? Mexican-American children in your classroom often are exposed to "traditional" family values and role models; Portuguese- and Nicaraguan-American children, however, may have experienced a more "modern" home life. This difference is due to the culture and politics of each homeland. African-American girls often have more self-esteem than their European-American counterparts. Filipino and Japanese immigrant children may have seen vastly different sex-role behavior—more gender equity in the Philippines, less in Japan.

Although teachers must be aware of ethnic differences, they must also be careful not to overgeneralize on the basis of ethnicity. Asian-American children clearly are not all alike, as any one who has had Hmong-American and Chinese-American children in class will tell you. Nor are European-, African-, or Arab-American children alike. Differences in religion and social class can have an enormous impact on the behavior and values of children who share a similar ethnic background. Middle-class whites generally share more cultural characteristics with middle-class blacks than with poor whites, for example. Native American children raised in families that emphasize acculturation to the mainstream American lifestyle, which is heavily influenced by European-American ethnicity, may view classroom and playground situations very differently than those who have been encouraged to maintain traditional values.

Let us define a few terms. A *culture* is the values, beliefs, and customs—in brief, the way of life or lifestyle—shared by a group of people or society. Culture is learned. One can belong to many groups, each with distinct cultural characteristics. For example, one is a member of a gender group (women), regional group (southerner), racial group (black), religion (Baptist), occupation (school teacher), social class (lower-middle), ability (hearing impaired), and ethnic group (southern, rural black). The cultural characteristics of each of our several affiliations overlap, always making for a complex cultural identity.

An *ethnic group* is a particular kind of culture group. All Americans are members of one or more ethnic groups. Members of an ethnic group share a common history, a sense of peoplehood and fate, and values and beliefs. Moreover, "members of an ethnic group usually view their group as distinct and separate from other cultural groups within a society."[16] More broadly, an ethnic group is a group distinguished by race, religion, or national origin. Many, many ethnic groups live in the United States, more than in most other nations. There are, for example, Vietnamese Americans, Anglo Americans, Mexican Americans, German Americans, African Americans, and Native Americans (e.g., Lakota Sioux). Irish Catholics are sometimes considered an ethnic group, as are Mormons, Midwesterners, Southern Baptists, and West Texans. The Pilgrims and Puritans of American colonial times were ethnic groups, as were the native groups they encountered.

An *ethnic minority group* has characteristics, usually both physical and cultural, that make its members easily identifiable to other groups. Very often, ethnic minorities suffer discrimination and subordination within a society. Arab Americans, Filipino Americans, Jewish Americans, and African Americans are examples. *Ethnocentrism* is the habit of judging other ethnic groups' beliefs and behaviors by one's own ethnic group's standards: comparing a "them" to an "us" unfavorably. In geography lessons focusing on societies that are quite different from the children's own society, the teacher will sometimes hear ethnocentric statements. These are good opportunities—"teachable moments"—to teach about human diversity, to provide instruction on the concept *ethnocentrism,* to encourage respect and empathy for people everywhere, and to inquire seriously into why a seemingly odd behavior can make complete sense to the people doing it. For example, when students learn that hungry families in rural India may not eat a readily available "food" (e.g., a cow), they may be incredulous.

Race refers to genetically transmitted physical characteristics that are innate and immutable. Race and ethnicity are often confused because in some cases they overlap. For example, the Japanese have physical characteristics that identify them as an Asian racial group. At the same time, the Japanese people have a language, tradition, common heritage, and history that give them an ethnic identity distinct from other Asians. A blond European baby boy who, at the moment of birth, was adopted and raised by a Japanese family would, as an adult, be ethnically Japanese in spite of the physical (racial) characteristics that he inherited from his European ancestors. Perhaps it would be difficult for this boy to be fully assimilated by the Japanese society because of his distinguishing physical characteristics. If so, this is because negative social values are being associated with the physical characteristics. This is *racism,* which is the practice of attaching nonphysical characteristics to physical qualities of human beings. This practice has been and continues to be quite common in the United States and many (probably most) other societies. Race and racism are problems not because of the reality of physical differences among human beings but because there are social values attached to those differences. Denying the prevalence of racism has never helped to end it.[17]

During the past three decades, dramatic changes have occurred in the racial, ethnic, and cultural composition of school populations. Inside our classrooms—as in U.S. society generally—the term *minority group* is quickly becoming factually inaccurate. Traditionally the term has been used loosely to refer to nonwhite and Hispanic people in the United States, but in a matter of decades the *numerical minority* will be the *numerical majority.* In the largest school districts in the nation, this is already the case.

GENDER

In 1920 the Nineteenth Amendment to the Constitution became the law of the land, and thereby women won the right to vote, a right enjoyed by most free white men since the founding of the Republic. Discrimination against women, however, did not end with the Nineteenth Amendment.

Many people have argued that school programs of the past contributed to discrimination against women because they reinforced conventional notions of male superiority. Where this can be studied with a degree of objectivity, as, for example, in analyzing school textbooks, the evidence is overwhelming that males had a clear advantage. They were consistently represented in positions of greater prestige and as being more courageous and more skillful than women. Women tended to be represented in subservient positions in social-service roles or in roles that require serving men, as, for example, secretarial service and nursing. Thus, discrimination against women became *institutionalized* in that both boys *and* girls came to believe in the superiority of the male. Such blatant sexist portrayal generally does not now appear in recently published textbooks and other instructional material.

Nevertheless, during the preschool, elementary, and middle school years, students continue to experience gender bias. Though sex-role stereotyping in curriculum materials has diminished significantly, children's interactions with one another and the teacher's interaction with them remains a serious problem. For more than two decades researchers have confirmed that gender bias is a serious problem from preschool through adult education. Three aspects of gender bias are especially serious and were recently documented in a study conducted by the American Association of University Women (AAUW) called *How Schools Shortchange Girls:*

Doonesbury

- Girls receive significantly less attention from classroom teachers than do boys.
- African-American girls have fewer interactions with teachers than do white girls, despite evidence that they attempt to initiate interactions more frequently.
- Sexual harassment of girls by boys—from innuendo to actual assault—in our nation's schools is increasing.[18]

Research on this problem suggests that there are "two worlds" in the classroom, one of active boys, the other of inactive girls: "Male students control classroom conversation. They ask and answer more questions. They receive more praise for the intellectual quality of their ideas. They get criticized. They get help when they are confused."[19]

Consider this example from a fifth-grade classroom that is getting out of hand. The teacher quiets down the commotion, then reminds students of the rule to "raise your hand." She tells her students the reason for the rule: "There are too many of us here to all shout out at once." Order is momentarily restored. Soon, Stephen shouts out:

Stephen: I think Lincoln was the best president. He held the country together during the war.

Teacher: A lot of historians would agree with you.

Mike (seeing that nothing happened to Stephen, calls out): I don't. Lincoln was okay, but my Dad liked Reagan. He always said Reagan was a great president.

David (calling out): Reagan? Are you kidding?

Teacher: Who do you think our best president was, Dave?

David: FDR. He saved us from the Depression.

Max (calling out): I don't think it's right to pick one best president. There were a lot of good ones.

Teacher: That's interesting.

Kimberly (calling out): I don't think the presidents today are as good as the ones we used to have.

Teacher: Okay, Kimberly. But you forgot the rule. You're supposed to raise your hand.[20]

As a result of interactions like these, boys often receive more instruction and better instruction than girls. When boys are praised, for example, it is more often for the kind of learning and thinking they are doing at the moment; consequently, it serves as valuable feedback that will affect achievement. When girls are praised, it is often with less specific feedback. Furthermore, when girls are praised or criticized in a more helpful, specific way, they are twice as likely as boys to receive it for following or breaking the rules of interaction, form, and appearance, as Kimberly was, rather than for the substance of their thinking and their work. "I like how quiet you are" is one message the girls get. "You are so neat" is another. "I love your margins" is another.

The major goal of gender equity in the classroom is equal opportunity to learn. Sex discrimination prevents children from having an equal chance to get attention, praise, constructive criticism, and, in general, *instruction*. Over the years, this lack of helpful attention adds up. By one estimate, girls receive 1,800 fewer hours of instruction than boys between preschool and college. The main theme of the studies on gender in the classroom is that girls are taught less often and less constructively than boys are.

LANGUAGE DIFFERENCES IN THE CLASSROOM

Another kind of difference that matters greatly for children and their teachers is linguistic diversity. Over 100 distinct language groups are present in the United States (see Table 2–1). You should be able to obtain information on languages spoken in your state by calling the state education office, or search the state-by-state information at the U.S. Census Bureau's website: *http://www.census.gov.*

When children come to school in most communities in the United States today, they find that most of the adults and classmates speak one language at school, English, and that one dialect, standard English, is preferred. Depending on whether their home language matches the school's, students might face an awesome communication and learning barrier. If the match is perfect, however, the effect is like having a red carpet rolled out for them. Many of the directions and explanations given in classrooms and on the playground are verbal; most reading materials are in English; and a child's social contacts with peers, which are crucial for social development, depend heavily on linguistic expression. The impact on a child who speaks little or no English can be enormous. Consider this reflection by a Chinese-American student:

> I started to hate myself when I failed to answer the teacher's questions. . . because I couldn't express my answers in English. Then I began to hate everything in the world, including my parents because they took me to this country.[21]

Or this one:

> I just sat in my classes and didn't understand anything. Sometimes I would try to look like I knew what was going on; sometimes I would just try to think about a happy time when I didn't feel stupid. My teachers never called on me or talked to me. I think either they forgot I was there or else wished I wasn't.[22]

Certainly not all limited-English-speaking children react this way. Some respond eagerly to the task of learning the new language, have a relaxed attitude toward the difficulties that inevitably arise, and make good progress learning English *and* academic content and skills. Such children most likely are those who are provided content-based instruction in their

TABLE 2–1   Common languages in the United States.

Here are the twenty-five most commonly spoken languages in the United States after English. The number of persons speaking that language is given along with the state with the highest *percentage* of speakers of that language.

	Language	Number of Speakers	State with Highest % of Speakers
1.	Spanish	17,339,172	New Mexico
2.	French	1,702,176	Maine
3.	German	1,547,099	North Dakota
4.	Italian	1,308,648	New York
5.	Chinese	1,249,213	Hawaii
6.	Tagalog	843,251	Hawaii
7.	Polish	723,483	Illinois
8.	Korean	626,478	Hawaii
9.	Vietnamese	507,069	California
10.	Portuguese	429,860	Rhode Island
11.	Japanese	427,657	Hawaii
12.	Greek	388,260	Massachusetts
13.	Arabic	355,150	Michigan
14.	Hindi	331,484	New Jersey
15.	Russian	241,798	New York
16.	Yiddish	213,064	New York
17.	Thai/Lao	206,266	Hawaii
18.	Persian	201,865	California
19.	French Creole	187,658	Florida
20.	Armenian	149,694	California
21.	Navajo	148,530	New Mexico
22.	Hungarian	147,902	New Jersey
23.	Hebrew	144,292	New York
24.	Dutch	142,684	Utah
25.	Mon-Khmer	127,441	Rhode Island

Source: U.S. Census, 1990 (*www.census.gov*)

home language, supplemented with English lessons and practice. The children who do especially well are often those whose command of the home language is excellent for their age, who are highly motivated to learn the new language, whose family support for second language acquisition is warm and unambiguous, *and whose teachers do not confuse the lack of proficiency in the new language with a learning disability.* Some of these children's parents and teachers may themselves be multilingual and move smoothly between languages and dialects, depending on the social situation.

It takes time, effort, and good opportunities to learn a second or third language.

Research shows that it takes about two years to learn a second language well enough to engage in face-to-face conversation. It takes three times as long, or longer, to develop the skills needed to learn subject matter. Readers of this book who are themselves bilingual will know well this distinction. It is one thing for an English-speaking student of French (as a second language) to engage in conversational French with a classmate or a waiter in a café. It is quite another to go to a French school where it is necessary to comprehend school books written in the French language and to grasp concepts from lessons delivered in French.

Finally, we arrive at the term *dialect,* which is a variation of a language spoken by members of a regional or ethnic group. Each variation has somewhat different rules of speech and meaning. Educators disagree on how best to deal with dialect variations in the classroom. Most seem to agree that speakers of nonstandard dialects should learn to speak standard English.[23] The reason is that social rewards, such as higher paying jobs and higher status, generally will follow. Teachers, however, should encourage students to *retain and use the home dialect as well.* The point is not to replace it. Like a first language, a first dialect should be regarded as a strength, not a deficit. Teachers and children who are bilingual clearly have an advantage in a modern, diverse, and global society; the same can be said for those who are proficient in more than one dialect.

CHILDREN WITH SPECIAL NEEDS

The logic of individualizing—knowing individual children and their cultures and seeing differences as differences, not deficits—extends to children with special needs. Children with special needs have abilities and disabilities that are exceptional: beyond the usual.

Educators and parents often believe these children require what is traditionally called "special education," the purpose of which, simply, is to help these children reach their potential.

It is important that children with disabilities not be denied access to the academic curriculum. For this reason, the teacher can expect one or more children with varying types of disabilities to be present in the classroom. This practice is popularly called *mainstreaming* or *inclusion,* and it is the school's response to laws requiring that such children be educated with their nondisabled peers to the maximum extent possible.

What the teacher can and will do with these children in the classroom depends on the individual child's knowledge, experiences, and needs and the kinds of support services that are available. It is quite clear that a child who is physically challenged but intellectually gifted will be taught differently than one who is physically normal but mildly or severely mentally retarded. If the classroom has an interpreter-tutor who can work with the child for part of the time, it becomes easier for the regular teacher to integrate that child into the day-to-day life and activities of the classroom.

In the case of a child who is severely disabled, the chances are good that a teacher trained in special education will prepare what is called an Individualized Education Program (IEP). The classroom teacher may be responsible for only a small part of the implementation of the IEP. On the other hand, in the case of a child with mild mental retardation, the teacher may have full responsibility for the preparation and implementation of the IEP. The regular classroom teacher, the special education teacher, and other support personnel must, of course, collaborate to ensure a coordinated program of instruction for the child.

The Individualized Education Program must take into account the child's present level of attainment or development. Therefore, an assessment will be done. Based on that information, the IEP stipulates the long-range goals to be met by the end of the year and the short-term objectives to be achieved in order to attain the long-range goals. The short-term objectives should be listed in the sequence in which they are to be achieved. Although the regular teacher may exercise some initiative in preparing the IEP, the program planning and development *must* include, on a firsthand basis, the principal or other school representative and the child's parent or guardian. (Teacher-prepared IEPs that are sent to the child's parent or guardian for signature are not acceptable in terms of federal legislation.)

The actual format of the IEP will vary from district to district although the substance of what is included will remain much the same. The sample form provided in Figure 2–1 on pp. 48–49 illustrates a standard IEP that includes components required by federal regulation.

Gifts and Talents

Even though each child is unique or exceptional in her or his own way, some children are singled out as *more* exceptional. Children with special gifts or talents have a remarkable degree of general ability and/or extraordinary specific abilities. Furthermore, they display advanced creativity and are highly motivated to achieve in the areas of their ability and talent. They will often persevere on a problem far beyond the point where other children lose interest or give up. Such children in the elementary grades usually handle subject matter easily because of their capacity to use language and understand abstract relationships. Their work is sometimes "over the top"—very advanced for their age. Here is the gifted pianist or poet in the fourth grade and the third-grade child who not only plants kernels of corn in milk cartons at the plant table, but, captivated by the fact that beans are an inexpensive and plentiful source of protein, brings to class the next week a well-worked-out plan for cultivating beans in greenhouses attached ingeniously to homeless shelters. She has attended to the details of light and moisture, researched the necessary building permits, and is asking how to raise the funds.

Recognizing giftedness is not always this easy. The state department of education or the local school district establishes criteria that teachers and administrators are asked to use. They usually are derived from a child's school achievement history, teacher observations, and scores on intelligence tests. Sometimes schools define as gifted any child who scores in the top 2 or 3 percent of their age group. Guidelines may be distributed to teachers with questions such as these: Who among your children has an extraordinary vocabulary? Who is remarkably (and perhaps annoyingly) observant? Who seems to know about many things the other children do not? Who tackles problems that other children do not even see?

Regardless of the availability of special programs for children with special gifts and talents, the regular classroom teacher will need to make provisions for them. Social studies is a curriculum area that is ideally suited to make such adjustments because of its open-ended subject matter. Below are a few suggestions, and readers wanting more will find the work of Sally Beisser and Carol Tomlinson helpful.[24]

- *Tiered assignments.* All children will be learning to understand and make maps, but the teacher may ask high-ability children to examine together the mapping problems faced by cartographers working in the field today, perhaps in space or on the ocean floor.

- *Independent study.* Follow the interests of the high-ability child and encourage independent studies in those directions. Perhaps the teacher has led an interpretive discussion of an entry in the Lewis and Clark journals (see Chapter 4). A student with remarkable spatial gifts might then independently create a relief map of the entire journey, and this could be the centerpiece of a submission to the state's History Day competition. Another child with a talent for writing or an unusual insight into the human condition might compare the journals of renowned journal authors (e.g., Anne Frank and Meriwether Lewis).

Disabilities and Challenges

Harvard psychologist Howard Gardner notes that we are all gifted and challenged simultaneously.[25] Perhaps you are a gifted violinist, but when your Chevrolet breaks down on the highway you are utterly mystified and do not even bother to look under the hood. Or you are mechanically gifted but cannot carry a tune. Just as some people are exceptionally gifted, others are exceptionally challenged. In America's elementary and middle schools are children who are mildly and profoundly *mentally retarded,* children who have *physical disabilities* (e.g., epilepsy, hearing impairment, cerebral palsy), *emotional and behavioral disorders,* and *communication disorders* (e.g., delayed language development, stuttering). Other children (sometimes the

FIGURE 2–1 Sample IEP form.

PIEDMONT PUBLIC SCHOOLS
INDIVIDUALIZED EDUCATION PROGRAM

Standard Form

Student _____ Birthdate _____
C.A. _____

Address _____ (include zip) Lives With _____ Relationship _____ Home Phone _____ Work Phone _____

Home School _____ Grade _____ IEP Conference Date _____ Projected Review Date _____

Teacher _____ Program _____ School _____ Date Enrolled _____ Terminated _____

I. SUMMARY OF PRESENT LEVELS OF PERFORMANCE
(Include statements of progress in each area from last reporting period)

ACADEMIC:

PHYSICAL:

SOCIAL:

II. ANALYSIS OF ASSESSMENT DATA
(Report of significant changes since initial IEP)

ELIGIBILITY CRITERIA: _____

PLACEMENT OFFICE ONLY:

_____ Date Enrolled
_____ Teacher
_____ Building
_____ Program Assigned

PROGRAM AND/OR REPLACEMENT CHANGE:

Team Leader: _____ Date: _____
Parent: _____ Date: _____

PROGRAM RECOMMENDATION:

Psychologist: _____ Date: _____
Parent: _____ Date: _____
Date: _____

FIGURE 2-1 *continued.*

III. STUDENT GOALS & OBJECTIVES

Academic Year _____

Special Classroom Teacher _____

Support Services _____

(Specify Service)

Name of Student	B.D.	Grade	Program	Building	Teacher	Date Enrolled	

Goals:	Initial Objectives:	Evaluation Criteria & Progress Notes (include pre-test, post-test data, and grades)	Date Started	Date Completed

_____
Signature of person or persons responsible for reporting progress on goals and objectives

_____
Parent Signature

_____
Date

same ones) will have *learning disabilities*. Learning disabilities pose challenges in specific aspects of functioning, for example, reading, writing, or thinking abstractly. Dyslexia is one well-known learning disability.

Please note: *Learning disability* is a much-overused term, dangerously so. No doubt too many children are made to endure this label. For example, limited-English-speaking students do not have a "learning disability"; they just do not know the second language well enough to understand their teacher. Children who belong to ethnic minority groups, especially African-American boys, are disproportionately labeled "learning disabled." This was especially true before a federal law was passed that prevented this sort of segregation, but it persists today. Some African-American parents have created separate schools for their children to protect them from racist practices like these.

Let us emphasize two cautions. First, learning challenges are not disadvantages unless the child is in a situation where the disability or disorder gets in the way. A child with a hearing impairment, for example, is not necessarily at a disadvantage when making a map of the classroom or playground. The violin-playing Chevrolet driver above, the one with a "mechanical disability," is not disadvantaged when he or she is eating dinner with friends.

Second, educators' conversations about exceptionality are loaded with labels that are double-edged swords. On the one hand, labels help educators speak precisely about teaching and learning; on the other, labels can be attached to children and "stick." When that happens, children may not be helped to achieve their potential, which, recall, is the purpose of special education. Rather, the label may be used as an excuse by teachers, administrators, and parents to not bother teaching children what they actually may be quite capable of learning. Figure 2–2 describes the Education for All Handicapped Children Act, PL 94-142.

MULTIPLE INTELLIGENCES

Q: Are you gifted or are you challenged?

A: You are both.

We conclude this demographic tour of today's diverse classrooms by taking a closer look at a fascinating idea mentioned earlier: Each person is simultaneously gifted and challenged. Howard Gardner's theory of multiple intelligences has become popular with teachers across the nation who are eager to individualize instruction for each child. Gardner proposes that intelligence is not a singular or general phenomenon, of which any one of us has more or less. There are seven intelligences, not one, and there may be more. "This is a preliminary list," Gardner writes. *"The real point here is to make the case for the plurality of intellect."*[26] Each of us has all of them to one degree or another: linguistic, musical, spatial, logical-mathematical, bodily-kinesthetic, interpersonal understanding, and intrapersonal understanding. Most people eventually develop all the intelligences to a fairly competent level, but some people are "gifted" in one or more areas and "disabled" or challenged in others.

There are many ways to be intelligent in each category. Table 2–2 describes each kind of intelligence very briefly and suggests related learning activities in which children might participate. The purpose of gearing activities to multiple intelligences (MI) is to tap into *all* children's current strengths and also to encourage them to develop strengths in new areas. Traditionally,

FIGURE 2–2   Know the law.

The Education for All Handicapped Children Act, known as PL 94-142, was signed into law by President Gerald Ford in 1975, to go into effect in 1977 with no expiration date. It passed both Houses of Congress by very wide margins—probably because the issue had already been settled by the courts. This law was amended in 1990 by the Individuals with Disabilities Education Act (IDEA). Changes to the law included the substitution of the word disabled for the word handicapped. In the same year, the Americans with Disabilities Act (ADA) recognized the civil rights of persons with disabilities.

   PL 94-142 is based on a philosophy of inclusion rather than exclusion. It embraces the "zero-reject" principle and frowns on the segregation and labeling of human beings. It shatters long-held assumptions about who is educable.

Main points of this legislation:

1. The availability of a free and appropriate public education for all children with disabilities between the ages of 3 and 21; school districts are obliged to search for and identify such children.
2. The maintenance of an Individualized Education Program (IEP) for all children with disabilities, prepared in cooperation with the parent or guardian, the teacher, and the school principal.
3. The guarantee of complete due process procedures.
4. The provision of special education and related services as needed in the "least restrictive" environment.
5. Nondiscriminatory testing, evaluation, and placement.
6. Placement in regular public school settings with nondisabled peers to the maximum extent appropriate and feasible.

activities emphasizing linguistic and logical intelligence have predominated in many classrooms. As a consequence, children with these strengths may have been advantaged while other children were not given sufficient opportunities to learn. Remember the red-carpet effect? Here is yet another way to roll out the metaphorical red carpet for each child.

By individualizing, teachers can help more children achieve greater understanding of the curriculum. The third-grade child who loves to dramatize can be put in charge of a short play about the first meeting of Spaniards and Pueblo Indians in what is today New Mexico, and the child who has not participated much in dramatics can be encouraged to take a role. Another child can head the team that writes (and revises again and again) the script. Second-graders assembling the classroom store can be measuring, writing, and counting. Others can be planning the grand opening ceremony, complete with songs and interviews with local officials played by classmates. As one advocate has written, multiple-intelligence teaching "encompasses what good teachers have always done in their teaching: reaching beyond the text and the blackboard to awaken students' minds."[27]

TABLE 2–2   Teaching with multiple intelligences.

Intelligence	Characteristics	Entry Points
Linguistic	Sensitivity to words, their meanings and functions.	Read and write about it, discuss it.
Musical	Appreciation of musical expression and ability to produce music.	Sing or hum it, drum it or rap it, listen quietly to it, compose it, find out what music has been written to express it.
Spatial	Keen perception of the visual-spatial world and ability to change initial perceptions into other forms.	Map it, draw it, visualize the whole procedure.
Logical-mathematical	Sensitivity to and ability to perceive logical and numerical patterns.	Quantify it, identify the lines of reasoning used, classify it.
Bodily-kinesthetic	Sensitivity to one's body movements and ability to control them.	Dance it, get your hands in it, build it, dramatize it.
Interpersonal	Sensitivity and capacity to respond to other persons' way of being (feelings, moods).	Tutor someone, collaborate with others, discuss it, conduct "oral history" interviews.
Intrapersonal	Access to one's own feelings and moods and the ability to discriminate among and draw on them.	Write about it in a response journal, find personal analogy to it.

Source: Adapted from Howard Gardner, *Frames of Mind: The Theory of Multiple Intelligences* (New York: Basic Books, 1983); *Multiple Intelligences: The Theory in Practice* (New York: Basic Books, 1993); and *The Disciplined Mind* (New York: Simon & Schuster, 1999).

Two cautions about multiple intelligence theory must be mentioned: trivializing the curriculum and stereotyping children. First, Gardner himself is now chagrined to learn that his MI theory is often "invoked to convey trivial examples, or to present important examples in an offbeat or anecdotal way ('Let's sing our time tables, children!' says the teacher. . .)." MI theory should be invoked instead to present "ideas that are consequential."[28] His worry is that MI theory becomes an end in itself rather than a means to an end—striving toward powerful curriculum objectives. Choose a powerful, mind-expanding curriculum first, he urges. Then think of the multiple intelligences as multiple "entry points" for helping individual students engage and achieve that curriculum. Every child should learn, for example, to use the methods of scientific inquiry to formulate and test hypotheses about the social and natural world. Some children might enter this domain of knowledge through discussion where they can hear the ideas of one classmate expressed alongside the ideas of another (Chapter 3). Other children might enter it by audiotaping then interpreting and writing an "oral history" of war veterans in their family or neighborhood (Chapter 4). Others might research the songs of war and peace—both the marches and the laments—while others delve into the mathematics of food production and distribution. The point is this: Keep your eye on the prize (worthy curriculum objectives) and use MI theory to help children achieve it.

A second caution: MI theory shouldn't be used to "peg" a child as this or that. "He is a musical learner, she is linguistic, he is kinesthetic" and so forth. Quite to the contrary, Gardner emphasizes that we are all gifted and challenged simultaneously: All of us have strengths and weaknesses across the plurality of intelligences in us, to be sure, but *nearly all of us become fairly competent in each intelligence area in our lifetimes.*

Conclusion

When teaching in a diverse classroom, you will be called upon to use more of, and add continually to, your professional knowledge and skills. As a result, your work should steadily become more rewarding and fulfilling. You will be stimulated to learn more and more about your children *and yourself.* Like us, you will probably conclude that you are yourself "gifted and challenged simultaneously." If you are open and curious, your conversations with children, colleagues, and parents will be fascinating and instructive. Your students will benefit because they have a teacher who genuinely appreciates them, who does not shy away from their cultural and individual differences, who does not see their differences as deficits, and who has high achievement expectations for each of them. At the same time, *you* will learn continually and enjoy one insight after another. This makes for a satisfying professional life, and it is just the sort of thing people are leaving other kinds of work to find.

OUR COMMON GROUND: THE AMERICAN DREAM

Ours is not a Christian nation, an Islamic nation, or Jewish or Buddhist nation. Rather, it is a constitutional democracy where people created a government that would protect their liberties, not force a common way of life on them. When we look at an American classroom in a public school, one thing we can be sure of is that the children do not share a common ethnic identity, home language, or a common set of abilities and talents. At parent night, we do not encounter families with a common set of political party preferences, religions, or experiences.

But with all this diversity is there nothing that unites us? There is. Our common ground is our shared commitment to the values and principles of constitutional democracy. First among these are the freedoms of religion, speech, and press and the commitment to equality and fairness. There is also the commitment to rule by law and to the expectation that each person will take responsibility for the common good of his or her community. This is called civic-mindedness or civic virtue. Without it there could be no democracy. After all, it is not enough that we look out for our *own* rights and liberties; democratic citizens must insist on *one another's* rights and liberties. This is the essence of mutual respect.

Discussion Questions and Suggested Activities

1. Demography and diversity are key social studies concepts, and we used them in this chapter to survey just one population: the children in our classrooms. Select another population, such as the college or university where you are taking this class or your workplace or favorite restaurant or shopping mall. What are its demographic characteristics? Is it, too, becoming more diverse?

2. What are your memories of racial, ethnic, and linguistic differences in your elementary classrooms when you were a child? What are your memories of gender bias?

3. Call your state department of education and one or two school districts to get local demographic data. What are the home languages of students in your state? What is the number of immigrant children, and which immigrant group is growing fastest?

4. Do you agree with the following statements? Take a position on each one and articulate your reasons.

   a. "The problem is not that some children are unready for school. Rather, schools too often are unready for children."

   b. "Teachers sometimes treat cultural differences in children as deficits. This is not right, and it is ethnocentric."

   c. "You shouldn't treat a child with a special gift as 'gifted' any more than you would treat a child with a learning disability as 'disabled.'"

   d. "I don't care if they're red, green, or polka dot. I just treat them all like children."

5. Develop a floor plan of a classroom that would lend itself to flexible grouping and multimedia learning activities.

Selected References

Au, Kathryn H. (1993). *Literacy instruction in multicultural settings.* Orlando: Harcourt.

Banks, James A. (1997). *Educating citizens in a multicultural society.* New York: Teachers College Press.

Darling-Hammond, Linda. (1997). *The right to learn: A blueprint for creating schools that work.* San Francisco, Jossey-Bass.

Delpit, Lisa. (1995). *Other people's children: Cultural conflict in the classroom.* New York: New Press.

Ford, C. W. (1999). *The hero with an African face.* New York: Bantam.

Gardner, Howard. (1993). *Multiple intelligences: The theory in practice.* New York: Basic Books.

Grossman, Herbert. (1995). *Special education in a diverse society.* Boston: Allyn & Bacon.

Ladson-Billings, Gloria. (1994). *The dreamkeepers: Successful teachers of African American children.* San Francisco: Jossey-Bass.

Pang, Valerie Ooka. (1995). Asian Pacific American students: A diverse and complex population. In James A. Banks & Cherry A. McGee Banks (Eds.), *Handbook of research on multicultural education* (pp. 412–424). New York: Macmillan.

Radencich, Marguerite C., & McKay, Lyn J. (1995). *Flexible grouping for literacy in the elementary grades.* Boston: Allyn & Bacon.

Sadker, Myra, & Sadker, David. (1994). *Failing at fairness: How America's schools cheat girls.* New York: Charles Scribner's Sons.

Tomlinson, Carol Ann. (1995). *How to differentiate instruction in mixed-ability classrooms.* Alexandria, VA: Association for Supervision and Curriculum Development.

Notes

1. Eugene E. Garcia & Rene Gonzalez, Issues in systemic reform for culturally and linguistically diverse students, *Teachers College Record, 96* (Spring 1995): 420.
2. Lisa Delpit, *Other people's children: Cultural conflict in the classroom* (New Press, 1995), 120.
3. Gloria Ladson-Billings, *The dreamkeepers: Successful teachers of African American children* (San Francisco: Jossey-Bass, 1994), 33.
4. Ibid., 31.
5. Lisa Delpit discusses this phenomenon in her wise book, *Other people's children: Cultural conflict in the classroom* (New Press, 1995).
6. Christine I. Bennett, *Comprehensive multicultural education: Theory and practice,* 3rd ed. (Boston: Allyn & Bacon, 1995), 223–24.
7. Kathryn H. Au, *Literacy instruction in multicultural settings* (Orlando: Harcourt, 1993), 12–13.
8. Ladson-Billings, *Dreamkeeper,* 19.
9. Teaching multicultural literacy to teachers, *Teaching Education, 4* (Summer/Fall 1991): 139–140.
10. See James A. Banks, *Teaching strategies for ethnic studies,* 5th ed. (Boston: Allyn & Bacon, 1991).
11. Howard Gardner, *The disciplined mind* (Simon & Schuster, 1999), 188.
12. California Department of Education, *Bilingual education handbook,* 2.
13. New York: McGraw-Hill, 1999.
14. See Marguerite C. Radencich & Lyn J. McKay, *Flexible grouping for literacy in the elementary grades* (Boston: Allyn & Bacon, 1995).
15. Ann Brown. Design experiments: Theoretical and methodological challenges in creating complex interventions in classroom settings. *Journal of the Learning Sciences, 2* (1996): 141–178. Roland G. Tharp & Ronald Gallimore, *Rousing minds to life: Teaching, learning, and schooling in social context* (Cambridge: Cambridge University Press, 1988).
16. James A. Banks, *An introduction to multicultural education* (Boston: Allyn & Bacon, 1998), 115.
17. Contemporary social scientists raise deep questions about the meaning of "race"—its use and misuse and the ways race matters to people. See Warren Crichlow & Cameron McCarthy's *Race identity and representation in education* (New York: Routledge, 1993) and Cornel West's *Race matters* (Boston: Beacon, 1993).
18. American Association of University Women, *How schools shortchange girls,* Executive Summary (Washington, DC: Author, 1992).
19. Myra Sadker & David Sadker, *Failing at fairness: How America's schools cheat girls* (New York: Charles Scribner's Sons, 1994), p. 42.
20. Ibid., 43.
21. Herbert Grossman, *Special education in a diverse society* (Boston: Allyn & Bacon, 1995), 145.

22. Ibid., 189.

23. See, for example, Lisa Delpit, *Other people's children: Cultural conflict in the classroom* (New York: New Press, 1995).

24. Sally R. Beisser, Differentiating the curriculum for the high-ability student. In L. Mann (Ed.), *ASCD curriculum handbook* (Alexandria, VA: Association for Supervision and Curriculum Development, 1997), 12.333-12.347. Carol Ann Tomlinson, *How to differentiate instruction in mixed-ability classrooms* (Alexandria, VA: Association for Supervision and Curriculum Development, 1995).

25. Howard Gardner, *Multiple intelligences: The theory in practice.* New York: Basic Books, 1993.

26. Ibid., 9.

27. Thomas Armstrong, *Multiple intelligences in the classroom* (Alexandria, VA: Association for Supervision and Curriculum Development, 1994), 50.

28. Howard Gardner, *The disciplined mind* (Simon & Schuster, 1999), 188.

Websites

http://www.census.gov/

http://www.familytreemaker.com/allsearch.html

http://www.usdoj.gov/kidspage/words.htm

http://www.usdoj.gov/kidspage/bias-k-5/index.htm

http://www.usdoj.gov/kidspage/bias-k-5/lunch.htm

PART TWO

The Social Studies Curriculum

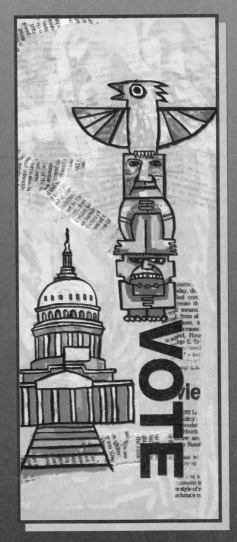

3

Citizenship Education and Democratic Values

Main Idea

There can be no democracy without democratic citizens, and educating democratic citizens is the primary mission of the social studies program. There are six dimensions of citizenship education. Attending to each will help nurture citizens who can create a better world.

Key Concepts

deliberation and decision making, voting, community service and action, citizenship knowledge, democratic values and dispositions (virtues)

Chapter Outline

- Why Citizenship Education?
- Citizenship Education: Six Dimensions
  - Deliberation and Decision Making
  - Voting and Elections
  - Community Service and Action
  - Citizenship Knowledge
  - Democratic Values
  - Democratic Dispositions and Virtues
- Conclusion
- Discussion Questions and Suggested Activities
- Selected References
- Notes

Chapter Snapshot

Mrs. Paley gathered the kindergartners at the rug area where they have their best deliberations. She put up a poster that read, YOU CAN'T SAY "YOU CAN'T PLAY" and asked the children, "Do you think we need this rule in our classroom?" They greeted the idea with disbelief. Hands shot into the air, and here began a long-term inquiry into public life—democratic life beyond family and friend groups. With two additional questions that she asked often (Will the rule work? Is it fair?), Mrs. Paley guided the discussion to issues at the heart of democratic citizenship in a diverse society. These kindergartners are engaged in the supreme act of popular sovereignty, the same as legislators: deliberating public policy.

 A favorite website http://www.kidsvotingusa.org/ This site helps young people get involved in elections. Click on "education" and "cool sites."

Democracy is not a machine that keeps running on its own. It is a human invention that must continually be reinvented by people. People become democratic citizens when they engage in this ongoing invention of democracy. Without democratic citizens, there can be no democracy. This chapter deals with the primary mission of social studies curriculum and instruction, which is to educate democratic citizens.

Democratic citizenship education aims to prepare children for a particular kind of relationship to one another and to the political community. While students will identify with diverse cultural and ethnic communities, religious beliefs, and family backgrounds, they share one political identity. This common political identity exists alongside multiple cultural identities. In American constitutional democracy, it is called *democratic citizenship,* or simply *citizenship.* According to the U.S. Constitution, in which the legal definition of citizenship can be found, citizens are persons who were born in the United States or who were born elsewhere and become citizens through a procedure called *naturalization.*

Children typically are introduced to the U.S. Constitution as part of the fifth-grade social studies curriculum. Many teachers incorporate the Constitution into their teaching and classroom management systems long before the fifth grade, but it is often during this grade that children are helped to read and interpret the Constitution. This is an important moment in the political socialization of the next generation, for the Constitution is the citizen's handbook and the nation's book of agreements.

A paraphrased version of the Constitution is usually included in fifth-grade textbooks. One appears in this text following page 72. Readers will note that it contains all the parts: the preamble, the 7 articles containing the rules by which citizens agree to live, and 26 changes or additions, called amendments. The first 10 amendments are together called the Bill of Rights.

Why Citizenship Education?

It may seem obvious that education for democratic citizenship is a worthwhile educational goal. Indeed, most school districts in the United States include it in their mission statements. Yet, citizenship education often gets overlooked amid the tremendous pressure to increase students' math and reading scores. Also, it is sometimes assumed that the knowledge and skills citizens need are by-products of the study of other school subjects. Alas, this is wishful thinking.

Democracy is a system for living together fairly and freely and for solving the problems that inevitably arise. But the knowledge, character, values, and skills citizens need for democratic living do not emerge without education. In a talk to teachers some years ago, writer and social critic James Baldwin warned that if children are not educated to live democratically, then they may well become apathetic or worse: They could become the next generation of people to sponsor a Holocaust such as the one in Germany in the 1930s and 1940s. Baldwin argued that the perpetrators of these crimes against humanity were very well educated and knew a great deal about reading, writing, literature, math, and science, but in spite of their education, they could not live democratically. They used their knowledge and skill to build not only great works of art and architecture, but concentration camps and a human nightmare. They swore allegiance to a tyrant and committed unimaginable atrocities against humanity. "The boys and girls who were born during the era of the Third Reich," Baldwin said, "when educated to the purposes of the Third Reich, became barbarians."[1]

Democracy requires that we educate children to the ideals of democracy, and those ideals require citizens of great character and civility. They require the ability to reason in principled ways, for example, to possess a deep appreciation for democratic values such as liberty, the common good, justice, and equality; to think critically and to resolve disputes in nonviolent ways; to insist on other people's rights (not only one's own); to cooperate with persons with whom one may not want to cooperate; to tolerate religious and political views different from one's own; and, indeed, to *insist* on the free expression of those views, as in the great democratic slogan attributed to French writer Voltaire, "I disapprove of what you say, but I will defend to the death your right to say it."

These skills are a tall order! What can elementary school teachers do? *They can do plenty.* As Polly Greenberg writes in *Young Children,* "Democracy is full of problems waiting to be solved." Teachers can encourage children continually to solve small problems cooperatively. They can form the habit of saying to a cluster of young children, "How can we solve this problem?" "What should we do?" "What's your idea?"[2] Such questions nurture cooperative discussion, decision making, and individual responsibility which, together, are *the* basic practices of democracy. Each primary grade classroom should have "the rug." The rug, according to elementary school principal Ethel Sadowsky, is "a spot where children gather on the first day of school to formulate the rules that will govern the classroom."[3] The rug is also used throughout the year as a place to discuss current problems and concerns. These are typical children's complaints that might be discussed on "the rug":

- One another's behavior: "She wouldn't let me play with them."
- Teamwork problems: "He never lets anybody else talk!"
- Fairness issues: "It's not right that the row closest to the door always gets to the playground first!"

Citizenship Education: Six Dimensions

There is general consensus in constitutional democracies that citizens need to be educated to understand and participate in majority rule, to respect minority rights, to care for the common good, to protect one another's freedoms, and to limit the size and scope of government. Still, wide leeway is left to teachers: Some conceptualize the citizen role mainly as one of compliance with authorities. Accordingly, they teach courteousness and obedience. Other teachers define the role in broader, more active and participatory terms. They teach students that it is their civic duty to vote regularly and only after informing themselves, to participate in civic decision making, and to engage in public service.

We recommend the second approach. In the early elementary grades, this means bringing children to the circle or "the rug" to discuss shared problems and concerns and to help decide the rules by which they agree to live in the classroom and the school. In intermediate grades, the rug is replaced with a class meeting or a classroom town meeting. It is the shared decision making about something that matters to each person in the group—civic discourse about a rule that will be binding on all—that teaches the citizenship lessons in this case.

The second approach means also that young persons are taught the importance of voting regularly and thoughtfully. As we will see later in this chapter, voting is a powerful public act. It expresses one's commitment to the ideals of democracy—that government ought to be "of the people, by the people, and for the people" as Lincoln expressed in his Gettysburg Address. Voting connects the voter to the broader political community that lies beyond one's smaller cultural communities (religious and ethnic groups, racial and linguistic groups, family and occupational groups, gender, sexual orientation, etc.). The act of voting helps create and sustain the citizen identity that must exist alongside these other identities. And, of course, one's own vote has consequences for everyone else: legislators and judges and presidents are elected or defeated; ballot initiatives are voted up or down; schools get more or less funding.

The power a citizen exercises in the act of voting, however, should be guided by knowledge (e.g., of law and government), democratic values (e.g., equality and liberty), democratic dispositions (e.g., civic-mindedness and honesty), and the citizen's own experiences in community service. *Children need to begin developing all of these in kindergarten.* Even community service, such as participating in canned food drives, simple as they are, gives children the opportunity to care for people they do not know, yet to whom they are related as members of the same community. Another way to develop these values is to have committees of children decide how to welcome new students and orient them to the playground, lunchroom, bathrooms, library, and bicycle racks.

These, then, are the basic dimensions of democratic citizenship education, six fronts in the battle against the cruelty of which Baldwin reminded us. They are deliberation (discussion and decision making), voting, community service and action, knowledge, democratic values, and dispositions (Figure 3–1). We explore each in the following sections. The first—deliberation—gets the most attention because it is the most basic and because so much of its foundation can be laid in the primary grades and then elaborated in the intermediate and upper grades.

FIGURE 3–1
Dimensions of democratic citizenship education.

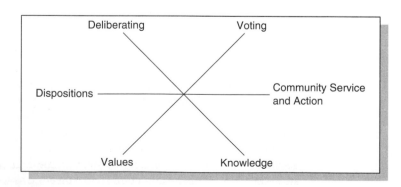

DELIBERATION: DISCUSSION AND DECISION MAKING

"After lots of talk, we decide on our rules."
—*Gretchen Calkins, third-grader*

Deliberation is discussion for the purpose of making a decision that will be binding on everyone. From the Latin *libra* for "scale," *deliberation* means "to weigh," as in weighing all the alternatives to make the best decision. Deliberation involves discussion because the alternatives are weighed *with others*. That way, one's own opinion about the alternatives can be examined alongside others' opinions and, if participants are open- and fair-minded, the group can challenge one another's views and, in time, forge a decision about what to do. Deliberation, then, relies on discussion, but not just any discussion; the discussion is about what "we" should do—for example, a classroom deciding on a playground rule, a community deciding about where to locate a park, or a play group deciding how to share toys.

Deliberation is probably the most important foundation of democratic citizenship. Contrary to sayings such as "Talk is cheap" or "Actions speak louder than words," deliberation should be appreciated as a wonderful and constructive alternative to violence. Compared to fighting over toys, or territory, or friends, or whatever differences, talking is the nonviolent bridge of choice. When children learn to talk through their disagreements on the playground and in the classroom, and later at work and on committees, by explaining, listening, negotiating, compromising, and forgiving, they are making significant progress toward democratic citizenship. The ancient Greeks, who were the first to experiment with democratic living, were in awe of the power of discussion. Athenian leader Pericles said, "Instead of seeing discussion as a stumbling block in the way of action, we think it an indispensable preliminary to any wise action at all." Discussion is not merely better than fighting; *discussion leads to wise action.*

Deliberation skills do not necessarily develop on their own; they need to be taught, practiced, and learned. Teachers can let children know that when they are brought to the rug, they need to practice the skills of good discussion. These can be posted:

> DISCUSSION SKILLS
>
> Listen as well as talk.
>
> Encourage others to participate.
>
> Criticize ideas but not people.
>
> Support opinions with reasons.
>
> Weigh alternatives.

These skills can be taught using a good skills-teaching procedure involving instruction and role playing, such as the one in Chapter 8. Let us look now at two well-known teachers and how they make deliberation a regular part of classroom life. In brief, they orchestrate their students' deliberations around classroom rule making.

Tarry Lindquist. Rather than posting skills, some teachers prefer to *elicit* them from students. Tarry Lindquist, for example, who is an elementary teacher in the Seattle area, describes her method of elicitation:

> I often start out in September by asking the class to brainstorm all the things we could do to make our classroom a terrible place, a place where no one would want to come, a place where we could guarantee no learning would occur.
>
> As we list the surefire ways to kill a classroom, each suggestion more outrageous than the last, we begin to build a community. Eventually, when we have exhausted our efforts, most sincere and many hilarious, I ask the class to picture a room like the one we've just described. I ask them, "What would you know if you stayed in a classroom like that one all year? What would you be able to do? How would you feel?" After that discussion, it doesn't take long to reverse the list, identifying what needs to happen to make our classroom a place of joy where all students want to be and where all students can learn.[4]

Mrs. Lindquist goes on to create with her students a sort of miniconstitution—a rule book, or what she calls an action plan for a "peaceful classroom." After much discussion and decision making, the plan is finalized. Each child signs it, as does Mrs. Lindquist. She sends a copy home. When misbehavior occurs, she can communicate with children and parents with the rule book in mind. "Do you recall the action plan we signed at the beginning of the year?" she might say to parents. "I am concerned that Nancy doesn't seem to be able to help the class reach this goal. Specific things about Nancy's behavior that have prompted my concern are. . . ." Mrs. Lindquist can now describe the behavior problem by referring to specific agreements written in the plan, such as "we are respectful of others" and "we listen and pay attention."

Vivian Paley. Another mentor on the art of conducting rich discussions with even the youngest children is Vivian Paley, who teaches kindergarten in Chicago. Mrs. Paley's approach is sometimes to *post* a rule for interaction, sometimes to *elicit* it from students, but most often to *propose* a rule. She tells her children a rule she is considering, not one she has decreed, and then engages them in an ongoing inquiry about the rule. The inquiry may last for months and focuses on two questions: Will the rule work? Is it fair? These questions are compelling ones for the children. They have memories and opinions immediately.

Our favorite example of this process is when Mrs. Paley informed her class that she was considering a new classroom rule. She put up a poster that read, YOU CAN'T SAY "YOU CAN'T PLAY." It was greeted with disbelief, she recalls. "Only four out of twenty-five in my kindergarten class find the idea appealing, and they are the children most often rejected. The loudest in opposition are those who do the most rejecting. But everyone looks doubtful. . . ."[5]

Mrs. Paley's approach to classroom discussion of rules strikes us as an elegant combination of two techniques: (1) She brings her students to the circle often to discuss a new rule she is planning. (2) She interviews older children to ascertain their views and then brings these views back to her kindergartners who, of course, are terribly impressed that *their* issues are of such interest to the older children.

Mrs. Paley began one discussion with her students this way: "I just can't get the question out of my mind. Is it fair for children *in school* to keep another child out of play? After all, this classroom belongs to all of us. It is not a private place, like our homes."[6] Notice here how clearly Mrs. Paley communicates that the classroom is a civic or public place and that how we conduct ourselves in such a place is somehow different. In public places, we have to be concerned with the *common good,* not just private interests. We are obliged to act with civility, to be civic-minded. "The children I teach are just emerging from life's deep wells of private perspective: babyhood and family," she says. Selfishness and jealousy are natural to both conditions. "Then, along comes school. It is the first real exposure to the public arena."[7]

Indeed, this is why deliberation is important. Discussion is a *civic* practice that introduces children to ways of behaving that are imperative if we are to have, as the Constitution calls it, "domestic tranquility" or what Mrs. Lindquist's class calls, simply, "peace."

Mrs. Paley: Should one child be allowed to keep another child from joining a group? A good rule might be: "You can't say 'You can't play'. "

Ben: If you cry, people should let you in.

Mrs. Paley: What if someone is not crying but feels sad? Should the teacher force children to say yes?

Many Voices: No, no.

Sheila: If they don't want you to play, they should just go their own way and you should say, "Clara, let's find someone who likes you better."

Angelo: Lisa and her should let Clara in. . . .[8]

Soon, Mrs. Paley trades classes with a second-grade teacher for a little while. She asks those children's opinions about her class's plan. "I've come to ask your opinions about a new rule we're considering in the kindergarten. . . . We call it, "YOU CAN'T SAY 'YOU CAN'T PLAY'." These older children know full well the issue she is talking about. Examples and some vivid accounts of rejection spill from their mouths. They are fully engaged in the discussion because it is a problem that they both recognize and feel. Many children believe it *is* a fair rule, but that it just will not work: "It would be impossible to have any fun," offers one boy.

Later, while interviewing a fourth-grade class, she hears these students conclude that it is "too late" in their lives to give them such a rule. "If you want a rule like that to work, start at a very early age," declares one fourth-grader. "Yeah, start it in kindergarten," someone says. "Because they'll believe *you* that it's a *rule.* You know, a law."[9]

Mrs. Paley takes these views back to the discussion circle in her own classroom. Her children listen, enthralled, to her retelling of the older children's thinking. They often revise their opinions as a consequence of hearing one another's arguments. In the Socratic spirit, gently, Mrs. Paley is forever challenging them to develop their own opinions, to support their views with reasons, and to listen carefully and respond to the reasoning of other children, classmates, and older children alike.

Listening to Diverse Views

This last detail is important: listening carefully to the reasoning of other children. Why does this matter? Principal Ethel Sadowsky reminds us that "children learn from peers who are thinking in different ways and at different levels."[10] This is the miracle of a good discussion about an engaging problem with a diverse group of children. *Research has shown that discussion stimulates growth in children's reasoning, and it is more likely to have this effect if each child (a) encounters and (b) listens to reasoning that is somewhat different from his or her own.*[11] Teachers should, therefore, encourage all children to speak during discussions, giving both opinions and reasons, and help all children to listen carefully to one another's opinions and reasons. Asking children regularly to paraphrase what others have said is a good way to build the listening habit. "Brandon, what was Neetha saying to the group?" "Jamal, were you listening as Myrna gave her reasons? Will you restate them for us, please?" Also, when two children share the same opinion but have different reasons, help the class notice this: "You two seem to agree, but for different reasons. Who else agrees, but for yet a different reason?"

Discussions of this sort help children develop their capacity to reason about moral issues. This is extremely important because democratic life requires a well-developed sense of what children call fairness (adults call it justice). To treat others as you yourself wish to be treated if you were in their situation is hailed as the supreme level of moral maturity in the world's great religions. One way to help children move in this direction is to engage them in discussions of fairness issues of all sorts, especially those involving rules that apply to all class members, as did Lindquist and Paley. Within these deliberations, teachers can help children listen to and grapple with reasoning that is different from their own. This is the kind of discussion that, in Pericles' words, produces "wise action."

Assessing Discussion

We devote an entire chapter to assessment later in this book, but it should be helpful to look at this matter now in the context of this treatment of deliberation and citizenship education. As teachers plan how they will find out what students have learned about a topic or skill, they must think about levels of proficiency or the *criteria* by which a performance can be judged. These criteria also serve as the objectives of instruction. Let's see what this means.

Social studies educators in Oakland County, Michigan, have carefully examined this issue and developed a guide for assessing the quality of a child's participation in discussions of civic issues.[12] A civic issue is a *public* issue—an issue that "we the people" face in common. Public issues range from simple matters such as how we behave toward one another in a classroom and whether we have a rule that you can't exclude classmates from your play to major policy issues that confront our communities today: Who is responsible for the poor? Are affirmative action policies fair? Should elected officials' terms be limited? Should students be tested for drug use before they can play team sports? What can be done about hate crimes? Teenage suicide? Teenage pregnancy? The epidemic of homelessness?

The Oakland County assessment emphasizes two dimensions of discussion, one *substantive* (the "what") and one *procedural* (the "how"). The substantive dimension refers to *what* children contribute to the discussion—the knowledge and information they bring to it and their ability to support opinions with reasons and analogies. The procedural dimension indicates *how* children participate—whether they invite others to contribute, for example, or make negative statements that inhibit others from participating. Figure 3–2 lists the substantive and procedural guidelines, and Table 3–1 arranges these into four levels of quality. An unacceptable performance in a discussion would mean that, on the substantive dimension, a child remained silent or made only irrelevant comments, and on the procedural dimension, the child made no comments to help the conversation along or made statements that lacked civility—they were negative in character.

A highly skillful contribution to the group discussion, on the other hand, is characterized by making no comments that inhibit other students' participation, *and* the child intervenes if others do this. Moreover, the child engages in sustained dialogue with others, both

FIGURE 3–2

Performance criteria for discussing public issues
Source: David Harris, "Assessing Discussion of Public Issues," in *Handbook on teaching social issues.* Ronald W. Evans & David Warren Saxe (Eds.). Washington, DC: National Council for the Social Studies, 1996, pp. 288–97.

THE SUBSTANTIVE DIMENSION
+ States and identifies issues
+ Brings knowledge to the discussion
+ Specifies claims or definitions
+ Elaborates statements with explanations, reasons, and evidence
+ Recognizes values or value conflict
+ Argues by analogy

THE PROCEDURAL DIMENSION
Positive
+ Acknowledges the statements of others
+ Challenges the accuracy, logic, relevance, or clarity of statements
+ Summarizes points of agreement and disagreement
+ Invites contributions from others

Negative
– Makes irrelevant, distracting statements
– Interrupts
– Monopolizes the conversation
– Engages in personal attack

talking and listening. On the substantive side, this child weighs multiple perspectives and considers what is best for everyone—the common good. Moreover, this child uses higher-order participation skills, such as drawing analogies and summarizing what has been said.

Teachers use this scoring guide to assess their students' current discussion abilities and, just as important, to help plan instruction. Perhaps a teacher will decide to teach the difference between positive and negative comments, followed by a lesson on how to encourage other children to participate and how to respond constructively to ideas they offer. Assessment guides of this sort, called *scoring rubrics* or *rating scales,* can be enormously helpful in planning instruction.

A much simpler discussion rating scale is shown in Figure 3–3. Teachers in the primary grades may wish to use this scale as may teachers in the intermediate grades until they become more adept at clarifying with children the more ambitious discussion guidelines used in Oakland County.

Teaching Decision Making

Many teachers already engage students in discussions of classroom rules and problems as well as community and world events. These discussions naturally revolve around decisions: Which rule is fairest? Which plan of action is wisest? What should we do? We recommend going further, however, to include teaching the decision-making process directly and explicitly.

TABLE 3–1   Scoring guide for assessing students' participation in discussions of public issues in grades 6–12.

	Exemplary (3)	Adequate (2)	Minimal (1)	Unacceptable (0)
SUBSTANTIVE	Weighs multiple perspectives on a policy issue and considers the public good; uses relevant knowledge to analyze an issue; employs a higher-order discussion strategy, such as argument by analogy, stipulation, or resolution of a value conflict.	Demonstrates knowledge of important ideas related to the issue; explicitly states an issue for the group to consider; presents more than one viewpoint; supports a position with reasons or evidence.	Makes statements about the issue that express only personal attitudes; mentions a potentially important idea but does not pursue it in a way that advances the group's understanding.	Remains silent; contributes no thoughts of his or her own; makes only irrelevant comments.
PROCEDURAL	Engages in more than one sustained interchange, or summarizes and assesses the progress of the discussion. Makes no comments that inhibit others' contributions and intervenes if others do this.	Engages in an extended interchange with at least one other person, or paraphrases important statements as a transition or summary, or asks another person for an explanation or clarification germane to the discussion. Does not inhibit others' contributions.	Invites contributions implicitly or explicitly, or responds constructively to ideas expressed by at least one other person. Tends not to make negative statements.	Makes no comments that facilitate dialogue, or makes statements that are primarily negative in character.

Source: David Harris, "Assessing Discussion of Public Issues," in *Handbook on teaching social issues.* Ronald W. Evans & David Warren Saxe (Eds.). Washington, DC: National Council for the Social Studies, 1996, pp. 288–97.

We have three reasons for recommending this. First, as we saw in Chapter 2, teachers must provide explicit instruction on the topics and skills they expect their students to demonstrate. To withhold instruction merely gives an advantage to children who already learned the skills at home or elsewhere while creating a disadvantage for children who did not. Second, the decision-making process offers many opportunities for higher-order thinking. When children ferret out all the alternatives for a particular decision and predict the consequences of each alternative, they are engaged in several important intellectual processes that will enable them to be more thoughtful citizens. Third, the decision-making process offers opportunities for values education as well. Groups and individuals choose an alternative typically because they value its consequences more than the others; similarly, conflicts can arise when values differ. Budding citizens in a diverse society need many opportunities to examine and wrestle with value conflicts, for they are an inevitable part of democratic life.

FIGURE 3–3   Rating scale for discussion in the primary grades.

(Primary Grades)	Always	Sometimes	Not Often
1. Helps make plans			
2. Listens to what is said			
3. Takes turns			
4. Gives own ideas			
5. Considers what others have said			

Children can be taught the decision-making process in four phases. Older children may not need to begin with the first phase.

First, the teacher helps children become aware of decisions and decision making. The children themselves make many decisions each day, as does their teacher. Decisions are being made throughout the school and community. Some of the decisions are *political*—that is, decisions about rules and laws by which "we the people" agree to live. Others are *social,* concerning fund raising for charities or welcoming new students to school. Still others are *personal*: What shall I wear? How should I spend my allowance?

Second, the teacher helps children "crawl inside" a decision, so to speak, to make a visual representation of it—a decision map. Decision maps show all the parts of a decision in relationship to each other: the occasion for the decision (usually called the problem), the array of alternatives that could be considered, and the consequences of each alternative.

Third, the teacher models good decision making for children. Standing in front of a "decision tree" (see Figure 3–4) sketched on the chalkboard or posted on the wall, the teacher can talk about how he or she decided on the next unit of study, for example, or how to handle a difficult class problem. With this "think-aloud" demonstration, children witness a decision being made thoughtfully and can then practice one themselves.

Fourth, the teacher can provide opportunities for students to practice decision making. The opportunities are too numerous to list here, but key areas are decisions about classroom rules and issues; decisions about classroom management (clean-up, play time, cooperative group work, work habits); and decisions about subject matter: Which reference resources will be best for this project? Will you use the tools to build a tower or a bridge? Will you make a model of Mt. Everest or Pikes Peak? Will you write about Harriet Tubman or Susan Anthony?

Lesson Plan 2 is geared to the first and second phases of decision-making instruction. Notice that it teaches the design of a basic decision map, shaped as a tree, while building children's awareness of the decisions they and others make.

When it is time in the second phase to introduce children to the skill of predicting consequences, two focus questions are helpful for organizing the lessons. First, what might be the consequences (effects) of each alternative on all the persons involved? This question focuses students' attention on each alternative and its possible consequences. It challenges students to think of everyone's interests, not just their own. Second, will the alternative help or

FIGURE 3-4   A decision tree.

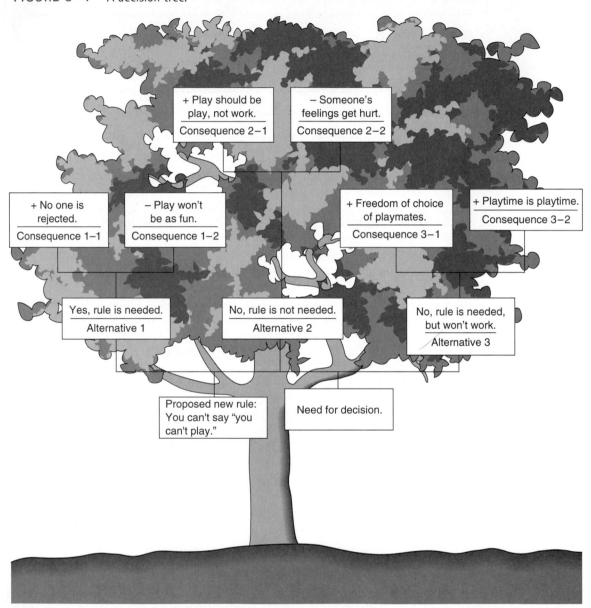

hinder the realization of democratic values, such as liberty, the common good, and fairness? This question asks students purposefully to bring the ideals of democracy into the heart of decision making. These values can act as powerful screening tools, causing children to reject an alternative because it unnecessarily curtails someone's liberty, because it treats people unequally, or because it fails to consider the welfare of the whole community.

Lesson Plan 2 MAKING A DECISION TREE

Grade 1–3

Time One class period

Objectives Children will become aware of the numerous decisions they make every day and the alternatives that are considered in each decision. They will learn a way to "map" such decisions.

Interest Building Remind students of a lively discussion they had recently about a rule, such as deciding on a rule for sharing books or playground equipment. Ask them to recall what was decided. Help them remember the alternatives (choices, options) that were considered. As they recall the alternatives, record them on the chalkboard using a "decision map" such as this:

Need for decision _____

alternative #1 _____

alternative #2 _____

alternative #3 _____

Lesson Development

1. Ask students to think of all the decisions they have made so far today: Whether to get up early or late; whether to have cereal, toast, or something else; what to wear; what to do upon arriving at the school building; whether to get to class early or just when the bell rang, and so forth. Record these on butcher paper and post.

2. Explain that decision making means choosing among alternatives. Select a few decisions that will not invade anyone's privacy, such as what to do upon arriving at school and whether to get to class early. Have the class help you map one of these decisions on the chalkboard, similar to the way you did this in the introduction. Then put children in pairs and ask them to map one or two more of these decisions. Ask the pairs to share their maps with the class.

3. Because you have been using the terms up to this point in the lesson, most children should by now have some understanding of their meaning. Check those understandings now. Ask several children for a definition of *decision* and *alternative*. Ask several others to suggest examples. Provide explanations as necessary.

4. Build awareness of decisions that others make. Ask one pair of children to list the decisions they think the school principal might make in a typical day; ask another pair to list the decisions the mayor might make; to other pairs, assign community helpers: the librarian, the curator of a museum, an athletics coach, an orchestra conductor, a police officer, a doctor, a firefighter, an ambulance driver, a health inspector, a newspaper delivery person.

Summary and Assessment Ask each pair to decide on one decision to share from step 4 above. As each pair shares, listen for any misunderstandings and provide explanations as needed. As they share, diagram each decision on a decision map. Post these on a bulletin board called "Decisions in Our Community."

Follow Up Ask the children to tell brief stories about *courageous* decisions that someone has had to make. Probe for the alternatives that person may have considered. Make decision maps for the decisions and alternatives.

Materials Posters and marker for decision maps in summary. Also, if children have difficulty coming up with stories of courageous decision makers, you may want to have some ready. You can draw on current news stories, literature the children are reading, and exciting historical examples: Harriet Tubman's decision to continue the underground railroad despite great dangers, the

Pilgrims' decision to sail for America, Jefferson's decision to write the Declaration of Independence.

Integration   *Writing:* As the weeks go by, have children make more decision maps based on material they are studying in math, science, and literature. As students work through math problems, for example, they must decide: multiply or divide? Writing also requires an endless stream of decision making. Each draft is the result of decision making: what to include, what to set aside, how to organize and present it. Invite an older student who likes to write to share his/her decision making with the class.

■   ■   ■   ■   ■

Student teams can be created to do this work on each alternative. Team 1 is asked to work with Alternative 1, Team 2 with Alternative 2, Team 3 with Alternative 3, and so on. As readers can see, decision making is challenging intellectual work, especially when students take seriously the task of predicting consequences. An elaborate decision map in the form of a decision tree is shown in Figure 3–4. Notice that it includes positive and negative consequences for each alternative.

VOTING AND ELECTIONS

Learning about voting is the second dimension of a citizen's education for democracy. Elementary teachers should miss no opportunity to involve their students in deliberation or voting. These two dimensions of democratic citizenship education go hand in hand because voting needs to come *after* deliberation, not before. Deliberation informs and empowers voting. Voting, then, should be seen as a *culminating activity* that comes after thinking with others about the issues and candidates. Without study and deliberation, children (and adults) vote without having thought about the power they are exercising.

Participating in real and "mock" elections—whether as voter, candidate, member of the press, delegate, representative, or campaign worker—afford students opportunities to learn many concepts that will "travel" with them into subsequent school years and into adulthood. Some of these are listed in Figure 3–5. Historical study is important, too, for voting rights did not come easily. The struggle for the vote can teach children a good deal about the American struggle for democracy *and equality.* Overall, it is important to help children understand that voting is a civic duty, that it was hard won, and that it should not be done casually but, instead, after study and deliberation.

The long struggle for voting rights. The words of Elizabeth Cady Stanton and Martin Luther King, Jr., can be posted in the classroom to help children grasp the importance of voting and the long battle their foremothers and forefathers had to wage for voting rights. Older children can write biographies of these and other voting rights activists (see Chapter 13). Stanton and King were amazing. Stanton founded the American Equal Rights Association in 1866 and 20 years earlier organized the Seneca Falls Convention, the birthplace of the women's suffrage movement. One of the convention's resolutions read: "It is the duty of

Summary of the
Constitution of the United States

PREAMBLE

We, the People of the United States, in Order to form a more perfect Union, establish Justice, insure domestic Tranquility, provide for the common Defense, promote the general Welfare, and secure the blessings of Liberty to ourselves and our Posterity, do ordain and establish this Constitution for the United States of America.

This is the meaning of the Preamble:

The people of the United States made the Constitution for the following reasons: (1) to set up a stronger government and a more united nation than the one that existed under the Articles of Confederation; (2) to ensure peace and justice among the people; (3) to defend the nation against enemies; (4) to help ensure the well-being of all the people; and (5) to make sure that the people of this nation will always be free.

ARTICLE 1
LEGISLATIVE BRANCH
Section 1: The Congress

The legislative branch, or Congress, makes the nation's laws. It is made up of two houses—the Senate and the House of Representatives.

Section 2: The House of Representatives

Members of the House of Representatives are elected for two-year terms. A representative must be at least 25 years old, a citizen of the United States for at least 7 years, and live in the state he or she represents.

The number of representatives a state has depends on the state's population. In order to find out how many people live in each state, the government must do a count of the population every ten years. This count is called a census.

Section 3: The Senate

The Senate is made up of two senators from each state. Each senator is elected for a six-year term. A senator must be at least 30 years old, a citizen of the United States for at least 9 years, and live in the state he or she represents.

The Vice President of the United States is in charge of the Senate but may vote only if there is a tie.

Sections 4–6: Rules

The houses of Congress set their own rules for their members. Each house must keep a record of its meetings and how each member voted.

To make sure that there is complete freedom of discussion in Congress, senators and representatives cannot be arrested for things they say while doing their jobs.

Section 7: How a Bill Becomes a Law

A suggested law, or bill, becomes a law when both houses of Congress agree to it by a majority vote and when the President signs it. If the President vetoes, or rejects, the bill, it can still become a law if both houses of Congress approve it again by a two-thirds vote.

Section 8: Powers of Congress

The powers of Congress include the power to: collect taxes; borrow money; control trade with other countries and among the states; decide how foreigners can become citizens; coin money; set up post offices; set up courts; declare war; set up an army and a navy; make all laws necessary to carry out powers granted to the government.

Sections 9–10: Powers Denied to Congress and the States

There are certain powers that Congress and the states do not have. Congress cannot, for example, spend money without telling how the money will be spent. The states cannot make treaties with other countries or coin money.

ARTICLE 2
EXECUTIVE BRANCH
Section 1: President and Vice President

The President and Vice President head the executive branch. Along with the people who work with them, their job is to carry out the laws made by Congress. They are elected for four-year terms.

The President and Vice President must be natural-born citizens and at least 35 years old, and must have lived in the United States for at least 14 years.

Sections 2–4: Powers and Duties

The President's powers and duties include: commanding the armed forces; appointing government officials; reaching agreements with other countries; and pardoning crimes. At least once a year, the President must tell Congress how the nation is doing. This is called the President's State of the Union message.

A President who commits a serious crime may be removed from office.

ARTICLE 3
JUDICIAL BRANCH
Section 1: Federal Courts

The judicial branch is made up of the Supreme Court and all other federal, or United States, courts. Federal judges are appointed for life.

Section 2: Duties

The judicial branch has the power to decide the meaning of the Constitution. It may decide if the actions of the other two branches are unconstitutional, or go against the Constitution.

Federal courts have a say in many cases, such as those having to do with the Constitution, federal laws, or disagreements between citizens from different states.

Section 3: Treason

Treason is a crime committed when a citizen of the United States betrays the country, especially in wartime.

ARTICLE 4
THE STATES
Sections 1–4: Dealings Among the States

All states must accept the actions, records, and court decisions of other states. When citizens visit another state, they must be given the same rights as citizens of the state they are visiting.

New states may be added to the United States. The United States government promises to protect the states from enemies.

ARTICLE 5
AMENDMENTS

The Constitution may be amended or changed, if Congress and three fourths of the states agree.

ARTICLE 6
SUPREME LAW, OATHS OF OFFICE, DEBTS

The Constitution of the United States is the supreme law, or the highest law, in the nation. Government officials must promise to support the Constitution. In addition, the government promised to pay back all debts owed before the Constitution was adopted.

ARTICLE 7
APPROVING THE CONSTITUTION

The Constitution was to become law when 9 of the 13 original states ratified, or approved, it. Special conventions were held for this purpose, and the process took nine months to complete.

AMENDMENTS TO THE CONSTITUTION (The first 10 are called The Bill of Rights.)

AMENDMENT 1
Freedom of Religion, Speech, Press, Assembly, and Petition (1791)

Congress cannot make a law setting up an official religion. It cannot stop people from practicing any religion they choose. Congress cannot take away freedom of speech or of the press. Congress cannot stop groups from assembling, or meeting together, peacefully.

It cannot stop people from petitioning, or asking the government, to end an injustice.

AMENDMENT 2
Right to Keep Arms (1791)

The people have the right to keep and carry arms, or weapons.

AMENDMENT 3
Quartering Soldiers (1791)

During peacetime, people cannot be forced to quarter soldiers, or let them stay in their homes.

AMENDMENT 4
Search and Seizures (1791)

People's homes and other property cannot be searched and seized unless the police have a search warrant.

AMENDMENT 5
Rights of Accused Persons (1791)

People who are accused of a crime cannot be forced to testify, or give evidence, against themselves. Their lives, freedom, or property cannot be taken away from them unfairly. The government may take a person's property for public use only if the person is paid for it.

AMENDMENT 6
Jury Trial in Criminal Cases (1791)

People accused of crimes have the right to a public and speedy trial with a jury. They have the right to be told the charges against them. They have the right to have a lawyer.

AMENDMENT 7
Jury Trial in Civil Cases (1791)

In most civil, or noncriminal, cases, people have the right to a jury trial.

AMENDMENT 8
Excessive Bail or Punishment (1791)

Bail must be reasonable for people accused of a crime. Punishments may not be cruel and unusual.

AMENDMENT 9
Other Rights of the People (1791)

The people have rights in addition to those listed in the Constitution.

AMENDMENT 10
Powers of the States and the People (1791)
Powers that are not granted to the national government and not forbidden to the states are left to the state governments or to the people.

AMENDMENT 11
Suing the States (1798)
A state government can be sued only in its own courts.

AMENDMENT 12
Election of President and Vice President (1804)
Electors vote for President and Vice President on separate ballots.

AMENDMENT 13
Abolition of Slavery (1865)
Slavery is abolished, or made illegal, in the United States.

AMENDMENT 14
Rights of Citizens (1868)
Every citizen of the United States is also a citizen of the state in which he or she lives. No state may pass a law limiting the rights of citizens or take away a person's life, liberty, or property unfairly. Every person must be treated equally under the law.

AMENDMENT 15
Voting Rights (1870)
No person may be denied the right to vote because of race.

AMENDMENT 16
Income Tax (1913)
Congress has the right to tax people's incomes.

AMENDMENT 17
Direct Election of Senators (1913)
United States senators are elected directly by the people of their states.

AMENDMENT 18
Prohibition (1919)
The manufacture or transport of liquor is prohibited, or banned, in the United States.

AMENDMENT 19
Women's Voting Rights (1920)
Women cannot be denied the right to vote.

AMENDMENT 20
Terms of Office (1933)
The President and Vice President take office on January 20. Senators and representatives take office on January 3.

AMENDMENT 21
Repeal of Prohibition (1933)
Amendment 18 is repealed, or ended.

AMENDMENT 22
Two-Term Limit for Presidents (1951)
A President may serve only two terms in office.

AMENDMENT 23
Presidential Elections for District of Columbia (1961)
People who live in Washington, D.C., have the right to vote for President and Vice President.

AMENDMENT 24
Poll Tax (1964)
No citizen may be made to pay a tax in order to vote for President, Vice President, senator, or representative.

AMENDMENT 25
Presidential Succession and Disability (1967)
If a President leaves office before the end of term, the Vice President becomes President. If the Vice President leaves office, the President suggests a person to fill the job and Congress must approve. If the President becomes too ill to do the job, the Vice President becomes Acting President until the President recovers.

AMENDMENT 26
Voting Age (1971)
Citizens who are at least 18 years old have the right to vote.

AMENDMENT 27
Congressional Salaries (1992)
Congress cannot change its salary until after the next congressional election.

FIGURE 3–5
Voting-related concepts.

Voting
Voter eligibility
Voter registration
Voting booth
Franchise
Suffrage
Women's Suffrage Movement
Freedom Riders
Civil Rights Movement
Polling place
Poll tax
Poll watchers
Secret ballot
Ballot box
Ballot initiatives
Election laws
Candidates
Campaigns
Perspective (point of view)
Press and press conferences
Public issues
Representation
Delegates and representatives
Constitution and Bill of Rights
Democracy and dictatorship
Majority rule and minority rights
Freedom of press and speech
Rights and responsibilities
Civic duty
Fairness (justice)

the women of this country to secure to themselves their sacred right to the elective franchise." Note the words *duty* and *sacred* used in connection with voting. A century later, women had the vote but blacks still did not—at least, not actually in many places. The Fifteenth Amendment to the U.S. Constitution in 1870 made it illegal to deny the right to vote to anyone because of race, but then whites invented poll taxes and other means to keep African-Americans from voting. Poll taxes were not made illegal until the passage of the Twenty-fourth Amendment in 1964. But even this did not solve the problem of actually registering black voters, particularly in the Deep South. "Freedom Riders" flocked to southern states in the early 1960s to help register black men and women, and many of them were imprisoned; some were shot. In Dr. King's words: "We must gain political power, and we must come to the point of being able to participate in government. No longer must we be willing to be disenfranchised. We must say, 'Give us the ballot.' We are determined to have the ballot, and we are determined to have it now."[13]

There are more ways to involve children in voting than there is room here to present them all. So, let us highlight what may be the most powerful ways.

Hold Real Elections

Hold elections for one or two classroom delegates to the school's Student Advisory Council. If your school doesn't have one, help get it started. Cottage Lane Elementary School[14] provides an excellent model. At Cottage Lane, these elections involve the whole student body in school governance, grades 1 through 6. There are two student advisory councils (SAC): "Little SAC" is for students in the primary grades; "Big SAC" is for students in grades 4 through 6. The school principal presides over both. "Our *one* purpose here," she always tells them, "is to identify problems and try to solve them."

Each class elects two of its members to serve on the council. These students are delegates, not representatives, and consequently must vote at SAC meetings as instructed by their classmates. One student, Douglas, clarifies the distinction: "We are delegates. We can't just say what we want or tell only about our own problems. We must bring notes from the class and talk about the class's problems at SAC meetings."[15] Therefore, the elections really matter to the class, and class meetings at which delegates are given instructions are a critical part of the program. The deliberation in these meetings can be authentic and lively. With this kind of program, even primary-grade children gain experience with electing and being elected, with majority rule, with the distinction between delegate and representative, and with deliberation on issues that are important to them.

Elections can also be held to decide on any number of classroom roles. When a committee is formed, members can be asked to elect a chairperson. The same applies to students in charge of watering plants and feeding classroom pets, guiding the class to the lunchroom, and welcoming a guest speaker in the main office.

Beyond popularity contests: Criteria. An election at school can be nothing more than a popularity contest in which students are elected on the most irrelevant criteria—gender, physical appearance, and athletic ability, for example. You can point out this problem to students and encourage them to identify relevant criteria for doing the job. "What knowledge or skills will our delegate to the student advisory council need?" Or, "Will the chairperson of our newsletter committee need any special skills?" Listen carefully as students respond, and you will learn how they are thinking about the job to be done. Ask a good writer to record the list on the board. Then help students prioritize items on the list.

Hold Mock Elections

Every four years in November is a presidential election; every two years is a congressional election. City, county, state, and school district elections often coincide with these, but sometimes are held at other times. Each election is an opportunity to hold a mock election.

A mock election is and is not a real election. It is not an actual election because one need not be a citizen or a registered voter or at least 18 years of age to participate, and the votes cast in mock elections do not actually elect anybody. It *is* a real election, however, because voting does occur, and so do all the learning activities that lead up to and prepare children for the voting, namely, deliberation, press conferences, speech writing, research on candidate positions, and so forth.

When children participate in mock elections, it is best to asure a secret ballot. Here, a refrigerator box is transformed into a polling booth. (Photo courtesy of Carol Hamilton Cobb, veteran kindergarten teacher at Gateway Scool, Metropolitan Nashville, Tennessee, Public Schools.)

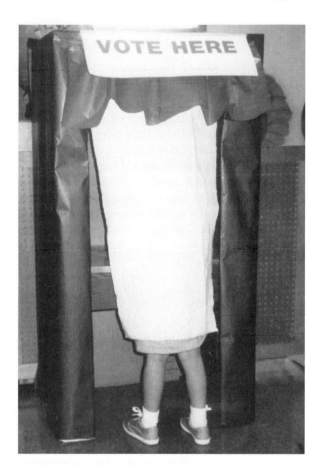

Tennessee teacher Carole Hamilton Cobb routinely conducts mock elections with her kindergarten children. They vote in local and presidential elections. But first they learn about the candidates and discuss some of the issues. Then they register to vote and receive a voter registration card, which they take to the polling place (in the hallway) on voting day. Meanwhile, they help make polling booths from refrigerator boxes, such as the one shown in the photo above.

Preparing for an Election

All sorts of learning activities help prepare children for an election, real or mock. Here are several.

Mock press conferences. Mock press conferences provide terrific opportunities for role playing and learning about elections. A committee can be formed to plan a press conference, gather information, and assign the roles (candidates, press, moderator, audience). Every student in class should have a role. Many can be members of the press: reporters representing television stations and newspapers. Tape recordings of press conferences can be made from television news programs and shown to students to give them a clearer idea of the real thing.

Guest speakers. Invite members of the press to share information and personal experiences on covering elections and campaigns and participating in press conferences.

Speech competitions. Here is another good opportunity to infuse language arts instruction. Help students study the general concept of speech writing and speech giving with some famous examples (e.g., Patrick Henry's "Give Me Liberty or Give Me Death"; King's "I Have a Dream"; Sojourner Truth's "Ain't I a Woman?"; and Lincoln's "Gettysburg Address"). Some will be found on video- and audiotapes. These speeches can be read aloud then dramatized by the class. Next, help students form the more specific concept of *campaign* speeches. These examples can be drawn from the speeches reprinted in the newspaper and seen on television. With this background knowledge, students are ready for a speech-writing competition of their own. Attend to these things: Select judges, decide on criteria for judging speeches, select topics, determine due dates and length (e.g., five minutes), select location and time, invite an audience, and prepare the audience.

Deliberation. Elections—real and mock—are another opportunity for students to practice the democratic skill of deliberating controversial issues with a diverse group of citizens (see Mrs. Paley's discussion of classroom rules earlier in this chapter). Prior to an election, the issues should be identified, studied, and thoroughly deliberated. Here is a good opportunity to teach newspaper reading skills (using the directory to find the editorials, skimming the letters to the editor, or interpreting political cartoons), to help students form the attitudes that voting is one's duty, and to show students that voting should always be *informed* voting.

In addition to the specific issues of the election, general voting issues can be discussed:

- What difference does one vote make?
- Are secret ballots really necessary?
- Should voting be required or voluntary?
- Should the voting age be lowered? Raised?

Field trips. Visit a city council meeting or a polling place. (Advice on conducting a field trip can be found in Chapter 9, "Resources.")

Issues-finding discussions. Before the election or press conference, the teacher can lead the class in several issues-finding discussions. The purposes of such discussions are to

- Help children form the concept of "public issues"—controversial, shared problems on which reasonable people have differing positions but must, nevertheless, reach a decision that will be binding on all. They can be classroom, school, local, national, or world issues.
- Assess what the children perceive to be the public issues that candidates should be addressing (taxes? drugs? crime? poverty? welfare? environment?).
- Decide what issues should be included in deliberative forums, press conferences (the issues about which candidates should and will be questioned), and voted on in the election. In preparing for a press conference, the teacher might ask: "What should the members of the press ask our candidates about?" Students can be prompted

FIGURE 3–6   Data retrieval chart.

	Public issue # 1 Location of new park	Public Issue # 2 Park play equipment	Public Issue # 3 Regulating dogs in the park
Candidate #1			
Candidate #2			

with reminders of local issues, for example: "Several of you have been concerned about the homeless people you see lying on streets. Do you want to ask the candidates for their ideas about that?" Or "The city council is trying to decide where to put the new park. Shall we ask the council candidates about that?" And "On what other public issues do you want to know their positions?"

Once issues have been identified, a data-retrieval chart such as the one shown in Figure 3–6 can be used during and after the press conference to help organize and record candidates' positions on the issues.

Visiting candidate websites. Candidates in national elections now typically have websites. Create a data-retrieval chart with students, similar to the one in Figure 3–6, to help them organize the information they collect across several candidates' web pages.

Bulletin boards. Fill the board with candidates' photos, issues, speeches, bumper stickers and campaign buttons, yard signs, editorials, and political cartoons—created by students and found in the newspaper, at party headquarters, and elsewhere.

Writing the classroom newsletter. So much reading and writing goes on in conducting an election, whether real or mock. It would be a shame for it not to be featured in a special "election day issue" of the classroom newsletter.

Newspapers in the classroom. Children can learn a good deal about the organization and contents of daily newspapers during mock elections that coincide with actual national or local elections. Here is the "teachable moment" for distinguishing between news stories, editorials, and letters to the editor, and between the literary genres of narrative (sometimes news stories are in narrative form), exposition (laying out the facts of the matter), and persuasive argument (in editorials and letters). Can your students find the "lead" in a news story? Children can be assigned to follow the press coverage of different candidates and to watch for the day when the city newspapers "endorse" one candidate over another and advise readers on how to vote on ballot initiatives. Call your local newspaper to find out about the Newspapers in Education program.

Visiting voting websites.

- KIDS VOTING USA is a nonprofit, nonpartisan, grassroots organization dedicated to securing democracy for the future by involving youth in the election process today. This website, at *http://www.kidsvotingusa.org/,* presents a good deal of information for teachers and students. Click on "Education" and examine the voting-related activities for each grade level. Also click on "cool sites" for links to the web pages of the Democratic, Republican, and Libertarian parties.

- At PROJECT VOTE SMART, hundreds of volunteers and student interns have labored "to provide their fellow citizens with the most crucial tool to citizens in a democracy: abundant, relevant information on those who govern us, or wish to replace those who already do." This website, at *http://www.vote-smart.org/education/,* also has lessons and links to other helpful sites. One lesson engages students in an inquiry on the question, "How do people decide who to vote for?"

COMMUNITY SERVICE AND ACTION

The real test of a social studies program comes in the out-of-school lives of children. If the school has provided new insights, improved skills, and increased civic-mindedness, such learning should be apparent in students' out-of-school behavior now as children and later as adults. One way to help bridge citizenship learning in school with citizenship experiences in the community and the world is through community-service activities.

This participation can be social or political in nature. If children are concerned with vandalism of school property, for example, they might volunteer to clean up and repair some of the damage. This is social action. But if they propose new rules to officials or request stronger enforcement of existing rules, this is political action. Both social and political action by citizens are important for the health of democratic communities. As Supreme Court Justice Louis Brandeis said early in this century, "The greatest menace to freedom is an inert people."

Community service activities can be spontaneous and short-lived, such as when the children learn of a fire at a nearby house and collect canned goods and clothing for the family. Activities can also be planned systematically and sustained over a longer period of time, such as the adoption of a creek or a section of the school grounds.

Examples of Community Service

The following projects have been done by real kids in real communities. Note that some are social, some are political, and some are both.

Saving a creek. The children at an elementary school near Everett, Washington, decided to do something about a dirty little stream named Pigeon Creek. The children were alarmed that Pigeon Creek had become so dirty that salmon stopped coming there to lay their eggs, so they "adopted" it.

The first thing the children did was to get an aquarium for their classroom and raise thousands of salmon eggs. Meanwhile, they worked with people in their community to clean up the creek. Litter was removed and the children put up "DON'T DUMP" signs. When the eggs hatched, the students released them in Pigeon Creek and monitored the creek to keep it clean.

These students "adopted" a block
near their school.

Getting out the vote.   One elementary school teacher from Salt Lake City, Barbara Lewis, has a unique way of impressing on her students the importance of voting. In her book for children about social action, she tells them:

> Do you know that a lot of adults are numb? They're numb from filling out forms, balancing checkbooks, changing diapers, and changing tires. In the process, many have forgotten the principles our country was founded upon. Many don't think their votes count for anything. . . . Imagine what could happen if kids attacked their communities in a campaign to shake adults out of the mothballs.[16]

Children can be *very* influential participants in get-out-the-vote campaigns. Distributed door to door, their flyers can read: "We can't vote yet. You can. Please do." By urging adults to register and vote, children can learn about voting eligibility, voting rates, and the role voting plays in representative democracies. Hopefully, the experience will encourage them to become regular voters themselves.

Teaching senior citizens about computers.   Clare Devine teaches at North Dover Elementary School in Toms River, New Jersey. Her students had learned about computers in the school's computer lab. They realized that many adults around them, especially older people, are nervous about working with these machines. Mrs. Devine and the children decided to offer a series of classes to seniors. Significant cooperative group work and planning were involved—both good opportunities for citizenship learning. In the computer classes, the students showed *their* "students" how to write to their grandchildren using word processing programs and how to communicate on the Internet, and they shared some of their favorite computer games.

Mrs. Devine liked how the project brought the two groups together. Did the seniors like the classes? "Yes, I think so. This year at the last class," reported Mrs. Devine, "they bought ice cream for everyone."[17]

Giraffes stick their necks out. Members of the Giraffe Club in LaConner Elementary School in LaConner, Washington, make this vow: "I promise to stick my neck out to make a difference. I will help people, animals, and my environment to make the world a better place to live."[18] The little giraffes do all manner of things to help people. (The address of the

FIGURE 3–7   Community service resources.

These national resources can help teachers plan community service projects. Local resources are just as helpful. Teachers can find out about them from local officials, the local chamber of commerce, and local chapters of 4-H, Camp Fire, Kiwanis, Rotary Club, and League of Women Voters.

American Bar Association, 541 N. Fairbanks CT, Chicago, IL 60611–3314. Phone: 312-988-5522.
American Red Cross, Program and Services Department, 2025 E St., N.W., Washington, DC 20006-5099.
American Society for the Prevention of Cruelty to Animals, Education Department, 441 E. 92nd St., New York, NY 10128. Phone: 212-876-7700.
Boys and Girls Clubs of America, 1320 Peachtree St., N.W., Atlanta, GA 30309. Phone: 404-815-5700.
Center for Civic Education, 5146 Douglas Fir Rd., Calabasas, CA 91302. Phone: 818-591-9321.
Center for Living Democracy, 289 Fox Farm Rd., Brattleboro, VT 05301. Phone: 802-254-1234.
Close Up Foundation, 44 Canal Center Plaza, Arlington, VA 22314. Phone: 800-765-3131.
Constitutional Rights Foundation, 601 S. Kingsley Dr., Los Angeles, CA 90005. Phone: 213-487-5590.
Educators for Social Responsibility, 23 Garden St., Cambridge, MA 02138. Phone: 617-492-1764.
Giraffe, P.O. Box 759, Langley, WA 98260. Phone: 360-221-7989.
Habitat for Humanity, 121 Habitat St., Americus, GA 31709. Phone: 912-924-6935.
Keep America Beautiful, Inc, 1010 Washington Blvd., Stamford, CT 06901. Phone: 203-323-8987.
National Association for Advancement of Colored People, 4805 Mt. Hope Dr., Baltimore, MD 21215-3297. Phone: 301-358-8900.
Volunteers of America, Inc, 110 S. Union St., Alexandria, VA 22314. Phone: 703-548-2288.

Giraffe organization and other resources appear in Figure 3–7.) One service they perform is gathering donations of food for people at Friendship House, a shelter for homeless people. Visit their website at *http://www.giraffe.org* .

Other Community Projects

Good neighbor club. Middle-grade students formed a Good Neighbor Club to help elderly residents in the neighborhood with yard work and errands.

Peer tutoring for citizenship. Your students can help welcome new children from other lands, not only into the classroom social system, but also into the processes of democratic citizenship. An immigrant child can be paired with an especially good citizen in your classroom—or one who needs to learn to be a better citizen. This "tutor" helps the new student learn to participate in class discussions and consider all alternatives when making a decision. Ask a resourceful parent to obtain a copy of the citizenship test preparation booklet from the federal courthouse. The peer tutor can go over the items with the new student and explain ideas, people, and places (e.g., national and local elections, representatives, and Washington, DC).

Adopt a part of the school. Frustrated by vandalism and litter on school grounds, fifth-grade children surveyed other students in the school to determine how many regarded this as a pressing problem. Results in hand, they wrote a proposal to the principal. Upon its approval, the children divided up the grounds by the number of classrooms in their school. Then they mounted a campaign to persuade each class to adopt one section of the school grounds as its own, regularly picking up the litter and painting over vandals' marks.

Civic letter writing. On a walk around the school, a second-grade class noticed that a main sidewalk was so badly damaged that children on their way to and from school had to walk into the street to avoid it. The class had practiced writing five kinds of letters: letters of support, letters giving information, letters requesting something, letters disagreeing with an action or opinion, and persuasive letters. They debated which kind was best for the current situation, eventually deciding to draft a letter to the city council *informing* it of the problem and *requesting* a repair.

Public information campaigns. Students can create posters and flyers for the school and neighborhood. These should be informational in nature, educating readers about a problem and suggesting possible or proven solutions the students think others should know about. Possibilities are fire safety in the home and at camp grounds, poisonous products in the home, and pet safety.

One group of fourth-graders was studying pollution problems in each region of the United States as part of their U.S. geography curriculum. One student brought to class a newspaper article about things that can pollute their front yards—weed killers and chemical fertilizers. Children playing in the yard and pets rolling in the grass can come into contact with these chemicals and track them into the house. They may develop rashes and become ill. These students produced a flyer that described the problem, listed information resources, and suggested remedies:

1. After using weed killers and fertilizers, water the lawn once a day for two days before allowing people or pets on it.
2. Take your shoes off before entering the house.
3. Don't use "weed and feed" products, which spread weed killer even where there are no weeds. Instead, pull weeds or use a spot sprayer.

The children printed the flyers and distributed them to the houses or apartments near their homes. Children, of course, should never go door to door without an adult supervisor. When this poses a difficulty, teachers rely on the classroom newsletter to get the word out to parents, school board members, and others on the class's mailing list.

CITIZENSHIP KNOWLEDGE

We have examined three categories of participatory democracy: discussing and deciding what to do about public problems (in the classroom, the community, and beyond); voting; and community service and action. If children learned to be good deliberators, well-prepared voters, and community servants, that would be terrific. But there is something better: knowledgeable deliberators, knowledgeable voters, and knowledgeable community servants. When participants possess a rich storehouse of knowledge about democracy and social life near and far, their discussions and decisions are more intelligent and their service projects more effective. As James Madison, one of the leading minds behind the U. S. Constitution and fourth president of the United States, wrote in 1788, "A people who mean to be their own governors must arm themselves with the power knowledge gives."

Informed participants have a keen respect for the facts. They are disposed to listen to facts rather than to prejudices, stereotypes, or the first thought that comes to mind. Moreover, they have learned ideas, examples, and analogies from their studies of other peoples' experience—people who may have lived long ago and far away. History is one of democracy's best teachers and a "precondition for political intelligence."[19] Knowing, for example, that other democracies have collapsed into hatred and tyranny when the people became apathetic or strained by an economic downturn is powerful information. Or knowing the history of the struggle for voting rights—that long after men won the vote, they kept it from women and African-Americans—may motivate some children to mount a voter-registration campaign in the school neighborhood.

Core Citizenship Ideas

Ideas, or what we shall know more precisely as *concepts* in Chapter 8, are the cornerstones of social studies education generally and of democratic citizenship in particular. *Democratic* is an idea, as is *citizenship*. Ideas are the basic mental tools that human beings think with. Without them, problem solving, reflection, and living could not proceed. Imagine going to the grocery store without the benefit of such concepts as *nutrition, cost,* or *fresh.* Or imagine being stranded on a remote island with persons who did not carry in their minds the ideas *cooperation* or *justice.*

Identifying the key ideas that children should develop for democratic citizenship is a task to which teachers need to devote a good deal of time. Fortunately, good advice is available. As we saw in Chapter 1, several sets of voluntary national curriculum standards have been published. One of these, published by the National Council for the Social Studies, includes *civic ideals and practices* as one of 10 subject-matter themes for the social studies curriculum. Examining the expectations for the early grades related to this theme (see the standards *Sampler* that accompanies this textbook), we see that emphasis is given to several ideas:

- Democratic government
- Common good
- Actions that influence public policy
- Rights and responsibilities of citizens

Another helpful source of citizenship concepts is the book, *National Standards for Civics and Government.* Some of the ideas this resource emphasizes are featured in the citizenship glossary in Figure 3–8. Teachers can help children develop such ideas first by providing examples of them drawn from children's literature, the newspaper, local and national elections, mock elections held in the classroom and school, and the social studies textbook and then by helping children see similarities among the examples. This teaching procedure, called *concept formation,* is detailed in Chapter 8.

We are *not* saying that this knowledge of democracy needs to be learned first, before democratic participation experiences begin. As anyone who spends time with young children knows, this would never work, even if it were a good idea. Children need to "learn as they go," experientially: identifying problems, discussing and debating them, defining them further; doing research and listening to stories to answer questions that were raised; then returning for more discussion, then more learning, and so on. In the midst of decision making, for example, when children realize they can identify only two alternatives, they are driven to do more research until they can describe several alternatives and how each affects various people in a diverse society. Participation skills and knowledge go hand in hand.

Simulation. A great way for the class to check its knowledge of democratic citizenship is to simulate a naturalization ceremony. When newcomers to the United States decide they want to become citizens, they must apply to the U.S. government. The process is called naturalization, and its culminating event is the ceremony at which the applicants take an Oath of Allegiance. Before this ceremony takes place, each applicant is required to pass a number of tests—of reading and writing ability, ability to understand English, and knowledge of some basic facts about democratic citizenship.

Children should attend a naturalization ceremony, if at all possible, and prepare for it by studying the Oath of Allegiance and by practicing the citizenship test. All of this can be simulated in the classroom:

1. The presiding "judge" asks the applicants to introduce themselves and tell where they are from and why they want to become U.S. citizens.
2. The judge then calls on another student, the "test giver," who administers the citizenship test orally. This can be done in teams (as in a spelling bee), in writing, or in groups in which the test giver asks one question to each applicant.
3. "Applicants" who pass the test proceed to reciting after the judge the Oath of Allegiance.

Students can practice for the citizenship test online at a website operated by the Department of Justice at *http://www.ins.usdoj.gov/exec/natz/natztest.asp.*

DEMOCRATIC VALUES

Children need to understand that democratic ideas and practices as they have developed in the United States rest on a foundation of democratic values. But what are values? They are a special kind of idea. They are ideas about the *worth* of something—some behavior, person, place, or thing. Values define for us what is worth striving for, what is right and desirable,

FIGURE 3–8 A glossary for democratic citizenship.

Bill of Rights. First ten amendments to the Constitution. Ratified in 1791, these amendments limit governmental power and protect basic rights and liberties of individuals.

Citizenship. Status of being a member of a state; one who owes allegiance to the government and is entitled to its protection and to political rights.

Civil rights. Protection and privileges given to all U.S. citizens by the Constitution and Bill of Rights.

Civil rights movements. Continuing efforts to gain the enforcement of the rights guaranteed to all citizens by the Constitution.

Common or public good. Benefit or interest of a politically organized society as a whole.

Constitutionalism. Idea that the powers of government should be distributed according to a written or unwritten constitution and that those powers should be effectively restrained by the constitution's provisions.

Democracy. Form of government in which political control is exercised by all the people, either directly or through their elected representatives.

Due process of law. Right of every citizen to be protected against arbitrary action by government.

Equal protection of the law. Idea that no individual or group may receive special privileges from nor be unjustly discriminated against by the law.

Founders. People who played important roles in the development of the national government of the United States. *Framers* are delegates to Philadelphia in 1787 who wrote the Constitution.

Freedom of expression. Refers to the freedom of speech, press, assembly, and petition that are protected by the First Amendment.

Freedom of religion. Freedom to worship as one pleases.

Government. Institutions and procedures through which a territory and its people are ruled.

Justice. Fair distribution of benefits and burdens, fair corrections of wrongs and injuries, or use of fair procedures in gathering information and making decisions.

Limited government. Constitutional government; a government created by the people to protect their individual rights and promote the common good. The opposite is *totalitarian* government.

Loyal opposition. Idea that opposition to a government is legitimate; organized opponents to the government of the day.

Politics. Process by which a group of people, whose opinions and interests are divergent, reach decisions that are binding on the group and enforced.

Representative democracy. Form of government in which power is held by the people and exercised indirectly through elected representatives who make decisions.

Rule of law. Principle that every member of a society, even a ruler, must follow the law.

Separation of powers. Division of governmental power among several institutions that must cooperate in decision making.

Suffrage. Right to vote.

Source: Adapted from *National Standards for Civics and Government* (Calabasas, CA: Center for Civic Education, 1994): 151–156. Reprinted by permission.

what is important, what is preferred, what constitutes worthy life goals, what may be worth sacrificing one's life for. Like other ideas, values are abstract conceptions (mental phenomena) and, therefore, cannot be observed directly. But they can be inferred from our decisions and our actions.

Basic democratic values include the individual rights to life, liberty, and the pursuit of happiness; the public or common good; justice; equality of opportunity; diversity; and responsibility. There is general agreement among Americans that such things are valuable. They are judged positively and are widely believed to be worth nurturing in our children. We saw in Chapter 1 that the Baltimore County schools selected 24 democratic values as the core of their character education program.

But can the *school* teach values in a democratic society? After all, this is a diverse society, and we don't wish to force our values on one another. The answer is simple: Yes, the schools can teach democratic values and they must. Democratic values are what we hold in common alongside our many differences. Democratic values are *public* or *general* values. They are expressed in our great public documents, such as the Declaration of Independence, the Constitution of the United States, the Bill of Rights, the Seneca Falls Resolution, and the speeches of Martin Luther King, Jr., Abraham Lincoln, and many others. Individuals who lead exemplary lives that reflect these general values are extolled as national heroes.

If children are to be socialized in accordance with these general values of society, they must be provided with examples of behavior that illustrate these values in action. That is, young people need to have encounters with idealized types—persons who illustrate by their way of life the values that society rewards and likes to see in its citizens. Because these general values are internalized by the majority of citizens, orderly social life can take place. We expect our fellow citizens to behave in ways that are predictable and consistent with the basic premises inherent in those values on which there is general consensus. Law enforcement agencies are provided to protect society from the minority of persons who cannot or will not live in accordance with the general values embraced by the majority. But no police force could possibly monitor the behavior of all citizens if they were not willing to comply voluntarily with the accepted rules of the society.

Lesson Plan 3, dealing with symbolic values, provides a good example of a lesson based on public or general values. These values are promoted through social studies in the following ways:

1. Daily life in the classroom that stresses consideration for others, freedom and equality, independence of thought, individual responsibility for one's actions, and the dignity of individual human beings.

2. The study of the history and development of this country stressing the ideals that inspired it and showing that a continuing effort is needed to move reality closer to those ideals.

3. The study of biographies of individuals whose lives reflect the general values of the nation.

4. The study of law, the justice system, and the U.S. Constitution.

5. The celebration of holidays that reinforce values and ideals associated with the holiday (e.g., Veterans Day, Fourth of July).

6. Thoughtful analyses of the meaning of such statements as the Pledge of Allegiance, the Preamble to the Constitution, the Bill of Rights, and the Declaration of Independence. (Here is another good opportunity to integrate language arts and social studies instruction.)

7. Building awareness of situations that are not in accord with values to which this society is committed.

8. Cross-cultural studies to illustrate differences in values from one society to another.

As we move from public values to *personal* values, the role of social studies becomes considerably different and, to some extent, less clear. Personal values are those values that influence the decision making of individuals in their own personal lives. To some extent they represent individual interpretations of general values, that is, the integrating of general values in the personal life of each individual. However, they also refer to cultural values and customs—for example, beliefs and practices that Catholics may have but Methodists do not, or that Buddhists may have that Jews do not, or that Mexican Americans may have that Cambodian Americans do not.

Personal values also refer simply to what individuals like or want to do—preferring films to television, blue to yellow, bicycling to jogging. Modern life in affluent, industrialized societies involves an incredible amount of choices: how to spend our time, what career to choose, what clothes to buy and to wear, where to live, what brand products to buy, what hobbies and leisure-time activities to pursue, and how to spend our money. Each decision is an expression of individual preferences. It should be obvious that the social studies program cannot promote personal values in the same way that it can promote general values.

DEMOCRATIC DISPOSITIONS AND VIRTUES

Dispositions, also known as character traits and virtues, are closely related to values. They are habits or inclinations that summarize a person's behavior and values. One may value honesty and courage and decency, for example, but only rarely behave honestly, courageously, and decently. On the other hand, if we describe a person as honest, courageous, or decent, we mean that *generally* he or she exhibits these traits and is inclined to behave these ways. It's one thing to be honest now and then; it's something quite different to be regularly and routinely honest. Such behavior has become a *habit,* a part of this person's character. If such habits were not widely formed by people, life would be chaotic and living together democratically would be impossible. The authors of the U.S. Constitution knew this. James Madison often said that if virtuous habits were missing from the people, then no amount of law, government, or police power would protect us from one another.

Teaching children to develop positive dispositions is what many today call *character education.* Others call it *moral* or *values education,* terms often used interchangeably. Whatever we call it, it is a long-standing tradition in American education (Figure 3–9). It has been called the "great tradition" not only in the United States but everywhere, for "the transmission of moral values has been the dominant educational concern of most cultures throughout history."[20]

Lesson Plan 3 — SYMBOLIC VALUES

Grade	4–6
Time	One class period
Objectives	Children will infer information about a country's values from symbols placed on its coins.
Resources	At least one coin for each child, preferably coins or facsimiles of coins, from several different nations.
Interest Building	Placing one coin in child's hand should build interest.

Lesson Development

Teacher: Boys and girls, for the past few days we have been studying the use of signs and symbols. At the close of our discussion yesterday we came to an important conclusion. What was it?

Tess: We said that we could tell what people considered to be important to them by the symbols and signs they use on their buildings and clothing.

Teacher: Yes. What was an example?

Kim: I liked the flag example. The stars stand for states, and that shows that in our country people think it is important that the states have power. It's not only the national government that has power.

Teacher: Thank you. Today you will have a chance to test that idea in a slightly different way. Each of you has a coin to use for a reason: Study the coin carefully, as you did the flag yesterday, and see how many things you can tell about the country just from what you see on the coin.

Ask children to examine very closely the coin in their hands. After they have had time to make their observations, ask the children what they have concluded. As these are presented, write them on the chalkboard. Have each child tell *why* the conclusion was made. Pass the coins about for other children to inspect. Items such as the following may surface in this discussion:

> These people believe in God.
>
> They believe in liberty.
>
> Men must be more important than women in this country.
>
> They construct large buildings.
>
> They speak more than one language.
>
> They have a queen.
>
> They like birds.
>
> They are a peace-loving people.
>
> They are proud of their wars and war heroes.

Assessment

Imagine that the United States is planning to issue a new coin and there is a contest to get the best design. You decide to enter the contest. The rules are these:
- Write down two ideas that best describe what people in our country think are important to them.
- Think of and draw symbols that could be used on a coin to show these two values.

Integration

Literature: Read aloud a children's literature selection that will deepen students' understanding of *values.* For example, Elinor Batezat Sisulu's *The Day Gogo Went to Vote* (Little Brown, 1994) tells the South-African story of Thembi who accompanies her great-grandmother, Gogo, to vote for the first time in 1994. What does Gogo value? Why?

Math and economics: In another direction, students may have questions about coins. What is their function? Compare the worth of different coins (penny, dime, quarter). Ask students what they think people did before there were coins or paper money. Read David Schwartz's *If You Made a Million* (Mulberry, 1994), with its pictures of coins and money.

■   ■   ■   ■   ■

Responsibility and Civility

What character traits are important to democratic citizenship? Perhaps the most important are individual responsibility and civility. *Individual responsibility* is the habit of fulfilling one's obligations to family, friends, teachers, and other citizens in one's community and nation. *Civility* is the habit of treating other persons courteously and respectfully, regardless of whether one likes them, agrees with their viewpoints, or shares their cultural or religious beliefs. Uncivil behavior is summed up by terms such as *rude, bigoted, ill-mannered, criminal,* and *hateful.* The willingness to listen generously to others, asking for clarification and elaboration, especially to persons one may not know well or not want especially to be friends with, is a hallmark of civility. If people are to walk the democratic path together, they must behave with civility toward one another.

FIGURE 3-9
Democratic dispositions and
virtues.

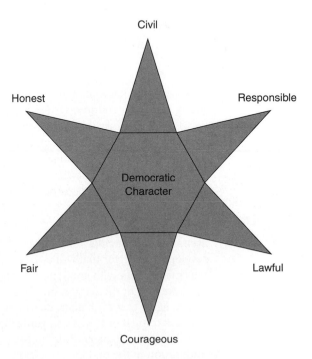

> The ancient Greeks defined the word *idiot* in a surprising way: *Idiots* were citizens who were concerned only with their private lives, preferences, and freedoms and paid no attention to the common good. They placed personal concerns way out in front of community concerns.

The virtues of responsibility and civility combine to mean something that is greater than the sum of the parts: civic-mindedness. Democratic citizens are disposed to think not only of their private interests and private affairs; they need to think also of the common good. The ancient Greeks defined the word *idiot* in a surprising way: *Idiots* were citizens who were concerned only with their private lives, preferences, and freedoms and paid no attention to the common good. They placed personal concerns way out in front of community concerns.

More recently, the brilliant French visitor to America, the sociologist Alexis de Toqueville, observed that Americans were at a "dangerous passage" in their history. They were at a point where they "are carried away and lose all self-restraint at the sight of the new possessions they are about to obtain." Getting "carried away" like this is dangerous, he warned, because it can cause people to lose the very freedom they are enjoying: "The more they look after what they call their own business, they neglect their chief business, which is to remain their own masters."[21] What did he mean by this—that our chief business is to remain our own masters? He meant that we need to maintain the kind of community that secures our freedom. Without democratic community—without civic life—there is no freedom. This is why the Greeks called it "idiotic" to ignore civic life.

We are each obliged, then, to be civic-minded. Children must be taught to enjoy the rights democracy affords them in such a way that their enjoyment does not become an obsession that harms the common good and ruins the very arrangement that protects those rights. This means they must be taught to pay attention to the democracy, to nurture it, maintain it, and help it grow; not to become so selfish as to become, well, "idiotic."

Courage

Courage is the habit of standing up for one's convictions when conscience demands. For young and older children alike, courage is required when "everybody is doing it," but one knows in one's heart that it is wrong. This applies to cheating, stealing, teasing, illicit drug use, lying—all the very real temptations of social interaction. Bringing children to the circle for a discussion of courage can be a wonder-filled event for the teacher who is curious about children's character development. Ask children to give examples of courageous behavior and courageous persons. You will learn a lot.

Fairness (Justice)

Even kindergartners have a keen sense of what is and isn't fair. But it is not necessarily a well-developed sense, for that will take time, experience, maturation, coaxing, a stimulating social environment with good models, and intellectual development.

As we saw in the section on "Deliberation and Decision Making," moral philosophers tend to agree that the highest development of the sense of fairness is expressed as the commitment to treat others as you yourself would want to be treated if you were in their situation. This is the "Golden Rule" in the Judeo-Christian faith, and the Mahayana doctrine of compassion in the Buddhist tradition.

Other Virtues

Other democratic dispositions such as being lawful, respecting the rights of others, being a critical thinker, and being patriotic are surely important. And no list of democratic dispositions is complete without honesty. "Honest Abe" Lincoln is an honored figure in American history, largely due to his reputation for truth telling; and whether or not George Washington actually chopped down that cherry tree, the famous line "I cannot tell a lie" resonates in the American citizen's value system. The mere thought that a politician is corrupt or that a military academy cadet has cheated is sufficiently jarring to make the evening news. Teachers can help children develop the *habit* of honesty by exhibiting it themselves, pointing it out in those who model it, and giving children plenty of opportunities to discuss with one another, in the style of Mrs. Paley earlier in this chapter, the challenge of being honest when "nobody else was" or when it was easier to avoid punishment by lying or cheating.

RELIGION AND THE SOCIAL STUDIES

Any discussion of values education and dispositions inevitably takes us to religion, because religions—if they have anything in common—are concerned with the inculcation of particular values and dispositions. Religions *at their best* are "the world's wisdom traditions. They look like data banks that house the winnowed wisdom of the human race."[22]

Yet, in keeping with the mandate of the First Amendment, schools in the United States have been diligent in their effort to maintain a separation of church and state. This can be cause for confusion.

Some observers, both liberal and conservative, believe that schools have been overly zealous in removing religion from the schools. As a result of this omission, a distorted understanding of history has been fostered. It is as though religion does not exist as an important force in shaping the affairs of human beings and their cultures, as if people's wisdom traditions didn't matter to them. Of course, nothing is further from the truth. Religion has had and continues to have a tremendous impact on history and human affairs. History on every continent is loaded with examples of religious hope giving comfort to oppressed peoples, religious wars and persecutions destroying countless lives, and persons with deep religious convictions who intervened to prevent wars and persecutions. Think of the Hindu Gandhi in India and the Christian Martin Luther King, Jr., in the United States.

Religion plays a critical role in the formation and maintenance of cultures (think of Shintoism in Japan, Judaism in Israel, animism among Native Americans, and Christianity in the African-American community) and in migrations (e.g., the Pilgrims). Religion plays a critical role also in civil war (e.g., in Serbia and Northern Ireland), conquests (e.g., Columbus and Cortés), nonviolent resistance (e.g., Gandhi and King), and the transformation of individual character (e.g., the practices of Christian or Muslim prayer or Buddhist meditation).

Modern, industrialized peoples are generally less defined by church doctrine than were pre-modern, agricultural peoples, and they tend to value *pluralism*, which permits persons of different religions to live and work and educate their children in the same community.

But still, religion is an enormous historical force to be reckoned with. Historians who study the past and sociologists and anthropologists who study the present typically make much of it. It is at best strange, then, for the school curriculum to ignore it.

Where does this leave the teacher? Most important, understand that the First Amendment prohibition is against teaching doctrinal religious beliefs; it does not disallow the *study* of religion as a powerful phenomenon of history and culture. Therefore, the study of religion as a social phenomenon constitutes a legitimate area of inquiry for social studies. Children cannot possibly understand historical events, such as the European colonization of the Americas or the Civil Rights Movement, without understanding the role of religion on all sides. Nor can they appreciate the fact that democracy, with its guarantee of religious liberty and its insistence on religious tolerance and pluralism, is so much better than the alternative: the religious warfare and persecution so common in nondemocratic societies. "Thanks in large measure to the Religious Liberty clauses of the First Amendment [to the U.S. Constitution], this country remains the boldest and most successful experiment in living with religious differences the world has ever seen."[23]

The challenge to teachers is to make religion a natural part of the social studies topics studied. Just as it is common to have children study the geography, government, and history of a selection of communities around the world, it should also be common for them to gather information about the religions practiced in these communities. This means that teachers need to become knowledgeable about the religions of people studied and how the lives of those people are affected by their religious beliefs. Closer to home, today's teachers need to know about the diverse religions embraced by the families of the children in their classrooms. As noted in the previous chapter, a teacher can display genuine respect for children's home cultures in many ways; attending a special event at a child's mosque, temple, or church is one way that is sure to be remembered by the child and the family. This is simple kindness, and it is good pedagogy as well. We called it culturally responsive instruction in Chapter 2.

Conclusion

Democracy is a difficult and often exasperating form of living together. But, as Winston Churchill said, it is better than the alternatives.

There can be no democracy without the democratic citizens who create it day by day. Educating these citizens is the primary mission of the social studies curriculum. We presented six dimensions of this task. Each should be part of the classroom life you create for students: Deliberating classroom rules and problems, voting in real and mock elections, taking action on school and community problems, developing the knowledge citizens need, understanding the values expressed in the documents and speeches that anchor our democracy, and developing the virtues that make democratic life possible. These are the civic expectations teachers should have for each and every student.

Discussion Questions and Suggested Activities

1. Through discussion with classmates, develop a set of guidelines to involve children in classroom decision making. In which decisions would you, and would you not, invite their participation? Then make a decision tree (see Figure 3–4) on a poster and take turns leading the decision tree lesson with classmates.

2. Compare the discussion/decision-making approaches of Ethel Sadowsky, Tarry Lindquist, and Vivian Paley. Then list some of the specific things they do that you might want to try. For example, Mrs. Paley *proposes* a new rule and has students *consider* it—deliberating its positive and negative consequences. She conducts an ongoing moral inquiry based on two questions: Will the rule work? Is the rule fair?

3. Divide the community service resources list (Figure 3–7) with five other students. Call or write to each service. Explain that you are seeking advice on starting up community service projects with your class and request materials. Be sure to indicate the grade levels of the children. If writing, use school letterhead.

4. Examine the levels of proficiency in the two discussion scoring guides (Table 3–1 and Figure 3–3). Compare and contrast them, and skip ahead to Chapter 10 to the section on performance assessment. Design a scoring guide for a decision-making or a community-service skill.

5. Develop a reading lesson on the U. S. Constitution. You might try leading an interpretive discussion of the Preamble or the First Amendment. Or you might plan a lesson to teach skimming, using the entire document. Perhaps you'll develop a competitive game for teams based on the U.S. Constitution.

Selected References

Anderson, Charlotte C., Gallagher, Arlene F., Mertz, Gayle, Zarnowski, Myra, Lindquist, Tarry L., & others. (1991, Sept./Oct.). Articles and a pull-out section on "Celebrating the Bill of Rights." Special issue of *Social Studies and the Young Learner, 4.*

Dewey, John. (1916). *Democracy and education.* New York: Macmillan.

Engle, Shirley H., & Ochoa, Anna S. (1988). *Education for democratic citizenship.* New York: Teachers College Press.

Evans, Ronald, & Saxe, David (Eds.). (1996). *Handbook on teaching social issues.* Washington, DC: National Council for the Social Studies.

Goodman, Jesse. (1992). *Elementary schooling for critical democracy.* Albany: State University of New York Press.

Greenberg, Polly. (1992, July). How to institute some simple democratic practices pertaining to respect, rights and responsibilities in any classroom. *Young Children, 47,* 10–17.

Haas, Mary, Hatcher, Barbara & Sunal, Cynthia Szymanski. (1992, Sept./Oct.). Teaching about the president and the presidential election. *Social Studies and the Young Learner, 5.* Special pull-out section.

Hahn, Carole L. (1998). *Becoming political.* Albany, NY: State University of New York Press.

Leming, James S. (1993, Nov.). In search of effective character education. *Educational Leadership, 51,* 63–71.

Lickona, Thomas. (1991). *Educating for character.* New York: Bantam.

Mosher, Ralph, Kenny, Robert A., Jr., & Garrod, Andrew. (1994). *Preparing for citizenship.* Westport, CT: Praeger.

Niemi, R. G., & Junn, J. (1998). *Civic education: What makes students learn?* New Haven: Yale University Press.

Paley, Vivian Gussin. (1992). *You can't say you can't play.* Cambridge: Harvard University Press.

Parker, Walter C. (Ed.). (1996). *Educating the democratic mind.* Albany: State University of New York Press.

Walzer, Michael. (1992). *What it means to be an American.* New York: Marsilio.

White, Patricia. (1996). *Civic virtues and public schooling: Educating citizens for a democratic society.* New York: Teachers College Press.

Notes

1. James Baldwin, A talk to teachers. In *Multicultural literacy,* ed. Rick Simonson & Scott Walker (Saint Paul, MN: Graywolf Press, 1988), 4.

2. Polly Greenberg, How to institute some simple democratic practices pertaining to respect, rights, and responsibilities in any classroom, *Young Children, 47* (July 1992): 10–17.

3. Ethel Sadowsky, Taking part: Democracy in the elementary school, in *Preparing for citizenship: Teaching youth to live democratically,* ed. Ralph Mosher, Robert A. Kenny, Jr., & Andrew Garrod (Westport, CT: Praeger, 1994), 153.

4. Tarry Lindquist, *Seeing the whole through social studies* (Portsmouth, NH: Heinemann, 1995), 35.

5. Vivian Paley, *You can't say you can't play* (Cambridge: Harvard University Press, 1992), 4.

6. Ibid., 16.

7. Ibid., 21.

8. Ibid., 18–19.

9. Ibid., 63.

10. Sadowsky, *Preparing for citizenship,* 153.

11. Thomas Lickona, *Educating for character* (New York: Bantam, 1991).

12. David Harris is the social studies curriculum coordinator for the Oakland County, Michigan, schools. A full description of this scoring guide appears in his chapter in *Handbook on teaching social issues,* edited by Ronald W. Evans & David Warren Saxe (Washington, DC: National Council for the Social Studies, 1996, 288–97).

13. Southern Christian Leadership Conference, Atlanta, 1990. (Reprinted from a speech by Dr. King on May 17, 1957.)

14. Read Principal JoAnn C. Shaheen's account in *Social Education, 53*(October 1989): 361–363.

15. Ibid., 361.

16. *The kids guide to social action: How to solve the social problems you choose, and turn creative thinking into positive action* (Minneapolis: Free Spirit Publishing, 1991), 87.

17. James A. Banks et al., *Adventures in time and place: Communities* (New York: McGraw-Hill, 1997), 337.

18. Giraffe organization brochure. Contact Giraffe at P.O. Box 759, Langley, WA 98260.

19. Paul Gagnon, History's role in civic education, in Walter C. Parker (ed.) *Educating the demo-cratic mind* (State University of New York Press, 1996, pp. 241–262).

20. Edward A. Wynne, The great tradition in education: Transmitting moral values, *Educational Leadership, 43* (December 1985/January 1986): 4. The most comprehensive resource book for character education is Thomas Lickona's *Educating for character* (New York: Bantam, 1991).

21. *Democracy in America,* Trans., George Lawrence; ed., J. P. Mayer (Garden City, NY: Anchor Books, 1969), 540.

22. Huston Smith, *The illustrated world's religions* (HarperCollins, 1991), 13.

23. Charles C. Haynes, ed., *Finding common ground* (Nashville: The Freedom Forum First Amendment Center, Vanderbilt University, 1994), 1–2.

Websites

http://www.kidsvotingusa.org

http://www.vote-smart.org/education/

http://www.giraffe.org

http://www.ins.usdoj.gov/exec/natztest.asp

CHAPTER 4

History, Geography, and the Social Sciences

Main Idea

The main sources of subject matter for the social studies curriculum are the disciplines of history, geography, political science, economics, sociology, and anthropology. The social studies curriculum integrates these areas, often leading with history or geography, and steers students toward becoming democratic citizens. The key to teaching these disciplines to younger and older children alike is to help the children *do* them as well as learn *about* them. Like the two wings of an airplane, neither is sufficient alone. The social science disciplines, after all, are not only collections of knowledge but ways of constructing knowledge.

Key Concepts

History, historical reasoning, primary source, knowing and doing history, geography, political science, economics, anthropology, sociology

Chapter Outline

- Teaching History
- Teaching Geography
- Teaching Political Science (Citizenship Education)
- Teaching Economics
- Teaching Anthropology
- Teaching Sociology
- Conclusion
- Discussion Questions and Suggested Activities
- Selected References
- Notes

Chapter Snapshot

A small group of fourth-graders was *doing* history as well as learning about history. The students were working on a script for a dramatic re-enactment of the famous meeting of Lewis and Clark with Sacajawea, a Shoshone, and her French-Canadian husband. Each time the children learned something else about the encounter, their teacher encouraged them to revise their script. She helped them search a Lewis and Clark website where they learned that the explorers had developed a ceremony they used when meeting a tribe for the first time. The children pored over this description, and the ceremony became a new scene in their drama. Other small groups of students dramatized the day Lewis and Clark's team set out on the Missouri River in 1804, the day they sighted the Pacific Ocean in 1805, and the day they returned to St. Louis in 1806. It was a remarkable journey. Lewis and Clark were good observers, and they kept journals, which students also got from the website.

 A favorite website www.pbs.org/lewisandclark/ This is the Public Broadcasting Service's website on the Ken Burns film of the Lewis and Clark Expedition. Click on "The Archive" and then go to "The Journals."

The subject-matter banquet table of the social studies curriculum in the elementary and middle school is loaded with offerings, each more tempting than the next. The center-pieces traditionally have been history and geography. These are taught together, usually, but sometimes, for increased clarity, separately. Children typically are introduced to the history and geography of their community, state, nation, and world in grades 3 through 6, respectively. Geography is easily integrated into historical study because historical narratives cannot be comprehended or constructed apart from their geographical settings.

We introduce the fields of history and geography in this chapter, along with political science, economics, anthropology, and sociology. These are the major sources of information, ideas, and issues for social studies lessons and units. Political science was the subject of the entire previous chapter on citizenship education, so we give it only brief coverage here.

Teaching History

History is the subject in which students learn stories about the past, learn how these stories are created, learn that these stories are created differently by different people, and learn to create these stories themselves, as historians do, using historical reasoning. The key to teaching history to children is to do two things, not one. Like the two wings of an airplane, these two work together and neither works alone. One is exposing children to historical narratives that others have written or told. We call this historical knowledge. The other is helping children to write and tell historical narratives of their own making. We call this historical know-how or historical reasoning.

If they are to do either of these things well, and to understand the difference between them, their teachers need themselves to understand what history is and why they should bother with it in the elementary and middle grades. After all, the school principal will be waving copies of reading and math tests at the faculty before addressing the importance of historical know-how and historical reasoning. Accordingly, we begin with the "why" and "what" of history and then return to the two wings of the airplane: absorbing and doing history.

RATIONALE

The famous child psychologist Bruno Bettleheim argued that elementary school children need "rich food for their imagination, a sense of history, how the present situation came about."[1] What is at stake here is *wisdom*. Without historical knowledge and know-how there can be no wisdom. Here, briefly, are five reasons for history instruction throughout the elementary school years and into adulthood. We believe they add up to wisdom.

1. *Judgment.* The first reason for history teaching and learning is that historical knowledge and know-how help people develop better judgment, especially the judgment needed for what is called "political intelligence."

   > Knowledge of history is the precondition of political intelligence. Without history, a society shares no common memory of where it has been, of what its core values are, or of what decisions of the past account for present circumstances. ... Without history, one cannot move to the informed, discriminating citizenship essential to effective participa-

tion in the democratic processes of governance and the fulfillment for all our citizens of the nation's democratic ideals.[2]

Just how do historical knowledge and know-how give us political intelligence? Mainly, they help us learn from others' experience. Martin Luther King, Jr., for example, learned from the experience of another social activist: Indian revolutionary Mahatma Gandhi (1869–1948). As Dr. King wrote, "Christ furnished the spirit and motivation, while Gandhi furnished the method."[3] What method? King is referring to the method of social action and protest he and others used successfully during the Civil Rights Movement. That method was a version of Gandhi's *Satyagraha:* nonviolent civil disobedience. King watched and read Gandhi closely, as did many in the Movement, for Gandhi's nonviolent protests in India had helped free the Indian people from British rule. Some of the same methods were then used in Montgomery, Birmingham, and Selma, Alabama, in the 1950s and 60s to challenge racist laws and customs. If you visit the King Center in Atlanta, Georgia, you will find that the bookstore is loaded with books by and about Gandhi. King's judgment, then, in formulating methods to end racial segregation in the United States was nurtured by his historical knowledge. Indeed, one way to help children celebrate the life and work of Dr. King is to study Gandhi's life and work.[4]

2. *Empathy.* A second reason for history instruction is that history builds children's knowledge of the world's peoples and the inclination to understand their struggles and appreciate their humanity. By learning about the diversity of the world's societies and their histories, children see that many, many people live differently than they do, *and that their own way of life is "different," too,* at least from the perspective of other peoples. Respect for the tapestry of human similarities and differences is a virtue that distinguishes the intolerant bigot who loves to hate from the good neighbor who seeks friendship with people alike and different.

3. *Imagination.* A third reason for history teaching and learning is that, as Bettleheim says, it is rich food for the imagination. History *enlarges* and *excites* children's imagination. It gives them experiences they have not actually had. In some cases, one is thankful for having been spared the actual experience; in others, one longs to have "been there." History, like other kinds of good literature, is by its nature expanding and liberating: It takes children to far-away places and far-away times, even to unknown destinations close to home. It puts them in the shoes of both the queen and the queen's slaves, the president and the pauper. It introduces them to decent people and horrible people, to inspiring ideas and despicable ones, and to remarkable events and ordinary life—all this around the world and across decades, centuries, and millennia. These people, ideas, issues, and values fuel the imagination like gasoline does an automobile engine; without it, there may be a spark but there is no combustion.

4. *Agency.* Agency means the power to take action, to *do* something about personal and public problems. History shows us that people are shaped by their circumstances; they are acted upon by social forces that often are beyond their control. Yet, history teaches us also that people make a difference. "Don't mourn, organize!" goes the old activist slogan. It's true: People make a difference. They can create organizations of like-minded people, they can form protest movements, they can discover cures for diseases,

they can treat others fairly, they can write letters and make laws, they can make speeches that rouse people to action for good (think of Dr. King) or ill (think of Hitler). Teachers should expose their students to many examples of people making a difference in their neighborhoods, the nation, and the world: men and women, boys and girls, famous and not. Historical study, then, helps children to see that just as they have been shaped by the past so will they shape the future for others. Whether by their actions or their inaction, they will do it. How do they want to shape the future? For what contribution do they want to be remembered? Ask them these questions often.

5. *The Long View.* There have been about 10,000 years of human civilization. Before that, for 10 times longer, humans were hunters and gatherers who roamed for food and shelter. About 8,000 B.C., a major change occurred in how people lived: agriculture. Agriculture triggered the beginning of settled village life and, with that, the beginnings of civilization. Since then, humanity has had two major lifestyles: agricultural (or traditional) and, very recently, industrial (or modern). The biggest difference between the two is the amount of time individuals and groups spend on food production. Securing food was the main event in agricultural societies; not so in industrial societies where advances in science and technology allowed most people to do other things. Families became smaller, students went away from home to school, and parents went away to work at things other than food production. Every facet of social life—from politics to religion—was transformed.

Humanity now shares a web of stories reaching all the way back to the first farming villages and stretching all the way forward through the Industrial Revolution to the space age and the global marketplace. *Feeling* this connection going all the way back and forward, sensing it, perceiving it, knowing it, having it pervade one's judgment— this is having the long view. This is long-term thinking.

The fifth reason, then, concerns the chief problem humanity faces today. Biologist-inventor Stuart Brand captures it well: "How do we make long-term thinking automatic and common instead of difficult and rare? How do we make the taking of long-term responsibility inevitable?"[5] The bizarre speed of current events, information overload, and runaway consumption and production unfortunately give even adults a pathologically short attention span. They are acting more and more like children, showing too little inclination to serve the long-term interests of the family, the community, and the planet. Historical study is one solution, for it introduces people to the long view.

Summarizing the five reasons for history instruction, we return to the single word *wisdom*. Students' encounters with distant times and places become part of who the children are. These encounters, and the meaning students make of them, are added to the inventory of knowledge they take with them to new situations and problems. History helps liberate us from the blinders placed on our vision by the circumstances of our lives. It broadens our horizons and extends our time frame back to those first villages, forward to the next 10,000 years, and out to people everywhere.

WHAT HISTORY SHOULD BE TAUGHT?

Let's turn to the matter of choosing themes and topics. The school district curriculum guide will probably list themes (e.g., time, continuity, and change) and topics (e.g., the American Revolution). These are probably adapted from recent national efforts to identify essential historical subject matter. Figure 4–1 lists eight curriculum topics suggested for study in grades K–4 by the *National Standards for History*. This is a good list. (For grades 5–12, this group suggests the chronological study of both United States and world history.)

While this is a powerful and comprehensive list of topics, another piece of curriculum advice should prove just as helpful. The chart in Table 4–1 summarizes the U. S. history knowledge on which fourth-, eighth-, and eleventh-graders are assessed by the National Assessment of Educational Progress (NAEP).[6] The group that produced this curriculum is composed of teachers and historians, liberals and conservatives, and members of both majority and minority ethnic groups. What is interesting here is that they *agreed* on anything: eight chronological eras and four themes to emphasize in each era. The themes include:

1. *Change and Continuity in American Democracy.* The development of American political democracy from colonial times to the present. This includes basic principles and core civic ideas developed through the American Revolution, U.S. Constitution, the Civil War, and the struggles over slavery and civil rights.

2. *The Gathering and Interactions of Peoples, Cultures, and Ideas.* The gathering of people and cultures of many countries, races, and religious traditions that have contributed to the American heritage and the development of American society.

3. *Economic and Technological Changes and Their Relation to Society, Ideas, and the Environment.* The transformation of the American economy from rural frontier to industrial superpower and its impact on society, ideas, and the environment. This includes the development of a market economy and the influence of geography, urbanization, science, and technology.

FIGURE 4–1   Historical topics for study in the early grades.

1. Family life now and in the recent past; family life in various places long ago.
2. History of students' local community and how communities in North America varied long ago.
3. The people, events, problems, and ideas that created the history of their state.
4. How democratic values came to be, and how they have been exemplified by people, events, and symbols.
5. The causes and nature of various movements of large groups of people into and within the United States, now and long ago.
6. Regional folklore and cultural contributions that helped to form our national heritage.
7. Selected attributes and historical developments of various societies in Africa, the Americas, Asia, and Europe.
8. Major discoveries in science and technology, their social and economic effects, and the scientists and inventors from many groups and religions responsible for them.

Source: *National Standards for History for Grades K–4: Expanding Children's World in Time and Space* (Los Angeles: National Center for History in the Schools, 1994): 29–30.

4. *The Changing Role of America in the World.* The movement from isolation to worldwide responsibility. This includes the impact of geography, resources, interests, and ideals on American foreign policy; relations between domestic politics and foreign affairs; and the influence of the American example on the rest of the world and of other nations on the United States.[7]

HISTORICAL REASONING

Passive absorption of this material is certainly not the point. Do you remember the opening "snapshot" of this chapter? A fourth-grade class was divided into small groups, and each was studying and dramatizing an event in the Lewis and Clark expedition (1804–06). Each time they encountered some new facts about their event (e.g., learning at the Public Broadcasting Service website that Lewis and Clark had a standard ceremony they enacted whenever they met a new tribe), their teacher encouraged them to revise their script for the dramatization. The point is that *the script the students were drafting and revising was a historical narrative of their own construction.* They were using historical reasoning to figure out what happened and to decide how to portray it.

This kind of reasoning, historical reasoning, is *interpretive* reasoning. Why? Because the past is over with, it *must* be interpreted. But what is "it" that's interpreted? There is a makeshift record of the past left to us in the form of what historians call "sources," and these

TABLE 4–1 U.S. History content outline by periods and themes.

Themes Periods	Change and Continuity in American Democracy: Ideas, Institutions, Practices, and Controversies	The Gathering and Interactions of Peoples, Cultures, and Ideas	Economic and Technological Changes and Their Relation to Society, Ideas, and the Environment	The Changing Role of America in the World
Three Worlds and Their Meeting in the Americas (Beginnings to 1607)				
Colonization, Settlement, and Communities (1607 to 1763)				
The Revolution and the New Nation (1763 to 1815)				
Expansion and Reform (1801 to 1861)				
Crisis of the Union: Civil War and Reconstruction (1850 to 1877)				
The Development of Modern America (1865 to 1920)				
Modern America and the World Wars (1914 to 1945)				
Contemporary America (1945 to Present)				

Source: *U.S. History Framework for the 1994 National Assessment of Education Progress (NAEP)* (Washington, DC: U.S. Department of Education, 1994):18.

are what gets interpreted. They are the "evidence" in historical interpretation. Historical narratives must be pieced together from this evidence. The evidence is found in the "sources": primary sources, artifacts, and secondary sources.

Primary sources are materials created (written, filmed, painted, etc.) during the time under study. These are eyewitness accounts such as those contained in the journals of Lewis and Clark. *Artifacts* are objects made by persons during the time under study, such as a medicine pouch carried by Sacajawea. *Secondary sources* are interpretations of these primary sources and artifacts. The Ken Burns film of the Lewis and Clark expedition and Stephen Ambrose's book about it, *Undaunted Courage* (1996), are both secondary sources. When you conduct a lesson or unit on the Lewis and Clark expedition, your students will need to work with primary and secondary sources as they compose a narrative description (a story) of what happened. When they do this, they are engaging in historical reasoning. Lesson Plan 4 suggests a way to teach the difference between primary and secondary sources.

Some primary sources will be collected for you in the textbook program and its ancillaries, some are available online, and local museums will often loan a few artifacts. A field trip to the museum may be arranged, and biographies (which are secondary sources) are probably in the school library or multimedia center along with photo collections and paintings.

Interpretive reasoning, then, is investigative reasoning. The historian—whether a child or a professional—conducts an *inquiry,* an *investigation.* It is a question-driven search for evidence and answers. There is a problem to be solved (e.g., Why did King decide on nonviolent resistance as the method? Were Lewis and Clark kind to the tribes they encountered?). Information must be collected and evaluated and a conclusion drawn. This conclusion is difficult to draw because, among other things, *there are gaps in the record.* Plenty of them. Furthermore, not all the information that is available is altogether credible. (Who said it? What was their agenda? In what direction did their bias run?) And that's not all. The author—whether your student or a professional—makes choices about what to pay attention to. "No historian tries to write a 'complete' account, and no one would have time to read one."[8]

Understandably, then, one student's interpretation will differ from another's, just as do the interpretations of professional historians. Historians disagree about almost everything, even such "basics" as the causes of the American Revolution, the meaning of Lincoln's Gettysburg Address, and Dr. King's role in the Civil Rights Movement. Consequently, history teaching is not a simple matter of teaching children "what happened." It is, rather, helping children, through reasoning, to *figure out* what happened: to reconcile competing primary and secondary accounts of the same event, to make sense of an old artifact, to bridge gaps in the record, to produce a credible and fair-minded account.[9]

TEACHING SUGGESTIONS

Now, what we said at the outset should make more sense: The key to teaching history to children is to head in two directions, not one. Like the two wings of an airplane, these two work together beautifully and neither works alone. Let's work on this distinction: In one direction, children are exposed to historical narratives that others have constructed; in the other, children are helped to construct their own narratives. Put in the simplest way, one is *absorbing*

Lesson Plan 4 PRIMARY AND SECONDARY SOURCES

Grade 5 or 6

Time One class period

Objectives To form an initial concept of what historians call primary and secondary sources and to interpret conflicting primary sources.

Interest Building Send a committee of students on an errand to the school library/multimedia center (e.g., to borrow the "best" dictionary). While they are gone, stage an event to which the students remaining in the classroom will be eyewitnesses. It should surprise students but not upset or disturb them. Two that have been used successfully rely on an unexpected classroom visit: (a) Ask the principal to come into your class unexpectedly, sneak up behind you and say "boo!" Surprised, you spill a cup of water. (b) Ask a colleague to come into your classroom unexpectedly and recite a poem very dramatically while you look on in surprise. Then, the unexpected visitor leaves.

Lesson Development

1. Explain to the class that this was a "pretend" event for the purpose of teaching an important idea about history.

2. *Primary source.* Ask students immediately to write down legibly an eyewitness account of exactly what happened. Tell them not to talk with one another, but to rely only on their memory. They should be sure to record all the details: the time at which the person came into the room, what he or she was wearing, saying, and doing; what the teacher did in response, the expression on his or her face, any words that were spoken, and all physical movements.

3. Congratulate students on having just written what historians call a *primary source.* When the committee returns with the dictionary, ask one of them to open it and read aloud the definition of *primary* (e.g., "first in time or order of development"). Explain that a primary source is one that is written at the time the event occurred by someone who was there.

4. *Secondary source.* Explain that secondary sources are accounts of an event written by a person or persons not present but who use primary sources as the basis for interpreting what happened. The committee that had been out of the room now is welcomed back and given the task of composing a brief written account of what happened. They have nothing to rely on but their classmates' primary accounts. Have each student read aloud his or her primary account and instruct the committee to listen carefully. After each eyewitness has spoken (and inevitably there are differences) the committee confers with one another and writes a secondary source, which is read to the class.

5. *Critique.* Ask the eyewitnesses to judge the quality of the secondary account. This should create some lively deliberation.

Summary Lead a discussion on this question: How and why did our primary sources differ from one another? Then, review the difference between the primary and secondary source.

Assessment

1. Ask students to write down the definition of a primary and a secondary source and to contrast the two. Ask several students to read their definitions aloud. Collect and read later.

2. Ask them to decide whether a diary is a primary or secondary source. (This will be difficult, allowing the teacher to see where the difficulties lie.) Have them hold up one finger for primary, two for secondary, a closed fist if they are not sure. Then listen

carefully to their reasons and any confusions. These will indicate what you need to clarify and whether the distinction needs to be re-taught.

Materials   Cup of water if you choose scenario (a) as described under "Interest Building."

Integration   *Reading and writing:* Following this lesson, concentrate your reading and writing instruction on primary documents. Letters and journals (of Columbus, of Abigail Adams, of Anne Frank, of abolitionists, of soldiers and nurses at battlefields, etc.) are especially interesting to children. Martin Luther King, Jr., wrote his most famous letter from a jail cell in Birmingham, Alabama. Lewis and Clark journal entries appear beginning on page 108. The children can write their own journal entries in response to these, or write a letter back to Abigail Adams, King, Columbus, or whomever's primary sources they read.

■　　■　　■　　■　　■

history, and the other is *doing* history. One is comprehending an historical account; the other is creating an historical account. The first is reading history; the other is writing history. The first is storytelling; the second is appreciating it. In the first, the student is the recipient; in the second, the student is author.

Absorbing: Exposure to Narratives Others Have Constructed

Good historical stories (narratives) abound. They have already been composed by someone else—a professional historian, a grandparent, a children's book author, or ancestors. They may be cherished stories that date back hundreds or thousands of years. Parents in the United States typically are disturbed when they think that the basic, civic stories of the founding and growth of this nation are not known by their children (e.g., the stories of the American Revolution, the Civil War, and the Civil Rights Movement). One "wing" of the history-teaching airplane emphasizes exposing students to such stories.

Exposure here means that students listen to the teacher or others read these historical narratives aloud or tell them from memory. Or students read these accounts themselves, discuss them with classmates, and tell them from memory. Of course, they are assisted in doing this with before- , during- , and after-reading/listening activities, which together aid children's comprehension of the story. Depth of understanding is encouraged as with any good literature instruction. Exposure, then, should not be dismissed as passive or superficial, for considerable intellectual effort is needed to really comprehend and interpret any story. Like music appreciation, story appreciation requires an active listener who is intellectually and emotionally awake.

Doing: Constructing Historical Narratives Themselves

The other "wing" of history teaching helps students actually to do the historical work themselves. On this wing, students are helped to compose (author; construct) historical interpretations using primary sources, artifacts, and secondary sources. Again, lots of assistance is needed. The teacher provides instruction on the inquiry process, teaching students about

hypotheses, evidence, and drawing tentative conclusions. The teacher also helps them to formulate good questions for their inquiries, teaches them about the different kinds of sources, helps them judge the quality of the evidence they find, and teaches them to draft, revise, and publish their interpretations.

The chart in Table 4–2 gives examples from each wing of history learning, and these are fleshed out in the examples that follow.

TABLE 4–2   The two wings of history learning: Absorbing and doing history.

Absorbing History (exposure; knowing about)	**Doing History (construction; composition)**
Listening to someone else read: • a primary document • a secondary source narrative • historical fiction Reading and examining: • a primary source document (e.g., diary, photo, newspaper editorial, speech) • a secondary source document • historical fiction Discussing the possible meanings of: • an artifact (e.g., a cave painting or other artwork) • a primary source document • a secondary source document • historical fiction Communicating the story to others by: • telling • dramatizing • singing • dancing	Using artifacts and primary and secondary sources, students will compose: • an autobiography • a biography • an oral history • an interpretative narrative (a story) of a current event in the school or local community • an interpretative narrative of some events in the recent past (e.g., the Montgomery Bus Boycott), the distant past (e.g., Boston Tea Party), or ancient times (the Trojan Horse) • a dramatic reenactment of an event

ABSORBING HISTORY

Let us examine several ways to help students learn about history. As the following examples show, learning about history is loaded with opportunities to improve students' comprehension skills.

Discussing the Meanings of a Primary Document

March 30, 1806, journal of Meriwether Lewis (*http://www.pbs.org/lewisandclark/archive/idx_jou.html*):

They have also a very singular custom among them of bathing themselves allover with urine every morning.

Can't you just imagine students hooting and hollering at hearing this? Ask them, *who* is bathing? (From this account alone, we don't know. Members of his corps? Members of a tribe he encountered? We have to search backward in the journal for evidence.) Ask them, *why?* Why in the world would anyone bathe with urine? Elicit hypotheses from students, and ask them what sources would help them find out which hypothesis is most likely true.

April 1, 1806, journal of Meriwether Lewis:

I purchased a canoe from an Indian to day for which I gave him six fathoms of wampum beads; he seemed satisfyed with his bargain and departed in another canoe but shortly after returned and canceled the bargain, took his canoe and returned the beads. This is frequently the case in their method of trading and is deemed fair by them.

How admirable that Lewis tries to understand what to him must have been a very annoying behavior. Ask your students if they would consider this "fair" today and why. Ask them to empathize with this custom—to assume it is intelligent—and see if they can imagine why it would be "deemed fair by them."

Listening to Historical Narratives (Fiction or Nonfiction) and Discussing Their Meaning

Young children can be gathered at the rug area to hear the story of "the shot heard 'round the world" at Lexington Green, which began the War for Independence. Older children can read it themselves or, taking turns, to one another aloud. Or there's the story of the Underground Railroad—the network by which enslaved Africans living in southern states were able to move, well-hidden, to the north. There's the story of the women who, against all odds, fought for and won the right to vote long after men had fought for it and won it for themselves. There is the coronation of Cleopatra, the assassination of Lincoln, the murder of Sitting Bull, and Custer's "last stand." There are the extraordinary stories of countless immigrants, both infamous conquistadors and anonymous stowaways, seekers of fortune and seekers of freedom. There are the stories of individuals who have died in wars defending their nations and of the innocent children caught up in them. There is the story of Martin Luther King, Jr., a pastor who rose to the leadership of the Civil Rights Movement, his learning from Gandhi, his relationship with his children, his wife, and Malcolm X. And, there is the story of Rosa Parks.

Mrs. Paley, the kindergarten teacher we met in the prior chapter was reading aloud to her students from Rosa Parks' autobiography about the Montgomery bus boycott. It was inspired by the now-famous incident in which Rosa Parks refused to give up her seat to a white man. The children were riveted. Afterward, they were eager to retell it, dramatize it, and talk about the consequences. Consider this excerpt from a discussion in which her kindergartners are considering the morality of segregating people by race. We can see them trying to distinguish between good and bad reasons for separating people from one another.

Wally: Martin changed all the rules.

Lisa: All the *bad* rules.

Fred: But not the one for the bathroom. The girls still have to separate from the boys.[10]

Role Playing

There may be no activity more powerful for developing historical empathy than to role-play the characters involved in a real historical happening. Display a photo, painting, or other visual representation of a historical event to help children imagine *being there* and read aloud a vivid description of the event from a piece of historical fiction, textbook, magazine, or encyclopedia. Assign children the roles of key persons in the scene. Coach them into the appropriate postures, expressions, and feelings. In this way, children can reenact Paul Revere's ride, the signing of the Declaration of Independence or the U. S. Constitution, or the coronation of Cleopatra. They can march for women's rights, conduct a sit-in at a segregated lunch counter, land on the moon, or surround Custer's troops at the Battle of the Little Big Horn. More ideas can be found in Vivian Paley's work with kindergartners in her book, *Wally's Stories* (Harvard, 1981), and in Douglas Selwyn's *Living History in the Classroom* (Zephyr, 1993).

Choosing Children's Literature

The four themes and eight chronological periods of U.S. history shown in Table 4–1 may take some readers of this book aback. "I don't know this material very well," is likely the first re-action of some readers who themselves may not have taken a course in history since high school. Teachers must know the material they want to teach, and it is well documented that teachers' knowledge of a subject shapes their teaching of it, often dramatically. Nonetheless, it is true that teachers themselves sometimes learn much of the material they will teach as they plan it. The children's social studies textbook and its teacher's guide are major sources of information for teachers. Trade books written for children are another source. Reading aloud Jean Fritz's stirring *China's Long March: 6000 Miles of Danger* during a unit on China will teach children and teacher alike much about China's geography, Mao's struggle against Chiang Kai-Shek, and the horrendous "long march." Reading aloud from Fritz's *Where Was Patrick Henry on the 29th of May?* and then having the children dramatically re-enact Henry's famous speech on liberty will teach children and teacher alike about both the orator and the events of 1775. The following children's trade books, geared to the four themes in Table 4–1, suggest the range of possibilities. Do you know which are fiction and which are not?

Theme 1: American Democracy

Jump Ship to Freedom, James and Christopher Collier (Delacorte, 1981).
Shh! We're Writing the Constitution, Jean Fritz (J. J. Putnam & Sons, 1987).
I Am Rosa Parks, Rosa Parks and James Haskins (Dial, 1997).

Theme 2: Gathering of Peoples

Indian Chiefs, Russell Freedman (Holiday House, 1987).
The Pilgrims of Plimoth, Marcia Sewall (Macmillan, 1986).
Tales from Gold Mountain: Stories of the Chinese in the New World, Paul Yee (Macmillan, 1990).

Theme 3: Economic and Technological Change

The President's Car, Nancy Parker (Crowell, 1981).
African American Inventors, Patricia and Fredrick McKissack (Millbrook, 1994).
Living in a Risky World, Laurence Pringle (Morrow, 1989).

Theme 4: America in the World

Sarah Bishop, Scott O'Dell (Houghton-Mifflin, 1980).
My Daddy Was a Soldier, Deborah Ray (Holiday House, 1990).
The United Nations, Harold and Geraldine Woods (Franklin Watts, 1985).
Sadako, Eleanor Coerr (Putnam, 1994).

Guidelines for selecting literature. Here now are four guidelines for selecting historical narratives (both fiction and nonfiction):

1. Does it tell a good story?
2. Is the story accurate in its historical detail, including the setting and the known events?
3. Is the interpretation sound?
4. Whose voices are missing? No narrative can include every perspective (Remember: no narrative is "complete"). But, because narrative can be a powerful genre, it is important to bring voices that are missing in one story to the forefront in another selection.[11]

Examining Artifacts

Children love to examine historical objects closely and handle them. Arrowheads from a native group, a facsimile of a slave contract or auction announcement, an army recruitment poster, a spinning wheel or spittoon, a manual typewriter or rotary telephone, a quill pen or piece of fool's gold, photos, a piece of traditional clothing, an old family Bible, an old butter churn, rice steamer, or tortilla press—any of these might be related to the instructional unit at hand. If an item is brought from home and is highly valued, it is best for the adult owner to bring it to school to show the children and tell them of its significance.

Local museums often have permanent displays of historical materials significant to the local community, state, and region. Increasingly, they package materials in a "museum treasure chest" that is loaned to the school. A phone call should provide needed information about this service. Also, artifacts can be viewed online. At the Smithsonian Institution's "Spotlight Biography" website (*http://educate.si.edu/spotlight/*), click on "inventors," then on Ben Franklin's printing press where you will see the press Franklin used in 1720.

Making a Time Line

A graphic way to help children "see" chronological time is to help them make time lines. As with understanding any narrative, fiction or nonfiction, the first challenge is to correctly sequence the events. The second challenge is to display graphically the *relative amount of time* between these events. As you read earlier, agriculture was invented 10,000 years ago, replacing a nomadic hunting-and-gathering lifestyle that had gone on for 10 times longer. Very recently (about 1900 A.D.) the Industrial Revolution revolutionized humanity again. How would you show on a time line these three events in the story of humankind in a way that captures the amount of time between them? (We give examples in the next chapter.)

Using Song and Dance

Collect folk and patriotic songs and dances of various eras of history. These will help children absorb the feeling of the era through a different "entry point," as Howard Gardner describes multiple intelligences (see Chapter 2). Present to another class "A Musical Pageant of American History."

Time Traveling

Plan imaginative trips back and forward in time, complete with a "time machine," travel brochures, and props.

This child is involved in the centuries-old process of churning and washing butter. Experiences of this type help children appreciate the ingenuity of human beings who lived in earlier times.

Speechifying

Depending on the event you or the children select for role playing, there may be a terrific speech that can be memorized and reenacted. Patrick Henry's famous speech before the House of Burgesses, for example, is the one that ends "But as for me, give me liberty or give me death!" And there is Sojourner Truth's "And, Ain't I a Woman?", Dr. King's "I Have a Dream," and Chief Joseph's "I Will Fight No More Forever."

DOING HISTORY

Now we turn to the other wing of the airplane where the students themselves learn to compose histories using the resources historians use: primary and secondary sources and artifacts. Teachers who plan to help their students work toward this objective will want to collect work samples along the way. A sample portfolio is shown in Figure 4–2 (and see Chapter 10, "Assessing Student Learning," for details). Following are examples of "doing history."

Composing a Dramatic Reenactment

Returning to our chapter-opening snapshot, recall that the students were not just retelling an episode from the Lewis and Clark journey that would help them absorb this moment in history. Beyond this, they were trying to get it just right, trying to figure out what really happened at that moment when Lewis and Clark met up with Sacajawea. This required students to construct an understanding of that meeting. They had to gather and judge evidence and draw a conclusion. Their conclusion would be "published" as a dramatization before classmates.

Noticing that they were relying on just two sources of information—the journals of Lewis and Clark and a fictionalized trade book narrative—their teacher encouraged them to find a third source. They returned to the website that has the journals and found, in another section, this secondary source description of the "meeting ceremony."

> Over the course of the expedition, Lewis and Clark developed a ritual that they used when meeting a tribe for the first time. The captains would explain to the tribal leaders that their land now belonged to the United States, and that a man far in the east—President Thomas Jefferson—was their new "great father." They would also give the Indians a peace medal with Jefferson on one side and two hands clasping on the other, as well as some form of presents (often trade goods). Moreover, the Corps members would perform a kind of parade, marching in uniform and shooting their guns. (from the PBS website of the Ken Burns film; *http://www.pbs.org/lewisandclark/native/index.html*)

Some will be saddened and angered by this information, believing it wrong for the expedition to claim the land for the United States. "That's stealing," one might say. The teacher can ask, "Well, *is it even true?* Who wrote this description? Go find out before you put it in your drama." Eventually, they revise their script to incorporate this ceremony, judging perhaps that it was enacted at the Sacajawea meeting just as it routinely was enacted elsewhere.

FIGURE 4–2   A "Doing History" portfolio.

Contents of my
"Doing History" Portfolio

_____
                                                                    Name

Type of History	Topic	Date/My Comments
Autobiography	My life	_____/_____
Oral history	A veteran's stories	_____/_____
Oral history	A classmate's move	_____/_____
Biography	President Lincoln	_____/_____
Cooperative Biography	Sojourner Truth	_____/_____

Oral History

Structured interviews or informal conversations with local persons of historical significance can be preserved as oral history by using cassette-tape recorders. Children are fascinated when old-timers talk of their exciting experiences in the early community. They are surprised to hear that the person now speaking to them marched in the Civil Rights Movement, bicycled across a desert or mountain range, fought in Vietnam, or helped change a community rule. This procedure has the added value of involving children, firsthand, in gathering historical data. The taped interviews, therefore, need to be planned, with questions written out and practiced first with classmates. After the data have been gathered, they need to be interpreted: Where does the story really begin? Where does it end? What is the chain of causation? Who influenced whom and how? Why did people act as they did? How did geography (climate, landforms, culture) influence events?

Paint

Paint a mural of some aspect of the history of the local community or state. Deciding what to paint, what to include and exclude, how to know what is true—these are the decisions that involve students in historical reasoning.

Models

Models can be made of many things: communities (the children's town as it looked 50 or 100 years ago, Mesa Verde, Tokyo, Plymouth), shelters (hogans, igloos, teepees, highrises, and longhouses), transportation (oxcarts, prairie schooners, trains, ships, and canoes), and means of long-distance communication (Pony Express, telegraph, radio, television, telephone, and Internet). Whether model building belongs to doing history rather than only absorbing it depends on whether the teacher involves the students in interpreting artifacts and primary and secondary sources. This is the evidence base with which students compose their model and defend it as fair and accurate—something every historian must be prepared to do. "How do you know that's true?" is a question the teacher must ask again and again, until the students themselves begin to ask it.

Snapshot Autobiographies

A meaty yet simple place to begin teaching the youngest students about the tools of historical inquiry is with the autobiography. A snapshot autobiography, as it is called, has students think of just four or five events that happened in the last two or three years. A special birthday, the first day in a new school, a move, a pet. A drawing of each makes the "snapshot." They are strung together, in sequence, with a very brief, written narrative description of each. The narrative description tells what is happening in that drawing. Add a title page and table of contents and the child has a complete autobiography. The children should be taught the vocabulary of chronology and asked to use it in each snapshot description, thereby locating it in time (e.g., "when I was four"; "one-and-one-half years later"; "that same month"; "the following year"). As appropriate for the developmental level of the children, encourage them to think more deeply about their audience, the events they will choose, and the interaction of the two; also, have them search for an artifact related to each event. For example, if a child has featured a move from one home to another as one snapshot in his or her autobiography, a good artifact would be an addressed and delivered envelope showing that mail was forwarded from the old to the new address.

Snapshot Biographies

After building some experience with autobiographies, children can be helped to write snapshot biographies of the historical figures they are studying. These might be biographies of courageous citizens, labor and business leaders, explorers, presidents, framers of the U.S. Constitution, women's suffrage and civil rights activists, heroes, villains, and other persons

My Last Three Years

1. ... My Dog
2. ... Our Move
3. ... The Fire
4. ... Relatives

We got Spotty when he was one month old and I was four. He chewed everything.

One and one-half years later we moved to Northeast 123rd Street. Then I was five and one-half.

That first month, we had a fire in the kitchen! Mom put it out with the red fire extinguisher.

The next year our relatives came for Thanksgiving. There were lots of us.

A snapshot autobiography

of historical significance. Also, these can be biographies of persons in their own lives: an aunt or uncle, a pastor or rabbi, a club leader, a brother or sister. Snapshot biographies focus on just four or five events with an illustration and brief description of each. Again, work with students on the vocabulary of chronology and deepen their understanding of the idea of primary and secondary sources. Chapter 13 explains how teams of children can together compose elaborate biographies.

Constructing a Classroom or Library Museum Exhibit

Children can engage in a major act of historical interpretation when they create a museum exhibit as the culminating project of an historical inquiry. The exhibit can be placed in the classroom or the school multimedia center. A curator from a local museum can come talk with the children about the process of selecting topics, artifacts, and documents for exhibits and discuss how to write the brief description that will be placed alongside each to help visitors understand what they are seeing. A field trip to a museum for this purpose would help, and "virtual field trips" on the Internet (see Chapter 9) to the Smithsonian or the National Archives will provide additional material.

Simulations

Classroom Curators is a published simulation game for grades 4–6 in which students create a classroom museum displaying artifacts from their parents' and grandparents' lives. The simulation game *Pilgrims* (grades 2–4) re-creates the Plymouth Colony in seventeenth-century Massachusetts. *Magellan's Shopping List* (grades 5–8) asks students to decide what supplies Magellan should have taken on his 1522 voyage.[12]

Teaching Geography

Geography's vantage point is not so much historical as it is *spatial*. The word *geography* derives from a Greek word meaning "writing about Earth." When we engage in geographical study, we learn not so much about the past as about the arrangement and interaction of people and places on Earth's surface. Geography brings the physical (e.g., landforms, climate, regions) and the human (culture, migration, interaction) together, and shows how they shape one another. You've heard of global warming? That is humans shaping Earth. You've heard of floods? That is Earth shaping people's lives.

So, welcome to space. Not only astronauts but all of us live in space. Maps help us know where we are in space, so maps are probably the most common kind of graphic representation found in geo*graph*ical study. Maps represent real images (a map of Japan is based on the actual physical image of Japan), which makes them easier for children to "read" than other kinds of graphics, such as bar graphs and pie graphs. Still, map reading is challenging for children because, first, they are only just at the beginning of learning about representations (symbols) and, second, even if they understand that maps represent/symbolize real things, they have not build up an adequate inventory of real forms. They may learn that /\/\/\ symbolizes a mountain range, but they very well may not have formed the concept of mountain range! Elementary and middle school teachers need to work continually, then, to increase students' understandings of the graphics and the real things—the mountains, deserts, climate zones, crops, and regions—to which they refer.

PURPOSES

Individuals need to understand the spatial settings of people and places on Earth for many reasons. The most basic reason is that people everywhere want to make sense of their lives: They want to know the nature of the world and their place in it. Great religions and literature grapple with this uniquely human need. "Humans want to understand the intrinsic nature of their home. Geography enables them to understand where they are, literally and figuratively."[13] There are also very practical reasons for having geographical knowledge and abilities: getting from home to school, for example. Travelers, explorers, military leaders, and entrepreneurs in search of natural resources all would be at a great loss without geographical tools and information. All of us need geographical knowledge to get where we want to go, to know where we have been, to understand the wants and needs of people in different places, and to grasp daily events in relation to their settings—a picnic in July in Phoenix, a flat tire in Minneapolis in February, a subsistence farmer on the horn of Africa, the American rebels' winter at Valley Forge. From a child's point of view, these practical needs for geographical knowledge spring to life when his or her parents decide to move their home from one place to another.[14]

THE GEOGRAPHY CURRICULUM: THE THEMATIC APPROACH

Is there any way a teacher can grasp the Earth-sized body of knowledge and skill called geography, at least well enough to do a good job of teaching it? There is. A set of curriculum guidelines was developed jointly by the National Council for Geographic Education and the

People everywhere strive to know the world.

Association of American Geographers. This group identified five *themes,* and they have since provided teachers and curriculum materials publishers with a meaningful framework for grasping this sprawling field and enriching geography learning for children beyond memory work alone. The five themes of geography are described briefly in the following list. Our students developed an acronym to help them remember all five: MR. HELP.

1. *Movement: Humans Interacting on Earth.* Human beings occupy places unevenly across the face of Earth. Some live on farms or in the country; others live in towns, villages, or cities. Yet these people interact with each other; that is, they travel from one place to another, they communicate with each other, or they rely on products, information, and ideas that come from beyond their immediate environment.

    The most visible evidences of global interdependence and the interaction of places are the transportation and communication lines that link every part of the world. These demonstrate that most people interact with other places almost every day of their lives. This may involve nothing more than a Georgian eating apples grown in the state of Washington and shipped to Atlanta by rail or truck. On a larger scale, international trade demonstrates that no country is self-sufficient.

2. *Regions: How They Form and Change.* The basic unit of geographic study is the region, an area that displays unity in terms of selected criteria. There are many kinds of regions. Some are defined by one characteristic such as a language group (e.g., the Cantonese-speaking region of China) or, more typically, a landform type (e.g., the Midwest or the Pacific Northwest). It is typical in the fourth grade for the social studies curriculum to concentrate on regions of the United States and, in the sixth or seventh, on world regions.

3. *Human-Environment Interaction.* All places on Earth have advantages and disadvantages for human settlement. High population densities have developed on flood plains, for example, where people could take advantage of fertile soils, water resources, and opportunities for river transportation. By comparison, population densities are usually low in deserts. Yet flood plains are periodically subjected to severe damage, and some desert areas, such as Israel, have been modified to support large population concentrations.

4. *Location: Position on Earth's Surface.* Absolute and relative location are two ways of describing the positions of people and places on Earth's surface. One of the great dramas in Europe's age of exploration was keeping sailors from being lost at sea as soon as they lost sight of land. "Launched on a mix of bravery and greed, the sea captains of the fifteenth, sixteenth, and seventeenth centuries relied on dead reckoning to gauge their distance east or west of home port. . . . Long voyages waxed longer for lack of longitude and the extra time at sea condemned sailors to the dread disease of scurvy."[15] So writes the author of *Longitude,* Dava Sobel, telling the story of John Harrison who developed the device that helps sailors locate their ships at sea. As you will see in the next chapter, there is much that children need to learn about location, both relative (Taiwan is off the coast of China) and absolute (Taiwan is at 120 degrees longitude and the Tropic of Cancer).

5. *Place: Physical and Human Characteristics.* All places on Earth have distinctive tangible and intangible characteristics that give them meaning and character and distinguish them from other places. Geographers generally describe places by their physical or human characteristics. Your classroom, for example, is a place with both physical and human characteristics. In Chapter 2, we emphasized the latter—the demographic makeup of the classroom. The physical characteristics all can be represented on maps.

Each theme is a concept that students should form as they work with multiple examples. Progress toward this goal can be made in every grade level of the elementary and middle school. As they study classmates' immigration from points around the world, Lewis and Clark's movement westward followed by the development of wagon trains and locomotives, the Native American movement eastward into America thousands of years before, the construction of interstate highways, and Mexican migration northward today, students are gathering the building blocks for understanding movement.

TEACHING SUGGESTIONS

The next chapter has many teaching suggestions for geography, so we will discuss only a few in the following sections.

Moving

Every year, tens of millions of Americans load their possessions into cars and trucks and move to new neighborhoods, near and far. A class can help orient a newly arrived classmate to the geography of the school grounds and community by creating maps, conducting guided tours, and preparing a "Welcome" brochure. Questions and answers in the brochure can be geared to the five themes of geography:

Movement. How did early settlers get to this place? How many newcomers arrive each year, and by what means of transportation? How many leave? Is there an interstate highway near?

Region. What regions is our town a part of and what are the regions *in* our town? What things do nearby towns have in common? What kinds of jobs do people in this region have? What is the highest and lowest average temperature in this region?

Human-Environment Interaction. What natural resources can be found here? How have people here changed the environment? Do we recycle anything? Where does our food and drinking water come from?

Location. Where is our school in our community? Why is it located there? Where is it relative to the park and city hall?

Place. What is it like here? What are this community's most notable natural and human-made features? What do kids do here for fun? What languages are spoken here? If you want to draw this place, what color crayons should you bring?[16]

Land and Water in the Neighborhood

Have children observe firsthand in the school neighborhood various water and land forms—lakes, creeks, islands, hills, gullies, slopes. Younger children can draw these; older children can draw them to scale and locate them on maps they create themselves. It is especially helpful if children can safely see firsthand the joining of a creek with a stream, or stream to river, or the confluence of two rivers. Where are the headwaters located? Where do they end up?

Schoolyard Geography

Divide the class into five teams and the school grounds into five spaces. Each team adopts a space for geographic exploration using MR. HELP.

Water Purification

Have children study simple methods of water purification in the classroom before taking them on a field trip to a water purification plant. Much of a town's water may come from a nearby reservoir, which can be toured.

Aerial Views

Take children to a high point (office tower; hilltop) where they can get an aerial perspective of streets and land and water forms. While there, help them sketch maps of the view, complete with legend and cardinal directions and drawn to scale. Before going, they should practice making maps of the classroom and playground.

FIGURE 4–3 Steps for drawing a world map.

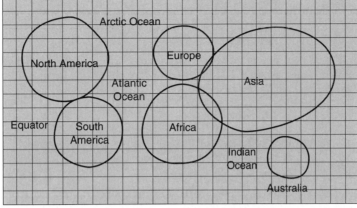

Six quickly sketched circles, roughly in the right places and in roughly proportionate sizes, make a working map of the continents. Asia is the biggest, Australia the smallest.

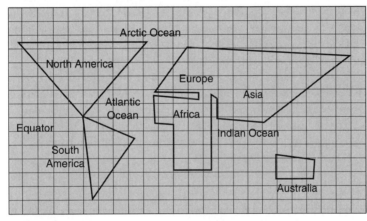

Turn the continents into squares, rectangles, and triangles. Remember that the Africa bulge is over the Equator, the Tropic of Cancer underpins Asia, and the Tropic of Capricorn cuts Australia in half.

Source: Geography for Life: National Geography Standards (Washington, DC: National Geographic and Exploration, 1994) 65. Reprinted by permission.

Drawing the World Map in 30 Seconds

Helping children get to the point where they can draw a world map from memory is, for them and their parents, a notable achievement. The task is not as difficult as it might seem, but the children must be provided ample opportunity to study world maps and to practice drawing their own. One helpful technique is to begin with circles (Figure 4–3).

Orienteering in the Library and Elsewhere at School

Have children start this activity by mapping the classroom. Then have teams of children make maps of the school's library or media center. They will learn where the card catalogue, the biography section, and the CD-ROM collections are located while symbolizing them on the map and in the map key. Polar directions should be included, and the maps should be drawn to scale. Then have students map the cafeteria, the playground, the school grounds. (Note: See the lesson plan in Chapter 9 on orienteering in the library.)

Excavations

A primary grade class can visit a nearby basement excavation for a new home. The children observe the various layers of soil, and the teacher calls their attention to the many roots found in the fertile topsoil. The class is able to obtain samples of the various strata of soil to take back to their classroom for an experiment in seeing how well plants grow in the various layers—an early beginning in the appreciation of soil conservation. The presence of earth-moving equipment suggests that human beings do things to modify the environment.

Weather and Climate

Weather and climate present another area of exploration. Children will have viewed weather forecasts on television, and it will have affected them in many ways that they will have noticed and cared about. In primary-grade classrooms, children will want to chart various weather data they observe each day. The teacher reads the daily temperature, or the children report the official daily temperature that they have heard over an early morning radio broadcast. These temperatures can be shown graphically, thereby applying knowledge of numbers and graphs. Over a period of several weeks or months the graph will show the changes occurring in temperatures and seasons of the year. Children can also record data dealing with wind velocities, cloud formations, precipitation, and similar subjects. They can even make their own predictions based on the data they have collected. Sensitivity to weather changes will again call attention to the changes in native plant and animal life as well as to the adaptations people make to changing seasons. Here the teacher can apply another technique of the geographer: recording data and using simple charts.

Simulations

Caravans (grades 4–6) has students form caravans that compete to gather museum artifacts from around the world. *Flight* (grades 5–8) has students race in airplanes across the United States in teams, taking weather into account and keeping journals. *Southwest* (grades 4–8) explores the lands and peoples of what is now the southwestern United States, culminating with a fiesta.[17] The wildly popular computer simulation *Where in the World Is Carmen Sandiego?* helps students develop geographical knowledge and skills. Students role-play detectives tracking down a notorious international criminal.

Children's Literature

The five themes of geography have been widely used as reference points for selecting children's trade books. The following sample suggests some possibilities.[18]

Movement

> *The Seekers,* Eilis Dillon (Charles Scribner's Sons, 1986).
> *Hector Lives in the United States Now: The Story of a Mexican-American Child* (HarperCollins, 1990).

Region

One Day in the Tropical Rain Forest, Jean Craighead George (HarperCollins, 1990).

Mojave, Diane Siebert (Crowell, 1988).

Human-Environment Interaction

Window, Jeannie Baker (William Morrow, 1991).

Roxaboxen, Alice McLerran (Lothrop, Lee & Shepard, 1991).

Location

My Place in Space, Robin and Sally Hirst (Orchard, 1990).

The Third-Story Cat, Leslie Baker (Little, Brown, 1987).

Place

Seeing Earth from Space, Patricia Lauber (Orchard, 1990).

Sarah, Plain and Tall, Patricia MacLachlan (Harper & Row, 1985).

Teaching Political Science (Citizenship Education)

Political science is a field of study that is concerned with questions dear to children's hearts. Can we all get along? How shall we deal with the conflicts and problems of living and working together? Does might make right? Do we need rules? Should rules be binding on everyone, even the leader or boss? What is the fairest way to make and enforce rules? To choose leaders?

When students are building knowledge about peoples and places on Earth (geography) and about the past (history), it is important that they ask these *political* questions, too. In this way, they construct a fuller understanding of a society—they gather more pieces of the puzzle. And the political piece is crucial: Without it, they are ignorant of the political system holding that society together. Is there a tyrant who won power by force and uses the police and military to keep everyone in line, jailing or executing those who disagree? Are the people afraid to speak out? Can they practice only the leader's religion? Are they prevented from joining clubs because the leader fears that opposition to his power will grow in them? There are plenty of tyrants in the world today. Ask your students, is this right? *Does might make right?* If not, *why not?* Should the government rule the people or should the people rule the government?

Mrs. Paley, recall, discusses these topics with her kindergartners. She begins by proposing (not posting) a rule for their consideration: "Should we have a rule that goes, You Can't Say 'You Can't Play'?" The students discuss this over several months; consequently, we have 5-year-olds doing the work of legislators: deliberating public policy. When her kindergartners get to the third grade where they study a set of communities on Earth, they are ready to begin looking at the political systems of these communities by asking questions:

- Who is the leader? How did he or she become the leader?
- Does the government rule the people or do the people rule the government? Do the people vote? How often?

- Do they have a *democracy* or a *dictatorship?*
- What are the rights and responsibilities of citizens in this place?
- What are the public values expressed on their coins, in their anthems, in their pledges of allegiance?
- Is there discrimination toward cultural and racial minorities? Are minorities treated fairly? Are women treated equally to men?
- Is there freedom of religion?
- Are the laws written down? Is there a constitution?
- Is government power divided up? (e.g., judicial, legislative, executive, local, national)

TEACHING SUGGESTIONS

Chapter 3 was devoted entirely to teaching suggestions related to political science. Let us briefly review the six dimensions of citizenship education presented there.

Six Dimensions of Citizenship Education

Deliberation. Give students opportunities to engage in sustained decision-making discussions about classroom life and problems. The decision is one that will be binding on all—a rule or law. Accordingly, keep prodding them, as did Mrs. Paley, with two questions: Is the decision fair (just)? Will it work?

Voting and Elections. Teach about elections and engage students in elections— real ones and mock ones.

Community Service. Community studies are a great way to integrate the teaching of history and the social sciences with the natural sciences. Communities are inevitably filled with problems. As your students come across them, help them think of ways to take action and do good for those in need.

Knowledge. To think well about community problems, students need to think *with* a knowledgeable mind. Look back to Chapter 3 at the glossary for citizenship (Figure 3-8). It contains key pieces of the knowledge citizens need (e.g., civil rights, constitution, democracy, rule of law).

Values. Revisit the distinction in Chapter 3 between personal values and public values. Public values, such as tolerance, are the glue that holds a diverse society together and forms the basis of community life. See the lesson plan on symbolic values involving coins in Chapter 3.

Dispositions and Virtues. James Madison observed that when virtues were missing from a population, then no amount of law or government or police would protect them from one another. Citizens without virtues are "idiots" in the Greek sense noted in the previous chapter. What are the key democratic virtues? We concentrated on six in Chapter 3: civil, courageous, lawful, fair (just), responsible, and honest.

Teaching Economics

Economics is the study of the production, distribution, exchange, and consumption of goods and services that people need or want under conditions of scarcity. You may want to read that sentence again, for it contains several key concepts of this field. In a modern industrialized society such as ours, needs and wants are many because individuals expect a high standard of living. Supplying these involves production, distribution, exchange, and consumption—all involving a web of relationships. When you flip the classroom lights on and off, ask students to think of all the people and resources that make possible this sudden illumination, then darkness, then illumination again. "We are consuming it, but who is producing and distributing it? How much money do they make? What kind of job is it?" These are good questions for a unit, "Who Produces What We Consume in Our Classroom?"

Basic economic concepts such as these are the central subject matter of economics. The group that has been working most diligently on what teachers can do to help students learn them is the National Council on Economic Education (NCEE). This group recently identified 20 content standards for economics teaching and learning and related benchmarks. Unlike the standards documents produced in history, geography, and civics/political science, the economics benchmarks are tied to specific lessons and curriculum materials. This is a useful resource! These instructional packages are all available from NCEE and on the CD-ROM *Virtual Economics*.[19] This ambitious resource has two main sections for teachers: a multimedia center with all sorts of economic education material and a library loaded with material linked to the 20 NCEE content standards. Also visit the website authored by the Omaha Center for Economic Education at *www.ecedweb.unomaha.edu.*

One key generalization that elementary and middle school children need to develop corresponds to the first of NCEE's standards. Its central concepts are scarcity, choice, and sacrifice:

> Productive resources are limited. Therefore, people cannot have all of the goods and services they want; as a result, they must choose some things and give up others. (*www.economicsamerica.org/standards/contents*)

Students who understand this should be able to do some very important things that are the foundation of economic theory: Identify when choices are needed and what they gain and what they give up when they make choices. Here are several fourth-grade benchmarks that specify this knowledge.

- People make choices because they cannot have everything they want.
- Economic wants are desires that can be satisfied by consuming a good, service, or leisure activity.
- Goods are objects that can satisfy people's wants.
- Services are actions that can satisfy people's wants.
- People's choices about what goods and services to buy and consume determine how resources will be used.
- Whenever a choice is made, something is given up.

- The "opportunity cost" of a choice is the value of the best alternative given up.
- Natural resources, such as land, are gifts of nature; they are present without human intervention.
- Human resources are the quantity and quality of human effort directed toward producing goods and services.

Once children begin to grasp these ideas, then they can make sense of additional ideas that incorporate them:

- Markets exist when buyers and sellers of goods and services interact.
- Governments provide certain kinds of goods and services in a market economy.
- The interdependence of peoples of the world and the division of labor among them makes exchange and trade a necessity in the modern world.
- Economic systems are usually mixed with both public and private ownership and with decisions made both by the government and by individual members of society.
- Unemployment imposes costs on individuals and nations.

TEACHING SUGGESTIONS

Are such ideas beyond the reach of elementary school children? Definitely not. "Many studies have been conducted over the years that provide evidence that children can learn economics when it is taught."[20] *The elementary and middle school program of economics instruction should concentrate on basic economic ideas such as those listed above, and situate them in broader units and in learning-by-doing experiences.* These ideas are easily integrated within broader unit topics such as "Life in Canada and Mexico," "Britain's American Colonies," or "Great Cities of the World." There will also be times when particular topics are selected because they have special usefulness in developing specific economic concepts. Units on the grocery store, airport, or the shopping mall in the primary grades are of this type and ordinarily focus on the distribution of goods and services.

Learning activities such as the following can be used to develop economic concepts:

1. *Examine ways that people depend on each other* in their families, neighborhoods, and communities. Relate this to the need for many different kinds of jobs and division of labor (see Lesson Plan 5).
2. *Compare work roles* of today with those in colonial times to discover differences between cottage-industry procedures and assembly-line production.
3. *Familiarize children with local goods and services production* through field trips and guest speakers.
4. *Use children's literature.* Just as there are children's trade books geared to history, geography, and citizenship education, so are there books geared to basic economic ideas. Delightful books for primary grade children are *If You Give a Mouse a Cookie* (Laura Joffe Numeroff, 1985), *Count Your Money with the Polk Street School* (Patricia Reilly Giff, 1994), *Bunny Money* (Rosemary Wells, 1997), and our favorite: *Uncle Jed's Barbershop* (Margaret King Mitchell, 1993).

5. *Learn by doing.* Whenever possible, economic ideas should be introduced with real-life experiences that actually engage students in economic decision making and require them to live with the consequences of their decisions. George Richmond and Marilyn Kourilsky have done brilliant work with real-life economic learning in classrooms in their books *The Micro-Society: A Real World in Miniature (1973)* and *Mini-Society: Experiencing Real-World Economics in the Elementary School Classroom* (1983), respectively. Researchers who have studied these programs[21] recommend that first-grade (and up) teachers set up a "real" classroom marketplace. This requires three things.

   a. *Money.* First, inject money into the classroom by paying play money daily to children for all the normal classroom chores and learning tasks (e.g., $1 for each book read, $2 for cleaning up, $1 for attending school).

   b. *Goods.* Second, inject goods into the classroom by opening a "factory warehouse" operated by the teacher. Students "buy" paper, pencils, crayons, toys, and other supplies from the warehouse.

   c. *Markets.* Third, inject market life into the classroom for 20 minutes each day. The children engage in dramatic play, in which they buy and sell the goods they have purchased from the warehouse as well as other goods and services they may produce. This will require them to set up "stores," "employees," "partners," and the like.

   Beyond setting up a marketplace, a whole *society* can be established with a municipal court, bank, and a city government (complete with a mayoral election). We are enthused about the microsociety program and hope readers will consider delving into it. The two books by Richmond and Kouridsky and the resources listed in the notes at the end of the chapter are highly recommended.

   Debriefing is crucial, for without it learning and retention are sacrificed. A debriefing *strategy* is needed. The one given in Figure 4–4 should work very well with most classroom simulations.

6. *Use prepared simulation games designed to teach economic concepts* (see Chapter 7 for an example concerning assembly-line production). Others include *Candy Market* (grades 3–5), in which the class holds a candy auction, and learns about supply, demand, and money; *Mini-Economy* (grades 3–6), in which students manage businesses, apply for jobs, and earn play money to spend at the classroom store; and *Kids' Town* (grade 3), in which students create a classroom economy using a salary schedule created by the class; jobs include tutors, carpenters, librarians, toy-makers, and farmers.[22]

THE WORLD OF WORK

The world of work is a subset of economic education, and elementary and middle schools have for many years included it in their social studies programs. In teaching about the work world, a systematic, integrated approach is probably more effective than special units spaced throughout the grades. Most who have been involved in curriculum work in this field suggest that *awareness building* should be a major goal of a program relating to the world of work in the elementary school. Children should *not* be encouraged to make occupational

FIGURE 4–4 Debriefing marketplace activities.

1. Have students describe in their own words *and role-play* a teacher-selected economic event from their market experience that day. (The teacher should choose an event that highlights the economic idea he or she is wanting students to learn, e.g., scarcity, opportunity cost.)
2. Ask students, "What is the problem here?" Help them identify and frame the problem in the selected event. For example, there are fewer units of a toy than the students want.
3. Teach the students new information about this problem and the related economic ideas. For example, teach the idea of *scarcity* and the necessity of choice making.
4. Help students use this new information as they think through the problem and plan for the next market day. For example, "Will toys still be scarce tomorrow? How should the few toys that are available be distributed?"

Sources: James D. Laney & Mark C. Schug, "Teach Kids Economics and They Will Learn," *Social Studies and the Young Learner 11* (November/December 1998): 13–17; and Marilyn Kourilsky, *Mini-Society: Experiencing Real-World Economics in the Elementary School Classroom* (Addison-Wesley, 1983).

choices when they are in elementary school. But they can begin to build a background of knowledge about a broad spectrum of occupations that will one day help them make an intelligent career choice. The major components of such a program follow.

Opportunity to Explore Work Values

Children need to see the connection between values that are stressed in school—such as responsibility, dependability, honesty, cooperation, and trustworthiness—and the world of work. They need to develop a sense of appreciation for a job that is well done. They need to learn what it means to take pride in one's work. It may be difficult for children who dislike doing "chores" to realize, but hard work done well seems to be an important source of contentment for humans.

Workplace Cooperation

Part of awareness building for the world of work is learning to work cooperatively and productively with persons with whom one may not have chosen to work. This reflects the reality of most job settings. For this reason, an important attribute of the instructional method called cooperative learning (Chapter 11) is *teacher-assigned work groups.* In this way, children gain experience at working well and solving interpersonal problems with classmates who are not necessarily their friends.

Workplace Competencies

Assign children to small groups and ask each group to brainstorm a list of skills and dispositions that, if developed by the children, would help them get and keep the kind of work they want. Second, have the groups share their lists on butcher paper with the whole class.

FIGURE 4–5   Workplace competencies.

Resources	Know how to allocate time, money, materials, space, and staff.
Interpersonal Skills	Know how to work on teams, teach others, serve customers, lead, negotiate, and work well with people from culturally diverse backgrounds.
Information	Know how to acquire and evaluate data, organize and maintain files, interpret and communicate, use computers to process information.
Systems	Know how to understand social, organizational, and technological systems; monitor and correct performance; design and improve systems.
Technology	Know how to select equipment and tools, apply technology to specific tasks, and maintain and troubleshoot equipment.

Source: The Secretary's Commission on Achieving Necessary Skills (SCANS), *What Work Requires of Schools: A SCANS Report for America 2000* (Washington, DC: U.S. Department of Labor, 1991).

Third, share with the class two economic trends: the internationalization of production, distribution, and consumption, and the changing technological skills required on the job. Give examples to help the children understand the trends. Fourth, ask the groups to revise their lists as needed, based on these trends. Fifth, share with the class the list of workplace skills and dispositions shown in Figure 4–5. Developed under the direction of U.S. Labor Secretary Lynne Martin and published in a report nicknamed the SCANS report,[23] this list contains powerful categories and thoughtful workplace competencies.

ACTIVITIES FOR STUDYING THE WORLD OF WORK

- *Inquiry.* Brainstorm a list of reasons people might have selected particular occupations. This list should include such things as "It provides me with a chance to be my own boss" or "I earn a good salary." Use the list as the basis for a survey the children distribute to working adults in your community. Have the adults choose three reasons from the list and rank them from most important to least important. Then help students organize and analyze these data and prepare reports for the classroom newsletter.

- *More Inquiry.* Conduct interviews to find out how adults in the community earn money. Have the children compile a list of categories for their questionnaire such as these:
    People Who Produce Things
    People Who Fix Things
    People Who Study Things (social scientists; naturalists)
    People Who Govern (members of any branch of government)

Lesson Plan 5 DIVISION OF LABOR

Grade 2 or 3

Time Two class periods

Objectives Children will form an initial concept of what economists call division of labor and build their awareness of jobs in the community.

Interest Building Read aloud from *Apple Picking Time* by Michele Benoit Slawson (1994), in which Anna helps her family with the apple harvest. Point out that Anna expects to be paid for her work at the end of the day (i.e., the concept *employment*) and that hers is only one of the jobs involved in getting apples from the orchard to our lunchboxes.

Have children discuss jobs they know about in their family or neighborhood by responding to these questions:

Do *you* have a job at home? What do you do? What is the difference between your job and the jobs of grownups?

Explain that during the next few days they are going to learn about different kinds of jobs in the community.

Lesson Development Have the children make a chart with the following headings:

Name of Job	Reasons for the Job
1. _____	_____
_____	_____
2. _____	_____
_____	_____
3. _____	_____
_____	_____

Instruct the children to take the chart home with them and complete it with the help of a parent, naming three different jobs in the community.

On the following day have the children compare and discuss their lists with each other.

Compile a list of as many different jobs as possible on the chalkboard. Children should pick one from their individual lists until everyone has had a turn to name one. Keep going as long as different jobs are named.

Have children discuss the need for a variety of jobs by responding to these questions:

1. Why do we have so many different jobs in our community?
2. Why couldn't each family do all these jobs itself?
3. Why do you suppose people in a community divide the work the way they do?
4. Do you mean that people who have these jobs have special skills? What do you mean?
5. Do you think people can do their jobs better when each person has a special job?

Tell the children that when people divide work so that each one does something special, we call that *division of labor*. Write this term on the chalkboard. Have students discuss this term using these questions:

1. Does anyone know another word for *labor*? (Children suggest *work* as a synonym for labor. This is discussed and examples are provided.)

2. Can anyone tell us in his or her own words what division of labor means? (Children respond that "division of labor means dividing the work.") This is discussed and examples are elicited.

Assessment and Summary

Have children tell in their own words how they see the division of labor in these places:

in their school	at the shopping center
in their families	in a hospital
in the supermarket	at the airport
at the post office	anywhere else they may have visited

Materials

One copy of *Apple Picking Time* (1994).

Follow–Up

Arrange a field trip to see division of labor at a supermarket.

Integration

Drawing: Have students make an accordion book on a division of labor they decide to study. Each illustration of the book should show, in correct sequence, a different job (e.g., picking grapes, processing grapes, wholesaling grapes, retailing grapes).

Literature: Ali Mitgutsch's *From Grain to Bread* (Carolhoda, 1983) shows the division of labor in bread making.

■   ■   ■   ■   ■

Help students organize and analyze these data and prepare reports for the classroom newsletter.

- *Awareness.* Here is a good assessment activity from which the teacher can find out students' conceptions of occupations and the world of work. Have them brainstorm a list of 25 to 50 jobs and occupations. In groups, have the children organize the data into only four categories, using any system they wish to devise. Have each group explain its system.

- *More Awareness.* After completing the previous activity, use the categories students devised to analyze the "classified" sections of local newspapers. What types of work are most available? Help them revise their categories as needed.

- *Still More.* To sensitize children to sex-role stereotyping, have them generate lists of occupations that are associated with males, those associated with females, and those that are neutral. Discuss these in terms of equality of job opportunity and whether or not a person's gender has anything to do with performance of the jobs listed in the male and female categories. Then have students analyze television commercials and newspaper and magazine advertisements to detect evidence of sex-role and racial stereotyping in certain occupations.

- *Division of Labor.* This is a concept best formed through actually doing it. Teachers often create a division of labor simulation in the classroom such as the assembly-line simulation presented in Chapter 7. Lesson Plan 5 illustrates how a primary grade teacher helped the class develop the concept *division of labor.*

Teaching Anthropology

Anthropology, with its several divisions, is often thought of as a unifying social science because it is by definition the study of human beings in their totality: their culture and environment. In the elementary grades, anthropology is often folded into geography. Geography, as we have seen, is concerned not just with the environment (climate, land and water forms) but with human-environment interaction. Anthropology is unique, however, in its steadfast concentration on the idea of *culture.* Culture is a uniquely human creation and, in addition to human physiology, it is the primary distinguishing attribute between humans and other animals. Ants live in groups, like humans and have complex social organizations, but they don't have culture. This means they don't *learn.* They don't need to learn because all the information they require for living is contained in their physical makeup.

Unique to anthropology, too, is its method of inquiry. Called *ethnography,* the method requires anthropologists to live within a culture other than their own and there to do *fieldwork:* observe, observe, and observe some more; write detailed notes on these observations; observe some more; write more notes. "The ethnographer," writes renowned anthropologist Clifford Geertz, "inscribes social discourse; he writes it down."[24] The emphasis, obviously, is on descriptive detail. Geertz, calls this "thick description." Ethnographies try to capture the stream of social happenings completely, both what was said and how, and what wasn't said and how. Ethnographies, therefore, often make for wonderful reading. If you haven't done so yet, look into Margaret Meade's *Coming of Age in Samoa* (1928), Ruth Benedict's *Patterns of Culture* (1934), or Shirley Brice Heath's *Ways with Words: Language, Life and Work in Communities and Classrooms* (1983).

Anthropological studies are often comparative. Cross-cultural studies show the wide range of capabilities of human beings: the modern surgeon and the tribal Shaman; preliterate and literate lifestyles; affluence and poverty; humanitarian behavior and cruelty and war; urban living and rural life; life in extremely cold areas and life in hot, desert regions. People are, therefore, highly adaptive in their behavior, capable of remarkable achievements, both rational and irrational. They can, within limits, control and shape their environment and build a culture. They rely on their ability to think, stand, manipulate objects with their hands, imagine, and innovate to solve problems of living. These characteristics result in great diversity among the people of the world in how they live, what they believe, and how they conduct their affairs. Nonetheless, people are all part of the human family; all are a part of humankind, and all have many common physical and social needs.

The following are sample generalizations from anthropology that have been used as organizing ideas in developing social studies units:

1. Every society has formed its own system of beliefs, knowledge, values, traditions, and skills that can be called its culture.
2. Culture is socially learned and serves as a potential guide for human behavior in any given society.
3. Although people everywhere are confronted with similar psychological and physiological needs, the ways in which they meet these needs differ according to their culture.
4. The art, music, architecture, food, clothing, sports, and customs of a people help to produce a national identity.

TEACHING SUGGESTIONS

The central concept of anthropology, *culture*, is so complex and comprehensive that it cuts across all of the social science disciplines and takes years to master. Thus, social studies units in every grade often contain a substantial amount of information that could be defined as anthropological even though it may not be made explicit in the curriculum.

Activities such as the following have been used by elementary and middle school teachers in studies having an anthropological emphasis. The essence of each activity is *observation*—to observe those things that we may no longer even notice because they have become familiar and mundane.

1. *Children's Literature.* As you will learn in Chapter 8 in the "concept formation" section, concepts are formed by noting similarities across examples of the concept. *Culture* is no different. Children need to absorb multiple examples of this complex idea before they can begin to construct the idea itself. Many children's trade books are available on specific cultures. After the children have at least three distinct cultures in mind, ask them how they are alike and different. List these on butcher paper and post it on the wall. Keep adding to it after additional cultures are studied. Sample books include *And It Is Still That Way* (about Hopi village life today, by Byrd Baylor, 1976), *The Egyptians* (Pamela Odijk, 1989), *The Flame of Peace: A Tale of the Aztecs* (Deborah Nourse Lattimore, 1987).

2. *Make the Familiar Seem Strange.* Ask students to observe something familiar—the lunchroom, the playground, or artifacts such as a postage stamp or coin. Ask them to see it as though for the first time so that it actually seems strange rather than familiar. This takes lots of practice. It may help if they pretend they are from outer space or from the distant past or future. The key question then is, What do you see? What is happening here? Like anthropologists, they should take field notes. (See Lesson Plan 3 in Chapter 3, in which students examine a coin, such as a penny, and attempt to infer what is valued in the society that made this coin.)

3. *Fieldwork.* Divide the class into five fieldwork teams. On each day of the week, a different team takes field notes on what its members see in the cafeteria. On Friday afternoon, field notes are compiled and a "thick" description called "Life in Our Cafeteria" is attempted. Following this, read aloud a thick description from an actual ethnography. (Or read one or two of the Lewis and Clark journal excerpts from earlier in this chapter and ask students to judge whether it is adequately detailed to count as a "thick description.")

4. *Tools.* Trace the development and use of certain everyday human tools: pencil, backpack, lawn mower, hammer, computer, television. Again, make the familiar seem strange.

5. *New Tools.* Study ways that inventions have changed civilizations (e.g., clocks, cell phones, television, backpacks).

6. *Charts.* Prepare data-retrieval charts to compare the use of resources, tools, technology, or other variables by different groups.

7. *Music.* Have students listen to music that is culturally different from what most of them are accustomed to. Japanese and Chinese melodies, for example, can seem strange from the perspectives of Europeans, South Americans, or Africans.

8. *Art.* Show slides of artwork that is culturally different from what most students are accustomed to. Art museums, particularly on college campuses, usually have slides to lend.

9. *Dig.* In the upper grades, participate in a simulated archaeological dig. A committee of students can "bury" on the school grounds artifacts that they believe represent life in your town today (current coins, stamps, bottles, fork, chopsticks, etc.—remind them that theirs is a culturally diverse town). The rest of the class then simulates an archeological dig. They excavate the artifacts and must make sense of what they find by trying to get inside the minds of the people who used them.

10. *Other Simulations. Nacirema* (grades 5–6) asks students to examine a supposedly alien culture that is really American (*Nacirema* spelled backwards) and compare it to the culture of the Bushmen of the Kalahari Desert. *Dig 2* (grades 4–8) is a simulation of an archeological dig but with a nice twist. Competing teams create a culture and bury representative artifacts on the school grounds for *each other.* Each team then excavates and analyzes the other team's artifacts, using them to reconstruct its culture.[25]

Teaching Sociology

Someone once quipped that economics is about how people have to make choices, and sociology is about how they don't really have any choices to make. Sociology is a broad social science that is especially concerned with social organization—the way people organize themselves into groups, subgroups, social classes, and institutions. According to sociologists, humans are *completely* situated in these organizations. Even one's supposedly "private" thoughts and fantasies utilize language and concepts derived from these organizations; therefore, sociologists say that we are to a great extent determined by them. Organizations shape even "deviants" or so-called nonconformists, for both are defined by the norms of these organizations. One cannot even be a deviant, then, without reference to these norms.

The following are major generalizations from sociology that have been used as organizing ideas to develop social studies units with a sociological emphasis:

- The social environments in which a person is reared and lives have a profound effect on the personal growth and development of that individual.
- Racism and sexism, like language and body image, are learned from these social environments. This learning process is called *socialization.*
- The family is the basic social environment in most cultures and the source of some of the most fundamental socialization.
- Social classes exist in every society although the bases of class distinction and the degree of rigidity of the class structure vary widely. Social class membership, like the family, shapes much of an individual's behaviors, values, and beliefs.
- Every society develops a system of roles, norms, values, and sanctions to guide and control the behavior of individuals and groups within the society. Deviancy is identified and dealt with in reference to this system.

TEACHING SUGGESTIONS

Just as anthropology is steadfast in its concentration on the concept *culture,* sociology is steadfast on the concept *groups.* The first three grades of school typically focus on three groups: family, neighborhood, and community.

In actual practice, the study of these groups is integrated with geography, history, and political science (civics). And a comparative approach is strongly recommended. Comparison, after all, is the gateway to higher-order thinking. And comparison allows students to grasp the tremendous variety of—differences among—families, neighborhoods, and communities around the world. The two basic teaching suggestions regarding sociology, then, are to integrate it with the other social sciences and organize learning activities that require comparison.

Take the first-grade topic "The Family." Children learn about the variety of this basic group in our society and elsewhere on Earth, some of its functions, and the roles of various members. A data-retrieval chart (like the one in Figure 4–6) posted on the bulletin board can support students' comparisons.

Of course, controversy swirls around the definition of family and the roles of family members. Is an unmarried couple a family? What about a married couple without children? Are gay and lesbian couples families? In the 1990s in the United States, something called "family values" was a political hot potato. Family life and the social norms and political debates that surround it are prime research subjects for professional sociologists. Most elementary school social studies curriculum materials, meanwhile, generally teach that there is no "typical" family.

FIGURE 4–6 Life in families.

LIFE IN FAMILIES				
	Where does this family live?	How many people are in this family?	What things are learned in this group?	What does each member do?
#1: Family in suburban Chicago				
#2: Family in rural Ethiopia				
#3: Family in rural China				

A photo of grandparents and a child will be placed next to a mother and three children and, next to this, a "traditional"-appearing family with a mother, father, two or three children, and a dog. All are labeled, "Families in Our Community." Next to this set of photos will be other photos of diverse families from around the world, large and small, rural and urban, agricultural and industrial. This set might be labeled "Families Around the World."

A child's own family will no doubt differ from those represented in texts as well as those represented in story and picture books. Ethnic, racial, religious, and social class differences will make a difference. Perhaps the school resource librarian will collect trade books on Latino families, Chinese-American families, Arab-American families, or rural and urban families. One of our favorite trade books about family life (maybe because we love tamales) is *Too Many Tamales* (Gary Soto, 1993). It shares a Latino family's preparation for Christmas dinner, with a hilarious incident involving a lost diamond ring thought to be in the tamale batter. *Pablo's Tree* (Pat Mora, 1994) tells of the special relationship between a grandfather and grandson. If the data-retrieval chart shown above is too difficult for the youngest children, or if information on families around the world is not readily available, a single story book can be used. In this case, the chart might look like the one developed by Mary Hurlbut Cordier and Maria A. Perez-Stable in Figure 4–7:[26]

FIGURE 4–7   Life in families.

	My Family	**Story Book Family**
Homes and family members		
Food, everyday and for special events		
Clothing, every day and for special events		
Recreation, home, school, community		
School, grade levels, size, special features		
Jobs, adults and children		
Contributions to America, as good neighbors		

In the second grade, another group—the neighborhood—is featured. Again, a comparative approach is recommended to show both differences and similarities. Now the first data-retrieval chart might look something like Figure 4–8.

Note that the questions at the top of the chart are essentially geographic: location, place, movement, and place again (recall the five themes of geography). Again, if this approach is too difficult for young children, or if information on diverse neighborhoods is not readily available, a data-retrieval chart could look like Figure 4–9:

FIGURE 4–8   Life in neighborhoods.

	Where is this neighborhood located?	What is life (work? play?) like here?	How do people and goods get around?	How does climate influence life here?
#1: A suburb in New York				
#2: A city in the Midwest				
#3: A farm town in New Mexico				

FIGURE 4–9   Life in neighborhoods.

	Where is this neighborhood located?	What is life (work? play?) like here?	How do people and goods get around?	How does climate influence life here?
My neighborhood				
The neighborhood in our book				

For a treatment of the group called *community,* look back to Chapter 1 where you will find the 10 themes of social studies applied to a course of study for the third grade called "Sharing Earth-Space with Others: Communities."

Peer groups and *peer pressure* are topics of great interest to upper elementary and middle school students, and a tremendous amount of sociological research has been done on them. Children's literature can be used to explore these concepts with your students. Three of our favorites are *Best Friends* (Loretta Krupinski, 1998), *Standing Up to Mr. O* (Claudia Mills, 1998), and for the teacher, *You Can't Say "You Can't Play"* (Vivian Paley, 1992).

SIMULATIONS

Disabled Society (grades 2–6) encourages children to participate in situations that help them understand and empathize with disabling conditions. In *The Numbers Game* (grades 5–12), the class is distributed proportionally to North America, Latin America, Asia, Africa, and Europe based on world population data. Cookies and crackers are then distributed, but based on each area's resources.[27]

Conclusion

The main sources of subject matter for the social studies curriculum, as we have seen, are the disciplines of history, geography, political science, economics, sociology, and anthropology. The social studies curriculum integrates these, often leading with history or geography, and points them toward the development of democratic citizens. The key to teaching history, geography, and the other social sciences to younger and older children alike is to help children build both knowledge and know-how. They must not only learn history but also learn to *do* history. The same is true of geography and the other social sciences. Like the two wings of an airplane, neither is sufficient alone. The *doing* of history, geography, economics, and so forth naturally requires reading and writing of all sorts; accordingly, a good portion of the language arts curriculum can be folded into the social studies curriculum. Whether helping children write snapshot biographies or detailed ("thick") descriptions of everyday events, or helping them read children's trade books or make maps and charts, it is not surprising that for many gifted teachers the language arts curriculum is achieved *within* the social studies curriculum.

In the next chapter, we look more deeply into social science teaching and learning, now concentrating on the "tools" they afford us.

Discussion Questions and Suggested Activities

1. Explain the airplane analogy as a representation of the two key ways of teaching and learning history. Try to think of a better analogy. If you think you have one, send it to the author in care of the publisher, Merrill/Prentice Hall, 445 Hutchinson Ave., Columbus, OH 43235.

2. As you read earlier, agriculture was invented 10,000 years ago, replacing a nomadic hunting-and-gathering lifestyle that had gone on for 10 times longer. Very recently (about 1900 A.D.) the

Industrial Revolution completely changed humanity again. Show on a time line these three events in the story of humankind *in a way that captures the amount of time between them.*

3. History is (choose one or more): (a) the recorded past, (b) a story about the past, (c) a set of methods for figuring out what happened in the past, (d) a set of sources for interpreting what happened in the past, (e) all of the above. [*Note:* We choose (e). The first option helps us understand that "prehistoric" does not mean "before anything happened," but before written records were kept. The second is true except that it would be better to say that *a* history is *a* story of the past, not *History* is *the* story of the past. The third and fourth answers make good sense, too, don't you think?]

4. Examine the *Curriculum Standards for Social Studies Sampler* that accompanies this text. In particular, read the performance expectations and the teaching examples given for history (theme 2), geography (themes 1, 3, and 9), economics (theme 7), sociology (theme 5), and anthropology (theme 1).

5. In the Sociology section, we mentioned the controversy that swirls around the concepts *family* and *family values.* How do you think families should be portrayed in curriculum materials to young people?

   A year-long program entitled MAN: A COURSE OF STUDY (MACOS) was an anthropology-based program developed during the 1960s for the fifth grade. It was widely acclaimed by scholars as a fine effort to build challenging social science concepts into the social studies curriculum. Yet, this program was thoroughly rejected by many parents and religious groups. They charged that it was "secular humanist" in its philosophy, that it promoted relativism in values education, and that it taught children to question the authority of their parents and church leaders. (True, serious anthropological study can do all these things.) Disregarding the specific issues of this particular program, however, discuss what you believe should be the appropriate role of parents in deciding the subject matter and procedures used in teaching social studies at the elementary and middle school levels. Do you have the same view regarding their role at the high school level?

Selected References

General

Cobblestone. Cobblestone Publishing, Inc., 7 School Street, Peterborough, NH 03458. Phone: 800-821-0115.

Gardner, Howard. (1999). *The disciplined mind.* New York: Simon and Schuster.

Laughlin, Mildred Knight, & Kardaleff, Patricia Payne. (1991). *Literature-based social studies: Children's books and activities to enrich the K–5 curriculum.* Phoenix: Oryx.

History

• **Curriculum Advice:** National Center for History in the Schools. (1994). *National Standards for History* (Vols 1-3: K–4 general; 5–12 U.S. History; and 5–12 World History). University of California at Los Angeles. Phone: 800-421-4246. Website: *http://www.sscnet.ucla.edu/nchs/standards.html.*

• **Research:** Levstik, Linda S. & Barton, Keith C. (1997). *Doing history: Investigating with children in elementary and middle schools.* Mahwah, NJ, Erlbaum.

• **Read a Good History Book:** Ulrich, Laurel Thatcher. (1991). *A midwife's tale.* New York: Vintage. Tells the story of midwife Martha Ballard (1735-1812).

• **Historical Reasoning:** Wineburg, Sam. (1999). Historical thinking and other unnatural acts. *Phi Delta Kappan, 80:* 488–499.

Geography

- **Curriculum Advice:** National Council for Geographic Education. (1994). *Geography for life: National Geography Standards.* Washington, DC: Author. Phone: 412-357-6290. Website: *http://www.nationalgeographic.com/education/standards.html.*
- **Research:** Stoltman, Joseph P. (1991). Research on geography teaching. In J. P. Shaver (Ed.), *Handbook of research on social studies teaching and learning* (pp. 437–447). New York: Macmillan.
- **5 Themes of Geography:** Salter, Christopher L., & Riggs-Salter, Cathy. (1988, Nov./Dec.). Five themes in geography and the primary-grade learner. *Social Studies and the Young Learner, 1,* 10–13.

  Stremme, Robert. (1993). Great geography using notable trade books. In Myra Zarnowski & Arlene F. Gallagher (Eds.), *Children's literature and social studies: Selecting and using notable books in the classroom.* Washington, DC: National Council for the Social Studies.
- **Read a Good Geography Book:** Sobel, Dava. (1995). *Longitude.* New York: Penguin.

Political Science

- **Curriculum Advice:** Center for Civic Education. (1994). *National standards for civics and government.* Calabasas, CA: Author. Phone: 800-350-4223. Website: *http://www.civiced.org/stds.html.*
- **Research:** Hahn, C. L., (1998). *Becoming political.* Albany, NY: State University of New York Press.
- **Six Dimensions of Citizenship Education:** See Chapter 3 of this text.
- **Read a Good Political Science Book:** Fukuyama, Francis. (1995). *Trust: The social virtues and the creation of prosperity.* New York, Free Press.

Economics

- **Curriculum Advice:** National Council on Economic Education. (1998). *Voluntary national content standards in economics.* New York: Author. 1140 Avenue of the Americas, New York, NY 10036. Phone: 800-338-1192. Website: *http://www.economicsamerica.org/standards.html*

  Kourilsky, M. L. (1983). *Understanding economics: Overview for teachers, experiences for students.* Menlo Park, CA: Addison-Wesley.

  Meszaros, Bonnie, & Engstrom, Laurie. (1998, Nov./Dec.). Voluntary national content standards in economics: 20 enduring concepts and benchmarks for beleaguered teachers. *Social Studies and the Young Learner, 11,* 7–12.
- **Research:** Laney, James D., & Schug, Mark C. (1998, Nov./Dec.). Teach kids economics and they will learn. *Social Studies and the Young Learner, 11,* 13–17.

  Schug, Mark C., & Walstad, William B. (1991). Teaching and learning economics. In James P. Shaver (Ed.), *Handbook of research on social studies teaching and learning* (pp. 411–419). New York: Macmillan.
- **Read a Good Economics Book:** Galbraith, John Kenneth. (1958). *The affluent society.* New York: Mentor.

Anthropology

- **Curriculum Advice:** Barnes, Buckley R. (1991, Jan.). Using children's literature in the early anthropology curriculum. *Social Education, 55,* 17–18.

  Little Soldier, Lee. Making anthropology a part of the elementary social studies curriculum. *Social Education, 54,* 18–19.
- **Research:** Nelson, Murry R., & Stahl, Robert J. (1991). Teaching anthropology, sociology, and psychology. In James P. Shaver (Ed.), *Handbook of research on social studies teaching and learning.* (pp. 420–426). New York: Macmillan.

- **Read a Good Anthropology Book:** Cole, Johnetta. (Ed.). (1988). *Anthropology for the nineties: Introductory readings.* New York: Free Press.

Sociology

- **Curriculum Advice:** Two chapters in Haas, Mary E., & Laughlin, Margaret A. (Eds.). (1997). *Meeting the standards: Social studies readings for k–6 educators.* Washington, DC: National Council for the Social Studies:

    Ladson-Billings, Gloria. I don't see color, I just see children: Dealing with stereotyping and prejudice in young children. (pp. 15–18).

    Nakagawa, Mako, & Ooka Pang, Valerie. Cooperative pluralism: Moving from 'Me' to 'We'. (pp. 115–117).

- **Research:** Nelson, Murry R., & Stahl, Robert J. (1991). Teaching anthropology, sociology, and psychology. In James P. Shaver (Ed.), *Handbook of research on social studies teaching and learning.* (pp. 420–426). New York: Macmillan.

- **Read a Good Sociology Book:** Bellah, Robert N. et al., (1985). *Habits of the heart: Individualism and commitment in American life.* Berkeley: University of California Press.

Notes

1. Quoted in Charlotte Crabtree, Returning history to the elementary schools, in *Historical literacy,* eds. Paul Gagnon & the Bradley Commission on History in the Schools (New York: Macmillan, 1989), 176.

2. *National standards for history for grades k–4: Expanding children's world in time and space* (Los Angeles: National Center for History in the Schools, 1994), 1.

3. Martin Luther King, Jr., *Stride toward freedom* (New York: Harper & Row, 1958), 85.

4. See the Gandhi archives online at *http://www.pitzer.edu/~dward/Anarchist Archives/bright/gandhi/Gandhi.html*

5. Stewart Brand, *The clock of the long now: Time and responsibility* (New York, Basic Books), 2.

6. *U.S. history framework for the 1994 National Assessment of Educational Progress* (NAEP) (Washington, DC: U.S. Department of Education, 1994), 18.

7. Ibid., vi–vii.

8. Linda S. Levstik & Keith C. Barton, *Doing history: Investigating with children in elementary and middle schools* (Mahwah, NJ: Lawrence Erlbaum Associates, 1997), p. 5.

9. Ibid., 92.

10. Vivian Gussin Paley, *Wally's stories* (Cambridge: Harvard University Press, 1981), 112.

11. Adapted from Levstik & Barton, (above) 95–96.

12. Sharon Pray Muir, Simulations for Elementary and Primary School Social Studies: An Annotated Bibliography, *Simulation and Gaming: An International Journal of Theory, Practice, and Research 7* (March 1996): 41–73.

13. *Geography for life: National geography standards* (Washington, DC: Geography Education Standards Project), 23.

14. Thomas T. Olkowski & Lynn Parker, *Moving with children* (Littleton, CO: Gylantic, 1993).

15. Dava, Sobel. *Longitude* (New York: Penguin, 1995), 13.

16. See Kids' questions about moving, in *Moving with children* (above), 37.

17. See Muir (above).

18. Belinda Y. Louie, Using literature to teach location, *Social Studies and the Young Learner 5* (January/February 1993): 17–18, 22; and Robert Stremme, Great geography using notable trade books in *Children's literature and social studies: Selecting and using notable books in the classroom,* ed. Myra Zarnowski & Arlene F. Gallager (Washington, DC: National Council for the Social Studies, 1993), 12–15.

19. Write NCEE at 1140 Avenue of the Americas, New York, NY 10035.

20. James D. Laney & Mark C. Schug, Teach kids economics and they will learn, *Social Studies and the Young Learner 11* (November/December 1998): 13–17.

21. Ibid., 15. See John D. Hoge's description of classrooms deeply involved in mini/micro-society programs: Try microsociety for hands-on citizenship, in *Social Studies and the Young Learner 10* (September/October 1997): 18–21.

22. See Muir (above).

23. The Secretary's Commission on Achieving Necessary Skills (SCANS), *What work requires of schools: A SCANS report for America 2000* (Washington, DC: U.S. Department of Labor, 1991).

24. *The interpretation of cultures* (New York, Basic Books, 1973), 19.

25. See Muir (above).

26. Latino Connections, *Social Studies and the Young Learner 9* (September/October, 1996): 20–32.

27. See Muir (above).

Websites

http://www.pbs.org/lewisandclark/

http://educate.si.edu/spotlight/

http://www.ecedweb.unomaha.edu

http://www.sscnet.ucla.edu/nchs/standards/html

http://www.nationalgeographic.com/education/standards.html

http://www.civiced.org/stds.html

http://www.economicsamerica.org/standards.html

http://www.pitzer.edu/~dward.AnarchistArchives/bright/gandhi/Gandhi.html

CHAPTER 5

Powerful Social Studies Tools: Time Lines, Maps, Globes, and Graphics

Main Idea

Making sense of time and place requires tools, both physical and mental. This chapter is loaded with them. From time lines to wall maps, charts, and globes, the social studies curriculum teaches children a wide variety of ways to read and represent information and ideas.

Key Concepts

Time, space, chronology, time line, location, globe, map, symbol, directions, scale, projection, chart, graph

Chapter Outline

- Developing a Sense of Time and Chronology
- Map and Globe Skills
- Teaching About the Globe
- Teaching About Maps
- Teaching Graphs and Charts
- Conclusion
- Discussion Questions and Suggested Activities
- Notes and Selected References

Chapter Snapshot

Three wall maps were taped side by side to the chalkboard at the front of the room. One is a Mercator projection, one a Robinson projection, and one a Peters projection. "This is the United States," the teacher said, pointing at the U.S. on the first map. "Right?", she asked. "Right!", the children cheered. "And so is this and this," she said as she pointed to the other maps. "Right?" "Right!" "But the *shape* of the U.S. is different in each," she continued. "Why is that? Come have a closer look and tell us what you think." The next morning, she hands a nice fresh orange to each student. "Peel this orange, like you were peeling the globe, then try to flatten out the peel on your desk. Tell us what happens and why."

 A favorite website http://www.nationalgeographic.com/maps/political.html This National Geographic site, with both physical and political maps, is a good place to begin a search for online map collections.

This chapter presents hands-on and minds-on conceptual tools that are important if children are to make sense of time and place—that is, history and geography. We suggest numerous ways to teach them, and we are confident that readers will think of many more. These tools promote in students an attitude of thoughtfulness about social data by requiring them to organize and analyze rather than only memorize.

The social studies curriculum operates within a space-time matrix that might be represented very simply as follows:

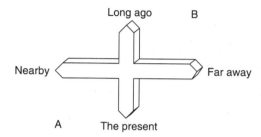

Experiences that could be charted at point A would be the least abstract and would usually be found in the primary grades. Experiences at point B would be more difficult to make concrete for children because they are remote not only in space but also in time. Because many children today have firsthand experiences that acquaint them with places beyond their immediate environment, it is not necessary to confine the social studies program to the local area. There can be some movement from the near at hand to the far away even in the early grades. This movement can be more difficult to do with the time dimension, however; hence the reliance on things that are known concretely—the family, the home, neighborhood, and community workers, for example—as vehicles for moving into the past. Examples include families now and long ago; homes the children live in today and the caves, castles, and manors of yesteryear; farmers now and then.

Many instructional aids can help us teach and learn about time and space. Time lines make chronology more meaningful. Graphs make quantitative relationships vivid and more understandable. Tables and charts help us organize our data and our thoughts. Globes and maps are indispensable tools for working with spatial phenomena. Refer to the color insert following page 168, which contains several types of maps that are used in elementary and intermediate schools. It is imperative that the social studies program teach children how to use these tools.

Developing a Sense of Time and Chronology

Children, of course, learn much about time through ordinary living outside of school. Undoubtedly most children would learn how to tell time and identify the days of the week and months of the year, and they would become familiar with terms ordinarily used in referring to units of time, such as *noon, midnight, afternoon,* and *morning,* even if these were not taught in school. The school program can ensure that these are learned correctly, however, and can provide children the opportunity to practice using them with the guidance of the teacher and more capable peers.

Nonetheless, the main thrust of the school program should be on those aspects of time and chronology that are *not* likely to be learned outside of school. These include (1) the more technical concepts of time and chronology such as *century, decade, fortnight, fiscal year, calendar year, generation, score, millennium,* A.M., P.M., B.C., and A.D.; (2) placing events in chronological order; (3) developing an understanding of the time spans that separate historical events; and (4) developing what in the last chapter was called the *long view* and, with it, the capacity for long-term thinking. References to *indefinite* units of time—such as "many years ago," "several years had passed," and "in a few years"—need special attention because they are apt to mean almost any amount of time to young children. Definite references to time can be made meaningful by associating them with units of time that are known to the children: their own ages, the length of time they have been in school, when their parents or grandparents were their age, and so on. The teaching of these relationships can and should take place within the context of social studies units, especially those that focus on history, and in connection with current news stories.

The development of time concepts should begin with time situations that are within the children's realm of experience. Children should be given help in learning to read clock time and in understanding references to the parts of the day, days of the week, months, seasons, and the year. Even though primary grade children make statements about things that happened "a hundred years ago," they have little comprehension of the real meaning of the expression and simply use it as a vague reference to something that happened in what seems to them a long time ago.

Time lines are often used to show how related events are arranged in chronological order and to show the relative amount of time that separates them. Teachers report success in helping children arrange events in proper sequence by using time lines. Using only a limited number of events that are clearly a part of the subject matter studied seems to enhance understanding.

Children can develop the concept of representing time on a continuum by first arranging events that they experience firsthand. They can make time lines that show things that happened to them yesterday, today, or are being planned for tomorrow. The amount of time included on the line can gradually be expanded to cover several months and then years. Time lines are more interesting to children if events are shown pictorially rather than simply as dots and dates. With upper-grade children, frequent use can be made of time lines in connection with historical studies of their home state and their nation. Figure 5–1 shows two simple time lines, one of events in the child's own life and one of Thomas Jefferson's life.

SOFTWARE

TimeLiner (Tom Snyder Productions) allows teacher and students to create, store, edit, merge, and print time lines. This is a wonderful tool! The time line, once created, can be represented in various forms—as a banner that stretches around the classroom or a list that runs down the classroom door. As students learn to use this program, their oral and written reports and their autobiographies and biographies should be expected to contain helpful and accurate time lines. We like to see a time line banner stretched around the classroom, with children adding new events and persons as the year progresses. Joseph Braun and his

FIGURE 5–1   Times lines: Autobiographical and biographical.

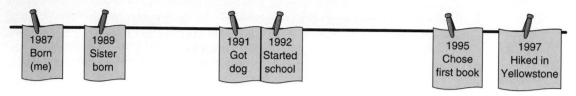

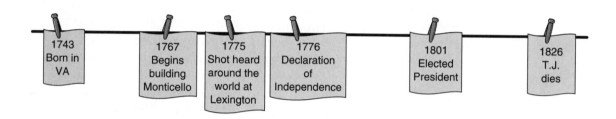

colleagues recommend that butcher paper be stretched below the time line and used to create a mural of key events. "Thus a living wall can be created, providing a visual record of any period of study."[1]

Map and Globe Skills Essential to the Social Studies Curriculum

Maps and globes are tools for representing space symbolically. The essential features of all maps and globes are a grid, color, scale, symbols, and a legend that explains the symbol system used. The ability to read and interpret maps and globes, like conventional reading, represents a composite of several subskills. These subskills can be inferred by analyzing the behavior of someone reading a map who is skillful at it. Probably the most widely used analysis is published by the National Council for the Social Studies. According to this source, the essential map-reading skills are:

1. Orient a map and note directions.
2. Use scale and compute distances.
3. Locate places on maps and globes.
4. Express relative location.
5. Interpret map symbols and visualize what they mean.[2]

DIRECTIONAL ORIENTATION

To deal with directional relationships on maps and globes, the child must first understand them in reality. The easiest directions to use are those that express relative location, such as *close to, near, over here,* and *over there.* These can be learned in the primary grades. The *cardinal directions* are also learned in the primary grades by having them pointed out and by referring to places that are known to children as being north of, east of, south of, and so on. Placing direction labels on the various walls of the classroom helps remind children of cardinal directions. They can associate east and west with the rising and setting of the sun. They can learn how a compass is used to find direction. While on field trips, children should be given practice in noting directions, observing especially the directions of streets and roads. Gradually, they learn the purpose of the poles, the meridians of longitude, and the parallels of latitude in orienting a map and noting directions. When maps with unfamiliar projections are introduced, children should be taught how to establish correct directional relationships on them.

USING MAP SCALES

In making a map, the cartographer tries to reproduce as accurately as possible that portion of the earth being represented. Because globes are models of the earth, they can represent the earth more correctly than can maps. No map can altogether faithfully represent the earth simply because the earth is round and maps are flat. The flattening process inevitably results in some distortion.

Scaling is the process of reducing everything in the same amount. Mathematical reasoning is involved, and here is a good opportunity for the math and social studies curricula to overlap. When one works with children in the primary grades, scaling should be done in the relative sense. Some things are larger or smaller than other things, and the maps should show their *relative size* as accurately as possible. For example, a 50-foot-high tree in the schoolyard should be about five times larger than the 10-foot-tall playground set. On conventional maps, three types of scales are used:

1. The graphic scale

2. The inches-to-miles scale

3. The representative fraction   1 : 250,000

Of these, the graphic scale is the easiest to use and can be taught at about third grade. The inches-to-miles scale is more complex. It can be taught in the fourth or fifth grades. The representative fraction is usually considered beyond the scope of the elementary school program.

As children become more global in their experiences, they will encounter map scales in metric measures. If metric measurement is used, the distance on a graphic scale would be recorded in kilometers. Likewise, rather than as inches to miles, the scale would show the relationship as centimeters to kilometers. The following graphic scale illustrates the same distance expressed in miles and in kilometers:

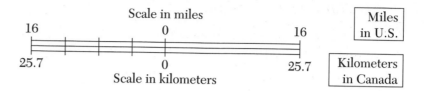

LOCATING PLACES

Location, recall, is one of the five themes of geography (the "L" in *MR. HELP*). The ability to locate places on maps and globes and to verbally express locations comes with a familiarity with these devices cultivated over a period of several years. Children first learn to locate places that are known to them on simple maps and layouts that they make in the classroom. In the early grades, too, children can learn the names and shapes of some of the major geographic features, such as continents, oceans, the equator, and the poles. Commercially prepared maps and globes designed for the lower grades are quite plain, having only a few features shown. Gradually, children increase their repertoire of known places they can find on the map and globe because of frequent references to the location of important cities, countries, rivers, mountains, and other physical features.

In the intermediate grades, children are taught to use coordinates to locate places. Local highway maps are well suited for use in teaching this skill because they deal with an area familiar to the children. One set of lines of the grid—perhaps the north-south lines—is identified with letters; the other set of lines is numbered as is done in Figure 5–2. The teacher can have the children find several places located on or very near to a north-south line, say D. Then several places can be found on an east-west line, say 6. If the teacher is clever enough to pick two coordinates that intersect on a major point of interest, the children will discover that some city or other important feature is located at the point where D and 6 intersect. Figure 5–2 is an example of an exercise of this kind. This experience provides readiness for the use of meridians of longitude and parallels of latitude in locating places on wall maps and the globe. At this stage, children are mature enough to understand why reference points such as poles, the equator, and the prime meridian are essential in locating places on a sphere.

The teacher needs to understand that there are two ways to indicate the location of any place: relative and absolute. *Relative location* is indicated by real estate agents when they tell you that the home is located "near schools and restaurants." They have told you where it is— sort of. They could add, "it is south of the university campus." Or, "it is northeast of the city, across the river." In each case, they are locating the house relative to other places. *Absolute location,* by contrast, is indicated by such statements as these: "The house is at the corner of Maple and Third." "Most of Australia lies between 120°E and 160°E, which places it between two lines of longitude."

Ask your students, "Where is our classroom?" and help them understand the two ways of answering this question. As homework, ask them to locate their home.

FIGURE 5–2

Intermediate grade children can learn to use a grid in locating places by using road maps that have coordinates of the type shown on this map. Test your own memory of place locations by responding to these questions:

1. What major city is located in square C2?
2. What major city lies near the intersection of the squares D1, D2, E1, and E2?
3. Describe the location of Savannah by using the coordinates provided on this map.

Check your answers by consulting a map of Georgia that shows cities.

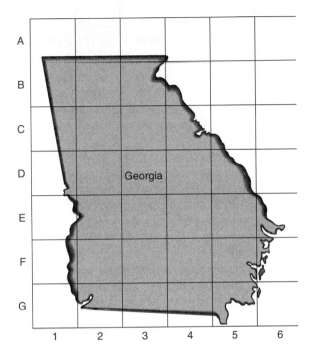

READING MAP SYMBOLS

Maps use symbols to represent real things: Dots of varying sizes stand for cities of different populations; color is used to represent elevation; stars indicate capital cities; and lines are used to show boundaries, coastlines, and rivers. Naturally, readers will not comprehend the messages of maps unless they know what these symbols represent. Children begin to learn their meanings early in the elementary school social studies program. The development of this subskill closely parallels that of locating places on maps.

Map and globe symbols vary in their abstractness. Indeed, some simple maps for children in the primary grades use symbols that are pictorial or semipictorial. These symbols either look like the object being represented or provide a strong clue as to its identity, as shown in Figures 5–3 and 5–4. It would not take much imagination, for example, to differentiate water areas from land areas on a globe simply on the basis of their color.

The instructional sequence to be followed in teaching the symbol system of maps is to move gradually from pictorial and semipictorial symbols on maps made by children to the abstract symbols used on conventional wall maps, globes, and maps that are included in the textbooks of the middle and upper grades. It is essential that children learn to consult the map legend or key to confirm which symbols are being used. In most cases, children in

FIGURE 5–3   Children can be introduced to the concept of symbols through pictorial representations that they encounter in real life, such as the ones shown here.

the middle and upper grades will be dealing with maps that use conventional map symbols, but special-purpose maps such as those showing vegetation, rainfall, population density, and so on often use symbols that are unique to the particular map.

It is always a good idea to make generous use of photographs of the areas shown on a map to help children associate the map symbol with what the place actually looks like. Similarly, when children go on field trips, they should be encouraged to observe carefully the appearance of landscapes, rivers, bridges, railroad tracks, and other features shown on maps. In time they will be able to visualize the reality that the abstract map symbols represent.

FIGURE 5–4
Examples of standard symbols used on maps.

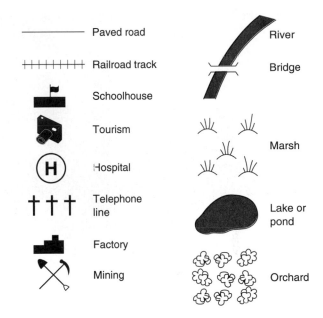

Paved road

Railroad track

Schoolhouse

Tourism

Hospital

Telephone line

Factory

Mining

River

Bridge

Marsh

Lake or pond

Orchard

Teaching About the Globe

Every social studies classroom should have a globe and use it often. In grades 1, 2, and 3 a simplified 12-inch globe is generally recommended because small children find this size easier to handle than the larger 16-inch one. For primary grades, the globe selected should have a minimum amount of information on it. It should not use more than three colors to represent land elevation or more than two colors to represent water depth. Only the largest cities, rivers, and water bodies should be shown. In the intermediate and middle grades, a 16-inch globe is recommended because of its easy scale of one inch to 500 miles. Moreover, its larger size allows more detail to be shown without the globe becoming a confused collection of symbols. Globes for intermediate and middle grade children will ordinarily use seven colors to represent land elevations and three colors to represent water depths.

The chief value of the globe in grades 1, 2, and 3 is to familiarize children with the basic roundness of the earth and to begin to develop a global perspective. Parents speak of places in the news, and the children wonder where those places are. They hear of wars and famines and wonder about their location. Perhaps a girl has just joined the class; her family has recently moved to this country from another part of the world, and she wants to show the class the location of her former home. The teacher will use situations such as these—and hundreds more like them—to acquaint children with the globe.

The teacher should help children discover other things about the globe, too—differences between water and land areas and that these are represented by different colors; the line that separates the water and the land is called the seacoast. Children may be shown pictures to help them visualize different kinds of coastlines. Similarly, the teacher extends their understanding

Globes invite inspection.

of other concepts—oceans, cities, rivers, and mountains. Children learn that most of the brown areas that represent land are on the half of the earth that has the North Pole and that it is here that the majority of the people of the world live.

In addition to the incidental references made to the globe, the teacher should use the globe frequently when teaching social studies and other subjects. For instance, in a reading lesson, children might find where their book friends "live." Thus, the globe can be used in a great variety of ways to lay a good foundation for more formal aspects of the teaching of these skills later on.

The following are examples of the types of learnings and experiences that can be planned with the globe for children in the lower grades:

1. Stress that the globe is a very small model of the earth. Good models look exactly like the real thing but are smaller. The globe is a good model of the earth.

2. Show the children how land areas and water bodies are represented on the globe. Have them find land areas and water bodies. Names of these need not be taught at this level, but children might already know the large water bodies such as the Pacific and Atlantic oceans, and it is good for them to begin hearing the names. Similarly, they might be familiar with North and South America, Africa, or the Antarctic, and these can be pointed out. Explain that all water bodies and land areas have names.

3. Have children discover that there is considerably more water than land shown on the globe. Ask them if they have any theories about why this is.

4. Show children the location of the North Pole. Explain that most of the land of the world is on the same half of the world as the North Pole. We call this the Northern Hemisphere or half.

5. Show children the location of the South Pole. Explain that most of the water areas of the world are on the same half of the world as the South Pole. We call this the Southern Hemisphere.

6. Explain that our earth is a planet, one of several spinning around the sun.

7. Show children how they can find their country, their continent, their state, and possibly their city on the globe.

8. Use the globe to find places that are familiar to the children—places they have visited on vacations, places in the news, homes of book friends and visitors from other countries, or places in the world from which some circus or zoo animals are brought.

9. Encourage children to handle the globe and to find places on it themselves.

10. If possible, visit a map site on the Internet. The National Geographic Society's map collection is a good place to start: *http://www.nationalgeographic.com/maps/political.html*

Lesson Plan 6 is an example of a plan used by one teacher to familiarize primary grade children with geographic concepts and skills using the globe.

As children move into the intermediate and middle grades, instruction in using the globe should take two forms. First, the teacher should take time from regularly scheduled unit activities to teach skills needed in reading and interpreting the globe. Second, in unit work and other classroom activities, there should be frequent reference to the globe and maps. Both of these aspects of instruction are important, and one should supplement the other. To hope that children will become skillful in using a globe or maps simply by making incidental references to them is wishful thinking. At the same time, formal lessons in using these devices without application of the newly acquired skills in purposeful situations is equally ineffective. The best arrangement is to provide for systematic instruction in the use of map- and globe-reading skills as a part of unit activities, reinforcing this with direct teaching of these skills as the need arises.

Maps may be used to find distances between points only under certain conditions, but the globe represents distances accurately and true to scale at all points on the surface of the earth. It is easy to place a flexible ruler on the globe and directly measure the distance between two points in question. Then refer to the scale and determine the actual distance between the two places. The air routes of the world use great circles because these are the shortest distances from place to place on the earth's surface. If nothing but flat maps are used, it is difficult to understand the concept of great circle routes and, therefore, of airplane routes. The globe can help clarify this concept (see Figure 5–5). In this connection, the *slated globe* (sometimes called the *project globe*) is useful because it is possible to write on the surface of it with a piece of chalk.

Globes are helpful, too, in establishing concepts of direction. It is not difficult to think of north as being in the direction of the North Pole when using a globe. On the other hand, this may be confusing if only a flat map is used. Furthermore, the relative direction of various parts of the earth can be better understood through the use of a globe. Many Americans are surprised, for example, when they learn that Great Britain lies in a more northerly latitude

Lesson Plan 6   USING THE GLOBE TO LEARN ABOUT EARTH

Grade 1 or 2

Time One class period

Objective To develop a familiarity with concepts relating to the globe.

Interest Building Give the children free time to manipulate a globe and explore it on their own.

Lesson Development The teacher directs the following questions to the children:

What shape is a globe?

Can you find the North Pole? Place your finger on it.

Where is north on a globe?

Where is south on a globe?

Is south the opposite direction of north?

What divides the north from the south?

Have any of you lived near the equator?

Is the equator really a line?

How much of the globe is north?

How much of the globe is south?

What is half of a sphere?

Does anyone know what we call the northern half of the globe?

Does anyone know what we call the southern half of the globe?

How can we tell water from land on the globe?

Does anyone know what we call these large pieces of land?

Can you find a continent in the Northern Hemisphere?

Can you find a continent in the Southern Hemisphere?

Are there any continents that are in both hemispheres?

Summary and Assessment How is the globe divided?

Can you name the parts of the globe we talked about?

Can you point to the Northern Hemisphere?

Can you point to the Southern Hemisphere?

Can you point to a continent?

Materials As many globes as are available so that each child can easily explore and manipulate the globe.

Integration *Literature:* Read aloud *Nine O'Clock Lullaby* (Singer, 1993). This picture book takes children on an around-the-world journey that introduces them to time zones. When it's 9:00 A.M. here, what time is it in Moscow? *Hopscotch Around the World* (Lankford, 1993) takes them globe trotting again, this time comparing 19 local variations on the hopscotch game.

Math: Use flexible rulers (or pieces of string) to measure the distances between the students' home state and places on the globe they want to visit.

FIGURE 5–5   Notice how differently the map and globe portray global relationships.

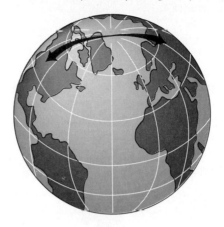

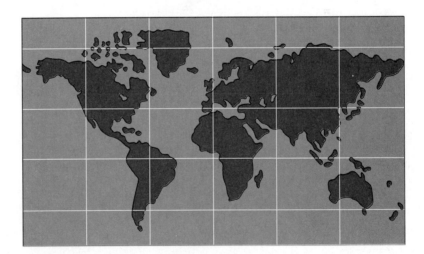

than do any of the 48 mid-continent states of our country; that Boston has nearly the same latitude as Rome; that our most westerly state is not Hawaii but Alaska; that our most southerly state is not Florida but Hawaii; that Moscow and Glasgow have approximately the same latitude, both being farther south than any city of Norway or Finland. These facts illustrate that one perceives the earth differently on a globe than on a flat map.

A definite advantage that globes have over maps is that they show the size and shapes of areas exactly as they appear on the earth's surface, whereas maps cannot. The classical examples of distortions in the size and shapes of land areas are Greenland on the Mercator projection and Australia on the polar projection. On the Mercator projection, Greenland appears as a very large area—larger than South America. On a polar projection, Australia appears to have a greater east-west distance and a shorter north-south distance than is actually the case. Notice the different shapes North America takes on various maps as

FIGURE 5–6

A land area such as North America may take a variety of shapes on maps, depending on the projection that is used. Professional cartographers continually search for more exact ways to show the earth's surface on flat maps. In 1988, its centennial year, the National Geographic Society selected a new map projection that more accurately represents the earth than did earlier projections. The new projection was developed by Arthur H. Robinson at the University of Wisconsin-Madison. The Robinson projection replaces the Van der Grinten projection that had been used by the Society for its world maps for more than five decades.

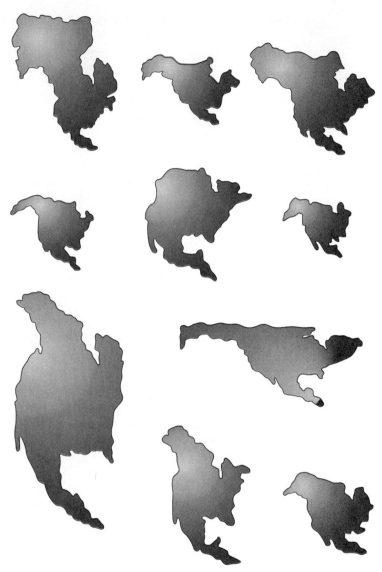

illustrated in Figure 5–6. A globe will show all these map shapes and sizes to be inaccurately represented. Therefore, a globe should be used with maps to prevent or correct misconceptions.

Teaching About Maps

A number of complex skills are involved in map reading and interpretation; therefore, early experiences with maps should be kept simple. This can best be done by using diagrams and maps that the teacher and the children make of their immediate vicinity. These experiences may take the form of a layout on the classroom floor, using blocks and other objects for houses, streets, trees, and public buildings. The layout can be done on a table, or the map can be drawn on a large piece of wrapping paper on the classroom floor. When the floor surface will permit, masking tape can be placed on the floor itself to represent boundaries, streets, or roads.

Opportunities to teach and apply these skills often arise in the everyday life of the classroom. For instance, children in one class learned about map direction when a new student joined the group. Soon after the child arrived, the teacher used a map to show the class the location of the child's previous home. They determined the direction the child's family traveled to reach their new home. The teacher then used a map of the local area and had the children discover the direction they travel when going from their homes to school each day.

TEACHING MAP SYMBOLS

A fundamental skill in map reading is to learn that a symbol represents a real and actual thing. The symbol may be arbitrarily chosen and bear no resemblance to the object represented, or it may be one that would suggest to the reader what is intended. A school might be represented by a small circle or by a small square with a flag placed on top. It is easier to associate the flag and square with a school than to associate the circle with it. The flag and square are, therefore, less abstract. With young children, it is better to use pictorial or semipictorial symbols of this sort than to use completely abstract ones. In teaching map-reading skills, one must remember that both reading and interpretive skills are involved, and the interpretive skills depend heavily on maturity and background knowledge. Primary grade children will do less with interpreting maps than they will with reading them.

The idea of objects representing other objects, people, or things is not new to the children; they have substituted symbols for the actual things many times in imaginative play. The teacher can begin by explaining that they are going to draw a map of the schoolroom, schoolyard, or some segment of the immediate vicinity. It is best if this can be done on the classroom floor, so the layout can be oriented exactly as it appears in relationship to the classroom; this sidesteps the matter of orientation to directions at this early stage. Trees, doors, playground equipment, parking areas, and other objects appear in relation to other objects, and

Have You Met Carmen Sandiego?

If not, you should. *Where in the World Is Carmen Sandiego?* may be the most exciting and useful piece of computer software available for geographical learning in grades 4 and up. It is a game that can be played alone, in small groups, or by the entire class. *Carmen,* you will discover, is thief of some of the world's great treasures. Students play the role of detectives hot on her trail across six continents and innumerable cities. Each on-site investigation produces clues that lead them on to the next city. Lots of geographical data are involved, all requiring interpretation and organization. The game is played using a database from *The World Almanac and Book of Facts.*[3]

DO-IT-YOURSELF MAP

This exercise can be used in the intermediate and middle grades for teaching or assessing map skills. The teacher can have everyone in class do the exercise as the directions are read, one step at a time. Directions can also be displayed with an overhead projector. When the maps are completed, the exercise should be discussed. Children can be invited to walk around the room to see maps drawn by their classmates. Maps can also be displayed on the bulletin boards.

Directions

1. On a clean sheet of paper, draw an outline map of an imaginary continent. You may make it any shape you wish, but you must include at least one peninsula and one bay.

2. Show a scale of miles in your legend for the map.

3. Draw east-west and north-south lines on your map.

4. Draw a mountain range running east and west across your continent, but include at least one mountain pass. Place the symbol you use for your mountain range in your legend.

5. Show a city in the northern half of your continent and one in the southern half. Make each one a seaport.

6. Show a railway joining the two cities.

7. Show three rivers on your continent; show a lake and a swamp. Place all the symbols you use for cities, rivers, lakes, and swamps in the legend.

8. Place a third city somewhere on your map where you think a city should be. On the bottom of your map tell why you think a city should be where you have placed it.

9. Show boundary lines that divide your continent into three large countries and one small country.

only the major ones should be included. The purpose of this experience is simply to show that it is possible to represent space symbolically and that symbols stand for real things. Their maps should have a title and a key to tell what the symbols stand for. This is the first experience in developing the skill of comprehending the significance of symbols, and it will be continued and extended as long as maps are used.

As the children become ready for more abstract symbols, such symbols will be introduced, taught, and used, as will more conventional map symbols. As a part of this instruction in the intermediate and middle grades, it is important to frequently use pictures and other visual aids that will help children visualize the area represented. It is helpful, too, to take children to some high point in the community where they can look down on an area and see what it actually looks like from above. In most localities it is possible to purchase inexpensive aerial photographs of the local community, and these can be used in studying map symbols and in making maps of the local area. The teacher also should take advantage of the many fine maps and photographs in social studies textbooks to acquaint children with the appearance of various areas, landscapes, surface features, land and water forms, and people-made things that are represented symbolically on maps.

TEACHING MAP DIRECTIONS

For reasons of simplicity, orientation to direction may be avoided in the children's first attempts at making diagrams or maps. But the need to orient a map properly for direction will become apparent to them if their classroom map is rotated. Being able to note and read directions is a prerequisite to serious map study, and this skill should be introduced fairly early, perhaps in the second grade. Children can learn the cardinal directions by having the directions pointed out to them. They learn which wall of the room is north, south, east, or west because the teacher may have placed labels on the walls. They learn that if one knows the direction of north, the other directions can be determined; for if one faces north, the direction of south will be to one's back, east to the right, and west to the left. To extend their ability to orient themselves, children should be taken outdoors and the directions pointed out to them. If this is done at noon on a sunny day, the children's shadows will point in an approximate northerly direction. After the children have this basic orientation to direction, subsequent mapwork should include reference to direction and should become increasingly more complex.

Finding directions on conventional wall maps can be facilitated with the aid of a globe and perhaps should not be taught much below the fourth grade. When this concept is introduced, it should be done through reference to north-south and east-west grid lines. Children are taught that north is in the direction of the North Pole and that south is in the direction of the South Pole. The poles can be easily found

Capital Punishment?

An old controversy in social studies is whether to require students to memorize the 50 states and capitals. John Hergesheimer, the editor of the newsletter of the California Council for the Social Studies, recently wrote an editorial opposing such a requirement in the new curriculum standards in that state. The editorial generated interesting responses, pro and con.

Con: "In each class I ask all of my students how many of them learned the states and capitals in elementary school. More than a majority of students in each class say they memorized those facts. Then I ask them how many of them can recite today what those states and capitals are. Out of more than 300 students, only three replied that they could. . . . Those three could 'sing' the states and capitals."

Pro: "Some teachers testify to tedium and failure, but in the instances with which

I am familiar, states and capitals were taught and learned with felicity. . . . There is no reason why any teacher should apologize for having students learn the names and location of the 50 states. The value of learning capitals is perhaps less tangible. . . . (but it) does give students a vocabulary of U.S. cities they would never know otherwise."[4]

by following the meridians of longitude. The east-west directions can be found by following the parallels of latitude. Generalizations such as "north is at the top of the map" and "south is at the bottom of the map" should *not* be taught because they are not correct and because they may be confusing when one uses a variety of different map projections. Similarly, references to north as "up" and south as "down" should not be taught in connection with either maps or globes. When we speak of the earth, the term *down* means toward the center of the earth and *up* means away from the center of the earth. Both terms should be taught only in that way. The matter of associating *up* with north introduces many instructional problems as children learn more of the geography of the earth. For example, if north is up, how can so many of the world's rivers flow north? The children will invariably ask why we say "way down South" or "the Land Down Under"; these can be explained as being colorful expressions and figures of speech similar to "way out West" or "out at sea" that have crept into our language but have nothing at all to do with direction itself. (See Figure 5–7.)

TEACHING MAP SCALE

Children can be helped to understand the need for map scales by indicating to them that maps must be small enough to bring into the classroom or carry in our backpacks and place in the glove compartment of the car. We cannot make maps as big as the area we wish to show, and who would want one that big? A map must be made smaller than the place it represents, and everything on the map must be made smaller in the same amount. Just as a photograph of the family shows everyone smaller in the same amount, so must the map; otherwise, it would not give a true picture. Children should learn that maps are precise and accurate tools. In primary grades, the scaling is not done in the mathematical sense, but the reductions are correctly made in the relative sense. That is, lakes would be larger than houses; streets, longer than driveways; cars, smaller than buildings; and so on. In intermediate grades, when children have had sufficient background in mathematics, they can deal with graphic reductions more precisely. They learn that wall maps have the scale printed on them and are taught how to read the various ways by which scale can be indicated. The experiences children have using map scales provide a good context in which to call their attention to distances between various places. Children can be helped to visualize these distances through an appreciation of the time needed to traverse the distances in question by air travel. These times may be obtained in time tables from commercial airlines.

TEACHING MAP INTERPRETATION

When children have learned the meaning of map symbols, are skillful in orienting a map to direction, and can recognize and use map scales, they are well on their way toward an understanding of the language of maps. This does not mean, however, that they find maps es-

FIGURE 5–7   This map illustrates why statements such as "north is at the top of the map" are incorrect. East-west lines or parallels of latitude have been omitted to draw attention to north-south directions. What questions might you pose to students studying this map?

pecially useful or that they regard them as a valuable source of information. The development of skills that deal largely with map language must be accompanied by associated interpretive skills. Proficiency in interpreting maps will vary considerably among the children. One who is skillful in map use has developed the ability to visualize what an area actually looks like when it is seen on the map. Looking at the map color, one in a sense "sees" the rugged Rocky Mountains of our West, the waving grainfields of western Montana, the rich farmlands of the Midwest, and the rolling countryside of Virginia. Because the child cannot visualize places not actually seen except in an imaginative way, the *generous use of additional visual material along with maps is suggested*. Good-quality pictures are especially important, and the class should see several pictures of an area to avoid fixing a single impression of the area in their minds. Filmstrips and slides can be used for the same purpose, and motion pictures and television are also excellent aids. Chapter 9, "Resources," provides many websites where students can see an array of maps as well as photographs of everything from the pyramids of Egypt to the Pilgrim settlement at Plymouth. As was previously noted, in the early stages of map reading, an excellent procedure is to have an aerial photograph of the local area as well as a conventional map. When these are placed side by side, the child can see how the area actually looks and how it is represented on a map. Stories and other narrative accounts are also useful in helping the child visualize areas represented on maps.

Activities such as the following can be used to relate the abstractions of maps to the reality they represent:

1. Observing local landscapes and geographical features, preferably from a high point.
2. Using pictorial and semipictorial symbols, especially at the lower grade levels.
3. Using three-dimensional models of the areas mapped; using blocks and models to represent buildings.
4. Making maps of the local area with which children are familiar.
5. Making generous use of pictures, films, and filmstrips of the areas shown on maps.
6. Relating aerial photographs (angle shots rather than perpendicular ones) to maps of the same area.

The types of information that can be read directly or inferred from map study can be classified as follows:

Land and water forms—continents, oceans, bays, peninsulas, islands, straits.

Relief features—plains, mountains, rivers, deserts, plateaus, swamps, valleys.

Direction and distance—cardinal directions, distance in miles or kilometers, relative distance, scale.

Social data—population density, size of communities, location of major cities, birth and death rates.

Economic information—industrial and agricultural production, soil fertility, trade factors, location of industries.

Political information—political divisions, boundaries, capitals, territorial possessions, types of government, political parties.

Human projects—cities, canals, railroads, highways, coaxial and fiber optic cables, telephone lines, bridges, dams, nuclear power plants.

COMPARING MAPS AND MAKING INFERENCES

Comparing different maps of the same place can be an insightful experience. In the fourth and fifth grades, teachers often have children compare vegetation maps with rainfall maps. They also have them compare maps showing the location of important resources, such as iron and coal, with maps showing the location of industrial centers, population densities, and so on. It is quite common to find special-purpose maps of the same region in the children's textbook, making comparisons easy. These provide excellent settings for critical thinking as the children can study the data presented on two or more maps, make predictions or hypotheses about these data, and then go on to the next step of verifying or rejecting their speculations.

Children in the intermediate and middle grades should study maps based on different projections and compare the shapes and sizes of known areas with those same areas as shown on the globe. This activity will familiarize them with the concept of distortion, which, in greater or lesser amounts, is present in all flat maps. Children should learn why distortion occurs and what cartographers have done to minimize its effect.

TEACHING MAP COLOR

The use of color has caused confusion for children trying to visualize elevations. Children seem to believe that all areas represented by one color are precisely the same elevation, not recognizing that variations in elevations occur within the limits of the interval used by the color representation. (See Figure 5–8.) Moreover, children develop the mistaken idea that elevations occur abruptly where colors change. Conventional color symbols give no impression of gradual elevations or depressions and create the illusion that changes are abrupt.

FIGURE 5–8   This diagram shows two methods of illustrating keys to colors, used to express elevations on classroom maps. Some teachers find it helpful to construct a three-dimensional papier-mâché model of the key to help students associate elevation with the color code.

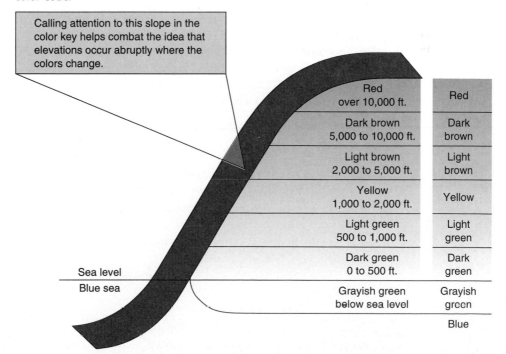

The use of a relief map helps show that changes in elevation occur gradually. Comparing colors of a wall map with elevations on a relief map helps children gain a better understanding of map color as used to represent elevations.

Landform maps are often used in social studies textbooks. (See the color insert following page 168.) The usual landforms shown are *plains, plateaus, hills,* and *mountains;* each is represented by a different color. Difficulty in using these maps arises when the child mistakenly thinks of the colors as representing elevations in absolute amounts. For example, there are high mountains and low mountains, yet on a landform map they may appear in the same color. Some high plateaus are actually higher in absolute elevation than some low mountains. Some hills may be lower in elevation than plateaus and plains. Children need to learn that landform maps show only where the plains, plateaus, hills, and mountains are located, not how high they are above sea level.

APPLYING MAP AND GLOBE SKILLS

Map- and globe-reading skills are learned through direct teaching and by application in situations in which the skill is normally used. In many instances, these processes can be combined. Let us say, for example, that children in a fifth-grade class read that "Permafrost is a condition found only in high latitudes." The teacher can use this encounter with *high latitudes* to teach map reading in connection with that concept. That is, class time can be taken to teach the meaning of *high, low,* and *middle latitudes* on maps and globes, and the teaching would occur in what we refer to as a functional or authentic setting. Teachers are encouraged to teach as many map and globe skills as possible in this way rather than to isolate the skills from their relevant subject matter. After direct teaching there must be a generous application and use of the skills if proficiency is to be developed and maintained.

Because these skills are *developmental,* one cannot expect to teach them once and assume that they have been learned. Most skills are introduced early in the grades and then are retaught, reviewed, or expanded later on. We expect that children will show increased proficiency and maturity in using these skills each year they are in school. Such development comes through continued teaching and use, not automatically through the natural process of maturation.

Below are map and globe activities that can be used to stimulate interest and at the same time teach important concepts and thinking skills related to map and globe reading.

1. After an on-the-spot observation of the school grounds or the immediate vicinity, construct a three-dimensional floor map of the area.
2. Locate the places where stories about children in other lands take place or where news events are occurring.
3. Find pictures in magazines and the textbook that illustrate various landforms: plains, plateaus, hills, and mountains.
4. Make maps of the same area, such as the playground or local county, using different scales for each map.
5. Plan a pretend trip to a distant place. Locate the destination in relative and absolute terms. Have small groups each develop a different route, one group heading east, another going west, another south, another southeast, and so on.

MAKING A TRIP MAP

The teacher showed children color photographs of several states and discussed the many interesting things that can be seen and done in the various states. Children shared some of their own travel experiences. The teacher provided the class with road maps of several different states and asked them to find places that might interest someone visiting those states. These places of interest were discussed briefly. Children were then asked to think about and select a state they would enjoy visiting. Choices were to be made by the next day.

The following day the children made their selections of states they wanted to "visit." Using a road map of that state provided by the teacher and using references available in and outside the classroom, they were to plan a route of travel through the state of their choice, making at least five stops at places that would interest a visitor. They were to mark these places with a large dot and write a short narrative description to accompany the map telling about the travel route, state or national parks, natural areas of interest, historical landmarks, or other items of interest. If the children preferred, they could prepare a verbal rather than a written narrative by using the cassette recorder in the classroom.

The children responded to the teacher's encouragement to be creative in describing their imaginary trips, and several prepared travel brochures and recorded travelogs. They began a classroom exhibit of their trip maps and narratives, and in a week the room resembled a travel agency office. This generated a considerable amount of discussion and sharing of ideas and, of course, numerous opportunities to learn from and about maps. The children acquired a great deal of information about their country, applied important skills (reading, research, writing, discussion, speaking), and developed an appreciation for the diversity and variety of their own country.

In addition to print sources in the school library (atlases, almanacs, trade books on individual countries and continents, etc.) and in the textbook, students can search the Internet. A good beginning site is *http://www.city.net/*

6. Develop a classroom exhibit of maps found in current newspapers and periodicals. Place captions under each that describe its unique features, errors, and projection.

7. Secure an outdated political map of the world and have the class compare it with a current one.

8. Use board games such as *Take Off* and computer software such as *Where in the World Is Carmen Sandiego?* to build and reinforce map and globe skills.

9. Develop an illustrated glossary of geographic concepts and terms.

10. Hold a regular "Monday Morning Geography Bee" using those concepts and terms. Teacher-assigned teams rehearse and compete, vying to spell and define the terms correctly. Figure 5–9 contains more than 50 terms. The teacher can select terms the children are ready for, and children can work on the definitions, using the textbook, dictionary, and other references, as they compile the illustrated glossary in item 9.

FIGURE 5-9   The Monday morning geography bee.

Select easier or more difficult terms from this list as appropriate.

absolute location	forest	migration
artifacts	globe	monsoon
barrier island	groundwater	mountain range
bay	hemisphere	multinational organization
biosphere	hill	nonrenewable resource
cartographer	hurricane	plateau
climate	hydrosphere	pond
contour map	industrialization	population density
creek	infant mortality rate	rain shadow
culture	interdependence	region
deforestation	lake	relative location
desert	landform	river system
developing country	latitude	scale
ecology	legend (key)	settlement pattern
equator	longitude	sustainable development
ethnocentrism	map	terrace
fauna	map projection	urbanization
fertility rate	mesa	
flora	metropolis	

Regular social studies unit work and the current events program provide natural settings for teaching map and globe skills. Children can use maps to record their data or observations as they study unit topics. They can think through the significance of the relationships they detect in maps. They can use maps to communicate ideas and findings to their classmates. It has been said that maps are the constant companions of geographers, and the same might be said about children as they engage in the social studies.

Teaching map and globe skills does require some special resources and equipment. Every classroom should have a globe and wall maps appropriate to the curriculum content of the grade. In third grade and above, all classrooms should have a wall map of the world. Outline maps are needed, and it helps to have available a three-dimensional relief map of the United States and of the home state. A class set of globes should be available in the resource center, shared by all classrooms. Additional equipment might include individual student desk maps, charts showing conventional map symbols, and special-purpose maps showing vegetation, crops, and natural resources. When children engage in map making, they will need to have available essential construction materials: boxes, blocks, butcher paper, black tape, tracing paper, colored pencils, pens or crayons, paints and brushes, papier-mâché, plaster, salt and flour, or other modeling material.

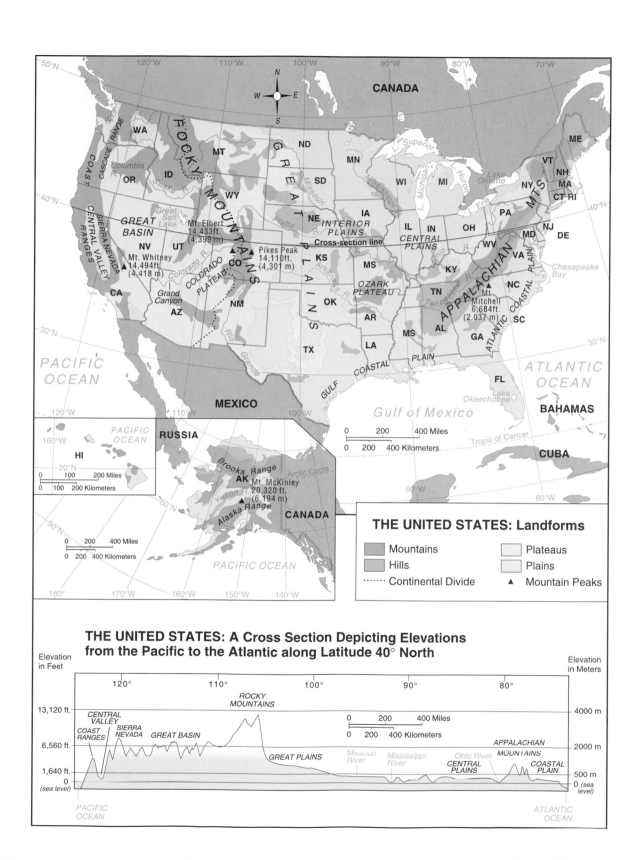

THE UNITED STATES: Landforms

Mountains
Hills
Continental Divide
Plateaus
Plains
▲ Mountain Peaks

THE UNITED STATES: A Cross Section Depicting Elevations from the Pacific to the Atlantic along Latitude 40° North

THE WORLD:
Political

ARCTIC OCEAN

160°W 140°W 120°W 100°W 80°W 60°W

80°N

GREENLAND
(Denmark)

ALASKA
(U.S.)

60°N

CANADA

NORTH

AMERICA

40°N

UNITED STATES

ATLANTIC

OCEAN

BERMUDA
(U.K.)

Area of inset

MIDWAY
IS. (U.S.)

Tropic of Cancer

HAWAII
(U.S.)

20°N

MEXICO

PACIFIC

GUYANA
SURINAME

VENEZUELA

OCEAN

FRENCH GUIANA
(Fr.)

COLOMBIA

Equator

0°

GALAPAGOS
ISLANDS
(Ecuador)

ECUADOR

TOKELAU
(N.Z.)

KIRIBATI

PERU

BRAZIL

SOUTH

W.
SAMOA

AMERICAN
SAMOA
(U.S.)

AMERICA

COOK
ISLANDS
(N.Z.)

FRENCH
POLYNESIA
(Fr.)

BOLIVIA

20°S

PARAGUAY

TONGA

NIUE
(N.Z.)

Tropic of Capricorn

CHILE

PITCAIRN
ISLANDS
(U.K.)

URUGUAY

ARGENTINA

40°S

FALKLAND
ISLANDS
(U.K.)

60°S

SOUTH
GEORGIA
(U.K.)

Antarctic Circle

80°S

ANTARCTICA

160°W 140°W 120°W 100°W 80°W 60°W

80°W

30°N

U.S.

Gulf of Mexico

60°W

BAHAMAS

ATLANTIC OCEAN

Tropic of Cancer

TURKS &
CAICOS ISLANDS
(U.K.)

CUBA

PUERTO
RICO
(U.S.)

ANGUILLA (U.K.)

20°N

ST. MARTIN (Fr./Neth.)

ANTIGUA &
BARBUDA

MEXICO

HAITI

DOMINICAN
REPUBLIC

BELIZE

CAYMAN
ISLANDS
(U.K.)

JAMAICA

MONTSERRAT (U.K.)

GUADELOUPE (Fr.)

VIRGIN ISLANDS
(U.S./U.K.)

ST. KITTS
& NEVIS

DOMINICA

GUATEMALA

HONDURAS

MARTINIQUE (Fr.)

ST. LUCIA

CARIBBEAN SEA

ST. VINCENT &
THE GRENADINES

BARBADOS

EL
SALVADOR

NICARAGUA

ARUBA
(Neth.)

CURAÇAO (Neth.)

GRENADA

BONAIRE (Neth.)

TRINIDAD
AND TOBAGO

10°N

COSTA RICA

PANAMA

VENEZUELA

COLOMBIA

GUYANA

90°W 80°W 70°W

0   200   400 Miles

0 200 400 Kilometers

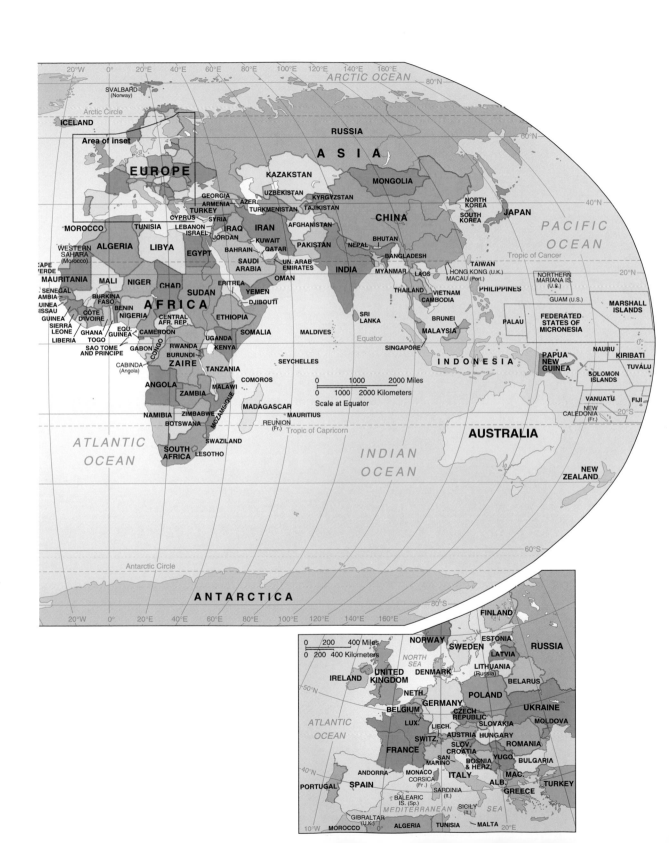

Dictionary of
GEOGRAPHIC TERMS

STRAIT (strāt) A narrow waterway that connects two larger bodies of water.

PLATEAU (pla tō´) An area of elevated flat land.

GULF (gulf) Part of an ocean that extends into the land; larger than a bay.

DAM (dam) A wall built across a river, creating a lake that stores water.

RESERVOIR (rez´ər vwär) A natural or artificial lake used to store water.

MESA (mā´sə) A hill with a flat top; smaller than a plateau.

CANYON (kan´yən) A deep, narrow valley with steep sides.

BUTTE (būt) A small, flat-topped hill; smaller than a mesa or plateau.

DUNE (dūn) A mound, hill, or ridge of sand heaped up by the wind.

HILL (hil) A rounded, raised landform; not as high as a mountain.

VALLEY (val´ē) An area of low land between hills or mountains.

DESERT (dez´ərt) A dry environment with few plants and animals.

COAST (cōst) The land along an ocean.

BAY (bā) Part of an ocean or lake that extends deeply into the land.

ISTHMUS (is´m əs) A narrow strip of land that connects two larger bodies of land.

PENINSULA (pə nin´sə lə) A body of land nearly surrounded by water.

ISLAND (ī´lənd) A body of land completely surrounded by water.

A SUMMARY OF MAP AND GLOBE SKILLS

Elementary and middle school children should develop map and globe skills associated with the following concepts and generalizations:

1. **Primary Grades**
   - A map is a drawing or other representation of all or part of the earth.
   - On maps and globes, symbols are used to stand for real things.
   - The earth is a huge sphere.
   - A globe is a small model of the earth and is the most accurate representation of the earth.
   - Half of the earth is called a hemisphere.
   - The earth can be divided into several hemispheres. The most common ones are the Eastern, Western, Northern, and Southern Hemispheres; land hemisphere and water hemisphere; and day hemisphere and night hemisphere.
   - Any part of the globe can be shown on a map.
   - Large bodies of land are called continents.
   - Large bodies of water are called oceans.
   - Terms such as *left, right, near, far, above, below, up,* and *down* can be useful in expressing relative location.
   - A legend or key on a map tells the meaning of colors and symbols used on the map.
   - Directions on a map are determined by the poles; to go north means to go in the direction of the North Pole, to go south means to go in the direction of the South Pole.
   - North may be shown any place on a map; north is *not* always at the top of a map.
   - The North Pole is the point farthest north on the earth; the South Pole is the point farthest south.
   - The scale on a map or globe makes it possible to determine distances between places.
   - Maps are drawn to different scales; scale ensures that all objects are made smaller in the same amount.
   - Maps and globes use legends, or keys, that tell the meaning of the symbols used on the map.
   - The cardinal directions are north, south, east, and west; intermediate directions are northeast, northwest, southeast, and southwest.
   - All places on the earth can be located on maps and globes. Different maps provide different information about the earth.

2. **Intermediate and Middle Grades**
   - The larger the scale used, the larger each feature appears on the map.
   - The same symbol may mean different things from one map to another; the legend tells what the symbols stand for.
   - The elevation of land is measured from sea level; some maps provide information about elevation.

- Physical maps can be used to determine land elevations, slopes of land, and directions of rivers.
- Parallels of latitude can be used to establish east-west direction and are also used to measure distances in degrees north and south of the equator.
- All places on the same east-west line (parallel of latitude) are directly east or west of one another and are the same distance north or south of the equator.
- All places north of the equator are in north latitudes; all places south of the equator are in south latitudes.
- The Tropic of Cancer and the Tropic of Capricorn are imaginary lines of latitude lying north and south of the equator. The part of the earth between them is known as the tropics.
- The Arctic and Antarctic Circles are imaginary lines that define the polar regions.
- The low latitudes lie on either side of the equator; the high latitudes surround the poles; and the middle latitudes lie between the low and high latitudes.
- Parallels of latitude, parallel to the equator, get shorter as they progress from the equator to the poles.
- Knowing the latitude of a place makes it possible to locate its north-south position on the earth.
- Meridians of longitude can be used to determine north-south direction and are also used to measure distances in degrees east and west of the prime meridian.
- The zero or *prime* meridian passes through Greenwich, a suburb of London.
- Meridians of longitude are imaginary north-south lines that converge on both poles.
- Meridians of longitude are *great circles* because they divide the earth into two hemispheres.
- The shortest distance between any two places on the earth follows a great circle.
- West longitude is measured to the west of the prime meridian from zero to 180°; east longitude is measured to the east of the prime meridian from zero to 180°.
- All places on the same north-south line (meridian of longitude) are directly north or south of each other and are the same distance in degrees east or west of the prime meridian.
- The latitude and longitude of any place determine its exact location on a globe or map.
- Longitude is used in determining the time of day at places around the world. The earth rotates through 15° of longitude every hour; the earth is divided into 24 time zones.
- Globes give such information as distance, direction, relative and exact location, and sizes and shapes of areas more accurately than flat maps can.
- Maps and globes often use abbreviations to identify places and things.
- An imaginary line through the center of the earth, running from pole to pole, is called the earth's axis; the earth rotates on its axis from west to east.
- Night and day are the result of the rotation of the earth.

- Maps and globes provide data about the nature of areas by using color contour, visual relief, and contour lines.
- All flat maps contain some distortion because they represent a round object on a flat surface.
- Different map projections provide different perspectives on the sizes and shapes of areas shown.

Teaching Graphs and Charts

Because of the widespread use of graphs and charts in social studies and in printed material outside of school, it is imperative that children develop the skills needed to read and interpret them.

GRAPHS

Graphs are used to illustrate relationships among quantities. These relationships may be spread over a period of time, thus showing trends. The most commonly used graphs are some variation of the *bar graph,* the *pie* or *circle graph,* and the *line graph.* Any of these graphs may include pictorial representations, thereby making them more interesting to young children and making the content less abstract. For instance, with primary grade children, stick figures can be used to represent children in a bar graph showing the number absent from class each day. It is easy to visualize the relationships of the parts to the whole in a circle graph, but to construct one accurately requires the ability to compute percentages, usually not possible in the elementary school grades. Modern elementary school textbooks make liberal use of graphs in presenting data, but children need to be instructed in how to read and interpret them. Because graphs can be designed to present distorted pictures of data, children in the intermediate and middle grades should be taught how bias can be introduced in a graph. (See Figures 5–10, 5–11, and 5–12.)

FIGURE 5–10

The drawing illustrates how the popular "pie" graph is sometimes used to create an incorrect impression. Because the sketch is shown in perspective, the sizes of the sections are distorted. Thus, sections that seem to be farthest from the viewer appear smaller than those in the foreground, although arithmetically they represent equal amounts.

FIGURE 5–11 It is important for children to learn that graphs can create false impressions. In these line graphs, the same data were used on three different grids, resulting in varying steepness in the slopes of the lines. Consequently, although the facts are the same, the rate of change appears markedly different.

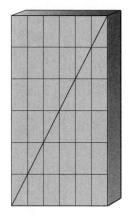

FIGURE 5–12

How much larger were profits in 2000 than in 1998? The chances are that you have said "about twice as large." This graph illustrates how wrong impressions can be conveyed. Careful examination of this graph will show that the 2000 profits are not even twice those of 1998. The basic error in this graph is that it does not show the first $500,000 of profit. A more accurate perception of the growth in profits can be made if the correct position of the baseline is established. Can you locate the place where the baseline should be?

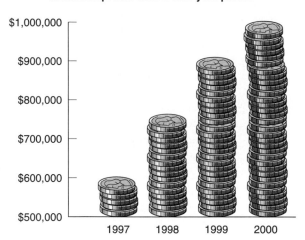

Growth in profits over a four-year period

Children can learn much about graphs and how to read them by constructing their own. Here, again, are the two wings of the pedagogical airplane introduced in the last chapter. Just as reading a history is one thing and writing one is another, reading graphs that others have made is one thing and making your own is quite another. Learner-made graphs should be encouraged as visual aids when students make oral written reports and for bulletin board displays. When the class takes a "class census" as suggested in Lesson Plan 1 (in Chapter 2), the information can be shown on a table. Then, after the additional classrooms have been surveyed, providing comparative information, a graph will help display the results. In making graphs, accuracy in the presentation should be emphasized rather than artistic perfection (see Figure 5–13).

CHARTS

Like graphs, charts are widely used to present ideas in a vivid and forceful way. *Data-retrieval charts*, as they are called by teachers, are widely used in social studies teaching, especially as aids to concept formation. They are employed throughout this text.

Note that data-retrieval charts are two-way charts, otherwise known as two-dimensional charts. Across the top are *focus questions* that guide students' examination of the *examples* that run down the left side. Here, again, in Figure 5–14, is a data-retrieval chart from the "Sociology" section in the prior chapter.

The advantage of this sort of chart is that it allows students and the teacher to keep track of and organize a large quantity of information across several examples. Without such a chart, the task of comparing and contrasting examples would be made difficult, perhaps too difficult for many students, and achievement would be sacrificed. Teachers who are able to get more learning from more students (note the two uses of *more*) rely on such techniques as this.

There are other kinds of charts. Charts are often designated as follows:

1. *Narrative Chart:* Tells a story; shows events in sequence. (*Examples:* how ears of corn become tortillas, stages of the development of civilization, how to use a computer, or the construction of homes.)
2. *Tabulation Chart:* Lists data in table form to facilitate making comparisons. (*Examples:* data placed in tabular form to show infant mortality rates, illiteracy rates, or per capita income among nations of the world.)
3. *Pedigree Chart:* Shows events stemming from a common origin. (*Examples:* a family tree, the development of a political party, or the history of language.)
4. *Classification Chart:* Groups data into various categories. (*Examples:* the various types of restaurants, types of personal services available, or different modes of transportation.)
5. *Organization Chart:* Shows the structure of an organization. (*Examples:* the three branches of government, the structure of a corporation, or the organization of a city government or a school district.)
6. *Flow Chart:* Shows a process involving change at certain points. (*Examples:* how raw materials are transformed into finished products or how scrap iron is converted into a usable raw material.)

The frequent use of charts in children's books provides a good basis for learning. In the process children not only learn how to read and interpret the chart, but also broaden their substantive knowledge and build their understanding of associated concepts.

FIGURE 5–13   Examples of graphs and data suitable for use with elementary school children.

Number of days the sun was shining at noon for the first five months

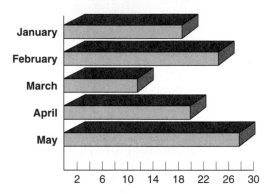

A class kept a record of the number of days the sun was shining at noon from the first of January through May. In January there were nineteen days when the sun was shining at noon; in February there were twenty–five; in March there were twelve; in April there were twenty; and in May there were twenty–eight days. These graphs show three different ways of showing these data. Graphs of this type can be constructed and used for study purposes by elementary schoolchildren. What inquiry questions might be based on these graphs?

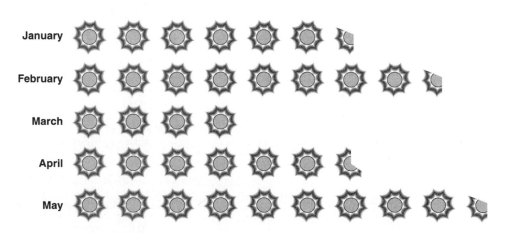

FIGURE 5–14 A data retrieval chart.

LIFE IN FAMILIES

	Where does this family live?	How many people are in family?	What things are learned in this group?	What does each member do?
#1: Family in suburban Chicago				
#2: Family in rural Ethiopia				
#3: Family in rural China				

Conclusion

The more one knows about the social studies curriculum, the more one realizes what an ideal place it is for the development of reading and writing skills and, hand-in-hand with them, higher-order thinking skills. Making sense of time and place requires all sorts of tools, both physical and intellectual. This chapter has presented and discussed many of them. From maps to globes, time lines to charts, the social studies curriculum teaches children a wide variety of ways to read and represent information and ideas.

Discussion Questions and Suggested Activities

1. Make a time line showing six events in your life. One event should be your birth, shown at the far left end; another should be the making of the time line today, shown at the far right. Select four other events, and place them between these two. Be sure to show the relative amount of time between the events as in Figure 5–1.

2. Secure a copy of the national geography standards, *Geography for Life,* and look in its glossary for definitions of the geographic terms given in Figure 5–9. Then, preview this excellent book and go online to where its author will introduce you to it and walk you through it. Go to *http://www.ncge.org/* then click on the tutorial.

3. Bring to class three wall maps of the world. These can be purchased for a few dollars at book stores or large drug stores or borrowed from the campus map collection. Try to get three different projections: Mercator, Robinson, and Peters. Help students compare and contrast their distortions of land and water. See the "snapshot" at the beginning of this chapter.

4. If you are teaching or have access to a class, try these activities.

   a. *Assessment.* Interview a class of children on the concepts *time* and *space.* Ask them for the meanings of such terms as *long ago, soon, century,* and *decade.* Then ask about *near, far, Southern Hemisphere,* and landforms such as *plateau, lake, bay,* and *mountain range.*

   b. *Proverbs.* Have the class think of as many popular expressions or proverbs as they can that have to do with time (e.g., "a stitch in time saves nine"; "time is money"). Conduct this activity for a period of days, and as phrases are suggested, place them on the bulletin board. Have children make drawings to illustrate them.

5. Make a chart or graph (your choice) to show how your time is spent during a school day.

Selected References

Carroll, Terry, C., Knight, Cheryl, & Hutchinson, Ed. (1998). Carmen Sandiego: Crime can pay when it comes to learning. In Joseph A. Braun Jr., Phyllis Fernlund, & Charles. S. White (Eds.). *Technology tools in the social studies curriculum* (pp. 77–86). Wilsonville, OR: Franklin, Beedle & Associates.

Carter, Roger. (1998). *Handbook of primary geography.* Indiana, PA: National Council for Geographic Education.

Hardwick, Susan W., & Holtgrieve, Donald G. (1996). *Geography for educators.* Upper Saddle River, NJ, Prentice-Hall.

Muir, Sharon Pray. (1985, Nov.). Understanding and improving students' map reading skills. *The Elementary School Journal, 86,* 207–216.

National Council for Geographic Education. (2000). *How to help children become geographically literate.* Indiana, PA: Author.

Sobel, David. (1998). *Mapmaking with children: Sense of place education for the elementary years.* Portsmouth, NH: Heinemann.

Notes

1. In *Technology tools in the social studies curriculum,* edited by Joseph A. Braun Jr., Phyllis Fernlund, & Charles S. White. (Wilsonville, OR, Franklin, Beedle & Associates, 1998), 93.

2. National Council for the Social Studies, *Social studies curriculum planning resources* (Dubuque, IA: Kendall/Hunt, 1991), 36.

3. For a helpful review of *Carmen Sandiego,* see the chapter by Terry Carroll et al. listed in "Selected References."

4. From Letters to the Editor. *Sunburst 24* (May 1999): 5.

Websites

http://www.nationalgeographic.com/maps/political.html
http://www.city.net
http://www.ncge.org

CHAPTER 6

Current Events and Public Issues

Main Idea

A program of teaching and learning about current events and public issues is required in each classroom, each year. Such a program will help rouse the children's civic dispositions and develop the knowledge needed to hold "the office of citizen."

Key Concepts

Current events, public issues, controversy

Chapter Outline

- Building a Current Events Program
- Four Strategies for Teaching Current Events
  - Daily Discussion of News
  - Decision Making on Controversial Issues
  - Teaching About Kinds of Controversy
  - Writing About Issues
- Teaching Enduring Public Issues
  - Poverty
  - Human-Environment Interaction
  - Crime and the Rule of Law
  - Peace and Understanding
  - Diversity and Prejudice
- Conclusion
- Discussion Questions and Suggested Activities
- Selected References
- Notes

Chapter Snapshot

The local television news and daily newspapers were dominated by the whale capture story, and Mr. Bower's students were upset. He asked them, "What do you want to do?" Their responses indicated that they didn't understand the matter well enough to choose an action. He suggested that they study it daily, using the same five-part decision-making process they used earlier in the year on another controversy. They began by identifying the facts of the case and then the issues of the case. Finally, they selected one of the issues for decision making, role playing, and action.

 A favorite website http://www.cnn.com Your local newspaper's website usually is the better option for local news and opinion, but this Cable News Network site has lots of information. Click on "local" for links to your local CNN television affiliates. (See also, *Scholastic News* Online: *http://www.scholastic.com/scholasticnews/index.htm.*)

A 10-year-old named Michael wondered what to do with his life. Seeking advice, he wrote to Buckminster Fuller, the philosopher, map maker, architect, poet, and inventor of the geodesic dome. "Bucky's" response was direct:

> Thank you very much for your recent letter. The things to do are the things that need doing; that *you* see need to be done, and that no one else sees need to be done.[1]

Bucky then tells Michael that doing what *he* sees needs to be done will naturally bring out his own, unique brilliance. He encourages Michael, closing the letter with this:

> You have what is most important in life—initiative. Because of it, you wrote to me. I am answering to the best of my capability. You will find the world responding to your earnest initiative.

The point of view in this chapter is that a program of teaching current events and social problems is a *must* in elementary and middle school classrooms. Such a program must be planned carefully and taught well. Without it, children are not likely to form citizenship dispositions that are critically important to the health of their communities, such as civic-mindedness and initiative. Without it, they may not have adequate opportunities to see the things that need doing, to respond, and, in turn, to develop their own talents.

Included in this chapter are strategies and activities for teaching children about current events. We also address a sampling of the enduring social problems—"public issues"—that make so many current events controversial: poverty, environmental degradation, crime, war and peace, and prejudice. When made appropriate to the ages and experiences of children and linked to social studies education, these events and issues can and should be taught in the elementary school. Readers concerned that young children are too young for current events and social problems need only look back to Chapter 3, where Mrs. Paley leads a year-long deliberation with her kindergartners on the public issue, *Should we have a rule that says you can't tell someone else that he or she can't play with you?*

PURPOSES

The first major purpose of current events/public issues teaching at the elementary school level is *to promote the habit of interest in current events and social problems.* This is no small undertaking. A market-driven, individualistic, affluent society encourages children to think of themselves and their families sometimes to the exclusion of minding the public square. This, recall, is what the ancient Greeks called "idiocy." Civic-mindedness is a virtue that must be cultivated, and one way elementary and middle school teachers can do that is by developing a regular, ongoing program of instruction involving daily news and issues.

Rational analysis of current events requires the use of a variety of skills and abilities:

1. To read and view news materials,
2. To discriminate between important and less significant news items,
3. To take a position on issues based on knowledge and critical evaluation of the facts, and
4. To predict likely consequences in terms of present developments.

Promoting the growth of these skills is the second major purpose of current events instruction at the elementary school level. These skills evolve over several years through the study of current events under the direction and guidance of capable teachers. It is unrealistic to hope for an adult population that can exercise critical judgment regarding social problems and issues unless individuals have at their command the fundamental abilities such action demands.

The third major purpose of current events teaching is *to help the child relate school learning to life outside school.* The constant reference to current events is good insurance against the separation of school activities from the nonacademic life of the child. Good teachers recognize that printed material begins to become obsolete shortly after it is written, and there is always a gap between the information contained in books and changing developments in the world. A generous use of current events materials helps to close this gap. Recognizing the need for timely information, some encyclopedia publishers issue annual supplements that include changes that have occurred during the preceding year. Because textbooks and supplementary books usually are not revised each year, teachers must depend on such sources as newspapers and magazines for the latest information on some topics.

Building a Current Events Program

The three most common methods of including current events in the elementary school program are (1) teaching current events in addition to social studies, (2) using current events to supplement or reinforce the regular social studies program, and (3) using current events as the basis for social studies units.

TEACHING CURRENT EVENTS IN ADDITION TO SOCIAL STUDIES

Ms. Hansen, who teaches fourth grade, plans to spend a few minutes each morning during the sharing period for the discussion of important news stories. She encourages children to bring news clippings from daily newspapers or from weekly magazines for the class bulletin board. Children are encouraged to bring news stories related to classroom work, and Ms. Hansen helps interpret these stories for the children by her comments and leading questions, such as

> "Do you suppose the new highway will help our town?"
> "What are the astronauts looking for on these expeditions?"
> "Why do you suppose the animals died when they were brought here?"
> "Can you show the class on the map the exact location of the explosion?"

Ms. Hansen uses a classroom news periodical and plans to spend one hour on it with the children each week. This consists of reading the material or portions of it, followed by a discussion. She varies the procedure from week to week and uses the suggestions provided in the teacher's edition that accompanies the periodical. (*Scholastic News* is a newsweekly for grades 1–6. For a sample issue, call 800-631-1586 or go online to *http://www.scholastic.com/ scholasticnews/index.htm.*)

This method has the advantage of providing a regularly scheduled time for news each day and for the classroom periodical each week. Such periods can be useful in building interest in current events and in teaching skills of reading and interpreting news stories. It has the disadvantage of isolating current affairs from the remainder of the school program, most especially from the social studies.

USING CURRENT EVENTS TO SUPPLEMENT SOCIAL STUDIES

Mr. Chung schedules his social studies period immediately following morning opening activities for his fifth-grade class. As a part of the opening activities, he gives students time to share news items. He often suggests parallels or analogies between events that happened long ago and events that they bring up during this time, thereby illustrating recurrent problems in the conduct of human affairs. For example, one student reported on a civil war in an African nation, and Mr. Chung asked whether that civil war was similar to our own in this country in the middle of the 19th century. Another student read aloud a news story on a terrorist incident at a military base abroad. He reminded them of the Boston Tea Party and asked if there was any connection between the two incidents. When the class was studying early European exploration, Mr. Chung related this study to present-day exploration in space. In addition to drawing these historical parallels, Mr. Chung brings to class news stories that he reads to students and interprets within the context of the topic under study. He seizes upon these stories as an entry point for applying social studies skills, such as map, graph, or chart reading. Because he integrates language arts and social studies instruction, he makes frequent use of editorials and news stories as writing samples.

The difference between this method and the one used by Ms. Hansen is that Mr. Chung is more explicit in making the connection between current events and social studies/language arts curriculum. He is concerned mainly with news stories that can support this curriculum. This method has the advantage of motivating greater student interest in the curriculum and displaying the relevance of the curriculum for understanding the current world scene. It has the disadvantage of restricting the range of news stories that are appropriate. Therefore, if this approach is used, the teacher should provide some opportunity to examine news items that are significant and timely, yet may not directly relate to the social studies unit under study at the time.

USING CURRENT EVENTS AS THE BASIS FOR SOCIAL STUDIES UNITS

Ms. Diaz likes to develop social studies units with her sixth-grade class around topics that are currently in the news. She schedules these between the regular units she is required to teach. During her years as a teacher, she has found that units of this type must be carefully selected because it is not always possible to find enough instructional material suitable for children that deals with topics in the news. Units that she has taught successfully in this way have dealt with gun control legislation, gangs, terrorism, contemporary explorers, new developments in science, current elections, and world organizations, such as the United Nations. When Ms. Diaz selects the unit topics carefully, she finds it possible to include much of the subject matter ordinarily included in her social studies curriculum under other unit titles. She believes that the use of current news happenings as a starting point for units does much to stimulate interest and discussion in her class.

Lesson Plan 7 ("The Nation Behind the Current Event") illustrates this third approach. An intriguing current event happening in another country is used as the springboard into learning the history and geography of that country. This method has the advantage of being highly motivating because it deals with subject matter that is of immediate interest. It also bridges school learning with life outside of school. It has the disadvantage of being difficult to plan because news events may not relate directly to the social studies curriculum. Also, news stories do not provide sufficient information on topics; therefore, other resources must be gathered.

Any of the three current events programs described here can be used successfully. Good programs devote time during the school day to study and discussion of current affairs that may be entirely unrelated to topics under study in the social studies units, and perhaps unrelated to any other curricular area as well. At the same time, in guiding unit work, the teacher will seek with enthusiasm the current events materials that will add strength and excitement to the unit. From time to time, too, the teacher and children can plan an entire social studies unit from current news developments. Units dealing with the concepts of energy, poverty, environment, safety, warfare, ethnicity, law and justice, housing, food production and distribution, elections, and discoveries frequently grow out of current events. When the social studies program includes these three methods, the teacher and class will use any or all of the procedures described in the following sections.

Four Strategies for Teaching Current Events

STRATEGY 1: DAILY DISCUSSION OF NEWS

Children enjoy discussing the news and should be given the opportunity to do so within the school program. It is fairly common for classes to have a morning meeting or sharing period at the beginning of each school day, during which time students can report news items. Children in the primary grades frequently report only news that affects them directly: Mom took a business trip, the family has a new baby, the pet cat had kittens, or other similar items of "news." As children mature, they move away from news items of concern only to them personally to news of more general interest.

In reporting, discussing, and analyzing daily news occurrences, elementary school children frequently report the sensational headline news that may or may not be particularly significant. Without guidance, children are likely to report murders or robberies or hold postmortems on the previous night's television programs. The teacher should help children evaluate the importance of news stories and teach them to discriminate between significant news and the sensational.

Lesson Plan 7 # THE NATION BEHIND THE CURRENT EVENT

Grade	6 or 7
Time	Seven class periods
Objectives	Students will learn about the country behind the current event—its geography (people, places, climate, landforms, resources), history (major turning points and pivotal people), government, and social life (religion, music and dance, family life, education, holidays and festivals). Also, they will refine their research and cooperation skills and learn to present a group oral report.
Interest Building	Seize upon students' interest in a current event that is happening in another nation. They may be interested in a famine that is reported on the evening news, a foreign policy crisis for the United States, a civil war somewhere, a natural disaster, or a terrorist incident. Use the daily newspaper to enlarge their understanding of the event (including news articles, editorials, cartoons, and letters to the editor). Use the five-step procedure presented in this chapter for helping students make a decision on what should be done about the event (e.g., should the United States send money? troops?). Hold a debate. Invite a guest speaker.
Lesson Development	Tell students that they need to understand the country behind the event—that any current event needs to be placed in its historical and geographical setting.
	Brainstorm a list of topics that would be suitable for small-group information-gathering projects. Have a student list the topics on butcher paper (see Sample Chart).
	Divide the class into teams of five students each. Teams meet and elect a leader; discuss, agree on, and sign up for a topic.
	Help students divide their topics into subtopics. Each team member is responsible for one subtopic, except for the chair who helps each team member search for information.
	Tell students they will have five class periods to gather information and two class periods to plan a team presentation. One team will present each day after lunch until all teams have presented. Give each student a copy of the assessment form and clarify (see Sample Assessment form).
	Review the procedure for taking notes and for properly citing the resources from which information was taken. Assign report dates.
	Monitor and guide the teams during the research days and the planning days.
Summary	Groups give their oral reports with each member contributing to the presentation. They field questions and comments from the audience.
Materials	• Text: *World Regions*
	• Reference books: almanacs, atlases, encyclopedias
	• Recordings: speeches, television specials
	• Internet: *www.nationalgeographic.com* (plus search the Web using the country and city names)
	• Trade books will depend on the country selected. For China, recommended books include *China, Here We Come!* (Tang Yungmei), *The Red Scarf Girl* (Ji-Li Jiang), *China's Long March: 6000 Miles of Danger* (Jean Fritz), *Two Chinese Families* (Catherine Edwards Sadler), *Red Star & Green Dragon: Looking at New China* (Lila Perl), *The People's Republic of China: Red Star of the East* (Jane Werner Watson).
Integration	*Literature:* Help students find biographies about political leaders, scientists, artists, and inventors from the nation under study, as well as the literature suggested in the "Materials" section.
	The arts: If students don't themselves suggest dance, film, and fine arts, show slides or videos that will stimulate interest in these things.

Sample Chart: A Nation in the News

Topics	Names of Group Members	Report Date
Family Life: Male/female roles, houses, urban/rural diversity, parents' work, children's schooling		
Geography: Land and water forms, climate, natural resources, major cities, transportation		
History: Turning points, key people, technological developments, economic development, invasions and wars		
Culture: Holidays and festivals, customs, religions, clothing, music and dance		
Government: Laws, elections, courts, leaders, participation by average citizens		

Sample Assessment: Nation in the News

	Exemplary	Adequate	Minimal	Missing
An introduction was given.				
Main ideas were clear.				
A conclusion was given.				
Visual aids were used.				
Teamwork was evident.				

Use of Daily Newspapers

Some teachers in the intermediate and middle grades find a daily newspaper helpful in promoting the goals of current events instruction. In units dealing with aspects of communication, the newspaper is an important learning resource. Students will profit from classroom instruction on the use of the newspaper that focuses on items such as these:

1. The organization of newspapers, purposes of various sections, where to look for certain kinds of information.
2. The nature of news stories, why some appear on the front page and others elsewhere.
3. The purpose and use of headlines.
4. Newspaper illustrations such as wire photos, maps, charts, graphs, and cartoons.
5. The editorial page and its function.
6. Detecting bias in news stories.
7. How to read a newspaper.

From time to time the teacher can devise practice exercises such as those described in this chapter to help students develop their skills in using a daily newspaper.

Many teachers have found the Newspaper In Education (NIE) program sponsored by the Newspaper Association of America (NAA) to be a useful resource in teaching current events and, more specifically, in using the newspaper. For information about the NIE program and the several materials available through it, contact your local newspaper or go to the website at *http://www.naa.org/foundation/nie.html*. The NIE program provides many teaching and learning resources. We especially like *The Newspaper as an Effective Teaching Tool*.

Use of Political Cartoons

Cartoons are an accepted form of social commentary. Responding to the cartoon's dramatic visual format, the reader projects meaning into the visual by virtue of his or her own experience (Figure 6.1). Cartoons are often humorous because they exaggerate, subjects are presented in caricature, and the cartoons are designed to show all the vices or virtues associated with a particular character in our culture. Cartoons are especially effective in calling attention to the ironies that surround our lives. They use humor to make a serious point.

Editorial cartoons are not necessarily humorous. Indeed, they are often biting in their comment on social issues. The techniques of symbolism, the use of familiar situations, exaggerations, satire, and caricature are used to present forcefully a single point of view. Political cartoons usually deal more with irony, hypocrisy, and cynicism than they do with humor. Such cartoons do not allow readers or the person portrayed in it an opportunity for rebuttal. Recognition of the fact that only one point of view is represented in cartoons is important in their interpretation. Older children need to be taught the general makeup of cartoons that deal with social and political problems and need the experience of evaluating their message critically. It is good for the children to present an opposite point of view from the one depicted in the cartoon.

FIGURE 6–1   This cartoon illustrates how much the reader must bring to such visuals if they are to have meaning. Ordinarily, we do not get new information from editorial cartoons. The artist relies on what we already know and provides a visual that places that information in a setting that conveys a powerful social, economic, and/or political message. (Reprinted with special permission of North America Syndicate.)

Controversy

There can be no doubt that the social studies teacher has a responsibility to include controversial issues in the current events and social studies curriculum. In so doing, the teacher has a strong ally in the National Council for the Social Studies. According to an NCSS policy statement on the subject, it is the prime responsibility of the schools to help students assume the responsibilities of democratic citizenship. To do this, education must impart the skills needed for intelligent study and orderly resolution of the problems inherent in a democratic society. Students need to study issues on which there is disagreement and to practice analyzing problems, gathering and organizing facts, discriminating between facts and opinions, discussing differing viewpoints, and drawing tentative conclusions. *It is the clear obligation of schools to promote full and free contemplation of controversial issues and to foster appreciation of the role of controversy as an instrument of progress in a democracy.*

When teaching a controversial issue, the teacher has a special responsibility to help children develop the disposition to be civil and open-minded, to evaluate sources of information, and to pursue multiple perspectives on a single issue. Young children are impressionable, and the habit of insisting on hearing all sides of an issue before taking a stand can be taught to youngsters by the teacher's example. If the class requests the teacher's own views on an issue, it is clearly the teacher's right to express them and to state the reasons for the position taken. The professional obligation remains, however, not to attempt to impose a personal point of view on the children on issues that are unsettled and on which there may be honest differences of opinion among well-informed persons. Instead, the teacher should encourage children to discuss the matter with other adults whom they respect whose views may be different. The child thus learns that there are honest differences of opinion among reasonable persons who consider problems in good faith. The children will respect the teacher who is willing to take a stand on issues, who gives reasons for the position taken, who insists that other positions be heard as well, and who accepts and honors different points of view.

STRATEGY 2: DECISION MAKING ON CONTROVERSIAL ISSUES

Daily discussion of the news is bound to expose students to controversial issues of all kinds. The news story found in Figure 6–2 is a good example of the types of controversial issues that can be found in nearly all communities, large and small. It is a *current event* because it is happening now. But it also involves *enduring public issues*—in this case, protecting the natural environment and deciding how best to navigate the perennial value conflict between individual liberty and the common good. Enduring public issues, also called *social concerns* or *social issues,* are what turn a current event into a controversial issue. By controversial, we mean that reasonable people will disagree over what needs to be done.

Not all current events are controversial. Many current happenings around the school and the community arouse little disagreement and debate: The school halls are swept nightly, the town garbage is picked up once each week, children go to school during the day, rice is eaten in many homes each evening, schools are closed for the summer, children are not allowed to run for the state legislature. Perhaps no one makes an *issue* of these humdrum events of daily life. Until someone does, they are not controversial issues. Once someone does, however, and someone else disagrees, then we have a controversial issue.

One of the best ways to teach current events is to select those that are controversial. In addition to the whale capture in Figure 6–2, here are several other current events that involve controversy:

- Establish city-wide curfew for persons under 18 years of age.
- Test athletes for illicit drug use.
- Choose new equipment for the playground.
- Allow animals to be used for medical research.
- A new orchestra hall (or sports stadium or jail) should be built.
- Remove a park for a shopping center.
- Remove a tree for a sidewalk.

FIGURE 6-2   A sample controversial issue in the newspaper.

Whale Capture Creates Wail

Seattle – Six killer whales are being held inside the Aqua Life, Inc. nets at Cook Inlet while Bill Holberg decides which ones, if any, will be kept for aquarium exhibits. Hundreds of people watched the capture from boats and shore yesterday afternoon.

The huge mammals swam slowly round and round inside two purse seine nets today, surfacing to "blow" for only moments. They stayed under for five minutes at a time.

GOVERNOR RECONSIDERING

Meanwhile, a political storm was gathering over the capture operation. The governor today interrupted her skiing vacation long enough to say that she was "reconsidering" the state's position on making the inlet a sanctuary for killer whales. The state's senior senator in Washington said that a declaration of support from the governor for a whale sanctuary would clear the way for protection of the sea animals. The senator also said, "Apparently this man [Holberg] had a valid permit. But there aren't going to be any more. This is the end!"

DEPTH CHARGES USED

Raul Santana, an assistant to the State Game and Fisheries director, watched the capture from about 50 feet away. Santana said Aqua Life, Inc. boats used "sonar, radar, and 'depth' charges" to drive the whales into smaller and smaller coves and finally into the nets. He said he watched three men in power boats racing across the water atop the whale school, "dropping 'depth charges' as fast as they could light them. I've never seen anything so disgusting in all my life," he said today. "This ought to be stopped right now."

A federal enforcement officer who supervised yesterday's operation said, "there is nothing in the permit that prohibits the use of such explosives."

USE OF CHARGES DENIED

Many citizens complained about the capture operation. An automobile dealer from South Harbor said he saw an airplane dropping "tomato can"-size cannisters that apparently exploded as the plane herded the whales. Sheila Moss, veterinarian for Aqua Life, Inc. said no such charges were used. She said the whale chasers used "firecracker"-type explosives thrown from boats to herd the whales. Holberg himself was aboard the Aqua Life, Inc. boat, KANDU, and was unavailable for comment.

COURT ACTION THREATENED

Environmentalists and others bitterly opposed the capture of the whales. Fred Russell, president of the state's largest environmental protection group, PROTEX, demanded that the whales be released. He said his group was prepared to take the matter to court if necessary to prevent Aqua Life, Inc. from keeping the creatures. "This is an outrage," he said, "and we are not going to sit by and let it happen."

Russell cited a Canadian biologist who found that only 65 killer whales remain in the Straits of Georgia and Juan de Fuca and Puget Sound. Earlier data had placed the number of whales at about 300.

OVERLAPPING JURISDICTION

The power to create a whale sanctuary rests with the federal government, but federal law says the governor of a state that contains the sanctuary may veto its creation. This overlapping jurisdiction sometimes creates confusion or results in no action being taken.

Until today, federal officials thought the governor opposed creation of a killer whale sanctuary in this area. The governor's staff said that no record could be found of the governor's ever having opposed such a proposal.

- Place metal detectors at school entrances.
- Serve only low-fat foods in the school cafeteria.
- Make gang membership illegal.
- Cut off public assistance to teenage parents.
- Cut off public assistance to large corporations.
- Ban sports utility vehicles from city parking lots.
- Permit freeway construction through a residential area.
- Require public school students to wear uniforms.
- Permit organized prayer in schools.
- Pass a dog leash ordinance.
- Ban cigarette machines throughout the city.
- Allow needle exchanges as an AIDS prevention measure.
- Close public swimming pools to save water for farmers.

These current events present good opportunities for teaching children how to deal constructively with controversy. We recommend the following decision-making procedure, which is based on the decision-making model presented in Chapter 3, "Citizenship Education and Democratic Values." Using a decision-making framework, teaching current events and social concerns serves a citizenship purpose: educating "we the people" to participate intelligently and constructively in community decision making. The procedure has five parts: (1) learning the facts of the matter, (2) identifying the controversial issues, (3) deliberating on one of the issues, (4) dramatizing the issue, and (5) sharing (publishing) the decision and reasons.

1. Have the children identify the *facts* of the case. In an examination of the captured whales news story in Figure 6–2, some of the facts are these:
    - Six killer whales were captured
    - The governor said she was reconsidering the state's policy
    - Raul Santana said he saw three men dropping depth charges
    - Sheila Moss said they used firecracker-type explosives
    - The state and federal governments both have jurisdiction over whale sanctuaries.

    When identifying the facts, it is important not to confuse them with opinions. Though the distinction is often fuzzy, children can develop a working understanding of the difference between facts and opinions. In the whale story, one would need further documentation that the explosives were of the firecracker type and that they were thrown from the hunters' boats, not dropped from an airplane.

2. Have students identify the *issues* in the case. Help them to identify a broad range of issues. Usually, issues involve conflicting values. In the whale case, the following are some of the issues. Notice that issues are stated as questions. People disagree on how to *answer* these questions, and this is why they are called controversial issues.
    - Should the capture of wild animals for uses in aquariums, zoos, and circuses be permitted? If so, to what extent, and why?

- Should animal hunters be allowed to use explosives?
- Was Holberg's permit "valid"?
- Should the captured whales be freed?
- Should governments, state or federal, protect wildlife? Or does this violate the constitutional principle of limited government?

3. *Select one of the issues* with the students. Make it an issue that requires a decision that the children can deliberate in the following way (see Chapter 3):

a. Identify a range of *alternatives*.

b. Predict the *consequences* for each alternative

c. *Discuss* which is the best alternative.

There is no need to rush toward a decision: The process of identifying alternatives and consequences, discussing them, and learning more about the issue is the primary objective here. Indeed, *slowing* the children's inclination to "jump to a conclusion" (a decision about what the community should do) is precisely what is needed here. As discussed in Chapter 3, we want them to grow in their ability and disposition to be thoughtful and reflective citizens, not reckless, uncivil, or ill-informed.

a. *Identify alternatives.* Let us assume that a group of children selects the fourth issue, should the captured whales be freed? Using a decision tree (Figure 3–4), the children can then be helped to identify alternatives. One group suggested these:

- Free the whales immediately and arrest Holberg.
- Free the whales immediately and pay Holberg for them with public tax money.
- Make courts decide if Holberg was acting lawfully.

b. *Predict consequences.* After identifying alternatives, the teacher helps the children predict consequences for each. The following consequences might be suggested:

- Holberg takes "we the people" to court, claiming that he was acting lawfully.
- The whales return to open sea and live happily ever after.
- Zoos across America close down because no one will collect zoo animals after reading what happened to Holberg.

c. *Deliberation.* After completing a decision tree on the issue, the teacher leads a discussion resulting in a decision about what should be done. The teacher might push students in the direction of a consensus, though this really is not necessary. The children may "agree to disagree" on the issue. (See Chapter 3 for suggestions on conducting discussions with children.) Roundtable discussions and panel discussions can be arranged in addition to whole-group discussions.

4. Issues such as this lend themselves well to *role playing* and *dramatic play.* Children can play the roles of Holberg, the governor, the senator, Santana, the federal enforcement officer, the automobile dealer, Moss, and Russell. Doing this helps make the event and the issues more concrete for children. Additional questions will be raised (this is inevitable), and the information can be secured by the students from the point of view of the role they are playing. Children can gather this additional data from the community by interviewing individuals and reading local news stories.

5. *Publish.* Something must be done with the students' deliberation on the issue. A report can be written for the classroom newsletter, of course, and a copy sent to the relevant government office. An accompanying "note from the teacher" should tell the audience that the main objective of this work is to help students learn a key democratic skill: taking and defending a position on an issue. Other objectives may involve the writing process, such as these "Follow-Up Activities" and "Strategy 4: Writing About Issues" on p. 194.

FOLLOW-UP ACTIVITIES

This decision-making strategy should not be limited to the use of newspaper articles. It is equally useful when the current event is a classroom or playground incident on which a decision is needed. It is also useful when children are considering the adoption of a new rule, such as Mrs. Paley's "you can't say 'you can't play'" rule (see Chapter 3).

A decision-making procedure used to examine a current event can generate a great deal of student interest. The teacher may wish to channel this enthusiasm into follow-up activities. These learning activities need to be related to the same event, yet they should expand the learning outward to incorporate additional ideas and skills. Several categories of follow-up activities are widely applicable. Below we exemplify each category with reference to the whale capture event.

> *Biography.* Study the lives of individuals who have dedicated themselves to the preservation of wildlife and other aspects of the natural environment: Rachel Carson, Jack Miner, John Muir, and local environmentalists. Then write a brief biography of this person.
>
> *Organizations.* Find out about the purposes and activities of organizations concerned about protecting the environment such as the Sierra Club, the National Wildlife Federation, the Environmental Protection Agency, and Greenpeace. Then write a comparison of these organizations.
>
> *Government/Jurisdiction.* Study the authority of federal, state, local, and voluntary associations in relation to the current event. For example, the whale capture event should lead students to local and state regulations concerning wildlife, conservation, and hunting. Then write a report, "Who's in Charge of What?"
>
> *Community Service/Action.* Use the event to build interest in developing a community service or action project, in this case dealing with ecology or conservation.

STRATEGY 3: TEACHING ABOUT KINDS OF CONTROVERSY

Discussions of controversial issues foster healthy disagreements, which in turn foster more discussion, more higher-order thinking, and more effort to apply what one knows. Consequently, disagreements should not be discouraged; rather, students should be prepared to take advantage of them—to learn more about the topic and one another and to practice reaching a consensus. An extremely helpful way to teach intermediate- and middle-grade students to learn from disagreements is to teach them occasionally to stop for a moment in the middle of a disagreement and to reflect on the *kind* of disagreement they are having. Doing so creates some cool distance from the disagreement, provides an opportunity to analyze the issue at hand, and to suggest what is to be done. The three most common kinds of disagreements, together with suggested methods for dealing with them, follow.

Factual Controversies

These disagreements over the facts of the case are sometimes called *informational disagreements* or *disagreements over the data.* Children may disagree about what Holberg was planning to do with the whales, whether depth charges were actually used, and so on.

Methods. To help children deal with factual disagreements, they can be taught to (1) reread the source of information, searching for relevant facts; (2) go to a reference resource, such as an almanac or encyclopedia; and (3) ask a credible authority for a judgment (e.g., ask the teacher, call the journalist who covered the story, or ask the librarian).

Definitional Controversies

These are disagreements over the meaning of a term. Even these can be quite heated. Children might disagree about whether Holberg was a "hunter," for example. Some children will argue that animal hunters kill whales for food or sport, whereas Holberg was searching for whales in order to sell them to an aquarium. When discussing homelessness, water pollution, welfare, crime, and other social problems, children will disagree over basic terms.

Methods. To help children deal with definitional disputes, they can be taught to (1) get a dictionary, (2) agree to accept the dictionary definition, or (3) tentatively agree to define the term in a particular way. Called *stipulation,* this last method is used in everyday situations when someone suggests, "let's say that (*a term*) means (*a definition*)," and the others involved in the conversation agree.

Value Controversies

These are disagreements about what is most important, right, best, or worthwhile. Typically, value conflicts arise as children (and adults) are trying to decide the question, what *should* the community do? In the captured whales example, value disagreements will arise as children discuss which alternative course of action is best.

Methods. To help children deal constructively with value disagreements, they can be taught to (1) clarify the values at stake, which involves asking one another questions such as "What do you mean?" and "What is important to you in this issue?" (2) Children also can be taught to give reasons for arguing that one alternative is more valuable than another. (3) "Agreeing to disagree" means the children realize there is a disagreement and it has not yet been settled. Nevertheless, everyone involved will continue to be friendly and civil toward one another. Citizens in a community or nation often disagree and must not become hateful or ill-mannered toward those with whom they disagree.[2]

STRATEGY 4: WRITING ABOUT ISSUES

Controversial issues present many authentic opportunities to improve children's writing. Writing letters to the editor of the classroom, school, or community newspaper is one good way to work with children on brief, persuasive writing. Another way is to send to local and national officials (the mayor, the school principal, a senator) an analysis of an issue and a suggested course of action. Letters can be sent conventionally or by electronic mail.

Perhaps our favorite writing technique for helping children think more deeply and creatively about current events and social problems is called the *dialogical essay.* As the name implies, the writer creates a dialogue about the choices that need to be made. This dialogue occurs inside the writer's mind, but only after the student has explored the issue orally with the class using the decision-making strategy above. Writing in this way helps the child sort out the opposing arguments on a controversial issue. This is far better than merely giving one's own opinion again and again, for it encourages students to examine the multiple perspectives on the issue.

One short-essay format has been found especially effective for this purpose.[3] Most children in the intermediate grades will have the necessary writing skills to compose such an essay, but clear directions are needed. The essay format, with directions, follows:

- *Paragraph 1.* Tell your reader that you are going to write an essay on this issue. Then tell your reader your position on the issue. Do not give any reasons yet.
- *Paragraph 2.* Give your reasons for your position. In other words, give good arguments that support your position.
- *Paragraph 3.* Give good reasons *against* your position. In other words, give good arguments that support the opposing position on the issue.
- *Paragraph 4.* Come to a conclusion. Now that you have thought about the reasons for and against your position, what is your position?

Other Activities

Many learning activities can be used profitably with the study of current events.

Internet. Your local newspapers and television stations most likely have Internet home pages. The newspapers typically provide news updates online plus (and this is very important to the students' study) online editorials, and letters to the editor. The students must search for these opinions if they are to grasp the multiple perspectives that attend a current event or issue. National news sites are operated by both CNN (*http://www.cnn.com*) and the company that produces the weekly current-events news magazine for grades 1–6, *Scholastic News* (*http://www.scholastic.com*).

Television. If a television monitor is available to the classroom, have the class watch one of the news summaries aired at the top of each hour. Keep track of CNN's coverage of an event that the children also are following in the daily newspaper or a weekly news magazine. Have the children compare the two and then hypothesize the causes of the different coverage. Keep a news bulletin board of this event. If CNN is not available, another television news source will do. (*Note:* This comparative approach is especially effective for dealing with a breaking news story or crisis with which the children and community are intensely concerned.)

Teachers help students learn to scrutinize, not watch passively, television news programs.

Conducting television news programs. Use this technique from time to time to dramatize news stories. Children can take turns as reporters, eyewitnesses, and public officials.

Making charts, maps, and graphs. Show increases in school population, steps in an event that led to a crisis, decline or increase in employment, the number of highway accidents over a holiday weekend, the route of a recent air flight of importance, and so on.

Keeping scrapbooks of news stories or pictures. Clipping and keeping the headlines from the evening paper for several weeks helps children to distinguish between news stories that are of continuing interest and those that are transitory in nature. Collections of news clippings can be a valuable resource if the topic selected is one that is likely to be in the news for several weeks or months. Careful selection of articles in the scrapbook will allow the class to follow the development of the news story.

Drawing cartoons to illustrate news. This can be used effectively with older children. Care must be taken to avoid having children draw cartoons that might be offensive to individuals or groups.

Giving reports. This is a widely used technique for handling current affairs by having individuals report news items to the class. Encourage students to create visuals for their reports, such as charts and graphs showing public opinion.

A food drive is a direct, compassionate action a class can undertake while studying the enduring issue of poverty.

Teaching Enduring Public Issues

We turn now to enduring public issues. These are controversial issues that do not just go away when the current event ends. Rather, the current event is the most recent incident in a long stream of incidents related to the enduring issue. As we have seen, children can learn to deliberate these issues—discuss them, make decisions, plan service/action projects, and send their advice to officials.

Issue-centered, also known as problem-centered, unit planning has been one of the most popular approaches to social studies education in the 20th century. The central focus of an issue-centered unit is an enduring public controversy that is sure to be as controversial tomorrow as it is today and was yesterday. It should be an issue that has challenged people throughout history and in many cultures, for example:

1. *Poverty.* Who is responsible for the poor?

2. *Human-Environment Interaction.* How much environmental harm should be allowed for the sake of human economic productivity? How much pollution should be permitted for the sake of providing jobs?

3. *Justice.* How should society punish lawbreakers? Are there better responses than "an eye for an eye"?

4. *Peace.* How can war be prevented? What can individuals do to increase peace and harmony among people?

5. *Diversity/Unity.* How can we keep our individual and cultural differences *and* be one people? How can we achieve *e pluribus unum?*

Note that the issues are stated as questions, and that the questions are mighty. They are *recurring* issues: people have grappled with them for years but never answered them once and for all. One of the responsibilities of being a member of "the public"—a citizen—is to tackle such problems. They are, of course, the sort of questions on which reasonable people will disagree; they lend themselves, therefore, to discussion and decision making.

With such a question as the unit's centerpiece, the teacher plans learning activities that inform the children's discussion, reading, and writing. This, then, is the instructional goal: to have children discuss, read, and write on the problem, and to *inform* these activities through study. Discussion without study, while not worthless (at least it activates prior knowledge), has none of the power and depth of discussions to which participants bring information, judgment, and competing viewpoints that they have read and heard elsewhere. Consequently, the problem-centered unit moves through iterations of discussion, study, and writing. In this way, social studies and language arts curricula are integrated.

POVERTY

Let us consider a sample unit that was built around the focus question, Who is responsible for the poor? Figure 6–3 shows that the children will endeavor to gather information from various disciplines to inform their decisions on this matter. The suggested procedure that follows can be altered considerably to suit a teacher's knowledge of the problem and related curriculum materials. Its focus can be shifted, for example, from a United States issue to an issue pertinent to another country, state, or community. Its essence, however, is discussion. There should be plenty of discussion. There also needs to be ample opportunity for students to reflect on the quality of their discussions.

HUMAN–ENVIRONMENT INTERACTION

Another enduring public issue, and one for which children have much natural concern, can be stated something like this: How can humans best live with the natural environment? Human consumption, especially in the affluent nations of Europe and North America, has already overwhelmed many ecosystems, and the developing nations of Asia, South America, and Africa are close behind. At the present rate, Earth will be overwhelmed by its human residents in the not too distant future.

FIGURE 6–3   Issue-centered units.

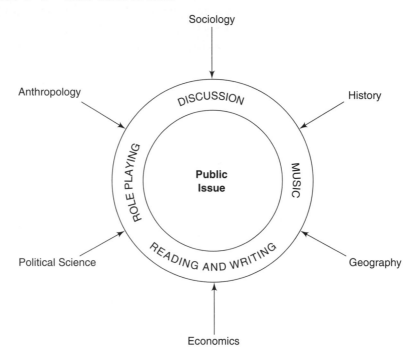

WHO IS RESPONSIBLE FOR THE POOR? (AN OUTLINE OF AN INTEGRATED ISSUE-CENTERED UNIT)

1. *Initial discussion* of the unit question followed by writing on the question in a "discussion journal" or "learning log."

2. *Instruction* on the characteristics of good discussion (see Chapter 3).

3. *Historical Study.* Using a time line that has been drawn on the board, the teacher describes for children several historical eras in which poverty was a problem and who did what about it.

   a. Poor African slaves living on plantations

   b. Poor immigrants

   c. Poor unemployed during the Great Depression

   d. A current, local example (rural or inner-city poverty; homelessness)

4. *Additional Data Gathering.* The class is divided into four committees. Each is assigned to one of the four examples listed in item 3. The committee's job is to find out more about its example and to give children a sense of the era by providing interesting facts about society at that time.

   Option. If the children are too young to conduct small-group research, the teacher can provide the additional information on each example using the same material the small groups would—films, stories, guest speakers, the textbook, primary documents, and references.

5. *Second discussion* of the question, now informed by historical information. Discussion followed by reflection on the quality of the discussion.

6. *Second writing in journals* on the unit question. Revise and share with peers.

7. *Additional Data Gathering.* Again using a small-group research format (option: teacher provides the data), the children divide group members among four social sciences: economics, sociology, political science, and anthropology. Each is given study questions and works with others from the other groups assigned to the same topic. (This technique, called "jigsaw," is explained in Chapter 11.) Study questions should be designed with the capabilities of students and available curriculum materials in mind. For example:

   Economics: For two or three of the examples, describe (a) who else in society was poor and (b) who was rich?

   Sociology: For two or three of the examples, find out (a) what conflicts occurred? (b) how were families affected by poverty?

   Political Science: For two or three of the examples, find out (a) did government help the poor? If so, how? (b) who else helped?

   Anthropology: For two or three of the examples, describe (a) how the lifestyle of the poor people—their culture—was different from the nonpoor and (b) an example of poverty in another nation.

8. *Third discussion* of the unit question, informed by the additional data.

9. *Third writing in journals* on the unit question. Share, revise, and publish.

One of the essential characteristics that distinguishes a modern, economically developed nation such as the United States from a less well-developed nation is its use of and dependence on various forms of energy. Modern nations have taken burdens off the backs of human beings and animals and have substituted inanimate sources of power and energy. The dependence on various forms of such energy—and in huge and escalating amounts—is absolute in modernized nations. Their economic systems cannot survive without it. They could not sustain their present standards of living if their energy sources were curtailed. Perhaps no topic is related more directly to the day-to-day lives of citizens than is energy.

Energy is, of course, related to the environment. The relationship occurs at all stages of the energy production–distribution–consumption sequence. Looking back to Chapter 4's section on "Economics," it becomes quite obvious that the central concept of that discipline, *scarcity,* which requires choice making and sacrifice, applies perfectly to a study of energy. Extracting energy sources such as coal, gas, and oil from the earth either scars or pollutes the environment. Processing the raw materials of energy into usable forms and delivering the finished products also do violence to the environment. Similarly, the consumption of energy in most instances has some environmental impact. Americans' love affair with high-consuming automobiles and, recently, even higher-consuming passenger trucks, makes a grand hypocrisy of their supposed concern for rain forests and the great outdoors. Thus, one of the profound social issues of our time is that of providing for the vast energy needs of our modern industrial society while at the same time preserving an environment that can sustain human and other forms of life at an acceptable level of quality.

When European settlers first came to North America, the incredible vastness and abundance of resources they found produced no concern in their minds for the environment or conservation. There was fresh water aplenty. Forests and trees were in such abundance that they were perceived as obstacles to land use. There was no shortage of places to dispose of solid wastes. There were no internal combustion engines or other devices creating large quantities of harmful hydrocarbons to pollute the air. The forests and streams were well stocked with wildlife and fish. What happened in the 300 years that followed provides us with a shocking case study of unbelievable exploitation and waste and an almost total lack of concern for the consequences of this behavior. All this is now too-familiar history.

Serious efforts to reverse this trend got under way about three decades ago. National and state leadership, combined with publicity in the popular press and, most importantly, concerned citizen groups, raised the consciousness of the general public to the violence being perpetrated on the ecosystem. More than that, these forces were successful in securing state, national, and local legislation that slowed the pace of environmental abuse. Scientific data relating to the use of certain energy-producing fuels raised the frightening possibility that the planet could experience something in the way of an "eco-catastrophe" in the foreseeable future. The most significant danger signals seemed to be those associated with (1) the use of fertilizers and pesticides, (2) the disposal of solid wastes, (3) air pollution, (4) water pollution, (5) radiation and radioactive substances, and (6) overpopulation.

Energy and environmental studies are, of course, not the sole province of the social studies. The subject is so comprehensive that it can be studied from many perspectives. It can be approached from the standpoint of science education, for, clearly, much of our polluted environment is a direct consequence of science and technology. Likewise, the subject is appropriate for health education because research has established relationships between air pollution and respiratory ailments such as asthma, emphysema, lung cancer, and bronchitis. Certainly, energy and environmental studies have geographical, esthetic, sociological, economic, and even political dimensions. Thus, the broad topic is highly appropriate for social studies programs because of its implications for human societies and human life. It is an ideal subject for interdisciplinary studies.

As with the study of poverty and other public issues, a program of energy and environmental studies should concern itself with three types of broad goals:

1. *Knowledge.* It should provide children with an opportunity to develop a basic understanding of the dimensions of problems surrounding energy and the environment, the causes and consequences of ecological disaster, the remedial measures now under way, the need for additional corrective legislation and action, *and* similar inputs of information that affect these important topics.

2. *Concern.* It should help children develop an attitude of responsible concern for energy use and the quality of the environment. It should leave them with the feeling that they have a personal investment in their natural surroundings—that energy and the environment truly are everybody's business.

3. *Action.* It should provide children with the opportunity to do something themselves about improving the environment. That is, if goals 1 and 2 are concerned with knowledge, thinking, and valuing, this goal constitutes the action dimension of the program.

In Chapter 13, we present an exemplary interdisciplinary environmental studies unit that was developed for use by third-grade teachers and students in Colorado. Readers may wish to read ahead at this point. In the boxed exercises that follow, however, we provide simple learning activities, not whole units, that are related to human-environment interaction issues. Beginning teachers have used these successfully with elementary school children.

CRIME AND THE RULE OF LAW

Now we turn from poverty and human-environment interaction to a third group of public issues. The United States has long held the distinction of being the most violent and lawless of all industrialized nations in the world. Moreover, in every category of violent crime—rape, murder, robbery, assault—the number of offenses committed by youngsters (children and teenagers) has increased substantially in the past decade. As well, youngsters increasingly are the victims of violent crime.[4]

What is causing this? That is a very good question to put to children in the classroom. As we will see in Chapter 8, such an *inquiry* teaches children to hypothesize at the same time that it teaches them to gather relevant data (information) and revise hypotheses as the data require. A planned program of law-related education (LRE) can help children focus on the problem of lawlessness and the idea of rule by law. Such a program should concern itself with broad goals such as these:

1. Develop an understanding of concepts that are basic to the legal system, such as liberty, justice, fairness, toleration, power, honesty, property, equality, and responsibility.

2. Develop an understanding and appreciation of the constitutional basis of the American legal system.

3. Develop a functional knowledge of how the institutions of the legal and justice systems operate.

4. Develop an understanding of and respect for the need for a system of law and justice as prerequisites for orderly and harmonious living.

ACTIVITIES RELATED TO HUMAN-ENVIRONMENT INTERACTION

Population

1. Using a checkerboard or other similar squares and kernels of corn, try doubling the number of kernels in each square, starting with one. How many kernels can be used before there is no longer room to double again? Discuss how this relates to population growth and its implications.

2. Encourage children to suggest problems that would be caused by an increase of twice as many persons in their environment.

3. Make a chart comparing the present-day population of a selected area with its population 20 years ago, 100 years ago, 200 years ago.

4. Become familiar with the web page of the U.S. Census Bureau. See Lesson Plan 1 in Chapter 2, "Taking a Class Census."

5. Construct a map showing areas of heavy population in the city, state, nation, or world. Identify sparsely populated areas. Have children give reasons for both conditions.

Air Pollution

1. Construct a map of the local region showing places of highest pollution. Explain why these areas have a high level of pollution.

2. Discover the major sources of air pollution. Present these on charts.

3. Relate air pollutants to health problems.

4. Have the class gather data associating smoking with lung cancer and other respiratory ailments.

Water Pollution

1. Discover major sources of water pollution in the local area. Prepare a chart showing those sources. Discuss. Present the chart to local government officials.

2. Make a map of a specified area through which a large river flows. Find out if or to what extent the river becomes polluted as it flows.

3. On a map of the United States, identify water bodies that once were contaminated but that have been rehabilitated.

4. Select a water body in the local area that is not available for recreation because of contamination. Plan a strategy to have it rehabilitated. Present the plan to local officials. Begin a movement to mobilize public opinion in support of such an action.

> ## Energy Use
>
> **1.** Through discussion, establish the relationship between increasing wants and needs and increased energy consumption. Find pictures from magazines to illustrate points. Advertisements for four-wheel drive passenger trucks can be examined.
>
> **2.** Develop a class project to encourage energy conservation in the children's homes (turning off lights, turning down thermostats, shutting off televisions and appliances not in use, and so on).
>
> **3.** Prepare a bulletin board display of energy-related news stories. Through discussion, establish the importance of energy to the everyday lives of everyone.
>
> **4.** Make a survey of their homes to identify energy uses that would not have been in homes 50 years ago or 100 years ago. Discuss in terms of new demands on energy resources.

In addition to inquiry-oriented units on crime, such simple activities as the following can make a difference in children's attitudes toward and knowledge of this enduring social concern:

Invite a local police officer to talk to the class about law enforcement, drug traffic, youth gangs, or some other real or potential problems in the community.

Bring in news clippings describing acts of vandalism; discuss the effects and costs of such behavior.

Discuss rights versus responsibilities along lines familiar to children such as "Can we go to the movies and talk out loud even if we disturb others?"

Research the latest legislation on drugs (upper grades). Find out if the legal penalties for drug abuse are the same for adults as for juveniles.

Take a field trip to a court, the state legislature, or a city council meeting.

Find out how a jury is selected. Invite someone who has recently served on a jury to speak to the class about the responsibilities and duties of jurors.

Conduct a mock trial.

Discuss citizens' rights and responsibilities in terms of specific cases that appear in the news.

PEACE AND UNDERSTANDING

We live in a world fraught with danger, which is likely to increase as modern instruments of destruction become available to more and more nations. Even a minor power, if armed with modern weapons, constitutes a threat to the entire world. To ignore the real danger that exists or to minimize it could result in disastrous consequences for the entire human population.

Perhaps through educational programs directed toward the understanding of others and toward a search for world peace, a more satisfactory method of resolving international disputes can be found than the oldest and least effective method, war. Many believe that a global perspective that engenders worldmindedness, therefore, is essential if humankind is to survive.

Teachers will need to be imaginative in exploring and discovering new avenues to a worldview. For example, when children in the primary grades are studying homes and home life, that is the time to begin developing the understanding that people all over the world need homes and that they build them in a variety of ways. Or when the food market is studied, time might be spent examining food markets around the world. Units on transportation and communication can, likewise, be expanded to familiarize students with these functions on a broader basis than the local community. Almost any topic has within it such possibilities for teaching global relationships.

If a school accepts global perspectives education as one of its primary purposes, it will concern itself with ideas such as these:

1. The interdependence of peoples.
2. The need for peaceful relations among nations.
3. Basic similarities and differences in peoples because of geographical, cultural, and historical considerations.
4. The philosophy and practice of respect for the dignity of the individual, regardless of race or other factors over which he or she has no control.
5. The need to develop a sensitivity to and respect for the cultures of other people, both within one's community and around the world.

The most productive teaching plan, as suggested earlier, is to extend each social studies unit in such a way that it includes global comparisons. Issue-centered units have great promise for helping children explore global problems. Such units can be planned on the question, how can war be prevented? Or, what can the individual do to increase peace and harmony in the world? Many other activities also have been used successfully. A sampling follows:

> *Use experiences from the everyday lives of children as a springboard for global studies.* Take *blue jeans,* for example. Here we have a fashion fad that began in the United States during the 1960s and suddenly spread worldwide. Responding to this demand, blue jeans factories were established in South Korea, Mexico, the Philippines, Hong Kong, and elsewhere. Or, take chocolate. What is it? How and where is it produced?

> *Keep instruction and experiences for primary grade children simple and child-oriented.* A major purpose of global studies in the primary grades is to develop the concepts of friendliness and neighborliness among the "human family." Learning experiences, therefore, should focus on the ways children in other lands live, play, dress, and eat. Social studies textbooks and children's trade books can be of tremendous help here. Jane Cowen-Fletcher's little book, *It Takes a Village* (Scholastic, 1994) offers a lovely story based on the African proverb, "It takes a village to raise a child." A girl must care for her younger sister while her mother sells fruit at the market.

Bulletin board. Expand the classroom's current events bulletin board to include news of "the country of the week."

Guests. Invite foreign-born local residents to the classroom to display photos, flags, and traditional clothes. Former members of the Peace Corps and persons who have lived at least a year abroad also have much to share.

Travel brochure. Have small groups prepare travel brochures on several countries. Children can role-play tourists and tour guides discussing a two-week itinerary.

Embassies. Have student committees write to embassies, consulates, airlines, or travel bureaus for material on the countries being studied.

Make direct contact. One of the best learning experiences for children who are studying the people of other lands is to have direct contact with someone from that country, especially a child their own age, who can answer questions about the clothes they wear, their schools and games, celebrations, and homes. With help from the teacher and their parents, children can correspond with children abroad, exchanging photos, news, and stories. Teachers who wish to have their students correspond with children in other lands may obtain information from local service clubs (e.g., Rotary).

DIVERSITY AND PREJUDICE

It is one thing to teach about differences around the world and another to teach about differences right here at home. The latter often is called *ethnic heritage studies* or *multicultural education.* As we saw in Chapter 2, the children in our classrooms come increasingly from diverse home cultures (defined broadly to include ethnicity, race, language, religion, and social class). Thanks to the trend toward inclusion of special-needs children in the regular classroom, the children we teach will become even more diverse. This gives teachers a tremendous opportunity to teach children firsthand about the meaning and value of diversity. Teachers can engage children in projects in which they play and work together and, thereby, develop habits of friendliness, cooperation, and appreciation for one another.

Like anything else we want to do well, multicultural education cannot simply be wished for; it must be planned. Teachers should direct the program of multicultural education toward the goal of improving the quality of human relations in the school, community, and nation. This includes not only educating children about the ethnic and racial heritages of the incredibly diverse people who call themselves Americans; it also means tackling the problem of prejudice head on.

Prejudice means pre-judging people and places; that is, judging them before they are known—before the facts are gathered. It is a type of ignorance. Before we meet someone, we might believe we know quite a bit about him or her based, perhaps, on stereotypes we hold about that person's group membership. Actually, we may know nothing at all about this person. When combined with fear, greed, and anger, prejudice has played a central role in all sorts of social problems, all manner of hate crimes, even the atrocities called "crimes against humanity," such as genocide. Prejudice has made slavery, the extermination of native populations, apartheid, the Holocaust, and the Japanese-American internment possible. It is a deep and pernicious problem that humans historically have had an extremely difficult time avoiding or overcoming. On the bright side, prejudice is a concept that children can learn, and they can learn it well enough to recognize it when they see it or read it. With the help of caring teachers and other adults in their lives, they may learn to courageously take a stand against it.

In Chapter 8, strategies for teaching any concept, such as prejudice, are explained. Many teaching suggestions related to diversity were also given in Chapter 2. Accordingly, we suggest at this point only a few additional activities.

Vocabulary

Teach children the meaning of the terms *prejudice, respect, stereotype, race, customs, religion,* and *tolerance.* Then read selections from newspapers, the textbook, children's trade books, and reference resources in which these terms are used.

Perspectives

The most powerful form of multicultural study for children in the intermediate and middle grades is to compare the perspectives of various cultural groups on a single event, historical or current. Newer social studies textbook programs often give multiple views on events. For example, both Native American and European perspectives on land ownership are given. Children's trade books can also be a great help. See the trade book examples of teaching multiple perspectives given in "Providing Multiple Perspectives" in Chapter 12.

Cooperative Groupwork

Create small, diverse working groups of children. Each group should contain as much heterogeneity as the composition of the class allows. During groupwork, help children cooperate on a meaningful and challenging task. The task will help take the attention off one another, placing it instead on the work to be done. The children will gradually get to know one another as a natural result of completing the task. The problems they have working together will be the usual ones of sharing, communicating, participating, listening, keeping agreements, and so forth, each of which is an opportunity to provide instruction on cooperation. Cooperative learning techniques are explained in Chapter 11.

Scrapbooks and Biographies

Make a scrapbook of outstanding individuals in an ethnic group. Include a list of their individual accomplishments *and what they have contributed to the whole society.* Help children build the idea that outstanding members of ethnic groups are good citizens; that is, they identify with and contribute to the whole society, not only their ethnic group. Examples abound: European-American, Eleanor Roosevelt; African-American, Sojourner Truth; Asian-American, Gordon Hirabayashi; Mexican-American, Caesar Chavez.

Bulletin Board

Have the class research its own ethnic origins. Show on a world map where their ancestors came from. These same countries can become the "country of the week" as suggested in the peace and understanding section in this chapter.

Demographics

Make charts and graphs displaying the changing population of the United States. Such data are available in social studies textbooks and reference resources in the library. Get information from the U.S. Census Bureau website (*www.census.gov*).

Guest Speakers

Invite representatives of various ethnic and racial groups in the community to your class. Ask them about their cultural roots. Be sure to include European-Americans; otherwise, children might develop the misconception that whites are somehow "neutral" (not members of ethnic groups).

Music and Art

Encourage children and their parents to share music and art that has distinct ethnic origins or particular meaning to the family. Invite an ethnic musicologist to the class to share information about music's cultural roots. Model for children that, regardless of your own ethnic or racial identification, you value many different forms of music and art.

Community History

Study the local community to discover whether Native American groups populated that area and which nonnative ethnic groups first settled there.

Holidays and Festivals

Write a letter or use e-mail to contact the local chamber of commerce. Inquire about the ethnic holidays and festivals that are celebrated locally. Make a classroom calendar of these events. See the "virtual field trip" to holiday celebrations abroad in Chapter 9.

Languages

Conduct a survey of the school or local area to find out the number of different languages spoken and identify each. To show that multilingualism is valued, develop an award for the person who speaks the greatest number of languages.

Conclusion

We began this chapter with a genius's letter to a fifth-grade boy named Michael. "Bucky" Fuller urged Michael to do the things that need doing, "that *you* see need to be done, and that no one else sees need to be done." This advice captures for us the soul of a current events curriculum: Help children develop an "eye" and an "ear" for current events and a "heart" for caring about the community. *Idiocy,* as the ancient Greeks taught, is the real threat to our lives, for *idiocy* means that one has neither this perceptiveness nor this heartfelt concern for the community as a whole. One has eyes, ears, and heart only for oneself and one's private concerns—one's family, friends, and recreation. Idiocy, then, meant to the Greeks something like selfishness and privacy all rolled into one. This was "idiotic" because it destroys the very community we need to secure the freedoms we enjoy.

A current events program is a *must* in elementary and middle school classrooms because, without it, children are not likely to form citizenship dispositions that are vital to the health of their communities. Without it, they may not have adequate opportunities to see the things that need to be done or to respond, and, in turn, to develop their own talents. We presented four strategies for teaching current events and then distinguished between current events and enduring public issues. The distinction, we believe, is worth reviewing for it indicates the difference between an article in yesterday's newspaper about a whale capture and the overarching problem of human-environment interaction that will assure that such stories appear in tomorrow's paper as well. We detailed five enduring issues (poverty, human-environment interaction, crime and the rule of law, peace and understanding, and diversity and prejudice) and encouraged the planning of integrated issue-centered units. An outline of one such unit was presented: "Who is responsible for the poor?"

In the next chapter, we turn to unit planning, and we return to it again in the final chapter, "Social Studies as the Integrating Core."

Discussion Questions and Suggested Activities

1. Three purposes were given for current events teaching in the elementary grades. Which of them is the most important? Why?

2. Three approaches to current events teaching were given in the examples involving Ms. Hansen, Mr. Chung, and Ms. Diaz. The latter featured a lesson plan for studying the nation behind the current event. Compare and contrast the three approaches. Which do you prefer?

3. Select a current event in the news today that you think might fruitfully be studied by children in a grade of your choice. Also select one of the four strategies given for teaching current events. Apply this strategy to the event you chose, designing a lesson or unit that centers on that event.

4. Select from those given in this chapter a public issue other than "Who is responsible for the poor?" Then, revise the issue-centered unit plan as needed for teaching that unit.

5. Select a news story from a daily newspaper and develop a five-part decision-making study similar to the one in this chapter concerning the captured whales.

Selected References

Bennett, Clifford T., Bliss, Donna, Defren, Marcia S., Heitzmann, William R., Holub, Brenda, & John E. Steinbrink. (1988, Sept./Oct.). Contributors to a special section on using political cartoons in the classroom. *The Social Studies, 79,* 205–227.

Case, Roland. (1993, Oct.). Key elements of a global perspective. *Social Education, 57,* 318–325.

Enloe, Walter, & Simon, Ken. (1993). *Linking through diversity: Practical classroom methods for experiencing and understanding our cultures.* Tucson, AZ: Zephyr.

Hahn, Carole L. (1991). Controversial issues in social studies. In James P. Shaver (Ed.), *Handbook of research on social studies teaching and learning* (pp. 470–480). New York: Macmillan.

Social Studies and the Young Learner (1990, Sept./Oct.). Vol. 3. The theme of this issue is social studies and the community.

Wells, James, Reichbach, Edward, Kossack, Sharon, & Dungey, Joan. (1987, Dec.). Newspapers facilitate content area learning: Social studies. *Journal of Reading, 31,* 270–272.

Notes

1. Buckminster Fuller, *Critical path* (New York: St. Martin's Press, 1981), xxxviii.
2. The three kinds of controversies are from Donald W. Oliver & Fred M. Newmann, *Taking a stand* (Middletown, CT: American Education Publications, 1972).
3. Walter C. Parker, Jane E. McDaniel, & Sheila W. Valencia, Helping students think about public issues, *Social Education, 55,* (January 1991): 41–44, 67.
4. National Issues Forums, *Kids who commit crimes* (Dubuque, IA: Kendall/Hunt, 1994).

Websites

http://www.cnn.com

http://www.scholastic.com/scholasticnews/index.htm

http://www.nationalgeographic.com

http://www.naa.org/foundation/nie.html

http://www.cnn.com

http://www.scholastic.com

http://www.census.gov

Planning and Teaching Social Studies

CHAPTER 7

Planning Units, Lessons, and Activities

Main Idea

Unit planning is the heart of social studies instruction. Within units are lessons and activities, which require planning, too, and are always aimed at the unit's objectives. Social studies units typically are integrated (interdisciplinary) because they incorporate two or three of the social sciences (e.g., history and geography) *and* require the teaching, learning, and flexible use of reading and writing skills.

Key Concepts

Unit, lesson, descriptive and behavioral objectives, learning activity, higher-order thinking, construction, simulation

Chapter Outline

- Planning the Unit
- Teaching the Unit
- Lesson Planning
- Five Ways to Enrich Any Unit
- Conclusion
- Discussion Questions and Suggested Activities
- Selected References
- Notes

Chapter Snapshot

For a manufacturing simulation in the unit "Working in Our Community," the second graders decided to make envelopes. One half of the class became *assembly-line workers,* the other half became *custom workers.* When all the preparations were completed, Mr. Allison gave the signal to start. Both groups began making envelopes. The assembly-line workers divided the labor, each student doing just one task. The custom workers each did everything. In 30 minutes, Mr. Allison stopped the production. Students were asked to study both the process and the results and to draw conclusions. To test their conclusions, they repeated the process.

 A favorite website http://infoseek.go.com/WebDir/Education/K_12/Resources_for_students/ Social_studies_for_students?sv=M6&svx=related. This site has a variety of already-reviewed Internet resources for use by students in their social studies units.

Dear Dr. Hahn:

This is a "fan letter." We think Mr. Allison is the best thing that ever happened to Lori. He was clearly the most creative, imaginative, and effective teacher she had during the seven years she attended your school. He always had the most unusual things going on in that room that would so hook the kids that they spent hours of unsupervised study on what they were doing. School-work seemed to be a sheer delight, strange as that may seem. They simulated law and justice procedures (Lori was a juror twice); they made butter churns and other pre-electricity technology and collected water in rain barrels; they went on a field trip to watch immigrants become citizens; there were art, music, and dramatic activities galore. Once they constructed a whole set of models of Native American villages from different regions of the country. This involved the children in an incredible amount of research. And there were always inquiries ("history mysteries," he called them)—tremendous interest grabbers. Children had to be told to go home after school. If not, they would stay until dinnertime working on that butter churn.

And through all this he taught reading and writing. In our other daughter's classrooms, reading and writing lessons were for some strange reason separated from social studies lessons; with Mr. Allison, however, Lori developed her reading skills by reading history, maps, plays, encyclopedias, folk songs, and speeches.

When we asked him how he did it, he looked sideways as though telling a secret. "Planning," was his reply. "Planning, planning, planning." We would have said it was charm or charisma or that he was a natural born teacher. But he set us straight. Please extend our thanks to him (again) for all the time he spent "planning, planning, planning."

Sincerely,

Joe and Erna Montoya

How do teachers like Mr. Allison develop stimulating programs of study for students in social studies? In a word: planning.

Such planning comes partly from a knowledgeable teacher who is able to select powerful social studies unit topics that also will require the development of children's literacy skills. Social studies units, when planned well, are almost always integrated/interdisciplinary units because, first, social studies learning almost always requires reading and writing. Children need to be taught to read maps, expository text material, primary documents, newspapers, reference books, and so forth. Second, social studies itself is already an integrated school subject. Social studies integrates history and the social science disciplines and, at times, the humanities. Third, many social studies units are animated by the same way of knowing that animates the science curriculum: inquiry (i.e., the scientific method of problem solving). When a unit centers on inquiry, the children are immersed in a problem or event (e.g., Why did the *Titanic* tragedy occur? Where did all the buffalo go? Where are Earth's largest rivers?). Then they formulate and test hypotheses, sift through evidence, and, finally, draw conclusions. We take a close look at inquiry teaching in the next chapter, taking the *Titanic* tragedy as one example.

Such planning also comes from an attentive and imaginative teacher who is able to listen, watch, and respond to children—to capitalize on their interests, curiosities, and home cultures. The teacher selects the topics of learning from the curriculum guide in combination with his or her own good sense and creativity and then encourages the children to raise questions and suggest activities. In this way the child, teacher, and curriculum meet.[1] Unit planning, then, is an interactive process (you, your colleagues, the curriculum supervisors, your students, and sometimes their parents). Also, unit planning involves the writing process: A unit is not planned in a single draft any more than a story or report is written in one draft. Revision is involved, and the unit is "published" when it is finally implemented. After it is implemented, it is revised again before being implemented the following year.

In this chapter, we turn our attention to planning social studies units, lessons, and activities. You will frequently be referred to prior and subsequent chapters in this text. This can be annoying, we understand, but it is unavoidable because social studies unit planning builds on *all* your knowledge of children, of social studies, and of teaching.

Social studies planning asks teachers to be four planners at once: a curriculum planner, an assessment planner, an activity planner, and a resource planner. The curriculum planner asks, "Which social studies subject matter is essential?" The assessment planner asks, "What evidence would indicate whether the essentials have been learned?" The activity planner asks, "What activities will engage my students' interest—both physically ("hands-on") and intellectually ("minds-on")—for a sustained period of time?" The resource planner asks, "What resources do I need and what resources do my students need? Where are they and how do I get them?" Figure 7–1 depicts these as four terms in an equation that adds up to social studies unit planning.

Teachers are not free to teach any topic they choose; rather, in most instances, the school district will supply a curriculum guide, district and state assessment expectations, a textbook for each student, some additional instructional resources, and a resource person such as a social studies curriculum coordinator or, more generally, a curriculum director. It is not

FIGURE 7–1 Being four planners at once.

Curriculum Planner	+ Assessment Planner	+ Activity Planner	+ Resource Planner	= UNIT PLANNER
What social studies knowledge, skills, attitudes, and values are essential?	What evidence will assure us that the essentials have been learned?	What activities will engage my students, both hands-on and minds-on, for a sustained period of time?	What resources do I need, what resources will students need, where are they, and how do I get them?	Choosing and organizing subject matter, planning lessons and assessments, designing related activities, and securing resources.

uncommon to find some subject matter required by the curriculum guide, some optional, and some to be chosen by the teacher. Subject matter chosen by the teacher is often within a general topical area that is required by the curriculum guide. The guide may read,

Grade 5 Social Studies:
One-year study of American history from pre-Columbian times through the U.S. Civil War. The year will conclude with a unit on either "Canada: Our Northern Neighbor" or "Mexico: Our Southern Neighbor."

Individual teachers, or teams of teachers, then select and organize subject matter within the general topical area. We will walk through an example later in this chapter.

But let us be careful not to skirt the issue of the teacher's *own* knowledge. Clearly, elementary school teachers need to develop their own subject matter understandings so that they are capable of teaching to the broad curriculum goals of the elementary school—history, geography, economics, law and government (civics), and the other social sciences: psychology, sociology, and anthropology. And that's just the social studies curriculum! There are also science, math, language arts, art, and music. The development of robust and flexible subject matter understandings is a career-long and lifelong enterprise: Good teachers love to learn.

Teachers who develop these understandings are better able to plan and teach. The deeper a teacher's knowledge of the American Revolution, for example, the better he or she can plan an integrated unit that has students role-playing the revolutionary "committees of correspondence" of the 1770s, which used letters to unite colonists to action against England; the better he or she can orchestrate teams of students to write biographies of key revolutionaries such as Jefferson and Washington and read the speeches, letters, and pamphlets of Patrick Henry, Abigail Adams, and Thomas Paine, the better he or she can introduce children to reading and writing their own historical narratives of key events—for example, of "the shot heard 'round the world" at Lexington Green and immortalized by Emerson:

> *Here once the embattled farmers stood,*
> *and fired the shot heard round the world.*

Or Paul Revere's ride the night before, remembered years later in Longfellow's famous poem:

> *Listen, my children, and you shall hear*
> *Of the midnight ride of Paul Revere,*
> *On the eighteenth of April in Seventy-five;*
> *Hardly a man is now alive*
> *Who remembers that famous day and year.*

Yes, teacher knowledge of subject matter matters.[2] And, the knowledge required to plan and teach a particular unit is dauntingly broad:

- General knowledge of history, the social sciences, and the humanities.
- Particular knowledge of the topic that will be planned and taught.
- Knowledge of the school and/or school district's curriculum expectations. (What kind of "Canada" unit is expected? The geography of Canada? The history of Canada? Customs, art, and literature, too?)

- Knowledge of assessment policies. (Is the teacher expected to develop American Revolution assessments him- or herself? Canada assessments, too? Is student knowledge of the American Revolution and Canada assessed on the state social studies assessment?)
- Knowledge of the children—development, home language, ethnicity and culture, gifts and talents, learning disabilities, hobbies, sensitivities, etc.
- Knowledge of teaching strategies—from knowing how to make difficult concepts intelligible to children, to knowing how to conduct an inquiry lesson, a skill-development lesson, or how to help students write original biographies of key historical figures.
- Knowledge of resources for the teacher's own study as well as for instruction: national standards documents, textbook program and teacher's guide, primary documents for "evidence" in historical inquiry, picture books and story books, biographies, community resources, computer resources.
- Knowledge of good rules of thumb for planning any social studies unit.

That's a lot of knowledge! Since no mortal human can possibly possess all this knowledge in relation to every curriculum topic, knowledge of *resources* stands out as the most important of all. While career-long and lifelong learning is an inescapable fact of teaching, knowledge of resources helps fill the gap between what we should know and what we do know. (Readers may want to skip ahead now to Chapter 9, "Resources.")

Planning the Unit

The *unit plan* is a long-range instructional plan that covers a period of 4 to 10 weeks, during which time the class studies some broad topic on an ongoing basis. The unit plan is a way of organizing resources, lessons, and activities for such an extended study. How units are planned and taught varies greatly from one teacher to another. "The art of teaching... consists precisely in resisting formulas," writes Howard Gardner.[3] What follows is a description of the essential components—and these are only rules of thumb—for planning a comprehensive unit. If you skim ahead, you will see there are five:

unit includes 5 essential components

1. Study the curriculum guide.
2. Survey the available resources.
3. Frame objectives.
4. Select and organize subject matter.
5. Think ahead to teaching strategies matched to the subject matter you selected.

STUDY THE CURRICULUM GUIDE AND TALK ABOUT IT WITH COLLEAGUES

A general, grade-level social studies topic can usually be found in the school, school district, or state curriculum guide, along with unit topics or themes. Typical unit topics for each grade were given in Chapter 1 (see pages 13–16). Looking back, for grade 3 the general topic is likely to be "Communities Near and Far, Now and Then." This suggests a comparative study of the communities where people live, integrating both geography ("near and far") and history ("now and then"). We might find six units lasting roughly five weeks each:

Grade 3, Communities Near and Far, Now and Then

Rural and Urban Communities	Community Workers
Oldest and Newest Communities	Our City's Government
Washington, DC: Our Capital	Beijing: China's Capital

A teacher employed by the school district located next door to this one, however, may find that the curriculum guide emphasizes the conceptual themes identified by the social studies curriculum standards produced by the National Council for the Social Studies, (NCSS). (See the accompanying *Sampler* and Chapter 1.) The general grade-level topic may again read "Communities Near and Far, Now and Then," but now the guide may require that the unit be developed to address themes, say, the first three themes. Each theme may help-fully be followed with one or more focus questions that suggest more specifically what the children should study:

Grade 3, Communities Near and Far, Now and Then

1. *Culture.* How do the ways of life of people living in our community differ from those of the people living in our sister cities in Japan and Kenya?

2. *Time, Continuity, and Change.* What were the turning points in our community's history? The oldest human communities were nomadic, then agricultural, then (very recently) industrial; what differences have these changes made in the lives of children? Parents? Grandparents?

3. *People, Places, and Environments.* Why is our community located where it is, and how would our lives be different if it was located elsewhere: on the edge of the sea, in a desert, on an island, or high in the mountains?

Let us turn to another grade and again compare a topical curriculum guide to a thematic one. For grade 5, where the general topic is American history, we might find 10 units with a suggested time frame of three weeks each:

Grade 5, American History

The American Land	Creating a New Nation
The Native Americans	The Civil War
European-American Encounters	Westward Expansion
The American Colonies and Slavery	The Industrial Revolution
War for Independence	Canada: Our Northern Neighbor

In the school district next door we could find the same general grade-level topic, "American History," but this time with the NCSS themes instead of unit topics. Let us say that this district specifies the first, second, third and tenth themes:

Grade 5, American History

1. *Culture.* What cultures have lived on the American land and how are they alike and different? When has there been cooperation among them? conflict?

2. *Time, Continuity, and Change.* What were the turning points in American history? Why are they "turning points"?

3. *People, Places, and Environments.* What are the major regions of the United States and how are they different from each other?

4. *Civic Ideals and Practice. Voting:* Who was eligible to vote at the time the Constitution was ratified? Who won the right to vote later; when and how? *Equality:* Has its meaning changed since 1492? Since 1776? *Liberty:* Should the community ever restrict individual liberty? If so, when?

SURVEY AVAILABLE INSTRUCTIONAL RESOURCES

If a school district includes particular topics in the social studies curriculum, it will ordinarily provide at least some of the necessary instructional resources. The amount of resources available will vary widely, however, from no more than an old textbook to a brand new multimedia textbook program with detailed teaching guides and an array of supplemental resources: maps and globes, Internet access, tradebooks and newspapers, and so forth. Resources availability generally increases with the community's income base: Affluent school districts have more than poor ones, sometimes resulting in huge differences in educational opportunity, which Jonathan Kozol called *Savage Inequalities* (HarperPerennial, 1992).

As an initial step in planning, the teacher should inventory the availability and adequacy of learning resources for the unit to be studied. In Chapter 9 of this book are gathered essential social studies resources:

- The school library (CD-ROMs, photos and slides, biographies, historical fiction, almanacs, atlases, maps, encyclopedias)
- Textbooks and their ancillaries (plays, literature anthologies, projects, map sets, worksheets, songs, CD-ROMs, audio- and videotapes)
- Community resources (field trips, guest speakers)
- Computer resources (virtual field trips, simulations)
- Newspapers and student news weeklies
- Map and globe collections

What the teacher finds will have a direct bearing on how the unit will be planned. Whereas instructional materials should not entirely determine the social studies program, the availability of essential instructional resources necessarily affects the teacher's planning.

Much difficulty is avoided in securing and using instructional materials when teachers plan well in advance what they will need. Books, recordings, pictures, films, and filmstrips must be requested early enough to ensure their arrival at the time they are needed. Usually, instructional resources must be ordered, reserved, or even secured before the unit begins.

FRAME OBJECTIVES

Instructional objectives make clear what children are supposed to *learn,* that is, what they should know and be able to do as a consequence of the unit of study. Objectives are the desired results of study. Well-stated objectives enable teacher and student alike to see more clearly how instructional activities relate to the purposes of study. Insufficient thoughtfulness about objectives is likely to lead to students being involved in activities that have neither purpose nor meaning or that have purposes that are not sufficiently worthy of students' time and energy. Another problem with poor objectives is that assessment of student progress is undermined.

Descriptive Objectives

Objectives may be framed as broad, general statements that describe what the children are expected to learn. The following are examples, selected from several different units, of such descriptive objectives:

As a result of a study of this unit children will:

- Learn to use simple research skills associated with gathering information.
- Understand that certain basic needs must be satisfied if human life is to be sustained, but that many wants can go unmet.
- Interpret legends on various maps.
- Develop the habit of previewing and skimming an expository text selection before trying to read it word for word.
- Understand that people around the world, however different they are culturally, are similar in many ways.
- Develop the skill of orienting a map to compass directions.
- Learn the central concepts of the legal system.
- Learn to formulate and test hypotheses relating to the causes of historical events.
- Understand the causes and effects of the American Revolution.

Behavioral Objectives

Descriptive objectives certainly provide purpose and direction for a study, and many teachers are comfortable with descriptive objectives of this type. Another way to frame objectives is also widely used and required in some places: The desired learning is stated in terms of *specific observable student behavior.* Such statements are called *behavioral objectives.* Now the teacher writes statements of expected student behaviors (sometimes called "performances") that are hoped to be achieved as a result of the proposed learning experiences. Stated in this way—as observable behaviors—their achievement can be assessed by an objective judge.

To achieve this degree of precision, teachers must use language that leaves no doubt as to what is wanted. Terms such as *comprehend, know, learn, interpret, realize,* and *understand* are not well suited for this purpose because they do not specify observable behaviors that would indicate whether or not the children do, indeed, comprehend, know, or understand. Terms that are more suitable for behavioral objectives are these:

name	explain why
choose	identify
illustrate	demonstrate
provide examples	define
write a narrative	point to
place in order	list
locate	sort examples and nonexamples
find	draw

Here are some examples of behavioral objectives:

As a result of a study of this unit children will be able to:

- Draw four different types of structures used as homes in the United States, in Australia, and in Mexico.
- Find examples of democracies and dictatorships in the newspaper.
- In the library, locate the CD-ROMs, the atlas, and the newspapers.
- List the main ideas of the chapter.
- Revise the first draft, creating a second draft.
- Show that they know how to use the index to find material in the textbook.
- Match causes to effects in an exercise relating to labor-management conflicts.
- Jot down the critical characteristics of the concept *culture.*

The use of behavioral objectives has accompanied the growing concern for accountability in education. Advocates of behavioral objectives argue that unless the child can actually do something to show what has been learned, one can only speculate about whether learning has taken place. Opponents claim that the use of behavioral objectives tends to fragment the social studies curriculum into bits and pieces of content and skills rather than to encourage the integration of learnings into larger wholes. They also argue that these objectives stifle teacher and student creativity, and that many significant outcomes of social studies instruction do not lend themselves well to behavioral definition. For example, who can say precisely what happens to a child while reading an exciting account of life in a rain forest? How does one define such learning behaviorally? And, should it be the same for all learners?

There is a midposition that suggests a limited use of behavioral objectives for those components of social studies that lend themselves well to definition in terms of observable learner performance. As we will see in Chapter 10, "Assessing Student Learning," the criteria that describe an exemplary performance are, in effect, behavioral objectives. In this way, framing objectives and planning assessments are two highly overlapping activities.

Certain work-study and inquiry skills lend themselves to framing in behavioral-performance terms: reading maps, making maps, using references, interpreting charts and graphs, forming and testing hypotheses. Social skills can also be of this type: participating in small-group discussion of a school problem, criticizing ideas rather than persons, moving quickly and quietly to team tables, sharing the work load. Some powerful knowledge objectives can also be stated behaviorally, such as arranging historical events in chronological sequence, showing how particular causes and effects are related, writing an original biography of an historical figure or narrative account of a turning point in history, drawing a conclusion based on data, providing examples and nonexamples of concepts, and so on. In the case of learnings that cannot be easily framed behaviorally, or should not be, the teacher may want to state instructional objectives in descriptive terms.

Whatever the form, the point is that objectives should indicate what the children are expected to *learn*. Objectives should not describe the activity (means) but the purpose (end) of having children engage in that activity. For example, the following are not appropriate instructional objectives because they simply describe activities that will be used by the children presumably to learn something that remains undefined:

> The children will view a film.
>
> The class will create a newspaper.
>
> Students will work in small committees.
>
> The children will draw a map of the local area.
>
> Teams will make progress reports.
>
> Children will make a model of a harbor.
>
> Children will role-play workers in a shopping center.

SELECT AND ORGANIZE SUBJECT MATTER

When teachers are asked, "What are you doing in social studies?" they often respond by naming the title of the unit or topic under study. For example, "We are studying Japan (or Canada, the Constitution, Africa, river systems, Gandhi)." Some teachers who favor the inquiry method of teaching social studies may name the central question that is driving the unit, for example: "We are investigating the question, 'What are the causes and effects of the American Revolution?'" The presumption is that these responses will communicate the nature of the study. The fact is that the title or topic or central question of a unit tells us something, but not much, about the main ideas of the study, the concepts and skills being developed, or the conclusions that students will be helped to reach, if any. The response, "We are studying Japan," at least tells us that Japan is being studied (in some unnamed way) as opposed to Canada or Tokyo or the U.S. Constitution or Early Civilizations or Rivers of the World, but that is all. In the inquiry question, we learn a little more, that the American Revolution is being studied and that its "causes and effects" are the focus of the study. This gives us an additional clue—and an important one—about the unit. Furthermore, we learn that it is a question-driven unit—an inquiry—which gives us an important clue about the kind of intellectual work students are engaged in.

Part of the task of organizing subject matter, therefore, deals with deciding on the focus of the study and determining which particular ideas (culture? government? inventions? cause-effect relationships?) and skills (map reading? inquiry? both?) will receive priority. Here now are two practical examples.

Example 1

Let us say that the fifth-grade curriculum guide in School District X calls for a unit on Canada. This guide is short and sweet.

District X
Grade 5: Unit 10: Canada: Our Northern Neighbor
This unit should provide children with a thorough understanding of the geography of Canada.

On the one hand, this is not very helpful to the teacher who must flesh out a unit with hardly any guidance on the details; on the other, the teacher is left with lots of room—freedom—to flesh out the unit as he or she sees fit. The sentence description focuses in on geography (as opposed to, say, the history and government of Canada), and then leaves it to the teacher to select and organize subject matter within this broad topic. Will the teacher decide to conduct an inquiry? If so, what will be the central question? Or if she decides to help her students develop a few powerful concepts, which concepts? The District X guide does not provide direction, so the teacher needs to choose the points of emphasis.

This task will require some work. Another fifth-grade teacher may have already developed such a unit plan, or the district or state education office might make one available. A new teacher certainly should ask other teachers at the building and the principal *and call on the school district social studies coordinator.* The curriculum coordinator often knows more than anyone else in the district about the "whats and wheres" of social studies unit planning. If the teacher regularly attends functions of the state social studies organization, he or she probably has met a teacher who specializes in Canadian studies or geography.

Because the guide settles squarely on geography, we recommend going directly to the five themes of geography found on page 118–119 in Chapter 4 of this book. Recall, these are five conceptual themes that were identified by a blue-ribbon task force of educators and professional geographers. Since the 1980s, they have helped legions of elementary and middle school teachers and children achieve, as the District X guide above states, "a thorough understanding" of the geographic characteristics of places all around the globe. These five themes, again, are Movement, Regions, Human-environment interaction, Location, and Place. (The first letters spell "MR. HELP," which might help you remember all five.) For additional self-study on geography, the teacher should also go to the best single resource, *Geography for Life: National Geography Standards.* This very popular and informative paperback book is written *to teachers* by the National Council for Geographic Education. The website and linked resources can be found at *http://www.nationalgeographic.com/education/standards.html.*

Example 2

School District Y, like School District X, calls for a unit on Canada to culminate the fifth-grade social studies curriculum. District Y's curriculum guide provides considerably more detail, however, and calls for a much more comprehensive study—not only the geography of Canada, but its history, cultures, government, and economic system. Note that the guide indicates both topical emphases *and* themes. The themes are those recommended by the National Council for the Social Studies (NCSS):

District Y

Grade 5: Unit 10: Canada: Land Giant of the Western Hemisphere

This unit should provide children with a comprehensive view of Canada as it is today. Enough historical perspective should be provided to help students understand the current separatist movement as well as Canada's relationship to England (independent, yet connected). The study is to be interdisciplinary with an emphasis on contemporary life. The unit should treat Canada as a whole rather than focus on a particular small sample of Canadian life and culture. Whereas the similarities between the United States and Canada should be studied (both modern, both culturally diverse, both regionally diverse, both capitalistic, both democratic, both with many natural resources), it is important to present Canada as a unique nation among nations. The longstanding tradition of friendship between the United States and Canada should also be stressed.

The central ideas that should emerge from the study of Canada and, before it, the United States are:

1. *Geography.* The physical features of an area influence settlement patterns and transportation routes. (NCSS theme #3)
2. *Culture.* Maintaining an ethnic identity is important to most members of any cultural group. (NCSS theme #1)
3. *Economics.* The use of available resources depends on the nature of the economic system, the values of people, and their level of technological development. (NCSS #7)
4. *History.* The early history of a country often helps to explain its current problems and ways of life. (NCSS theme #2)
5. *Government.* Democracies come in all shapes and sizes (some even have monarchs!), but they share important attributes that make them all democracies. (NCSS themes #6 & 10)

How does the teacher select subject matter about Canada that will be in accord with the broader study suggested by this curriculum guide? Just one of the five "central ideas" in District Y's unit refers to the entire focus of the district X unit! Clearly this is a more comprehensive unit and an integrated one as well. (Does that make it a *better* unit? What do you think?[4])

To select subject matter for such a broadly focused unit, the teacher, as before, needs to do some work. This time, though, the work needs to span the social sciences (five social sciences were named in the district guide) and the closely related NCSS curriculum themes. Help is available! The NCSS themes can be studied online at *http://www.ncss.org/links/home.html* and there are numerous teaching resources linked to each theme. And, don't forget the standards *Sampler* that accompanies this book. Also, each of the social sciences were introduced in Chapter 4, and the history, civics, economics, and (as we saw above) geography curriculum frameworks, with linked resources, can be found online. Much material will be found on Canada in the school and public library, the children's textbook, and online.

Take heart. The long-term advantage to preparing a comprehensive, integrated unit of this sort on Canada is that much of the study and preparation you do for Canada will transfer to planning integrated units on China, Egypt, Russia, Kenya—all other countries! This is not to say that Canada represents other the countries of the world. It *doesn't!* It is a modern, developed, huge, regionalized, bicultural, capitalistic, democratic country, and many other countries are none of these things. Rather, this is to say that *the work you do to understand the five themes of geography and the 10 integrated themes of social studies will pay off handsomely in virtually any social studies unit you might plan. These themes are fundamental and enduring.*

Let us assume that the teacher has done some self-study and talked with colleagues and the district curriculum coordinator and then decides on a set of main ideas that will be developed in the Canada unit:

1. Canada is a huge country with a unique northern geographic location.
2. Canada is a highly industrialized and technologically advanced country.
3. Canada is an urbanized country, rapidly becoming a nation of city dwellers.
4. Canada is a democratic nation with an elected parliament, a queen, and a federal system of government.
5. Canada is a multiethnic country with two predominant linguistic groups and many religions.[5]

> The work you do to understand the five themes of geography or the 10 integrated themes of social studies will pay off nicely in virtually any social studies unit you will ever plan. These themes are fundamental and enduring.

After the teacher has selected the main ideas, such as those listed here, she can identify the specific concepts and subject matter that students will study to help them draw these conclusions themselves, as shown in Table 7–1.

Other Objectives

Thus far we have discussed subject matter selection only in terms of facts and ideas—that is, knowledge objectives. But what about skills, attitudes, and values? How do they fit into the picture? Unless the curriculum guide specifically indicates which skills, attitudes, and values are to receive attention—and usually it does not—the matter is left to the judgment of the teacher.

Objectives that deal with skills, attitudes, and values are developed concurrently with knowledge objectives. In the Canada unit, map and globe skills (see Chapter 5) would be a necessary part of main ideas 1, 2, and 3. Deliberation skills (Chapter 3) are needed to discuss the trade-offs of urbanization in main idea 3 and biculturalism in main idea 5. All the main ideas will require information searches, which in turn will provide the need to teach and learn inquiry skills. These information searches will also require instruction on reading and note-taking: previewing and skimming for particular topics, for example, and carefully noting sources so that they can be found again quickly and so that credit is given fairly and properly.

Previewing and skimming typically are not taught or learned as part of the school's basic reading program. Word recognition is often the objective of the basic reading program, in comparison to which previewing and skimming are advanced reading skills. Also, narrative text is often the focus of basic reading instruction, and previewing and skimming would spoil the story. (No one wants to know how the story ends before they get there.) But in the social studies world of nonfiction expository (informative; explanatory) text, previewing and skimming are essential to comprehension and to skillful inquiry.

TABLE 7–1   Essential elements of a unit on Canada.

Main Ideas	Concepts – *Understanding of main idea.*	Study synopsis
big picture 1. Canada is a huge country with a unique northern geographic location.	Region Location (absolute, relative) Coastline, Heartland Landforms (bay, archipelago) Natural and political boundaries Demography	Map work on location and size of Canada, dominant land forms, climates, and population distribution, physical and linguistic regions
2. Canada is a highly industrialized and technologically advanced country.	Natural resources Minerals Raw materials Technological change Tradeoffs	Inquiry on the development of Canadian resources for export and domestic use, rise of Canadian industry, people's occupations, birth and death rates, trade-offs (e.g., pollution)
3. Canada is an urbanized country, rapidly becoming a nation of city dwellers.	Metropolitan area Trading center Manufacturing center Urban environment Inner-city poverty	Inquiry on causes and effects of Canadian urbanism—cities gaining influence over the lives of all Canadians, problems of urban sprawl, inner-city poverty; case study: Toronto
4. Canada is a democratic nation with an elected parliament, a queen, and a federal system of government.	Democracy Parliament Federalism Monarchy Commonwealth Anthem	Narrative history of Canada. For example, like the U.S., it once was a British colony; government—like the U.S., Canada is a federal democracy, but with differences: parliament, provinces, monarch; Canada's independence: 1867, 1982; anthems: "O Canada!", "God Save the Queen."
5. Canada is a multiethnic country with two predominant linguistic groups and many religions.	Race and ethnicity Bilingual Bicultural Heritage Immigration	Inquiry on Canadian bilingualism; effects of bicultural life on social, political, and economic decision making; status of native peoples ("First Nations") in Canada

As for note-taking, information searches take students across many sources of infor-mation—print, electronic, and personal. Students must become skillful at keeping accu-rate and detailed records of this journey. The name of the book where the data was found needs to be recorded, along with author, publisher, city, and date. If information was found online, whether through e-mail or at a WWW site, this source, too, needs to be recorded in full. In the case of a website, the path to the information used must be cited: one or more web addresses will probably suffice. If interviews were conducted, names, dates, and duration must be recorded along with the questions asked and the responses given.

Attitudinal objectives can hardly be ignored because the curriculum guide states explicitly, "the longstanding tradition of friendship between the United States and Canada should also be stressed." Generally when studying other countries and continents, the teacher should encourage children to take a warm and sympathetic stance toward the peoples found there. Compassion—in this case for the struggles of people everywhere to feed and clothe their families and to build a decent life—is an enormously important attitudinal objective. In no case should the teacher mock or dismiss the customs that are encountered in world geographical studies or tolerate the same from students.

Values and values conflicts will come into the study if the teacher decides to help children examine the trade-offs involved in Canada's becoming an urbanized country, exploiting its resources, polluting the environment with unnecessary consumer goods, conquering its native people, maintaining an official bicultural position, and so on. Discussions can be planned and discussion skills taught in relation to these controversial issues (see Chapters 3 and 6).

The use of a planning format such as the one shown in Figure 7–.2 can be helpful for coordinating knowledge, skills, attitudes, and values objectives. If a careful job is done in completing the four cells in the first row, the task of selecting resources and planning activities will be made easier.

REVIEW TEACHING STRATEGIES

The next chapter is devoted to teaching strategies tailored to teaching social studies concepts, skills, and inquiry. Teaching strategies are powerful instructional *tools,* and they have a purpose: to help more of your students learn more of the subject matter—learn it more deeply and more meaningfully—than would be possible without these tools. The word *more* is used four times in that sentence, and for this reason a powerful set of tools is needed. It is popular now to think of teaching strategies in terms of another metaphor, too—as *scaffolds.* Scaffolds help painters and window washers reach higher than they otherwise could. Similarly, teaching strategies help more students achieve more of the curriculum than they otherwise could.

When planning a unit, experienced teachers bring teaching strategies to mind as they select and organize subject matter. Having chosen "geographic region," "technological change," and "inner-city poverty" as three concepts to be developed in the Canada unit, a teacher might bring to mind the teaching strategy called *concept formation,* which is tailor-made for this purpose. Wanting the narrative history of Canada to be compelled by a question that will motivate students to gather and learn how to analyze large amounts of information, and create a narrative history themselves, the teacher seizes on the *inquiry* strategy. Having targeted the reading-research skills of previewing and skimming, the teacher brings to mind a *skill-development* strategy.

These three strategies, concept formation, inquiry, and skill development, are detailed in Chapter 8. In Chapter 6, you examined several strategies for teaching current events. In Chapter 13, you will find a wonderful strategy for helping the class write original biographies of key historical figures. In Chapter 3, you encountered strategies for leading discussions of classroom rules.

FIGURE 7–2 Social studies unit planning (integrated).

This form can be used in developing unit plans. Note that it contains five components: (1) the various learnings to be achieved; (2) the resources to be used; (3) learning activities; (4) the relationship to the rest of the curriculum; (5) assessments.

Unit Title: _____ Inclusive Dates: _____

Overview: _____

_____

Main ideas to be developed: Key Concepts:	Related Skills: a. reading/writing: b. democratic participation:	Related Skills: c. study and inquiry: d. intellectual:	Related Attitudes and Values:
Resources: a. textbook: b. multimedia: c. community: d. library:	Activities: a. reading/writing: Formative Assessment:	Activities: b. music and drama: Formative Assessment:	Activities: c. construction and simulation: Formative Assessment:
Summative Assessment:		Other Curriculum Connections (Science, Math, Literature, Art):	

Teaching the Unit

There are three basic phases in teaching any unit: the beginning, the middle, and the end. We look at each now. What is important to grasp here is that the first and third phases are not to be ignored or slighted, and the learning activities during the second phase must be related clearly to the unit objectives.

PHASE 1: LAUNCHING THE UNIT

Poor teachers do not plan the unit, mediocre teachers plan the middle of the unit, great teachers plan the beginning, the middle, and the end. That is, they surround the middle with a thoughtfully constructed opening and closing.

A good beginning launches the unit successfully. Building and sustaining the interest of children in a topic are continuing responsibilities of the teacher, but are especially important when beginning a new unit of study. This involves much more than simply getting started. It requires arousing the curiosity of students, assessing their present understandings, exploring with them some of the possibilities for study presented by the topic, and, in general, setting the stage for learning to take place. The students' "multiple intelligences" should be considered when launching a unit, too. Music might be a good entry point for some students, a good story could be better for others, a dramatic reenactment for still others. "The pedagogical decision about how best to introduce a topic is important," Howard Gardner writes. "Students can be engaged or turned off in quick order."[6]

Before the unit is actually undertaken, the teacher should post material in the room to rouse interest in the coming unit and to indicate the relationship of the new topic to previous work. There should be books, photos, and other materials in the room to catch a child's eye and to allow for browsing in free-reading time. A learning center can be placed in the corner of the room to house these books and photos. A map of Canada is there, too, along with the classroom computer with web addresses for Canadian museums and major cities. These environmental stimuli, together with dramatic play and construction activities create interest and will encourage the children to want to learn more about the topic.

Dramatizations and Constructions

Some teachers use dramatic play successfully in the initial stages of the unit. What child has not "been" a firefighter, a cowhand, a teacher, a jet pilot, a soccer champion, a doctor or nurse during the fanciful and imaginative play of early childhood? Let us assume that a primary class is beginning a unit on transportation. The teacher suggests that the children show through creative dramatics what the workers at an airline terminal do. The children become excited about this and want to start immediately. Props are improvised. Under the teacher's guidance, they begin to plan and play, but they soon discover that they do not really know enough about the situation to present it accurately. They do not know who the workers are at the terminal, let alone what each worker does. Now they have identified a problem they can understand and can go about their inquiry with genuine purpose. The children's purpose has to do with getting information in order to do the dramatic play, whereas the teacher's purpose is to have them learn basic ideas about the airport, jobs, division of labor, and the concept of transportation. Although the example given applies to a primary grade, the procedure can be used at any level.

Through dramatic play at the beginning of a unit (in the middle, too), children can be helped to achieve all sorts of social studies objectives. The biographies of famous Americans, for example, can be dramatized with great effect. Kindergarten teacher and writer Vivian Paley, whom you already met in Chapter 3, does this masterfully. In one lesson, she gathered the children at the rug to act out events in the life of Martin Luther King, Jr. "The story of

History lessons should often feature dramatic reenactments. They are engaging, and they challenge students to take the perspective of the people they are studying.

King's struggle evoked strong feelings among the children," she says. "The indignities of being told where to sit, where to play and with whom, where to go to school, and where to eat seemed to echo some of the children's own complaints."[7] One child, a boy named Wally, wants the class to act out one of King's speeches. In it, King describes the feelings of his young daughter, Yoki, when she was told she could not enter an amusement park. "My mother told me to bring you this record," Wally said. "She says you'll like the speech about the little daughter." Mrs. Paley has the children listen and then immediately dramatize this scene. With this beginning, the children are ready (curious, motivated) to study the Montgomery Bus Boycott. They dramatize it, too.

Listening to children's dramatization, teachers can assess their understanding of events as well as their sense of history and their ability to empathize. "Which character did you like best? Why?" "How do you suppose that person felt? Have you ever felt that way?" "Can you think of another event that is like this in some way?" "Now, let's place these events in order. Which happened first?" "How long ago was that?"

Of course, drama isn't the only activity with which to launch a unit. Other activities can be used in a similar way to motivate work, to develop purposes, and to give children reasons for doing the things they do. Construction activities, about which we will say more later, are often used in this way. If an individual or a class is to build something, they have to learn what goes into it, how it works, and how it is or was used. Children can build model bridges or ports, for example, perhaps a new one in their city and an ancient one in Greece—all in preparation for an integrated social studies/science unit, "Mighty Rivers of the World." Such a unit can take students into cultures on every continent of the world and deep into the natural realm of rain, mountains, lakes, and animal habitats. It can also take them to human attempts to control nature: dams, canals, gardens, and water purification systems. But it all has to begin somehow—with a field trip to a local bridge, perhaps, followed by a construction project on bridges. Or a dramatization. Imagine the possibilities.

Here is the point: The careful teacher *plans* the beginning phase of any unit. For here, at the launch, the children's prior knowledge is activated, curiosity is sparked, purposes are set, and a need-to-know attitude is aroused.

PHASE 2: DEVELOPING THE STUDY WITH LEARNING ACTIVITIES

The development phase of a unit of study is composed of purposeful learning activities that are sequenced wisely. Good elementary and secondary teachers of social studies have developed two "habits" that are essential to this phase of the unit: framing objectives before selecting activities and involving students in selecting and planning activities.

First, activities are means to ends. They are used to help children learn something worth learning. It is imperative, therefore, that the teacher frames objectives *before* deciding what activities are to be used. This may sound terribly obvious, but anyone who teaches (and is honest about it) will admit to sometimes leading children in activities that were engaging but not purposeful. Hands-on, perhaps, but not minds-on. That is, the activity did not help students achieve worthy objectives. It was "busywork," perhaps, or "merely interesting"— interesting without being meaningful, active without being intellectually challenging. The remedy for this problem is a habit, and that habit is to clarify the learning objectives before imagining or selecting activities. The planning format shown in Figure 7–2 is designed to help you form this habit. Used as suggested, the upper portion dealing with objectives is completed before the activities are selected.

Second, good unit development typically provides for the involvement of children in planning instructional activities. This is in keeping with attaining and maintaining student engagement in the unit. Having them participate in planning can do much to overcome the feeling that they are only "doing assignments for the teacher." Such participation allows them to identify psychologically with the unit activities, and they may suggest ideas that the teacher would not have imagined.

Here is an example. A fifth-grade teacher and her class undertook a unit called "Life in Colonial America" prior to the unit, "Revolution!" One objective concerned learning that many different kinds of highly specialized labor were needed in a colonial New England town. The teacher led students in a lengthy decision-making activity to plan this phase of the unit. A chart, shown in Figure 7–3, that summarized their plans was then posted on the wall:

FIGURE 7–3   Class Plan.

Jobs in a Colonial New England Town

- Each of us will select a different job from New England town life.
- Each of us will find out what skills and responsibilities each person has and how and where he/she learned them.
- Each of us will share our role with the others in the class by dressing up like the person, showing something the person may have created or used, making a bulletin board or diorama, or preparing a dramatization.

Some of the jobs in a colonial New England town are:

candlemaker	homemaker
blacksmith	merchant
weaver	shipbuilder
farmer	minister
school teacher	fisherman
miller	barrister
carpenter	tanner
lawyer	doctor
watchman	innkeeper
printer	cooper

What we want to find out about our jobs

- What skills did the person need?
- What training was necessary to do the job?
- How much money did the person make?
- How was the person paid?
- How many people will need the services of that person?
- What special equipment or resources did the people use in their job?
- Would you like to have done this job or performed this service?

Now let us examine a number of different types of activities. Although children of all ages need many firsthand experiences to extend their understanding of social studies concepts, older children have a greater familiarity with the world of things, words, and people and can, therefore, profit from vicarious experiences to a much greater extent than primary grade children. Furthermore, older children can use reading as a tool for learning in the social studies whereas young children are less able to do so. The physiological and psychological makeup of the primary grade children makes necessary the use of learning activities that involve them actively in firsthand experiences. Ten types of learning activities for all grade levels along with an example of each are listed on pages 233–234.

SELECTING ACTIVITIES

When selecting a social studies activity, the teacher should consider these criteria:

1. The activity is useful in achieving a social studies objective.

TEN TYPES OF LEARNING ACTIVITIES

Dramatic Activities

During their study of the Thanksgiving holiday, Ms. Paley's kindergarten class dramatized the story of colonists learning from helpful Wapanoag Indians how to plant corn, using fish fertilizer.

Construction Activities

Ms. Kim's class studied early people and constructed tools and utensils with sticks, rocks, and vines they gathered in nearby wooded areas. Each child demonstrated the use of the implement.

Sharing Activities

Mr. Johnson's second graders studied their seashore community and worked on the concepts *natural resources* and *manufactured goods.* Using a sandbox and things that each of them had gathered or collected with their families, they created a model of a seashore. The children talked about what they had brought and where their items had come from. They discussed whether the items were natural or manufactured.

Experiments

Ms. Womble secured samples of various grains—oats, corn, barley, wheat—while studying food production with her class. The children compared the appearance and taste of each type of grain and then planted some to compare germinating time and appearance of the first shoots.

Listening Activities

In Mr. Potts's class, the focus of study was Native Americans. Mr. Potts read a Native American legend and, using the legend as a clue, asked them to decide what the people valued in their lives.

Discussion Activities

Ms. Montoya's sixth-grade class had a regular time set aside for current events discussion. During the Canada unit, students decided to collect newspaper articles that reported on U.S.-Canada cooperation or conflict and to have discussions of the conflicts.

Art Activities

A fourth-grade class studying the regions of the United States searched for art works that captured the essence of each region. Then an art teacher from the high school visited the class to discuss each art work.

continue

Field Trips

A day was spent at the state fair during the study of their state. The children noticed what products were displayed and grouped them by (a) what region of the state they were from and (b) whether they were natural or manufactured.

Virtual Field Trips

After searching for the three branches of government in the U.S. Constitution, the class "visited" each one on the Internet. They started with the executive branch and a tour of the White House (at *www.whitehouse.gov/*), visited the legislative branch (at *www.house.gov/* and *www.senate.gov/*), and then searched for the judicial branch, entering "Supreme Court" in the "Search" box.

Processing Activities

During a study of colonial history the class divided into groups to make soap, dip candles, bake bread, churn butter, make dyes, and weave.

2. The time and effort expended can be justified by the learnings that occur.
3. It clarifies, enriches, or extends the meaning of some important concept.
4. It requires children to do careful thinking and planning.
5. It is an accurate and truthful representation.
6. It is within the capabilities of the children.
7. It is reasonable in terms of space and expense.
8. The needed materials are available.

FORMATIVE AND SUMMATIVE ASSESSMENT

Assessment means finding out what students know and can do in relation to the objectives. It's about evidence—gathering evidence to indicate what learning is occurring. An entire chapter is needed to address assessment. (Please skip ahead to Chapter 10 if you'd like.) For now, we wish to make just two points about assessment and unit planning.

First, *throughout* the unit the teacher and the children should frequently evaluate how well the unit is progressing toward its objectives. This is *formative* evaluation conducted to diagnose student learning difficulties and to plan instruction. Much of this day-to-day, along-the-way evaluation is, and ought to be, informal. As activities are planned, undertaken, and concluded, the teacher sees children working well or poorly and adjusts the instruction accordingly. She senses whether children are interested in what they are doing. Through observation and feedback, she gauges the extent to which progress is being made toward the achievement of objectives. Short teacher-made tests can be used to check how well specific areas of content and skills have been learned. Performances can be staged in which the behavior exhibited indicates what progress is being made. With this assessment information, the teacher may decide that much learning is taking place but the students

This unit on Greece came alive with dramatizations, artwork, and construction activites.

aren't enjoying learning. She adjusts the plan. Or she may think to herself, "Hmmm, this is definitely a hands-on activity but it's not 'minds-on.' They don't seem to understand what they are doing or why it is important." Again, she adjusts the plan.

Assessment of learnings, therefore, should not be associated only with the conclusion of a unit, but should be an important part of ongoing instruction. Of course, the end of a unit provides a time to judge the extent to which the overall objectives have been achieved. This is *summative* evaluation, and both informal and formal evaluation procedures are appropriate for this purpose. A culminating performance assessment may be planned; portions of the unit test provided by the textbook program may be used as well. As a rule, learning activities should result in some product (sometimes called an "artifact") that can be placed in each child's unit portfolio as evidence of learning. It might be a map drawn accurately and with good legends, a team-written biography of one of the heroes of the Civil Rights Movement, an annotated list of Internet addresses searched during an inquiry, or photos of a classroom museum exhibit. In the case of a single product made cooperatively with others, a description of it, perhaps with a photograph, can be used.

The second point to be made about assessment at this point was introduced in the section above called "Framing Objectives." The framing of objectives and the planning of assessments can often occur at the same time. This is so because the objectives of the unit— the targets at which teaching and learning are aimed—often serve also as the criteria against which student performance on assessments is judged. An example: If students are expected to understand the idea that "Canada is a democratic nation with an elected parliament, a queen, and a federal system of government" (the fourth main idea in Table 7–1), then at the same time this objective is framed the teacher needs to be thinking about the evidence that will be needed to determine when and whether this idea has, indeed, been learned by the student. Perhaps students will be expected to role-play the queen and parliament members in ways that accurately depict their relationship. Perhaps there is a paper-and-pencil test, too, that checks students' understanding of that relationship and their ability to articulate an answer to the question, "In a federal system of government like Canada's, which has more power: the national government or the local (provincial) governments, and why is this so?"

This second point is simply that when objectives are framed, the teacher is wise to frame them in the same terms that their achievement will be determined. This is certainly not an earth-shaking idea! Nonetheless, the practice is rare, which makes sometimes for a serious "disconnect" between unit planning and unit assessment.

PHASE 3: CONCLUDING THE STUDY

As a class nears the end of a unit, the teacher should plan a series of activities that help children summarize what they have learned. Summative assessments will be conducted. "Show-and-tell" opportunities and writing in response journals will surely be involved. A "sidewalk fair" in a local shopping mall could be a good outlet for sharing what has been learned in a comprehensive unit.[8] What is important about closing a unit of study is the opportunity to teach children to draw conclusions and to summarize what has been learned. It is also the time to identify what children found to be of special interest to them and to identify areas where additional study is needed. Concluding activities can and should serve as bridges to new studies.

Summary

There are three basic phases to teaching any unit. The first and third phases ensure an effective "launch and landing," so to speak, and they should not be ignored or slighted. Good openings and closings matter tremendously to achieving a unit's objectives because they launch students into the study and help them summarize what happened. Of course, the learning activities during the second phase must be related clearly to the unit objectives; otherwise, the classroom may be filled with activity but not *learning*. There's a big difference. Things get done, but enduring understandings are not developed. Read again through the letter from parents with which we opened this chapter. They are amazed at both the activities and the learning in Mr. Allison's classroom.

Lesson Planning

Thus far our discussion has concerned itself with planning and teaching a unit—a parcel of work that might take several weeks to complete. But day-to-day plans are needed as well. Teachers must extract from the unit plan shorter instructional sequences that may last anywhere from a single day to several days or a week. Usually these are called *daily lesson plans*. These plans must be complete in every detail, correctly sequenced, with contingencies anticipated and accounted for. As the teacher prepares such plans, he or she is rehearsing mentally how the lesson is expected to proceed, step-by-step. This rehearsal is worth its weight in gold.

There are four basic components of plans of this type. These are

1. The objectives that identify what children will *learn*
2. The three basic phases of any lesson (a beginning, middle, and end)
3. Assessment(s) to indicate what learning has been achieved and
4. Needed instructional materials and resources.

The example in Lesson Plan 8 shows how daily lesson plans can be constructed. Other lesson plan samples can be found throughout this text. They vary in the ways they attend to the four basic components, but they all attend to each of them. Pay special attention to the excellent plans from Colorado that are featured in the final chapter of this book, "Social Studies as the Integrating Core." Four lessons from a third-grade, integrated social studies/science curriculum called "Explore" are featured. Note that they rely heavily on the teaching strategies called concept formation and inquiry. (Please skip ahead now if you'd like.)

An experienced teacher sometimes will brag to a student teacher that "I don't use a lesson plan." The beginning teacher should not be confused by such claims. Most likely this teacher has internalized the four components of the lesson plan. In this case, the teacher most definitely does use a lesson plan, but does so automatically. The plan is held firmly in mind rather than on paper. (Another possibility, of course, is that the teacher making this claim mistakes activity for learning.)

> Experienced teachers sometimes brag to new teachers that they don't use a lesson plan. The beginning teacher should not be confused by such claims.

It is important to grasp that the basic idea of a lesson plan is to help teacher and students progress through the three phases of any instructional sequence: beginning, middle, and end. Accordingly, each class period should provide for three, objectives-related instructional movements: (1) getting ready, (2) work-study, and (3) summary and assessment. Teachers usually begin the social studies instructional period with the entire class in one group. At this time the previous day's progress is reviewed, plans for the day's work are outlined, and work objectives are clarified. A reading lesson focused on a selection from the textbook, a letter, speech, or other primary document may follow for the purpose of providing needed information for the work-study period to follow. The children then turn to their various tasks while the teacher moves from one child to the next or from one group to another, guiding, helping, clarifying, encouraging, and suggesting. The teacher will terminate the work period sufficiently early to assemble the entire group once again to discuss progress, to assess learning, and to identify tasks left undone that must be continued the next day.

As the children complete their various work projects and are ready to share them with the class, time will be arranged for them to do so. On some days the children may spend the entire period sharing, giving reports, discussing, and planning. Other days may be spent entirely in reading and research or, judiciously, on worksheets the teacher has prepared or taken from the textbook program. And on other days part of the group may be reading while others are preparing a mural and still others are planning a panel discussion, television news program, or musical.

Lesson Plan 8   GROUP MEMBERSHIP

Grade	2
Time	Two class periods
Objectives	Children will learn to identify human groups and will become aware of reasons people are grouped together.
Interest Building	Display five pictures of groups. Underneath each, write what type of group is represented. (Ideas: soccer team, birthday party, family, class, scout troop)

Lesson Development

1. Ask the class to think of one word that describes all the pictures. Elicit the word *group*.
2. Generate a simple definition of a human group.
3. Have children think of the names of several more groups. Suggest that they include groups to which they belong. Write these on chalkboard.
4. Lead a class discussion on "What are the reasons people are grouped together?" Place students' ideas on a chart as follows:

Human groups

What are some groups that we know about?	Why are these people grouped together?
Family	love, help each other
Team	to play games
Class	to learn
Birthday party	for fun
Scout troop	camping, making things, helping others

5. Discuss ways that groups can be identified. Look at the five original pictures for clues. Some clues might be: clothing/uniforms, symbols/mascots, official names, special songs, distinguishing looks, or languages.

Summary	Bring the concept of *group* into the children's immediate experience by asking the following questions: Is this class a group? How do you know? Why are we grouped together? What are your reasons for being a member of this group?
Assessment	Have old magazines available and ask children to cut out a picture of a group. Have each child tell something about what the group is doing. As they make their presentation, have them finish this sentence: "I think that these people make a group because. . . ." Use the pictures to make a collage on the bulletin board.
Needed Materials	Five pictures of different groups for display purposes. White butcher paper and felt pen to make chart. Old magazines or newspapers that have pictures of groups. Option: personal camera
Follow-up	Have children bring in personal photos of groups to which they belong and share them with the class. If possible, take a photo of the class group and have a print made for each child.
Integration	Groups are key to the science curriculum, too. There are herds of cattle, flocks of geese, packs of wild dogs, and schools of fish. Among plants, there are also groups (vegetables, trees, shrubs, evergreen, etc.)

The need to take time at the end of the work period to summarize what has been learned or to review work that has been accomplished should be underscored. Clearly understanding the objective or purpose of a learning activity and having knowledge of progress made go hand in hand. Unless the teacher spends some time crystallizing what has been accomplished or learned, the children may work for days without feeling that they have learned anything or that they are getting anywhere. Some teachers find it worthwhile to place these daily summaries on charts that serve as a visual log of the unit work as it progresses. Such logs are helpful in the culmination and may also be useful in assessment activities associated with the unit.

JUDGING THE ADEQUACY OF A LESSON PLAN

Teachers are never as well prepared as they might have been, given more time, more resources, and more knowledge. Lesson planning is an open-ended process that can go on endlessly. Many teachers can recall, as student teachers, staying up half the night preparing a half-hour lesson to be taught the next day. Although such effort is commendable, it cannot be sustained for any length of time. At some point, the teacher must decide that the lesson is "good enough" and then be able to turn to other matters with a clear conscience.

It is not always easy, especially for beginning teachers, to know when they have reached the point of diminishing returns in lesson planning. The checklist in Figure 7–4 can be useful in deciding whether all-important aspects of the lesson have been given appropriate attention in the planning process.

Five Ways to Enrich Any Unit

We turn now to five ways to enrich units of study. Briefly, these are reminders to pay close attention to reading and thinking in your unit planning (that is, to use the social studies unit to improve your students' reading and thinking abilities) and to engage students in meaningful learning by *doing*. It is essential to make social studies learning active and involving: hands-on and minds-on. Toward that end, we highlight three forms of learning activities—construction, simulation, and music and drama—that are especially promising.

After you have drafted a basic unit plan using the guide in Figure 7–2, return to this section of the chapter. Review the five ways and return to your plan, creating a new draft that incorporates some or all of them. Remember, unit planning involves the writing process: draft, revise, draft again and, eventually, "publish" it by implementing it.

Five ways to enrich any unit:
1. Incorporate reading instruction.
2. Incorporate higher-order thinking.
3. Incorporate construction activities.
4. Incorporate simulations and role playing.
5. Incorporate music and drama.

FIGURE 7–4   Lesson plan checklist.

Lesson plan checklist

✔ 1. Do the lesson objectives state clearly what the children are expected to learn? Am I clear in my own mind what I want them to understand and be able to do?

✔ 2. Do the learning activies for the lesson relate directly to these objectives? Will the children learn what they are supposed to learn by doing the things they are asked to do?

✔ 3. Do I know how the lesson is to begin? What is the very first thing I will do? Say? What next? Then what?

✔ 4. Have I written down the focus and follow-up questions that I plan to ask? Do I have them in the order I plan to ask them? (See Chapter 8, "Asking Good Questions.")

✔ 5. Do I have all the needed instructional material? Equipment? If I am planning to use a machine, have I arranged to get it? Do I know where the electrical outlets are in the room? Will I need an extension cord? Screen? An extra bulb?

✔ 6. Are there specific directions I am planning to give the children regarding what they are to do? If so, do I know what they are?

✔ 7. If I am going to group the children, are the group member assignments written on a poster or an overhead transparency? Do I have productive work planned for all the groups all the time?

✔ 8. Do I know how much time will be needed for each component of the lesson?

✔ 9. Have I provided for differences in rate and level of learning among children? Do I have productive work-study activities planned for those who complete their assignments quickly?

✔ 10. Have I planned how learning is to be assessed—formatively and summatively?

✔ 11. Do I know how the lesson is to close—that is: What will I do? What will I say? What do I expect the children to do and say?

✔ 12. Have I considered whether the lesson will require changes in the room environment, movement of furniture, and so forth?

✔ 13. Have I planned for any follow-up activity?

✔ 14. Do I recall the plan for a classroom/school emergency?

INCORPORATING READING INSTRUCTION

The information searches that are at the core of most social studies units make reading and writing skills central, not peripheral concerns. This is why nearly any social studies unit is an integrated unit if reading and writing instruction are incorporated. *Previewing* and *skimming* before reading and *summarizing* after reading are key skills for these information searches. Learning to preview a website or a text chapter before slogging through it is a powerful comprehension strategy for the nonfiction, expository material commonly found in social studies units. Previewing is "looking before you leap"—always a good practice. To follow previewing with skimming for information and main ideas further aids the reader. It builds up additional prior knowledge before reading any portion of the text word by word.

At the other end of reading is the enormously powerful (and difficult) skill of summarizing what has been read. Summarizing requires prioritizing and condensing. It requires readers to sift through the information that's been gathered to determine which is more and less important and which is more and less encompassing. These are difficult judgments to make because they require background knowledge and experience—more than the reader may have available on the topic at hand.

What to do? Teach summarization slowly but continually. It is a good idea to build summarization practice into every lesson as part of the closing phase. Summarization practice can be prompted with a simple direction from the teacher: "Now, let's summarize what we learned today. What information that you gathered today might be most important to our objective?" In the case of Canada: "What information have you found that best helps you predict whether Canada will remain unified or divide into French and English-speaking nations?" About the American Revolution: "Who can summarize the reasons the colonists decided to declare their independence from England?" Another way to prompt summarizing is to ask students to write a single sentence that captures the main idea of all they read today. For example, "Complete this sentence: Canada probably (will; will not) divide into two nations because _____." Or, "The colonists decided to declare independence from England because _____."

Of course, prompting a practice session is insufficient when students do not know the skill well enough to practice it. In the following chapter, you will learn a flexible strategy for teaching any skill, and Chapter 12 of this book discusses previewing, skimming, and summarizing at some length. The point here is to encourage you to think of social studies units as places where reading and writing instruction can *and must* occur. They must occur here for two reasons: because many children will not be capable of doing this kind of reading and writing without instruction and practice, and because reading and writing—literacy—cannot be properly developed without students engaging in challenging subject matter applications. One can't read reading or write writing, after all. The panic in some school districts over teaching children word-recognition skills (the bottom rung of the literacy ladder) sometimes causes educators in these schools to forget to take students upward and outward from there.

INCORPORATING HIGHER-ORDER THINKING SKILLS (HOTS)

A second way to enrich any unit is to increase the quality of the intellectual work you will ask your students to do. Like reading and writing, higher-order thinking skills (HOTS) do not develop spontaneously. They develop because children *need* them in the ongoing work of the class and because children are taught what they are and helped to use them well. Occasional special lessons on HOTS are necessary but not sufficient for their proper development; they must be applied in activities that invite them and nurture them.

As we have seen in previous chapters and will see in the next chapter, several thinking skills are particularly necessary to the subject matter of social studies. Any of them can be brought to the heart of social studies units, lessons, and activities:

Concept Formation

- Organizing information on data-retrieval charts
- Summarizing similarities across examples of a concept
- Classifying (applying a concept to new material)

Inquiry

- Forming hypotheses
- Gathering relevant data/evidence
- Hypothesis testing (judging if hypotheses are warranted)
- Drawing conclusions based on evidence

Deliberation

- Identifying and weighing alternatives
- Understanding the perspectives of other persons
- Making decisions

Of course, not all skills will be required by every social studies lesson. But across one or two units, one should see balanced and systematic attention being given to them. In a unit involving inquiry, children naturally will be making and testing hypotheses; to extend concepts, they will be classifying; to decide on the fairest classroom procedures, they will be engaged in decision making.

INCORPORATING CONSTRUCTION ACTIVITIES

Most children love to make things. They build villages and castles in the sand at the beach, make boats to float in the pond and creek, and sew clothing for dolls and make birdhouses to hang near a window. These natural, sensory-motor, kinesthetic play activities are valuable for children in and of themselves. They give countless opportunities for thinking and planning as well as for creative expression, socialization, making and using tools, physical activity, and the development of coordination. Children need many experiences of this type. In social studies, however, these values are only incidental to the chief purpose, which is to extend and enrich meaning of some aspect of the topic being studied. The excellence of the final product is, likewise, not a major concern. What is important is the learning that has occurred as a result of the construction activity.

It is possible to use construction activities to motivate children's work and to establish more clearly children's purposes for doing things. For example, the teacher of a primary grade conducting a study of the dairy farm might suggest that the class construct a model farm in the classroom. Naturally, the children will want to make their model as authentic as possible; therefore, a considerable amount of research will be necessary as they proceed with the building of the farm. In fact, they cannot even begin unless they know what they want to do. This gives them a genuine need for information. The children's purpose in this case may be to learn about the dairy farm to be able to build a classroom model of it. The teacher's purpose, however, is to have children form accurate concepts and understandings of a dairy farm; the construction activity is being used as a vehicle to achieve that goal.

There is no limit to the items that children can make in projects related to the social studies. The following have been used successfully by many teachers:

Model furniture
Books
Musical instruments
Simple trucks, airplanes, boats
Puppets, marionettes, and paper bag dolls
"Television set" with paper-roll news programs and biographies
"Computer" with paper-roll WWW sites
Looms for weaving
Hats, crowns, headdresses, and wigs
Maps (pictorial, product, landform, floor)
Candles and soap
Baskets, trays, bowls
Preparation of foods (making tamales, jelly, butter, ice cream)
Ships, harbor, cargo
Grocery store
Scenery and properties for stage, dioramas, panoramas
Decorations for holidays around the world
Pottery, vases, dishes, cups
Covered wagons
Post office
Hospital
Fire station
Dairy farm and buildings
Playhouses
Model Sioux or Pueblo villages
Birdhouses and feeding stations
Seedboxes, planters
Murals
Production of visual material needed in the unit, such as pictorial graphs, charts, posters, displays, bulletin boards

The following four suggestions should help you use construction activities in teaching social studies. In brief, they are:

1. Clarify the purpose of the activity with the children.
2. Plan methods of work with the children.
3. Provide plenty of time each day for beginning and ending the work.
4. Use the construction and relate it to the unit under study.

Clarify the Purpose of the Activity with the Children

The practice of having children make stores or maps without knowing why they are performing these activities is open to serious question. At the beginning of such an activity, therefore, the reasons for planning it should be discussed and understood by all. Also, the purposes for the construction should be reviewed from time to time during the activity.

Plan Methods of Work with the Children

Construction activities involve working in groups, using tools, perhaps hammering and sawing or other noisy activities, and somewhat more disorder than is usually found in classroom work. This means that rules and standards concerning the methods of work need to be established and understood. The teacher and the children should discuss and decide what the rules of work are to be. Group discussions and decision making about rules that will be binding on all, recall, constitute citizenship education at its best. These rules might concern:

1. How to get and return tools and construction materials.
2. Use of tools and equipment, including safe handling.
3. Things to remember during the work period: talking in a conversational voice, good use of materials to avoid waste, sharing tools and materials with others, doing one's share of work, asking for help when needed, and giving everyone a chance to present ideas.
4. Procedures for cleanup time. It is good to establish a "listen" signal to get the attention of the class. It can be playing a chord on the piano, turning off the lights, or ringing a small bell. When the listen signal is given, children should learn to stop whatever they are doing, cease talking, and listen to whatever announcement is to be made. In this way, the teacher can stop the work of the class at any time to call their attention to some detail or get them started at cleanup.

Provide Plenty of Time Each Day for Planning, Assessing, Working, and Cleaning Up

Before work on the construction activity is begun each day, time should be spent in making specific plans. This will ensure that everyone has an important job to do and that the children know their responsibilities. This time also allows the teacher to go over some of the points the class talked about during its previous day's assessment. "You remember yesterday we had some problem about which group was to use the tools. Which group has the tools today?"

During the work period the teacher will want to move from group to group observing, assisting, suggesting new approaches, helping groups in difficulty, clarifying ideas, helping children find materials, and supervising and guiding the work of the class. Children will be identified who need help in getting started, those who are not working well together, those who seem not to be doing anything, or others who may be having difficulty. The teacher will keep an eye on the time and stop the work of the class in time to ensure a thorough cleanup.

An important part of each period is the assessment that occurs after the work and cleanup. During these times, the teacher will want the class to evaluate its progress on the construction as well as the way children are working with each other.

"Were we able to make progress in building our store today?"

"Did anyone see signs of unsafe handling of tools today?"

"I wonder if the mountains aren't too high on Julie's group's map. Did you check that against the picture in your book?"

Some attention should be given to progress on the construction, methods of working together, and problems that need attention the next day.

Use the Construction in Some Way and Relate It to the Unit Under Study

When constructed objects are completed, they should be put to good use. A market in the classroom, for example, gives the children an ongoing opportunity to play customer, grocer, checkout person, delivery person, and various community officials—health inspectors, fire and safety advisers, and the tax authority. By rotating these roles, every child gets the opportunity to make change, to make decisions about supply and demand, to see firsthand the interdependence of the store and the community, and even to practice interviewing and preparing a resume for different jobs.

Storyline

One of the most imaginative construction activities originated in the elementary schools of Scotland and has children create a story together.[9] Called Storyline, the procedure builds on children's prior experience and their love of storytelling, scissors, and glue. There are four interlocking parts. First, a curriculum-related setting for the story is created. In a unit called "Our Community's Needs," the teacher might tell children about a fictitious community in the American southwest that is facing another year of water rationing. Working with the children, the teacher adds sufficient detail so that a shared visual image of the community is created. Second, characters for the story are created. Children are placed in small groups to cut and paste paper-doll families who live in the community. Responding to the teacher's questions (How large are the families? What are their physical characteristics? What kinds of homes do they live in?), the children decide what kind of families to create. Written descriptions of the families are posted with the paper dolls on the classroom wall, thus creating a vivid and highly personal mural representing the families in this community.

Third, the teacher suggests a number of curriculum-related episodes with which the small groups must cope. The teacher might suggest, for example, that a young child in the community, one the children have created, wants to know what the rules are so that he or she doesn't break any accidentally. Now the small groups deliberate the community's laws and post them on the mural. Next, the teacher might tell the class that an exchange student will be joining each family. The small groups decide where the visitor is coming from and then gather information about that country and decide what the visitor will be most eager to see in their own community. Next comes the water rationing problem. What are the community's priorities? Should larger families get more water? Should the golf course be closed? By whom should these decisions be made? Finally, the teacher might introduce the concept of trade, asking the families what goods they will produce and which goods must be imported and purchased with money, which is kept in the bank, which is robbed. The police and courts get involved, and so on. Finally, the children invite an audience, perhaps their own families, to come to class and experience the narrative they have created, with its evolving mural on the classroom wall.

After the presentation, a committee of students can tell the audience what the class learned from the experience—what objectives were achieved. This will require several planning sessions and discussions with the rest of the class. But it will be worth the effort because parents, like the Montoyas in their letter that began this chapter, will want to see that exciting activities *result in learning.* Storyline is a long-term construction activity. To assure that the time is well spent—to assure that learning occurs—careful planning is required so that the setting and episodes around which the children build this imaginary world are related directly to challenging curriculum objectives. This is the first and foremost criterion, recall, for selecting activities.

INCORPORATING SIMULATIONS AND ROLE PLAYING

A fourth way to enrich any unit is to plan a simulation that will deepen students' understanding—through experience—of one or more of the unit's main ideas. In Chapter 4, classroom simulations were suggested for history, geography, economics, anthropology, and sociology. Here, we provide an example of a classroom simulation, this one dealing with the economic concept *production.*

A fifth-grade class was studying the concept of assembly-line production in its unit on the growth of industry in the United States. In the discussion, the children contrasted assembly-line production with custom-made, individually built products. The class listed the strengths and limitations of each method of production:

Assembly Line

Strengths

1. It is faster.

2. Every product is the same.

3. Can be produced at low cost.

Weaknesses

1. Sameness makes for an uninteresting product.

2. Production can be slipshod because no one person is responsible for it.

3. The sameness of the work makes for a boring job.

Custom Built

Strengths

1. "One of a kind" product.

2. Product made to fit needs of buyer.

3. Work is less boring to the workers.

Weaknesses

1. Buyers cannot be sure of the product's quality because each is different.

2. Fewer people can afford to buy the product.

3. It takes longer for workers to become skillful in doing all the tasks needed to make the product.

The teacher pointed out to the class that each of the items they listed could serve as a hypothesis that they might be able to test. "Is it really true," she asked, "that assembly-line production is faster? Do workers on an assembly line become bored more quickly than those who make the whole product themselves? Do workers take greater pride in their product if they do it all themselves and sign their name to it? How could we test the truth of the statements?" The teacher and the children decided they could test their hypotheses by using a simple simulation involving the manufacture of envelopes.

The class was divided into two groups: one would be assembly-line workers; the other group would be custom workers. The teacher provided cardboard templates, or patterns, of an outline of an envelope, scissors, paste, and used ditto paper that would be needed to manufacture envelopes. After the pattern was placed on a piece of paper, its outline could be traced and could then be cut, folded, and pasted to make the finished product. The assembly line was arranged according to a division of labor as follows:

ASSEMBLY LINE

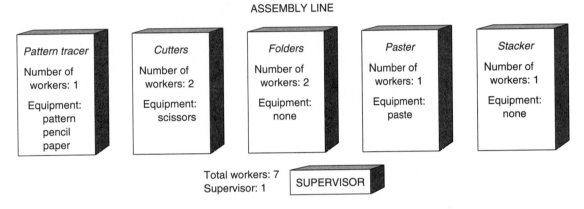

The custom workers consisted of seven individuals (the same number as on the assembly line) and a supervisor. Each of the seven workers had his or her own pattern, paper, pencil, scissors, and paste and was required to do all the steps necessary to make an envelope. These children would be required to put their own name on each envelope they produced and were encouraged to personalize their own product.

All children in both groups took turns, and all participated in the activity. The supervisor from each group could make changes and substitutions as needed. Three children served as a quality control panel that would accept or reject finished products in terms of quality of workmanship.

CUSTOM CRAFTSPERSONS

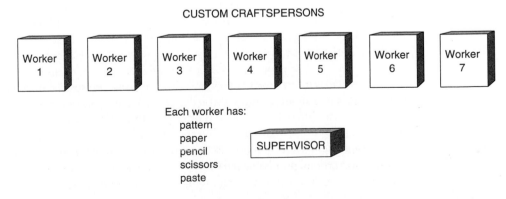

When all preparations were completed, the teacher gave the signal to start, and both groups began manufacturing envelopes. After a half hour, the production was stopped, and the debriefing took place. Children were able to test their hypotheses in terms of the data they generated through the simulation.

We have here an example of a simple simulation. It is a strategy designed to reconstruct as closely as possible some of the essential characteristics of the real thing. Simulations are enthusiastically accepted by those teachers who pursue innovative approaches to social studies teaching. The simulation may be a simple one devised by the teacher, as described here, or it may be one of the growing number of commercially prepared simulations and games now available.

Sharon Pray Muir provides an annotated list of nearly 200 simulations appropriate for use in grades K–6 that deal directly with social studies concepts and processes.[10] Muir's collection is a treasure! (See if the library carries this journal and make a copy the article. Create a "simulations" file.) To accommodate the typical classroom, it concentrates on simulations that can be played with large groups. Included are the title, recommended grade levels, and bibliographic information so readers can readily locate or order each simulation. Some appear in journals, newsletters, and magazines, which can be read in libraries for free; others can be purchased. Muir also indicates the social science discipline with which the simulation is associated. Several of the simulations she includes are those we described in Chapter 4, grouped by discipline. For computer simulation suggestions, see Chapter 9.

INCORPORATING MUSIC AND DRAMA

Music activities not only enrich social studies learning but contribute to the school's music program itself. Singing, listening, dancing, and playing musical instruments from cultures near and far add meaning and firsthand experience to social studies learning.

For almost any social studies unit, the teacher will find appropriate and related songs for children to sing. Singing gives the child an emotional feeling for the material not likely to be obtained in any other way. Like construction activities and simulations, singing allows children to shine in different ways, and it allows some children to shine perhaps for the first time. (See the discussion of multiple intelligences in Chapter 2.) Through singing, the child senses the loneliness of the cowboy, the relief and happiness of a frontier housewarming, the tragedy of slavery, or the sadness of a displaced people longing for their homeland. Folk songs can be springboards to the study of a period in history, of the lifestyles of minority ethnic groups, and of central themes such as human-environment interaction (sailing and hiking songs; fishing songs), civic ideals (hopeful, protest songs), production (workers' songs), and nationalism (patriotic songs). Singing is an experience that can broaden children's appreciation of people everywhere. In the study of communities around the world, the teacher will want to use the songs of various national groups. This provides opportunities to learn more about a culture through the language of music. (See Figure 7–5).

"Music from different cultures can offer us information and an entry point to understanding a people who may have lived thousands of years ago or thousands of miles from us."[11] The African-American gospel tradition is inseparable from the history of enslavement. "Oh Freedom" and "We Shall Overcome," for example, are synonymous with the Civil

FIGURE 7–5

Comparing national anthems: "O Canada!" and "The Star-Spangled Banner." What are the similarities in the ideas expressed within the two anthems? differences?

Lyrics of "O Canada!"
O Canada!
Our home and native land!
True patriot love in all thy sons command.
With glowing hearts we see thee rise,
The True North strong and free!
From far and wide,
O Canada, we stand on guard for thee.
God keep our land glorious and free!
O Canada, we stand on guard for thee.
O Canada, we stand on guard for thee.

Lyrics of "The Star Spangled Banner"
("The Defense of Fort McHenry")

Oh, say can you see, by the dawn's early light,
What so proudly we hailed at the twilight's last gleaming?
Whose broad stripes and bright stars, through the perilous fight,
O'er the ramparts we watched, were so gallantly streaming?
And the rockets' red glare, the bombs bursting in air,
Gave proof through the night that our flag was still there.
O say, does that star-spangled banner yet wave
O'er the land of the free and the home of the brave?

Rights Movement. Listening to Native American flute and drumming, children of all backgrounds can appreciate that pitch and harmony are not universally applicable attributes of the concept *music*. Contemporary folk songs such as "Little Boxes," "This Land Is Your Land, This Land Is My Land," "Detroit City," and "Sittin' on the Dock of the Bay" convey powerful social messages. Cowboy songs such as "I Ride an Old Paint," "The Night Herding Song," and "Git Along Little Dogie" have both lyrics and melodies that are hauntingly reminiscent of the lonely life of this American folk group. "The Yellow Rose of Texas," "When Johnny Comes Marching Home Again," and "Over There" are associated with significant conflicts of this nation (Texas independence, the Civil War, and World War I, respectively).

Teachers interested in learning more about the use of folk songs in the classroom should write to John W. Scott, P.O. Box 264, Holyoke, MA 01041, or to Diana Palmer, 433 Leadmine Rd., Fiskdale, MA 01518, for information about the newsletter entitled *Folksong in the Classroom*.

And drama? We are so enthused about the possibilities of dramatizations in social studies units that we could say it all again. But, instead, lets just simply refer you back to the section, "Launching the Unit," where we recommended dramatic play as a promising way to beginning a unit.

Conclusion

Unit planning is a lengthy and involved matter. It seems to sprawl every which way. In this chapter, we presented rules of thumb for *planning* the unit, followed by rules of thumb for *teaching* the unit. The latter included *activity* selection. Then came the *lesson* planning section followed by five ways to enrich any unit.

Each section asked readers to consult other chapters in this book, for example, the teaching strategies in Chapter 8, the resources in Chapter 9, assessment in Chapter 10, and teaching literacy skills in social studies in Chapter 12. We apologize for the inconvenience such skipping about may cause, but it cannot be avoided since the whole book is pertinent to unit planning.

At one point, we asked readers to look ahead to the final chapter of this book, which builds directly on the present one. In a sense, it is an extension of this chapter. Two ambitious teaching plans will be found there, and they are presented in full detail. One integrates language arts and social studies to help children read and write original biographies, in this case of the 19th-century abolitionist and women's rights advocate Sojourner Truth. The other, called "Explore," is a four-lesson unit plan that integrates social studies and science to help students construct a "unifying idea": *the decisions made by human beings influence the survival of other living things.* Both plans deserve your scrutiny. Both should stretch your thinking about unit planning, teaching strategies, tying learning activities to unit objectives, lesson planning, and curriculum integration. You may want to pay special attention to the second plan, "Explore." It is a remarkable, challenging, field-tested third-grade unit. In just three well-designed lessons, students construct three concepts needed to construct the unifying idea: the scientific method (inquiry), living things, and survival needs of living things. In the fourth lesson, they make decisions about how to help living things survive and, beyond survival, to reach their potential.

Both plans in Chapter 13 are focused on essential subject matter, they hold students to high expectations, they are aligned with the mission of social studies to empower democratic citizens, and they represent integrated unit planning at its most powerful. Just as important, both are do-able: They are feasible for beginning teachers who are willing to spend time planning. They are, in short, good models that build on the foundation laid down in this chapter.

We close by looking again at the last paragraph of the parent letter to the school principal with which we opened this chapter:

> When we asked him (Mr. Allison) how he did it, he looked sideways as though telling a secret. "Planning," was his reply. "Planning, planning, planning." We would have said it was charm or charisma or that he was a natural born teacher. But he set us straight. Please extend our thanks to him (again) for all the time he spent "planning, planning, planning."

Discussion Questions and Suggested Activities

1. Select a unit theme or topic that would be appropriate for a grade of your choice. Then identify three or four main ideas that could be developed in such a unit. Complete a unit planning chart such as the one shown in Figure 7–2. Think creatively about using drama in launching the unit, then incorporating reading, construction, simulation, and music in the development phase.

2. Develop a lesson plan related to the unit plan you developed in response to question 1. Use the simple format suggested in Lesson Plan 8 and elaborate on it as needed.

3. Write one or two behavioral objectives for the lesson you developed in response to question 2.

4. You have probably discovered by now that there is no standard unit or lesson plan format. Discuss unit and lesson plans and how to prepare them with your supervising teacher or another teacher you know. If possible, bring to class a sample of a lesson plan used by that teacher. In class, compare several types of plans.

5. Demonstrate for your classmates how you would proceed with a construction activity of some type (e.g., making butter, dipping candles, creating a model Cherokee village).

Selected References

Brophy, Jere, & Alleman, Janet. (1991, May). Activities as instructional tools: A framework for analysis and evaluation. *Educational Researcher, 20,* 9–23.

Katz, Lillian G., & Chard, Sylvia C. (1991). *Engaging children's minds: The project approach.* Norwood, NJ: Ablex.

Lindquist, Tarry. (1997). *Ways that work: Putting social studies standards into practice.* Portsmouth, NH: Heinemann.

Muir, Sharon Pray. (1996, March). Simulations for elementary and primary school social studies: An annotated bibliography. *Simulation and Gaming: An International Journal of Theory, Practice, and Research, 7,* 41–73.

Selwyn, Douglas. (1993). *Living history in the classroom: Integrative arts activities for making social studies meaningful.* Tucson: Zephyr.

Wharton-Boyd, Linda F. (1983, Winter). The significance of Black American children's singing games in an educational setting. *Journal of Negro Education, 52,* 46–56.

Wiggins, Grant, & McTighe, Jay. (1998). *Understanding by design.* Alexandria, VA: Association for Supervision and Curriculum Development.

Notes

1. See John Dewey's plain and helpful essay, *The child and the curriculum.* In has helped generations of teachers make peace between the child-centered and subject-centered impulses within them.

2. The seminal contemporary research on this point was done by Lee Shulman (Those who understand: Knowledge growth in teaching, *Educational Researcher, 15,* (1986): 4–14), and Sam Wineburg (The psychology of learning and teaching history, in R. C. Calfee & D. C. Berliner (Eds.), *Handbook of educational psychology,* 423–437, New York: Macmillan, 1996).

3. Howard Gardner, *The disciplined mind* (New York: Simon & Schuster, 1999), 209.

4. We think this is clearly a more comprehensive unit, but not necessarily a "better" one. Perhaps District X focuses on the other "central ideas" earlier in the year during the units on American history. Often a tighter focus is just what students need. At any rate, moving freely between planning broad comprehensive, integrated units and narrowly focused short-term units seems to us the wise course. (The "middle way" often is the best way in curriculum planning as in life and politics.)

5. Adapted from CONTACT #60, Canada Studies Foundation, Toronto, 1983.

6. Gardner, 186.

7. Vivian Gussin Paley, *Wally's stories* (Cambridge: Harvard University Press, 1981), 108.

8. See Barbara Hatcher & Mary Olson, Sidewalk social studies, *Social Education, 48,* (September/October 1984): 473–74, 485.

9. Margit E. Mcguire, Conceptual learning in the primary grades: The Storyline strategy, *Social Studies and the Young Learner* 3 (January/February 1991): 6–8.

10. Sharon Pray Muir, Simulation games for elementary and primary school social studies: An annotated bibliography, *Simulation and Gaming: An International Journal of Theory, Practice, and Research 7* (March 1996): 41–73.

11. Douglas Selwyn, *Living history in the classroom: Integrative arts activities for making social studies meaningful* (Tucson: Zephyr, 1993), 150.

Websites

Favorite: *http://www.infoseek.go.com/WebDir/Education/K_12/ Resources_for_students/Social_studies_for_students?sv= M6&svx=related*

http://www.nationalgeographic.com/education/standards.html

http://www.ncss.org/links/home.html

http://www.whitehouse.gov

http://www.senate.gov

CHAPTER 8

Three Great Teaching Strategies

Main Idea

Three time-honored, field-tested teaching strategies are presented. Each is tailored to a particular kind of social studies subject matter: concepts (e.g., *democracy*), skills (e.g., *map reading*), and inquiry (e.g., *Who lived at Mesa Verde?*). Each is a powerful tool for providing high-quality instruction, and each relies on the teacher's skillful use of questions.

Key Concepts

teaching strategy, concept, example, classifying, fact, inquiry, hypothesis, conclusion, skill

Chapter Outline

- Teaching Concepts
- Teaching with Inquiry
- Teaching Social Studies Skills
- Asking Good Questions
- Conclusion
- Discussion Questions and Suggested Activities
- Selected References
- Notes

Chapter Snapshot

The central theme of Dylan Coulter's third-grade integrated curriculum is the concept *community*. He uses the concept-formation strategy to teach this concept to his students. The examples they study are their own community, its "sister city" in Japan, and three communities that are detailed in the social studies textbook: Mesa Verde, Washington DC, and Los Angeles. After students have formed the concept, Mr. Coulter uses a skill-teaching strategy to help them learn how to take and defend a position on a controversial issue. Then the class conducts a poll of the parents to determine their community's most pressing issue. Following this inquiry, the students study and write editorials on that issue, in which they practice taking and defending a position.

 A favorite website www.titanic.cc/index.htm A *Titanic* site with many links for use with the inquiry strategy.

Why a separate chapter on teaching strategies? After all, teaching strategies can be found in every chapter of this book. Chapter 6 alone has several for teaching current events and controversial issues, and Chapter 13 presents two methods of curriculum integration. The reason is that we want to introduce you to three "classic" strategies. These are popular and time-honored instructional methods that are matched to core social studies subject matter. "Subject matter," recall, is education jargon for the *what* (not the *how*) of teaching and learning—the *curriculum,* which includes knowledge, skills, attitudes, and values. In social studies, the core subject matter includes facts, of course, and concepts, the social-science method called inquiry, skills, and democratic values and attitudes. The three strategies we present in this chapter are tailored to concepts, inquiry, and skills (see Table 8–1).

These strategies are powerful instructional tools with which you can help children learn much of the essential subject matter of social studies. You can think of them as scaffolds,[1] without which students probably will not learn as much or as well or be introduced to ways of thinking that will make them stronger learners.

That last point is important. These teaching strategies not only teach subject matter, they empower students *as learners.* In a school where the faculty is committed to empowering students as learners, the students not only know more each year but increase each year *in their ability to know.* They gradually become better researchers, questioners, and thinkers. Esmé Raji Codell, in her witty and irreverent book about her first year of teaching in Chicago, captures this general idea: "The difference between a beginning teacher and an experienced one is that the beginning teacher asks 'How am I doing?' and the experienced teacher asks 'How are the children doing?'"[2]

Teaching Concepts

In everyday parlance, the term *concept* is used to mean *idea,* as when someone says, "my concept of 'happy marriage' is not the same as yours." In social studies the meaning is the same: Concepts are ideas. Social studies concepts often embody an elaborate meaning that evolves with experience and learning over many years. Sometimes a child's initial understanding of a concept includes misconceptions that in later years must be corrected. Consider a kindergartner's concept of *history,* for example, or *family* or *freedom* or *money,* compared to an eighth grader's or a twelfth grader's or yours. Let us explore briefly the meaning and implications of concepts for teaching and learning social studies and then turn to a great way to teach them.

TABLE 8–1   Matching teaching strategies to the nature of the subject matter.

Subject Matter	Teaching Strategies
Concepts	Provide examples and help students grasp the attributes common to each.
Inquiry	Have students test hypotheses with data and draw conclusions.
Skills	Break the skill into its parts, explain and model each part; provide plenty of practice and application opportunities.

WHAT ARE CONCEPTS?

If asked to tell what a village is, most adults would probably say something along this line: "A village consists of a group of persons living in a rural area in a cluster of homes smaller than a city or a town." For most purposes this is an adequate definition to make communication possible. But *village* had a much more elaborate meaning for the native Americans of British Columbia, as explained in Margaret Craven's novel *I Heard the Owl Call My Name*. On the boat trip north, the young priest, Mark Brain, recalls what his bishop had told him about the village:

> The Indian knows his village and feels for his village as no white man for his country, his town, or even for his own bit of land. His village is not the strip of land four miles long and three miles wide that is his as long as the sun rises and the moon sets. The myths are the village and the winds and the rains. The river is the village, and the black and white killer whales that herd the fish to the end of the inlet the better to gobble them. The village is the salmon who comes up the river to spawn, the seal who follows the salmon and bites off his head, the Bluejay whose name is like the sound he makes—"kwiss-kwiss." The village is the talking bird, the owl, who calls the name of the man who is going to die, and the silver-tipped grizzly who ambles into the village, and the little white speck that is the mountain goat on Whoop-Szo.
>
> The fifty-foot totem by the church is the village, and the cedar-man who stands at the bottom holding up the eagle, the wolf and the raven! And a voice said to the great cedar tree in Bond Sound, "Come forth, Tzakamayi and be a man," and he came forth to be the cedar-man, the first man-god of the people and more powerful than all others.[3]

This is a superb example of a concept because it illustrates the richness and depth of meaning that can inhere in a single word label: in this case, *village*. It also illustrates how vital *experience* is in developing such meanings. It is doubtful if anyone who did not actually grow up in the village culture of these Native Americans could understand and appreciate the full meaning of *village* as they conceptualize it. Yet the novelist does very well in conveying the meaning by skillfully building word images for us of things that are familiar because they come out of our own background of experience.

As we have said, concepts are ideas. Ideas are abstract categories or classes of meaning—abstract because they are removed from specific examples. For instance, *island* is the word label for a geographic phenomenon whose attributes are (a) land (b) completely surrounded by water. Kauai is one specific example of such attributes. There are thousands of other specific examples of the concept *island*. But to know that Kauai is an island (that is, a body of land completely surrounded by water) is not to know very much about that beautiful outcropping of land in the Pacific. Concept definitions, therefore, tell us only about those qualities or attributes that a group of examples *has in common*. They do not tell us about the unique features of particular examples. The concept (the idea) refers to the attributes shared by all examples. And that is the most concise definition of concept: the critical (important) attributes shared by all examples. Put a little differently, concepts are "categories into which we group phenomena within our experience."[4] Concepts (e.g., *island*) help us group the phenomena in our world into meaningful categories. But they are meaningful only to the extent we deeply understand the examples to which they refer (e.g., Kauai).

Concepts may deal with concrete places, persons, objects, institutions, or events or ways of thinking, feeling, and behaving. Here are a few more concepts and some examples of each that would be appropriate for study in the third grade.

Island
Kauai
Cuba
Fiji

Mountain
Mt. Everest
Pike's Peak
Mt. Fuji

Technology
Steamboat
Morse Code
Airplane
Computer chip

Community
Mesa Verde
Washington, DC
Los Angeles
Tokyo

Public Issue
Should adults be required to vote?
Should zoos be allowed?
Should we have a new class rule: "You can't say 'you can't play' "?

Migration
Oregon Trail
Ellis Island immigration
The Great Migration
San Diego immigration

Justice (fairness)
Taking turns
Lining up for recess
Writing down the rules
Applying rules equally to everyone

Note that each of the 10 curriculum standards developed by the National Council for the Social Studies (see the standards *Sampler* that accompanies this text) is a concept or a group of two or three concepts:

1. Culture
2. Power, authority, and governance
3. Time, continuity, and change
4. Production, distribution, and consumption
5. People, places, and environments
6. Science, technology, and society
7. Individual development and identity
8. Global connections
9. Individuals, groups, and institutions
10. Civic ideals and practice

Similarly, the five themes of geography described in Chapter 4 are concepts:

1. Movement
2. Region
3. Human-environment interaction
4. Location
5. Place

When teachers become familiar enough with concepts that "they know one when they see one," they can teach more effectively: *Recognizing that a curriculum objective centers on a concept, teachers can then reach into their toolbox of strategies for one that is tailored to concepts.*

Here, at last, is the time-honored strategy for teaching concepts, called "concept formation." It begins by helping children experience multiple examples of the concept to be learned and then helping them grasp the critical attributes all the examples have in common. This is, in a nutshell, the key to concept teaching. After we present concept formation, we will briefly consider two variations: a concept teaching strategy called "list, group, and label" and another called "concept attainment." If you have time to learn only one, however, "concept formation" is it.

CONCEPT FORMATION

A fifth-grade class will be learning the concept *democracy*. It is one of the central concepts for understanding United States history, which is the subject matter emphasis of the fifth grade. The teacher, Kenneth Bailey, has assessed his students' preinstruction understanding of this idea by asking a few diagnostic questions:

> What is democracy?
>
> Is the United States a democracy? Why?
>
> Are our weekly classroom meetings democratic? Why?
>
> Can you think of another example of democracy?

In this way, Mr. Bailey learns that his students have no concept of democracy save vague notions of "voting" and "elections." With this information in hand, he builds an introductory concept-formation lesson.

First, he assembles three or four examples of democracy that will be the building blocks of the concept. He decides to use the governments of the United States, Mexico, and Canada because the textbook has information on them. For the fourth example, he wants something less "bookish," more experiential; he selects the democratic classroom meeting his students have each Monday afternoon.

Using the concept-formation strategy, students will build an understanding of democracy "from the bottom up" by studying each example, comparing and contrasting them, and then summarizing how they are alike. The similarities among examples are the critical attributes of the concept. The critical attributes common in the United States, Mexico, Canada, and Mr. Bailey's classroom meetings are these: the majority rules (laws are made by all citizens or their representatives), minority rights are protected, and laws are written down. These are the three attributes students eventually should summarize under the name "democracy." Is the resulting concept as complex as the one formed by college political science majors? Of course not, but it would be quite an achievement for fifth-grade children. Lesson Plan 9 shows the teacher's plan for achieving this result.

Lesson Plan 9   # DEMOCRACY: A CONCEPT-FORMATION LESSON

Grade	4–8
Time	Two to four class periods
Objectives	Children will form the concept *democracy* and then apply it (reinforcing and revising it as needed) by determining whether additional items are or are not examples of democracy (classifying).
Interest Building	Remind students of a recent classroom meeting in which a vote was taken to resolve a class or school issue. Lead a discussion on the question, "Is majority rule always fair?"

Lesson Development

Step 1

Studying multiple examples. Create a data-retrieval chart that contains the four examples down the left column and focus questions across the top. These questions focus students' attention on the critical attributes.

A Data-Retrieval Chart for the Concept Democracy

FOCUS QUESTIONS

Examples	Does the majority rule? How?	Are minority rights protected? How?	Are the laws written? Where?
United States			
Canada			
Mexico			
Class meeting			

Direct students to use this chart to record information they find on each example. Provide time in class to find the information in their textbooks and complete the chart. Direct them to finish the chart as homework. Suggest that they look for regular elections in response to the first question and push them to find out *who* can and cannot vote.

Step 2

Noting differences. The next day, verify that all the needed information on the four examples has been gathered and recorded. Then ask students, "In what ways do these four governments differ?"

Step 3

Noting similarities. Ask, "In what ways are these four governments all alike?" Record their responses on the chalkboard for use in the next step. (*Note:* This is the phase of the lesson where students themselves identify the critical attributes of the concept *democracy,* which are the similarities across the examples.)

Step 4

Summarizing. Direct students to "take a few minutes now to jot down a summary of these similarities in one, complete sentence. Let's begin the summary with, 'These are all ways of governing that . . . ' " Now students compose their own definition of the concept, working with the list of similarities still on the chalkboard from Step 3. Allow time for sharing and listen carefully to the concepts they have formed. Provide feedback and correction as needed. Students then compose a second draft, taking more care to include all the critical attributes of *democracy* in their summaries.

Step 5

Labeling. Ask, "What is a word you might use to describe governments like these? Be creative—invent a word if you like. Make sure it captures the essence of this kind of government." After eliciting several nicknames, tell students that the conventional label for this kind of government is *democracy.* Then use your desk dictionary to read aloud the etymology of this Greek term.

Step 6

Application: classifying. Now that students have built a rough idea of *democracy,* it is time to reinforce and extend it to the application activity called *classifying.*

Classifying 1. Ask students to read the brief description of the Plymouth Colony in their textbooks and then to decide whether it was a democracy. Ask for a show of thumbs (thumbs up for "Yes, it was a democracy"; thumbs down for "no"; thumbs sideways for "not sure"). Then ask for reasons.

Classifying 2. Give students information about two or three other governments (China's, Denmark's, Japan's) and ask them to decide which of them, if any, is a democracy. This time have them write down their reasons. Then call on several students to share their decisions and reasons.

Classifying 3. Form teams of three to four students and direct each team to brainstorm a fictional example of a democracy. Have them imagine themselves shipwrecked on an island with no chance of rescue; hence, they must create a society from scratch. Remind them to look back at their summaries to be sure the example they create has each of the attributes all examples of democracies must have. Have the teams share their fictional examples and tell why they are democracies.

Classifying 4. Tell students that you will describe an organization that is not an example of *democracy.* The students' task is to describe the changes that would be needed to make it into a democracy. (Describe a modern military dictatorship or a Little League baseball club.)

Summary Call on several students to review the critical attributes of democracy.

Assessment Any of the four types of classifying in Step 6 will serve as a precise assessment of the extent to which students have formed the concept. The proof is not in the decisions they reach (thumbs up; thumbs down) but in the *reasons* they give.

Materials Copy of data-retrieval chart for each student. Textbook section on Plymouth Colony and other examples and nonexamples as required.

Integration *Literature:* Voting captures the essence of "democracy" for young children, and children's trade books on voting are plentiful. *The Ballot Box Battle* by Emily Arnold McCully (Dragonfly, 1998) about women winning the right to vote in the United States or *The Day Gogo Went to Vote* by Elinor Batezat Sisulu (Little, Brown, 1996) about a black woman voting in South Africa for the first time in 1994.

Math: Voting in class meetings provides an opportunity to work with fractions and proportions (e.g., "two-thirds of us were for the playground rule; one-third was against it").

■   ■   ■   ■   ■

Classifying

Classifying is an integral part of the concept-formation procedure. It is the method by which students *apply* the concept they have formed. Classifying is a type of higher-order thinking that requires students first to recall the critical attributes of a concept and then determine whether those attributes are present in a new situation. This new situation is bound to be different from the examples studied initially to form the concept; accordingly, students need to decide if any of the differences really matter as far as the concept is concerned.

There are four basic forms of classifying. Each was used in Step 6 in Lesson Plan 9, and every teacher of every age of student needs to know them and is wise to use them frequently:

Four Types of Classifying

1. Deciding whether a new item is an example.
   (The teacher asks, "Is this an example?")
2. Distinguishing examples from nonexamples.
   (The teacher asks, "Which of these are examples?")
3. Producing examples.
   (The teacher directs, "Find or make an example.")
4. Correcting nonexamples.
   (The teacher asks, "What changes are needed to make this an example?")

The four types of classifying can be used both before and after concept instruction. When used before, it is for the purpose of assessing the extent to which students have formed a particular concept. A teacher may be thinking that a class needs a concept formation lesson on *peninsula.* But, not wanting to waste their time, she first assesses their understanding by using classifying. Let us say she decides to use the first type: Pointing to Florida on the wall map of the United States, she says, "I'm curious. Who can tell us whether this piece of land here in the state called Florida is a peninsula? Why don't you take a minute to think about it. Then give us a thumb up if you think it is, a thumb down if you think it isn't, and a thumb sideways if you're not sure. Remember, 'Not Sure' is an honorable position to take if you, indeed, are not sure." In a class of 25, she sees two thumbs up, two down, and 21 sideways. She then elicits their reasons, for without reasons she has learned almost nothing. "Those of you with your thumbs sideways, what makes you unsure?" Some say they've never heard "that word before." Another thinks a peninsula "is more like a lake." And so forth. The two thumbs up actually don't know the concept, it turns out. They're claiming Florida is a peninsula but for all the wrong reasons. The two thumbs down think it is not a peninsula, but their reasons reveal they haven't formed the concept either. Hence, she decides to work up a concept-formation lesson.

When classifying is used *after* instruction on a concept, it is for the purpose of strengthening the concept and providing students the opportunity to *use* it—to apply it to new items. Of course, if students haven't formed the concept, they will be unable to apply it. Noticing this, the teacher will have assessed that their understanding of the concept is too weak to simply "move on" to the next topic; accordingly, she will need to reteach the concept, probably in a different way. This time, she might incorporate cooperative groupwork at Step 1.

Incorporating Cooperative Groupwork

At Step 1 in concept formation, students can be placed in cooperative teams of four students each. Each member of the group takes responsibility for gathering information on one of the four examples. Sherry takes Mexico, Jim takes Canada, Mie takes the classroom meetings, and Reno gets the United States. (Or, in the case of the peninsula lesson, one takes Florida, another takes the Olympic peninsula, etc.) Because one member of every other team is studying the same example, these students get together in an "expert group" to work on their example together (see Chapter 11 for details). Every team member thus leaves his or her team to work with other students responsible for the same example. Eventually, experts return to their teams where they teach their example to teammates. In this way, everyone studies all examples—which is crucial for concept formation: remember, a concept is a summary of attributes shared by all examples.

For Steps 2 through 5, it is a good idea to work with the whole class as Mr. Bailey did. But for *classifying*, teams can again be convened to work through the four activities.

A VARIATION ON CONCEPT FORMATION: LIST, GROUP, AND LABEL

We would be remiss if we did not share a delightful and often usable variation on concept formation called "List, Group, and Label." Imagine a primary grade class that has just returned from a field trip to a supermarket. Back in the classroom, the teacher asks the children to list as many things as they can remember having seen in the supermarket. As they name items, the teacher writes them on the chalkboard—for example, eggs, bread, beans, meat, butter, checkout person, stock clerk, watermelons, candy, store manager, dog food, cat food, ice cream, and so on.

After listing the things they saw, the teacher asks them to examine their list to see if certain things seem to go together. "Can these items be put together in groups that have something in common?" They catch on quickly, and soon they are suggesting which items can be placed in the same group. Dog food and cat food are put together.

Having placed items that seem to go together in the same group, children are then asked to think of names or labels for these groups. In the foregoing example, a name for that group would probably be "pet food." The children should develop a name or label for each of the groups. Figure 8–1 shows a sample list, groups, and labels.

The "List, Group, and Label" strategy can be used in many ways to teach concepts in social studies. It can also be played as the game called "Things You See at _____" (at the zoo, at the mall, at the swimming pool, in the neighborhood). As students gain more practice, they begin to more skillfully note similarities among items. Consequently, they group and regroup items in more interesting and more subtle ways, using the same item in more than one group. One student can create a group and ask the others to guess the common attribute on which it was formed. For example, can you identify the similarity on which the following group was formed?

Apples
Oranges
Eggs
Ice cream

FIGURE 8–1
List, group, and label.

List	Group	Label
eggs	-milk	"cow food"
tomatoes	-ice cream	
brooms	-butter	
mops	-hamburger	
sponge		
dog food		
lemon cake	-brooms	"cleaners"
hamburger	-mops	
lettuce	-sponges	
chile		
apples		
cat food		
milk	-cookies	"sweets"
cookies	-ice cream	
ice cream	-sherbet	
sherbet	-oranges	
frozen pizza	-lemon cake	
butter		
oranges		
checkers	-checkers	"workers"
sackers	-sackers	

(*Possible responses:* each is a food; each begins with a vowel.) Here now are a few additional questions that call for listing, grouping, and then labeling. Each builds geographic awareness.

- Suppose a visitor from another country spent a day at our school; what would he or she see?
- What did you see on our walk through the neighborhood?
- What are all the ways you have seen goods and people being moved from one place to another?
- How many things can you list that are manufactured in our state?
- What are some land forms in North America?
- What natural resources do we depend on in our everyday life?

ANOTHER VARIATION ON CONCEPT FORMATION: CONCEPT ATTAINMENT

There is another variation on concept formation, which is less discovery oriented and more direct, but still powerful. This approach is sometimes called "concept attainment."[5] Let us say that a sixth-grade class has been studying the economic development of nations in the Third World. The teacher, Ms. Rush, wants her students to develop the concept *moderniza-*

tion and helps them do so in the following way. Note that she does not first give them examples to study and then lead them to a discovery of the concept based on the examples' shared attributes, as in concept formation; rather she *tells* them the attributes and then provides examples and nonexamples and helps students distinguish between them. She begins by writing the concept label and critical attributes on the chalkboard:

Modernization Involves

1. The use of technology to control nature's resources.
2. The use of inanimate sources of power and energy.
3. The use of tools to multiply the effects of human energy.

Ms. Rush then explains the meaning of each of the three attributes by using large pictures. She shows the class specific examples of modernization—situations in which technology is applied to the control of resources, where inanimate power and energy sources are used, and where tools multiply human energy. She calls these "examples" and makes the presence of all four attributes clear in each of them. Children's questions are discussed and problems are clarified. Ms. Rush then provides the class with a series of pictures in which modernization, as defined by the particular attributes, is *not* evident. She identifies these as "nonexamples" of modernization and tells students they need to understand *why* they are not examples of modernization. Each photo is explained, and the missing critical attributes are discussed. Questions are encouraged and answered carefully.

Having satisfied herself that the children understand the attributes that indicate modernization, the teacher presents the class with another set of pictures, but this time the students themselves must distinguish examples from nonexamples of modernization and explain their decisions (this is classifying, type 2). These pictures are discussed in detail. The teacher then provides the class with back issues of *National Geographic* and asks them to find photo examples and nonexamples of modernization and to tell why each is or is not an example (classifying, type 3). Finally, the teacher evaluates the children's understanding of the concept by having them identify examples and nonexamples from a new set of pictures (classifying, type 2 again).

This variation on concept teaching is less construction-oriented than the first two. In this case, the teacher provides the attributes of the concept in advance rather than having learners construct them in the process of study at Steps 3 and 4 of the concept-formation strategy. In summary, then, concept attainment has seven steps:

1. Teacher tells students the label for the concept (*modernization*).
2. Teacher lists the critical attributes of the concept.
3. Teacher provides examples (each has the attributes).
4. Teacher provides nonexamples (each is missing one or more attributes).
5. Teacher presents more examples and nonexamples, has the children decide which is which, and has them tell why or why not each was an example.
6. Teacher has children find examples and nonexamples on their own.
7. Teacher evaluates students' ability to use the attributes in identifying examples and nonexamples.

Preparations are made to deeply teach the concept *village* in a unit called "Village Life Around the World."

SUMMARY

Concept formation and its two variations help children learn multiple examples of the concept to be learned and grasp the critical similarities among all the examples. This is the heart of concept teaching. In concept attainment, the children do less of the construction work themselves; the teacher does more for them. It is therefore a somewhat easier strategy to use, and you may wish to try it before the others.

BUT WHAT ABOUT FACTS?

Before we leave the subject of teaching concepts, we should address one question that may be on your mind: What about facts in concept teaching?

Facts are data or information. Facts can be observed using the senses: A child can see that a pueblo home is made of pinkish mud. She can feel the straw sticking out of the adobe brick. She can hear the slow beat of the drum. She can taste the fry bread and smell the burning sage. These are facts. There are millions of facts that students could be asked to learn.

FIGURE 8–2   The relationship of facts, examples, and concepts.

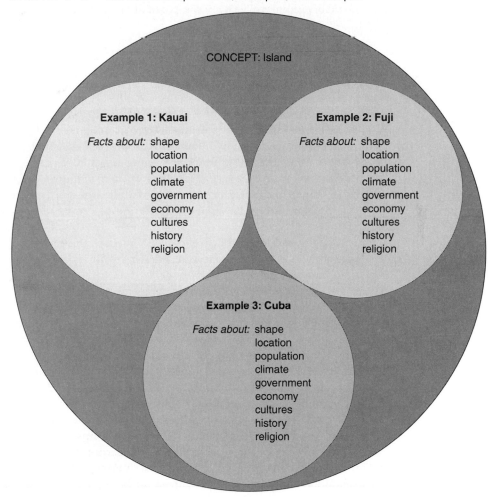

CONCEPT: Island

Example 1: Kauai

Facts about: shape
location
population
climate
government
economy
cultures
history
religion

Example 2: Fuji

Facts about: shape
location
population
climate
government
economy
cultures
history
religion

Example 3: Cuba

Facts about: shape
location
population
climate
government
economy
cultures
history
religion

Concepts, on the other hand, are ideas that exist only in our minds. They cannot, therefore, be observed using the senses. They are made up of examples, *and examples are bundles of facts.* The fact that adobe is used to make pueblo dwellings, that it is made from the soil found in some parts of the southwestern region of what is now the United States, that an adobe home feels remarkably cool inside though the sun shines bright and hot overhead—these facts together make one example of the concept *human-environment interaction.* The Lakota Sioux portable shelter made of buffalo hide is another, and the Woodland Iroquois' long house is yet another. Figure 8–2 shows the relationship of facts, examples, and concepts.

You can see, then, that concept learning involves a good deal of facts learning. Concepts are composed of examples, which are composed of facts.

Teaching with Inquiry

The inquiry process is also called the *scientific method* or *problem solving* and, in the field of history, historical interpretation or historical reasoning (see Chapter 4). Call it what you will, it is the chief method used by historians and scientists to develop new knowledge and correct old, mistaken knowledge. Even young children can learn inquiry; their incessant "why" questions show that the motivation to inquire—the wonder—is fully alive. Teachers can help children become more skillful inquirers by engaging them in inquiry often, both as part of daily classroom life and as a way of learning social studies subject matter.

Children who have developed their inquiry abilities are able to draw conclusions based on evidence and judge whether conclusions drawn by others are supported by evidence. This is the essence of inquiry.

When they learn to inquire skillfully, students learn to explore historical (and other social studies) problems by making an educated guess about the problem and then searching for evidence that would justify one conclusion over another. More specifically, they learn to hypothesize, search for evidence, draw conclusions, and evaluate the strength of conclusions. For this reason, numerous thinking-skills experts exalt the inquiry process as the highest form of higher-order thinking, what they call *critical thinking*.[6] Students learn that evidence varies in its *credibility* (believeableness) and that there are usually competing accounts of any one event. Their teacher is forever pestering them with the questions "How do you know that's true?" and "Do your sources agree?" And, "If not, how did you decide?" Gradually, thanks to such teachers, students will come to ask these questions themselves. They will develop a healthy respect for facts, a steadfast aversion to "jumping to conclusions," and an eagerness to spot prejudices and root them out. These are habits or dispositions that are among the most valued goals that we have for children's learning. For this reason, even beginning teachers should make it a priority to involve children in inquiry experiences.

The general inquiry procedure is this: The teacher engages students' interest in the problem for study and has the children pose hypotheses about it. Then the teacher designs activities in which the children gather information and compare it to these hypotheses. As they do the comparisons, the children learn to discard, add, and revise hypotheses, as the facts require. Eventually, they draw conclusions. Let's look at the process step by step.

1. The teacher engages students in a problem related to a curriculum objective. This is accomplished using a few photos, a newspaper headline, a film clip, a compelling story, or some other interest-building technique. Here are a few problems drawn from a school district's social studies curriculum guide.

Problem	Curriculum Objective (excerpt)
Who really "discovered" America?	First peoples in the Americas
What happened to the Anasazi at Mesa Verde?	Pre-Columbian civilizations in America; human-environment interaction
Why did the Titanic tragedy occur?	Changing social life during the Industrial Revolution; transportation
Why did the Pony Express end suddenly?	Inventions that change everyday life; communication technology
Why is there poverty in rich nations?	Comparative economic systems; social class
Why do so few adults vote in the United States?	Comparative political systems; citizenship rights and responsibilities
Who benefits from advertising?	Media literacy; production and consumption; needs and wants

2. The teacher elicits hypotheses (reasonable guesses) from students about the problem and records them on the chalkboard or butcher paper taped to the wall.

   A teacher might say to students, "We know that the *Titanic* hit an iceberg, but *why* do you think this great 'unsinkable' ship did that?" She draws hypotheses out of students and writes them in large print on butcher paper taped to the wall:

   HYPOTHESES:

   The Titanic hit the iceberg because there was no radar.

   There was poor visibility that night.

   The lookouts were asleep or at a party.

   The ship was bombed by the other ship company, lost control, and hit the iceberg.

   Competition between companies made the captain speed.

   Over-confidence made him reckless.

3. Students gather information (evidence) through reading, oral reports by classmates, field trips, guest speakers, interviews and surveys, the Internet, audio- and videotapes, films, paintings, teacher read-alouds and presentations, and the like. This data gathering could take anywhere from a day to a few weeks, depending on how much data are available and how much of it the teacher wants students to gather, organize, and analyze. This research should involve multiple information sources and, if possible, both primary and secondary sources.

4. Students organize and interpret the information and draw conclusions. The most efficient way to do this is to organize the information (evidence; data) around the hypotheses. That is, students evaluate the hypotheses using the information that has been gathered and draw conclusions as to which hypotheses are best or least supported

by the evidence. As with any scientific study, there will be disputes among the researchers. This is good! Challenging one another's claims and conclusions is central to the activity called science.

5. The conclusions are published—they are made public. Whether in the classroom newsletter, a report to the school principal or town mayor, or a presentation to younger students, the results of scientific inquiry are always shared. The audience members can then accept or reject the conclusions presented based on their own interpretation of the evidence. This is how knowledge is constructed, corrected, and reconstructed over time.

Here now are two quite different examples of inquiry teaching. The differences display the breadth of approaches possible within the concept *inquiry;* however, they share the critical attributes necessary to be called inquiry lessons. The first concerns a third-grade class that has been studying the concept *advertising.* Notice how this teacher has students assemble numerous examples, elicits their hypotheses about the value of advertising, and then has them search for information that confirms or denies these hypotheses. The second is an inquiry lesson plan on the causes of the *Titanic* tragedy. It is one of our favorite plans, and we have used it many times. Both examples adhere, more-or-less, to the inquiry model presented above. For additional examples of inquiry teaching, combined in a unit plan with concept formation, readers can skip ahead to Chapter 13 and study the integrated third-grade science-social studies unit called *Explore.*

INQUIRY EXAMPLE 1: WHO BENEFITS FROM ADVERTISING?

A third-grade class has been introduced, using the concept-formation strategy, to the concept *advertising.* Sensing that the children's understanding is still quite weak, the teacher selects the following inquiry strategy to strengthen it.

First, children are asked to search for as many different examples of advertising as they can find. This search uncovers newspaper and magazine advertisements, classified ads, radio and television commercials, billboards, signs on transit buses, signs in public buildings, direct mailers, catalogs, and others. These various methods of advertising are discussed in terms of (a) their purpose; (b) the audience to which they are directed; (c) the extent to which they are local, regional, or national; and, (d) perhaps most important, the nature of the appeal. To help students perceive and think about the appeal, the teacher asks: How did the cartoonish cigarette hawker Joe Camel appeal to children? How does the "Marlboro Man" appeal to boys? How does the outdoorsy, four-wheel drive sports-utility vehicle commercial on television appeal to people who drive mainly in urban and suburban areas? How do slender clothing models appeal to girls? Anthropologists, it should be noted, are hired by advertising companies to study a segment of society and decide how a product can be made to appeal to it. The teacher might videotape advertisement examples from the evening television news hour and bring them to class for study.

These activities will surely generate student interest. Now, the teacher moves toward the inquiry question. Maybe this one: "Who benefits from advertising, and how do they benefit?" In response, the children develop the following hypotheses that they record on butcher paper and post on the wall:

HYPOTHESES:

1. Advertising helps consumers because it informs them about new products and their prices.

2. Effective advertising makes people want things whether they are needed or not. It benefits only the sellers.

3. Local advertising has a more direct effect on sales in local stores than does national advertising.

The children begin searching for information that would support or reject these hypotheses. Much of their information gathering relies on interviews and is done outside of school by interviewing consumers, local merchants, and conducting telephone and e-mail interviews of representatives of advertising agencies. This process forces them to explore related subconcepts such as needs and wants, promotion, audience, client, market, layout, theme, and sales appeal. In time, they are able to form some tentative conclusions relating to their hypotheses.

INQUIRY EXAMPLE 2: WHAT CAUSED THE TITANIC TRAGEDY?

The teacher shows students a replica of the headline in the local newspaper dated April 15, 1912. It reads, " 'Unsinkable' Greyhound Sinking Off Newfoundland." She tells her students that the headline is referring to the sinking of the luxury ocean liner, the *Titanic*. Due to the hugely popular recent film by James Cameron, they bubble with excitement. She asks them why they think such ocean liners were called "greyhounds" and why the present tense "is sinking" was used. Then she shows them a 10-minute film clip from the Cameron film of the *Titanic* tragedy or from the earlier (1958) film *A Night to Remember,* or from one of the several documentaries now available on videotape. This accomplishes Step 1—engaging their interest in the inquiry. Then she has students hypothesize about the *causes* of the tragedy. She selects the inquiry's focus question: "Why did the *Titanic* tragedy occur? We know it hit an iceberg, but why?"

Lesson Plan 10 presents the lesson plan she used. Notice that the teacher in this lesson provides the information to students rather than having them conduct research themselves. This is because she wants to familiarize them with the basic inquiry process, using a highly motivating topic. In the next unit, she plans to help them to use the inquiry process again, following the same five-part plan used with the *Titanic* inquiry, only now they will add considerable Internet and library research. In this way, they gradually build their inquiry skills throughout the year.

Note also that in the *Titanic* plan the teacher provides information a little bit at a time—in chunks, or data sets. This way, children can be helped to evaluate their hypotheses and draw tentative conclusions after *each* chunk of data. This is a highly effective strategy with younger and older children alike. It is a vivid way to give children a memorable experience of the power of data, a little at a time, for they see hypotheses vanish from the chalkboard as a new chunk of data is considered.

Lesson Plan 10	CAUSES OF THE *TITANIC* TRAGEDY: AN INQUIRY

Grade 4–8

Time Two to four class periods

Objectives Children will understand that an event such as the *Titanic* tragedy can have multiple causes. They will learn to formulate and revise hypotheses as new information is encountered and to draw conclusions based on evidence.

Interest Building Show a 1912 headline of the sinking of the *Titanic* and a clip from a documentary or fiction film of the tragedy, or photos of the *Titanic* gathered from magazine articles about the sinking of the ship and recent expeditions to explore it at the bottom of the Atlantic. Tell students the story of the *Titanic*—that it was billed as luxurious and "unsinkable" but hit an iceberg and sank on its first voyage.

Lesson Development

1. Ask students why they think a ship this great with a captain so skilled might have hit an iceberg on its maiden voyage. What *caused* the tragedy? List their reasons on the board under the title *hypotheses.* If needed, suggest some possibilities: captain was asleep, terrorism, lookouts were at a party, crew was not expecting icebergs in those waters at that time of year, captain was overconfident, design flaws in the ship.

2. Ask each student to jot down the hypothesis that he or she thinks might be true. Then ask everyone to share his or her favored hypothesis with the class.

3. Give students more information, one chunk (5 to 10 minutes) at a time. Begin with a set of information on the ship's design; then move to such things as the weather conditions that night, the captain's experience, the *Titanic's* sister ships, the way ships communicated and received warnings in those days, icebergs, social life aboard the ship, the lifeboats, the ship's cargo, the competition between the shipping lines, and so forth.

   Important: Between each set of data, pause and ask students to examine the list of hypotheses on the board. Have them remove, add, and revise hypotheses in light of the information they are getting. This is the core activity of the lesson.

4. Draw the inquiry to a close. Ask students to return to the hypotheses they jotted down at the beginning of the lesson. Have them revise these as needed to reflect what they now believe to be true. The new statements are "conclusions" based on data. Have them begin their conclusions as follows: "I conclude that the main reasons the *Titanic* tragedy occurred are . . . ." Encourage them to build multiple causes, not just one, into their conclusions.

Summary Tell the class that this process of revising conclusions ("changing our minds") in light of new data is the essence of science. It is the meaning of *open-minded* and it is the opposite of *jumping to conclusions.* Now ask students what information they can imagine that would cause them to revise their conclusions yet again.

Assessment (a) Collect and read the conclusions students wrote at Step 4 and evaluate them on the extent to which they were based on data gathered in Step 3. Invite students to place these conclusions in their portfolios and to begin a subsection called "inquiries." (b) It will also be interesting to find out what students now perceive to be the meaning of such phrases *as jumping to conclusions* and *closed-minded.* Also, see if they can write down the inquiry sequence they experienced in this lesson. Listen to their responses and provide assistance as needed:

1. Become familiar with the problem.
2. Develop hypotheses.
3. Gather and organize information.
4. Use the information to test each hypothesis.
5. Draw conclusion based on the information gathered.

Follow-Up Repeat the inquiry sequence with other more specific questions that will surely arise: Why were there not enough lifeboats? What was the last music played by the band? Why did rescue ships not arrive sooner? What difference did social class make and why? Begin to teach students ways to evaluate the quality of information: What was the source? Did the author have an agenda? Is information on the *Titanic* found in the *National Geographic* equivalent to information found in the *National Enquirer?*

Materials *Titanic* websites (e.g., *titanic.cc/index.htm*), the textbook, encyclopedia, magazine articles, books about its sinking and the expeditions to find it, film clips from *A Night to Remember* (1958) or the more recent James Cameron film, *Titanic.*

Integration *Music:* The heroism of the eight band members who kept playing to calm the passengers as the ship foundered is a study in itself. The funeral of their leader, Wallace Hartley, was attended by 30,000 mourners in his home town of Colne, Lancashire (England). A mystery remains: What was the final music they played? Primary sources disagree. The contenders are "Autumn" and "Nearer, My God, to Thee." Invite a music teacher (or a parent who is a musician) to visit the class and help students listen to recordings of both of these songs.

Literature: There are many trade books, both fiction and nonfiction, narrative and expository, on the *Titanic* tragedy. See *Titanic: The Disaster that Shocked the World,* by Mark Dubowski (DK, 1998) for younger children and, for older, *Titanic: Destination Disaster* by John Eaton and Charles Haas (Norton, 1987). The latter deals with the music question in detail. Film: As mentioned above.

■   ■   ■   ■   ■

Teaching Social Studies Skills

One of the main causes of poor skills among children—whether cooperative skills, thinking skills, reading and writing skills, research and study skills, or whatever—is, not surprisingly, lack of instruction. The systematic and sequential development of skills is of utmost importance to children because skills are among the tools with which they continue their learning. Inadequately developed skills tend to retard learning in many areas of the elementary and middle school curriculum, particularly in the social studies. Inadequate achievement in the social studies can, in many cases, be traced to poorly developed reading skills, inquiry skills, discussion skills, inability to read maps and globes, poor work-study skills, and inability to use reference materials. Therefore, a well-balanced program in the social studies needs to provide for systematic instruction to ensure the development of these skills.

Skill implies proficiency: the capability to do something well. Skills are commonly classified as motor, intellectual, and social. We do not deal with motor skills in this book, but social and intellectual skills are considered throughout. *Social skills* include forming small groups for cooperative work and functioning well within them. Social skills also include citizenship skills, such as discussion and decision making. Such skills are the subject of Chapters 3, 6, and 11. *Intellectual skills* are dealt with in nearly every chapter of this book. Reading and making maps, globes, time lines, and graphics are the skills discussed in Chapter 5. Numerous reading skills are discussed in Chapter 12.

In the present chapter alone we have encountered the intellectual skills needed to form concepts and conduct inquiry:

Intellectual Skills in Concept Formation

- Gathering data on each example
- Organizing information on data-retrieval charts
- Noting differences and similarities across examples
- Summarizing similarities
- Classifying (applying the concept in new situations)

Intellectual Skills in Inquiry

- Hypothesizing
- Gathering and interpreting data
- Evaluating hypotheses in light of data
- Drawing conclusions

All skills have two characteristics in common: They are developmental, and they require practice if they are to be mastered. To speak of skills as being developmental means that they are learned gradually over a period of years. Furthermore, they are never really learned to completion although there usually comes a time when the learner has mastered them sufficiently for most purposes; however, one could continue refining these skills throughout one's lifetime. Thus, teachers should not assume that skills are taught and learned only once in some particular grade. All teachers need to assume some responsibility for the teaching and maintenance of social studies skills.

No amount of explanation or meaningful teaching will make children proficient in skills. In the ordinary study of a topic, there will be numerous opportunities to practice skills in the daily work-study activities of the class. In this way, the children improve their skills as they develop their understanding of concepts and subject matter. Skills are learned more effectively when they are closely related to actual situations in which they will be used.

The basic skill-teaching procedure is fairly clear-cut. The learners should first understand what is involved in the skill, how it is used, and what it means. Providing a good model of its use is helpful at this point. Second, the learners need to work through a simple application of the skill, step by step, under careful teacher guidance. This is essential to verify that they understand what is involved and are making a correct response. Third, they need to actually use the skill in a purposeful way. This first application of the skill should be kept very simple. It is a good opportunity to assess their understanding of the skill and provide feed-

Students test their hypotheses by gathering data from a website.

back. Fourth, the learners need additional guided practice, only now the level of difficulty can be increased a little. Continue to assess and provide feedback. Fifth, students need continued practice in using the skill in various functional settings. Gradually increase the complexity of the tasks in which students use the skill and encourage improved use of the skill. Sixth, continue to provide practice opportunities intermittently. These steps, along with an example of their application, are provided in Lesson Plan 11.

It is important to remember that skills should not be taught or learned outside a content framework. The content connection is most obvious in the case of work-study skills such as finding information, arranging information in usable forms, using maps, globes, and graphics, and organizing information. Such skills have no purpose outside of a functional setting where they are used to learn about peoples and places, form or extend concepts, conduct inquiries on problems, develop democratic dispositions, and other valued curriculum goals. The integration of content and skills applies to intellectual skills and groupwork skills as well. Higher-order thinking processes such as summarizing, classifying, inquiry, and decision making must be put to work in content learning if they are to be taught with integrity and authenticity. Accordingly, teachers should not set out to teach these important processes without giving ample consideration to the subject matter in which they are to be applied. Teaching the needed skills explicitly using a lesson plan such as the classic one provided here *and then using them*—that is the proper approach.

USING A NEWSPAPER DIRECTORY: A SKILLS LESSON

Grade 3–8

Time Two to three class periods

Objectives Children will learn to use a newspaper's directory and then apply the skill to finding information in several different newspapers

Interest Building Engage students in a brief discussion of a controversial issue in the news, something pertinent to them. Then ask a few questions to determine what they know about the location in newspapers of related news stories, editorials, and political cartoons. Then produce a class set of the day's newspaper.

Lesson Development

Step 1

Make sure children understand what is involved in performing the skill. Show them how it is used. Provide them with a good model of the skill in operation.

For example, for a lesson on using a newspaper directory, hold up the newspaper and show how difficult and time-consuming it is to find some bit of information if one has to leaf through the entire paper to find it. Have children try their hand at finding items without using the newspaper directory. Show how easily one can find information with the aid of the directory.

Step 2

Break the skill into components and arrange them sequentially. Develop the teaching sequence step by step, having the children do each component as it is presented and explained. Supervise carefully to make sure their responses are correct.

The following are some ways you might develop a lesson on using a newspaper directory:
- Acquaint children with various sections of the newspaper: general news, classified ads, sports, editorials, letters to the editor, weather, and so on.
- Teach children the specialized vocabulary associated with the newspaper: vital statistics, obituaries, market quotations, headline, byline, dateline, syndicated, and so on.
- Teach children what items are included in the various categories listed in the directory and how they are arranged. For example, what is included in the arts and entertainment section? How are the classifieds organized?
- Provide a newspaper for each member of the class and have the children locate easy items using the directory. Such items might include the television schedule, sports, and the comics. Supervise to make sure everyone is performing the skill correctly.

Step 3

Have children perform a simple variation of the skill under your close supervision. This will ensure that they are performing the skill correctly.

For the lesson on using a newspaper directory, follow Step 2 immediately with an exercise requiring children to locate items using the directory. Supervise and assist as needed. Check responses.

Step 4

After it is established that the children are performing the skill correctly, provide for supervised practice, using simple variations that ensure success.

For the lesson on using a newspaper directory, assign children to find information in the next day's newspaper. This should be done on their own without teacher supervision. Check responses.

Step 5

Gradually increase the complexity of the variation of the skill and begin having children apply the skill in situations in which it is useful. Continue this procedure until the desired level of proficiency is achieved.

For the newspaper directory lesson, bring to class copies of different newspapers from the one used thus far in which slightly different directory formats appear. Assign children to find information in these papers without teacher assistance to see if they can transfer and modify their skill from one situation to another. Check responses. (This can be done in trios—one paper per group.)

Step 6

Follow up. Continue to have students practice the skill at regular intervals, largely through functional application to maintain and improve performance.

For the newspaper directory lesson, have children continue to use the directory to locate needed information. Observe the accuracy and extensiveness of use of the directory. For example, when teaching a current event, have students locate relevant articles, editorials, and letters to the editor.

Summary Review the name of the skill. Then have several students demonstrate it.

Assessment Note the informal assessment that was part of the opening "interest building." Following the skill lesson and using a different newspaper (e.g., the next day's), observe students as they locate "as quickly as you can" the following sections: movies, sports, editorials, editorial cartoon, television schedule, national news, local news, classifieds, obituaries, and help wanted section in the classifieds.

Materials A newspaper for each student

Local newspaper website (e.g., *http://www.denverpost.com/index.html*)

Integration *Reading:* This lesson infused reading instruction into the social studies curriculum. Capable newspaper reading also requires the reading skills of previewing and skimming (see Chapter 12). Social studies is the ideal base for reading instruction, with its wide spectrum of content: narrative, exposition, biography, argument, and multiple perspectives.

■   ■   ■   ■   ■

Asking Good Questions

The teaching strategies presented in this chapter all rest squarely on good questions. Each of these three teaching strategies (five, if you count the two variations on concept formation) assumes that the teacher is a skillful question asker. Asking good questions, then, is not a separate teaching strategy so much as it is *a component of any good strategy*. Looking back at concept formation, we see that the teacher's questions make up the scaffold students stand on at each step. At the noting similarities step, the teacher asks, "In what ways are these four governments all alike?" At the next step, another question invites students to summarize these similarities into a single statement. At the next, a question elicits the concept's label, which is a label for this summary. Each question initiates a particular kind of intellectual work, in a particular sequence, culminating in the formation of a concept and then testing and extending it with still more questions: classifying.

Looking back at inquiry, a carefully placed question invites students to hypothesize about causes of a historic event. This is the essential question for the whole inquiry process. Another question initiates data gathering and another elicits conclusions. The same goes for teaching skills, current events, and so on: Questions are the teacher's constant companion and the handiest and most powerful of tools. *They direct the intellectual work of students.* We are not suggesting that they replace love, patience, and curiosity; these are not replaceable. But whether the subject matter is a concept such as *democracy* or *shelter,* an inquiry on causes of the Civil War or the sinking of the *Titanic,* a skill such as map reading, or more likely, a combination of these in a unit of study, a toolbox of good questions is arguably the teacher's best friend.

PURPOSES OF ASKING QUESTIONS

Questions serve five purposes. They *assess,* they *focus attention,* they *guide thinking,* they *follow up* on students' responses, and they *facilitate participation.* A good understanding of these purposes is the first step to asking good questions; therefore, sample questions are given in relationship to each purpose.

Assessment

"In the end, it is more interesting listening to pupils and trying to understand why they see things as they do than it is to hear one's own voice trying to push them into giving the right answer."[7] Questions help curious teachers listen to students and, thereby, learn how and why they see things as they do. In other words, questions help teachers know children and ascertain their understanding of concepts, inquiry, and skills. They also help teachers assess whether students understand what they are to do and their reactions to demonstrations or explanations. Examples:

- Are playground games *democratic?* Should they be?
- What is this photo (story, paragraph, film, art print) saying?
- Before beginning, let's review the instructions. What are you to do first? Keesha? Michael?
- What did you learn from that demonstration? What would you have done differently?

Focus Attention

"What proves to be effective is not telling the child the right answer, but guiding him or her towards the right considerations."[8] Teachers use questions to focus students' attention on a particular topic—that is, to guide their thinking to these matters, not those. This is done both in a moment-to-moment fashion during instruction, such as when the teacher shifts students' focus from noting differences to noting similarities during the concept-formation sequence: "Now that we have identified some of the differences among the examples, how are they all alike?" Questions also enter into planning, such as when a teacher plans one question that will guide a two-week inquiry unit: "Why did the *Titanic* tragedy occur?" or "Who benefits from advertising?" Reflecting back on the teaching strategies addressed in this chapter, focus questions played a key role. For example, here is one focus question per strategy:

- *In concept teaching:* "What is a word you might use to describe governments like these? Be creative—invent a word if you like. Make sure it captures the essence of this kind of government."
- *In inquiry teaching at Step 2:* "What caused the *Titanic* tragedy? We know it hit an iceberg, but why?"
- *In skill teaching:* "How can the directory be used to locate information in the newspaper?"

Promote Thinking

Different questions promote different kinds of thinking. Research conducted over the past several decades on classroom questions reveals that teachers use a high percentage of questions that stimulate only recall of information that has been read or discussed in class. These questions are lower-level questions because they involve simple memory rather than higher-order thought processes that require some manipulation of information such as application, analysis, synthesis, interpretation, or evaluation. Lower-order questions can be easily identified because they often begin with *who, what, when,* and *where.* These questions are important, to be sure; we have already discussed the importance of facts. The problem is that they are overused, with a corresponding decreased use of questions that prompt higher-order thinking. Questions that prompt higher-order thinking help children achieve higher levels of understanding and skill: being able to construct and apply concepts, distinguish examples from nonexamples, test hypotheses, draw conclusions, and use skills in contexts different from those in which they were initially practiced.

- *Lower (memory):* "Describe majority rule in Canada and Mexico."
- *Higher (compare and contrast):* "How are these governments alike and different?"
- *Higher still (classifying/application):* "Create a fictional democracy that is different from those we've studied, though still possessing all the attributes of a democracy."[9]

Follow Up

Questions elicit responses. What to do with those responses, how best to respond to them, brings us to the fourth use of questions. Generally speaking, the most powerful follow-up questions are those that cause students to go further with their initial response. There are three main types of follow-up questions:

- *Clarify:* "What do you mean by _____?" (a term the student has used)
- *Elaborate:* "Tell us more about _____." (something the student has said)
- *Verify:* "How do you know that is true?"

Participation and Inclusion

Questions can help teachers increase student participation in the lesson and include all students.

- *"Talk with your partner about your response to that question, and in a moment I will ask several of you to share with the whole class."* The teacher lets the children know they will be held accountable for responding, thus causing more of them to attend to the task. Also, the sharing technique gets all children involved and allows sufficient time for the children to think. The teacher can roam around, giving feedback, praise, and correction as needed.

- *"How many of you think that advertising benefits mainly the consumer? Show one finger if you agree, two if you disagree. Then I'll ask several of you for your reasons."* All students are involved in the decision because of the finger-voting technique, and all know they could be asked to give reasons.

- *"Thanks, Nathaniel. How did some of you others respond?"* The teacher uses this question to acknowledge one student's response and invite other children to speak.

IMPROVING QUESTIONING SKILLS

All skills require practice if proficiency is to be achieved; asking good questions is no exception. A teacher is in a position to practice question asking daily, and colleagues can be invited to observe and provide feedback. One way to begin such practice is to write out the focus questions for a lesson and carry them on a clipboard during class. Also written on the clipboard are the standard follow-up questions (Figure 8–3). These are *clarify, verify,* and *elaborate.* They are taped to the clipboard because they are used to follow up regardless of the focus question. No matter the topic, teachers should encourage students to elaborate and clarify their understandings and be able to back up their conclusions and beliefs with evidence and sound reasoning.

Here now are several specific suggestions for improving your questioning skills.

1. Consciously reduce the number of factual-recall questions you ask and increase the number of questions that require higher-order thinking. Also, use and teach the *vocabulary* of higher-order thinking, terms such as *classify, analyze, hypothesize, summarize,* and, of course, *think.*

2. Don't confuse instructional questions with management directions. When you mean to give a direction, such as "sit down," say "sit down." Indirect commands given as questions ("Are you ready to sit down now?") can be confusing to children, especially those who are culturally different from the teacher or not native English speakers.

3. Match questions to the purpose they are to serve. Questions that call for yes-no responses are not appropriate when an elaborate response is desired. Discussion questions should not be used for homework or independent study.

4. Provide adequate time for children to respond. Ask the question *before* calling on a child to respond and tell students to take time to think. This requires all children to form their own response. Asking children to jot down their response before calling on individuals to respond aloud gives everyone time to collect their thoughts.

FIGURE 8–3
Use a clipboard to improve your
questions.

Focus Questions
1. What goods does our classroom
   store produce?
2. What services...?
3. What are some similarities and
   differences between goods &
   services?

Follow-up Questions:
CLARIFY: What do you mean?
VERIFY: How do you know?
ELABORATE: Tell us more.

5. Vary the way you acknowledge responses. In addition to "uh-huh," "all right," and
   "o.k.," ask a follow-up question: "Tell us more about that" or "What do you mean
   by _____ ?" Avoid always acknowledging responses with positive evaluations
   such as "right," "great," or "very good." Using these terms less often gives them more
   credibility with students.

Conclusion

Teaching strategies can be found in every chapter of this book. Why, then, a separate chapter? We wanted to introduce you to three "classic" strategies that are tailor-made for some of the core subject matter of social studies: concepts, the inquiry process, and skills.

These strategies lift up or "scaffold" students into ways of thinking, knowing, and doing that otherwise might be beyond their reach. As such they empower students *as learners*. When a learner knows how to form and then think with concepts, test hypotheses and draw conclusions, and develop and refine skillful behavior—that's power. *And note that the skills required by concept formation and inquiry are the very skills to which the skills-teaching strategy can be directed.* In other words, the first two strategies are skills-rich strategies; to use them, teachers need to pay attention to the skills students already possess *and need to learn* in order to form concepts and conduct inquiries. The skills-teaching strategy is ready-made for that purpose.

Asking good questions was not considered here to be a fourth, separate teaching strategy (though it certainly would be reasonable to do so). Rather, we treated skillful question-asking as a *component* of each of the other three strategies. Whether the subject matter is a concept (e.g., *village; democracy*), an inquiry (e.g., on the causes of the American Revolution or the sinking of the *Titanic*), or a skill (e.g., map reading; using the newspaper directory), or more likely a combination of these in a unit of study, a repertoire of good questions that serve different purposes is indispensable.

Also indispensable is knowledge of resources. We take up this topic in the next chapter.

Discussion Questions and Suggested Activities

1. Select a unit topic from the following list and name three concepts that might be included in such units. (Look back to the first section of this chapter and to Chapters 1–6.)
   • People change the earth (K–8)
   • School living (K)
   • Families and their needs (grade 1)
   • The shopping center (grade 2)
   • Life in the city (grade 3)
   • Our home state (grade 4)
   • The American Revolution (grade 5)
   • Crossroads of the world: The Middle East (grades 6–7)
   • Colonial America (grade 8)

2. Interview individually two or three children from a grade in which you have a special interest to determine their understanding of selected social studies concepts. Use a straightforward procedure and everyday concepts. For example, you might ask, "What does the term *prejudice* mean to you? Can you give me some examples of prejudice?" (or use *history, justice, cooperation, democracy, long ago, the future,* or geographical terms such as *environment, island,* or *rain forest*). These interviews will provide you with firsthand knowledge of what it means to transform an otherwise complex idea into a form that is sensible for elementary school children. Write up your findings to share with classmates and potential employers.

3. What are the essential differences among how one teaches concepts, skills, and the inquiry process?

4. Using the lesson plan for teaching a skill, apply each step to a skill of your choice for a grade in which you have a special interest. Share your examples with others in class.

5. Five purposes of question-asking were given in the section called "Asking Good Questions." For a unit you are imagining or planning right now, apply each of these purposes. For example, plan one or two "classifying" questions (review the concept teaching section) for the purpose of assessing students' knowledge of a concept before teaching it. Then plan a focus question and follow-up questions for a discussion you plan to lead. Fine-tune the focus question so it promotes the kind of thinking (intellectual work) you want students to do. Plan several questions/directions that will increase student participation.

Selected References

Beyer, Barry K. (1995). *Critical thinking.* Bloomington, IN: Phi Delta Kappa.

Brooks, Jacqueline Grennon, & Brooks, Martin G. (1993). *The case for constructivist classrooms.* Alexandria, VA: Association for Supervision and Curriculum Development.

Brown, Ann. (1996). Design experiments: Theoretical and methodological challenges in creating complex interventions in classroom settings. *Journal of the Learning Sciences, 2,* 141–178.

Joyce, Bruce, & Weil, Marsha. (2000). *Models of teaching.* 6th ed. Upper Saddle River, NJ: Prentice-Hall.

National Council for the Social Studies. (1994). A vision of powerful teaching and learning in the social studies: Building social understanding and civic efficacy. In *Curriculum standards for social studies.* (pp. 155–177). Washington, DC: Author.

Parker, Walter C. (1991, Jan./Feb.). Teaching an idea. *Social Studies and the Young Learner, 3,* 11–13.

Taba, Hilda, Durkin, Mary D., Fraenkel, Jack E., & Mcnaughton, A. H. (1971). *A teacher's handbook to elementary social studies: An inductive approach.* Reading, MA: Addison-Wesley.

Notes

1. A scaffold helps students reach higher and learn more—to perform closer to the ceiling of their abilities. See James Wertsch, *Voices of the mind: A sociocultural approach to mediated action* (Cambridge, MA: Harvard University Press, 1991). Also, Ronald G. Tharp & Ronald Gallimore, *Rousing minds to life* (Cambridge: Cambridge University Press, 1988).

2. Esmé Raji Codell. *Educating Esmé* (Chapel Hill: Algonquin, 1999), 191.

3. Margaret Craven, *I heard the owl call my name* (New York: Doubleday, 1973), 19.

4. Peter H. Martorella, Knowledge and Concept Development in Social Studies. In *Handbook of research on social studies teaching and learning,* edited by James P. Shaver (New York: Macmillan, 1991), 370–384.

5. See Hilda Taba et al., *A teacher's handbook to elementary social studies: An inductive approach* (Reading, MA, Addison-Wesley, 1971), and Bruce Joyce & Marsha Weil, *Models of teaching,* 6th ed. (Upper Saddle River, NJ, Prentice-Hall, 1999).

6. See Barry K. Beyer, *Critical thinking* (Bloomington, IN: Phi Delta Kappa, 1995) and Richard Paul, *Critical thinking* (Rohnert Park, CA: Center for Critical Thinking and Moral Critique, 1990).

7. Rosalyn Ashby & Peter Lee, Children's concepts of empathy and understanding in history, In *The history curriculum for teachers,* edited by Christopher Portal (London: Falmer, 1987), 86.

8. Ibid.

9. A system for asking higher-order questions called Bloom's Taxonomy was widely used by teachers in the decades after its publication in 1956 and is still used by many. It has fallen somewhat from favor in the past 10 years, however, following the "cognitive revolution" in educational psychology. This movement focuses less on the *kind of question* students are being asked than on the *quality of the task* they are being helped to perform. Forming a concept, conducting an inquiry, and applying a skill are three great constructive-intellectual tasks, the accomplishment of which *necessarily* involves students in higher-order thinking. Bloom's Taxonomy, however, is still a valuable tool and many teachers find it very helpful. See Benjamin S. Bloom et al., *Taxonomy of educational objectives. Handbook I: Cognitive domain* (New York: David McKay, 1956). For a concise criticism, see Richard Paul's chapter, "Bloom's taxonomy and critical thinking instruction: Recall is not knowledge," in his book *Critical thinking* (Sonoma, CA: Center for Critical Thinking, 1990), 421–428.

Website

http://www.titanic.cc/index.htm

CHAPTER 9

Resources

Main Idea

Different kinds of resources for teaching social studies are presented, and a multimedia approach is favored. The teacher is encouraged to use a wide range of instructional resources because inquiry and concept formation require extensive information searches and because not all children learn in the same way. Also, different resources may provide competing viewpoints on the same subject; there may be discrepancies or inaccuracies that go undetected when a single source is used.

Key Concepts

Instructional resources, multimedia approach, competing viewpoints

Chapter Outline

- The School Library (Multimedia Center)
- Textbooks
- Community Resources
- Computer Resources
- Newspapers
- Map and Globe Collections
- Multiple Resources: Grappling with Competing Viewpoints
- Curriculum Guides
- Conclusion
- Discussion Questions and Suggested Activities
- Selected References
- Notes

Chapter Snapshot

Mrs. Santana, a veteran second-grade teacher, says to her students on the second day of class: "Welcome again, children. Today, we're going to learn to learn. Because you are Mrs. Santana's students, you will become experts at finding needed information quickly in our library, in our newspaper, on the Internet, and in our textbook. Did you know that many people cannot find their way around in these resources? They are like blind mice unable to find the cheese. Not you. You will become experts."

 A favorite website http://www.loc.gov This is the home page of the Library of Congress. Click on "Thomas" and "American Memory."

Children cannot learn concepts or skills, nor can they conduct inquiries in history or geography, without multiple sources of information. Therefore, we encourage a multimedia approach. Information sources (media) for the social studies can be grouped into two broad categories: (1) reading materials and resources (textbooks, encyclopedias, reference books, computer databases using text, electronic mail, magazines, primary documents, newspapers, classroom periodicals) and (2) nonreading materials and resources (pictures, films, filmstrips, computer databases of art prints and photos, recordings, field trips, simulations, maps, globes, and community resources of all types). Together they provide the information base for social studies teaching and learning.

What teachers use to teach their students

In selecting any instructional resource, teachers must keep uppermost in their minds the objectives to be achieved. The particular resources selected should move children most effectively in the direction of those objectives. Teacher will want to use a wide range of instructional media for any or all of the following reasons:

1. Not all children learn in the same way; different media are able to appeal to the learning styles and home cultures of different learners.

2. Teaching strategies that stress inquiry and problem solving require extensive information searches and, therefore, resources.

3. The reading range among children in most classrooms is great, averaging three to five years in the lower grades and five to 10 years in the middle and upper grades.

4. Each medium has peculiar strengths and limitations in the way it conveys messages.

5. The impact of a message is likely to be stronger if more than one sensory system is involved in receiving it.

6. The use of a variety of media has motivating and interest-generating qualities.

7. Different sources may provide different perspectives on the same subject; there may be discrepancies or inaccuracies or omissions that go undetected if a single source is used.

The School Library (Multimedia Center)

The collection of resources in the school library makes it one of the teacher's best friends when it comes to social studies teaching and learning. The wide variety of reference materials there (such as almanacs, atlases, and encyclopedias) combined with the historical fiction collection and the biographies and picture books make it a treasury of information, ideas, and, in the case of historical fiction, sympathetic journeys into the lives of people long ago and far away.

But one teacher's treasury is another teacher's desert. We are continually surprised at the number of teachers who do not realize the library's potential as an instructional aid. Often the reason is simple lack of *familiarity* with its materials combined with personal lack of *experience* actually using library materials. For these reasons, it is imperative that new teachers explore the school library themselves and help their students do the same.

The best way we know to accomplish this is to make library exploration an adventure in orienteering. *Orienteering* is a timed cross-country, territorial competition in which participants begin at point A and try to reach point B using a compass and map. What a fitting analogy for exploring the library! Lesson Plan 12 provides an example of how a teacher might use orienteering for second or third graders.

Textbooks

The policy of school districts that calls for furnishing free of charge the same basic textbook for every child in a class is based on the moral and legal principles of equal treatment and equality of opportunity. For this reason, textbooks are widely used and will doubtless continue to be widely used for years to come. It is apparent from their continued, widespread use that most teachers perceive the textbook as both a valuable and a manageable teaching tool in social studies. It is important, therefore, that the beginning teacher learn how to make the best use of these books.

Elementary school social studies textbooks actually are textbook *programs.* That is, they are more than a textbook. They contain an array of resources, some inside the book and some outside. In the textbook are primary documents, artwork, narrative histories, vocabulary lessons, skill lessons, explanations of all sorts, and questions and activities. Ancillaries are common as well: CD-ROMs, videotapes and videodisks, project books, giant maps that can be spread out on the classroom floor, smaller maps with washable surfaces that are placed on each student's desk, and anthologies of speeches, plays, and short stories. These ancillaries surround the textbook like satellites and are brought into lessons as the teacher sees fit. The *Teacher's Edition,* too, contains a wealth of resources. There are lesson and unit plans, overviews and summaries, focus questions and follow-up questions, additional background information on the subject of the lesson, website suggestions for online Internet activities, reading and writing lessons, connections to the literature curriculum (and other curriculum integration ideas), student projects, guest speaker and field trip suggestions, role-playing suggestions, discussion topics, classroom museum ideas, and both formal and informal student assessments. Some teacher's editions even have bar codes that tie into an accompanying videodisk. The teacher simply touches the code with a bar code reader and the videodisk is cued to a feature related to the reading students are about to do—a tour of modern-day Mesa Verde perhaps, the Taos Pueblo, or the Alamo.

A textbook program, then, is *a resource of resources* that beginning teachers otherwise would have to gather on their own. Considering all that teachers must do in a day (from teaching reading and math to teaching social studies and science; from mending hurt feelings to phoning parents), we believe the social studies textbook program is an indispensable aid to teaching and learning. Without it, social studies tends to be slighted. It is moved to the end of the day, the end of the week, or the end of the year, and the social studies curriculum is diluted to a point where it is no longer authentic. A busy teacher cannot easily assemble the rich stew of primary documents, explanations, examples, charts and maps, narratives, artwork, and the lesson plans for using these things. The wisdom that history affords, the social intelligence that geography affords, and the democratic values that civics affords—all are put at risk.

Lesson Plan 12	# ORIENTEERING IN THE LIBRARY (MULTIMEDIA CENTER)

Grade 2 or 3

Time Three class periods

Objectives To "break the ice" with the library and librarian. That is, to orient children to the school library, to help them feel comfortable there, to practice interacting with the librarian, and to group and label some of the contents of the school library.

Interest Building Tell the children about orienteering competitions in your area—perhaps across a forested area or a plateau, depending on local geography. Show them a map and pass around a compass and help them imagine the challenge of finding their way across a strange, new territory using these two tools. Then draw the analogy to the school library. Ask who knows this territory and what they know about it. Tell them that, with your help, they are going to become the school's library experts, familiar with each nook and cranny, each plateau and canyon.

Lesson Development Brief the librarian on the following activity and make an appointment to bring the class to the library. Secure the librarian's permission to post the cardinal directions in the library: a sign saying "north" on the north wall, another saying "south" on the south wall, etc.

Divide the class into teams. Ask each team to choose an interviewer who will ask questions to the librarian. Have them also decide on two questions for the interviewer to ask: one "where question" about the location of something in the library (e.g., Where is the biggest dictionary? Where is information about the Pony Express?) And one "how question" about how to locate something without asking the librarian (e.g., How can we find out where Pony Express information is located without asking you?). Then have the interviewers practice asking the two questions with teammates playing the role of the librarian.

Take the class to the library at the appointed time. Have the children sit in teams. Direct each interviewer to ask the team's questions. After all the questions have been answered, give teams the opportunity to actively experience the answers they received (e.g., go to the dictionary and open it up; load the CD-ROM with the Pony Express information).

Back in the classroom, lead the class in a list-group-and-label activity (see Chapter 8) dealing with the information provided by the librarian. If there were five teams with two questions each, there will be a list of at least 10 items. Ask children to group this information together based on similarities they see (e.g., electronic databases, biographies, books on the north wall, posters on the south wall).

Assessment/ Summary Distribute grid paper and ask students to sketch from memory a map of the library showing the locations of various references. Have them put a *compass rose* on their maps showing the cardinal directions. Collect and observe these: On the next day, hand the maps back unmarked and take the class to the library to revise the maps as needed. Then, distribute new grid paper on which students draw a revised map of the library to place in their map portfolios.

Materials Grid paper for each child, map and compass for displaying

Integration *Outdoor sports. Orienteering* is also a term for an increasingly popular outdoor sport in which participants use maps to find their way. Ask if any of your students are involved in organized orienteering events. (There are special programs for children.) Invite a parent orienteer to the class to show students how it applies to finding one's way around the school's multimedia center. Find out more about it on the Internet at

http://ourworld.compuserve.com/homepages/james_baker/ or

http://www.williams.edu:803/Biology/orienteering/o~index.html

■   ■   ■   ■   ■

Yet, clearly, a textbook is *only* a resource. A teacher should be its master, not its servant. This is the case with any resource.

TEACHING THE ORGANIZATION OF THE TEXTBOOK

Skillful readers have learned to investigate the organization or structure of a textbook before diving into the first page of the first chapter. In fact, this investigation (the skill called *previewing* or *surveying*) is one behavior that distinguishes the more from less skillful reader of expository texts—whether an elementary grade student or a graduate student in college. Rather than turning to the first page of the first chapter, utterly in the dark about the way the book is put together, the skillful reader first stands back and takes in the whole scene, so to speak. She surveys the table of contents in front, studies the chapter titles, finds the index in the back of the book, locates a large "reference section" near the back containing a glossary, atlas, and dictionary of geographic terms. She finds that the book's main sections are called units and that these are subdivided into three chapters, each having three lessons. She discovers that there are chapter and unit study aids (e.g., overviews and summaries), that pictures have explanatory captions beneath them, and that key vocabulary words are listed at the beginning of each lesson and reviewed in each chapter review. Knowing these things *in advance* boosts comprehension.[1] A lesson plan for teaching the skill of previewing appears in Chapter 12.

Left unguided, a child is not likely to investigate a book's structure. Consequently, we are firm believers in teaching students to do this. Previewing a text is a *skill*. As such, the teacher can use the skill-teaching strategy presented in Chapter 8. Figure 9–1 illustrates the organization components that are commonly found in social studies textbooks.

Community Resources

It is in the local community that the teacher should sow the seeds of a lifetime study of human society. Here the social processes that function a thousand times over in communities around the world may be observed firsthand. In the local community, the child is introduced to geographical concepts, to the problems of group living, to government in operation, to the production and distribution of goods and services, and to the rich historical heritage—the migrations, struggles, and stories—of the peoples who live there. In most American communities, the

FIGURE 9–1 Organizational structure of social studies textbooks.

USING YOUR TEXTBOOK

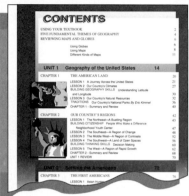

TABLE OF CONTENTS
Lists all parts of
your book and tells
you where to find
them

Your textbook contains many special features
that will help you read, understand, and
remember the people, geography, and history
of the United States.

TRADITIONS
Lessons which will give you a deeper
insight into the history and culture of
the United States and its neighbors

REVIEWING MAPS AND GLOBES
Reviews skills that will help you use the maps in your book

FIVE FUNDAMENTAL THEMES OF GEOGRAPHY
Introduces important themes of geography that will
help you to compare, to contrast, and to understand
the regions and people you will study

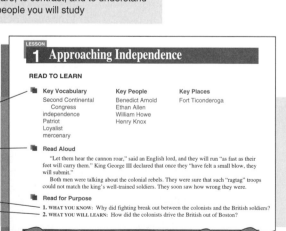

LESSON OPENER

Important vocabulary, people, and
places introduced in the lesson

Lesson introduction

Asks you to think about what you
already know from previous lessons
or your own experience

Question you should keep in
mind as you read the lesson

Source: Communities Near and Far (New York: Macmillan/McGraw-Hill, 1995): 2–3. Reprinted by permission of The
McGraw-Hill Companies .

REFERENCE SECTION

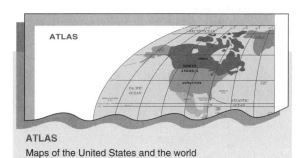

ATLAS
Maps of the United States and the world

GAZETTEER
Location and pronunciation of the major places discussed in your book and page where each is shown on a map

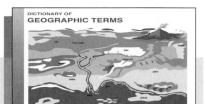

DICTIONARY OF GEOGRAPHIC TERMS
Definition and pronunciation of major geographic features

GLOSSARY
Definition and pronunciation of all Key Vocabulary and page where each is introduced

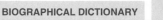

BIOGRAPHICAL DICTIONARY
Identification and pronunciation of important people discussed in your book and page where each is introduced

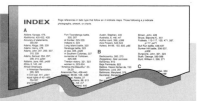

INDEX
Alphabetical list of important people, places, events, and subjects in your book and pages where information is found

child can see evidence that it is possible for persons of varied backgrounds, nationalities, religious faiths, and races to live and work together harmoniously, not by overcoming their difference but by living with one another respectfully with their differences intact.

The teacher may use local community resources in two basic ways. One is to bring some portion of the community to the classroom; the other is to take the class out of the school to some place or person of importance in the community. Either way, the children are interacting with and gathering information from the community. With guidance from the teacher, children can incorporate this information into investigations (inquiries) they are conducting and concepts they are building.

Teachers also use community resources when children bring materials from home for bulletin boards or for their construction projects. Here is yet another way to help children acknowledge and respect family-to-family diversity. Children who have immigrated from another country or moved from another state or city will have lots to say about the geographic themes *Movement* and *Place*. Children whose home language is different from the language of the school can be encouraged to bring for show and tell items that bear writing in the home language. Of course, they should be praised for speaking two languages rather than only one, and students who speak only English can be encouraged to practice another. The personal experiences children have in the community and share with the class are likewise a common use of community resources.

Teachers also use community resources when they obtain books from the public library. When this is done, the teacher should seize the opportunity for map study: Have students locate on a map just where this library is located and find out the location of the library closest to where each of them lives. (Here is a chance to practice with "relative location"—see Chapter 5. "Is your home south of the public library or north? Is it near or far from it? How far?") A librarian from such a library can be invited to the class to talk about the public library(ies) in town: their locations, holdings, and similarities and differences.

GUEST SPEAKERS

The teacher must always select with care the persons who are invited to spend time with the class for instructional purposes. The teacher should plan to spend some time with the visitor sufficiently far enough in advance to brief the guest on the activities of the class, the purpose of the visit, and the points to be discussed and stressed. The guest should be encouraged to bring visuals of some sort: slides, photos, charts, or maps. A pilot can bring flight maps or aerial photographs of the earth. A mail deliverer can bring a route map. Likewise, the children must be prepared for the visitor, listing questions they would like to ask, and be aware of general courtesies that should be extended to classroom guests. Handled in this way, persons from the community can make a significant contribution to the instructional program in the social studies. Those who might be used either for the purposes of interview or as classroom resource visitors include:

- Persons with special skills: weavers, potters, jewelry makers
- Armed forces personnel
- Exchange students

- Persons with interesting hobbies
- Members of the local historical society
- Newspaper reporters, editors, staff writers
- Members of service organizations
- County agents
- Representatives of environmental and conservation groups
- 4-H and other club leaders
- Early inhabitants of the community
- Professional persons: rabbi, pastor, doctor, lawyer, software developer
- Members of the local business community: bankers, shop owners
- Union officials
- Representatives of local industries (docks; timber; manufacturing)
- Travel agents (think of them as "applied geographers"!)
- Recent immigrants or other newcomers to the community
- Artists who work on public murals or public sculptures
- Commercial pilots (more "applied geographers"!)
- Community helpers: firefighters, police officers, librarians
- Government officials representing the three branches
- Judges (a municipal court judge; a federal judge)
- Legislators (city council members; state legislators)
- Executives (the mayor; the county commissioner)

Bringing a lawyer to the classroom to talk about law and government is a great way to introduce your students to the concept of law as well as to a "real, live person" who deals with the law everyday. The American Bar Association will help you contact a local lawyer who is both willing *and prepared* to visit your classroom. Visit the ABA's website at: *www.abanet.org/publiced* or fax them your question at 312-988-5494.

The key to hosting a successful visit to the classroom by a community member is to plan well the three phases of the visit: before, during, and after.

Before the Guest Arrives

Before the guest arrives, the teacher and students need to prepare to get the very most out of the visit. Before a visit by a city council member, for example, they build background knowledge by reading about the structure of city government in the textbook, dramatizing a city council meeting, and following newspaper accounts of council decisions. They also practice interviewing and plan the interview questions. The Welcome Committee who meets the guest at the main office is appointed and plans what they will say.

During the Visit

During the visit, the teacher helps students demonstrate courtesy and curiosity while enacting the interview or other activity they had planned.

Attorney David Wolowitz visits with second graders in Concord, N.H. "I find the children's enthusiasm to be infectious and their candor refreshing," he says. (Courtesy of *Law Matters*, American Bar Association Division for Public Education.)

After the Visit

After the visit, the learnings are reviewed and organized and a full report is "published"—whether prepared in cooperative teams and published in the classroom newspaper or written individually and placed in student portfolios. A follow-up committee writes a "thank you" letter telling of the class's plan to publish a report on the guest's visit and promising to send a copy when it is completed.

FIELD TRIPS

As a matter of principle, it is advisable to take elementary school children into the community only for the experiences that cannot be duplicated in the classroom. For example, it is usually better to arrange to have a person bring photographs of early life in the community to the school and speak to the children there than it is to take a class of 20 or 30 children to a home. On the other hand, the process involved in canning fish or cranberries or tomato juice cannot be observed in the classroom; the children must be taken to the cannery if this process is to be observed firsthand. There they will see vivid examples of the economic concepts they are forming and refining in class: production, distribution, division of labor, and cooperation.

Whenever children are taken off the school site, the teacher must attend to several exceedingly important details. As with guest speakers, attention must be paid to the three phases of a field trip: before, during, and after.

Adequate planning will help the teacher anticipate some of the problems that may arise in connection with the field trip and will help make the trip educationally worthwhile. Poorly planned field trips are worse than none at all, for they lack purpose, may jeopardize the safety of the children, may cause poor public relations between the school and community, and can break down learnings the teacher should have been trying to build in the classroom. Although the field trip should be pleasant for everyone (including the teacher), it is first of all an educational experience, and its primary objective is not that everyone have a joyous outing. Good planning will ensure that the trip will be both a pleasant and an educational experience. The suggestions on pages 296–298 will be helpful in achieving that goal.

Every community has places that can be visited by classes and thereby can contribute to the enrichment of history, geography, and all of social studies. These will differ from place to place, but any of the following could be used:

State historical society displays	Aquarium
Historical sites, monuments	Library
Flood plain, eroded areas, dam sites	Refinery
Razing of a building	Fish hatchery
Hospitals	Museums
Weather bureau	Public health department
Warehouses	Local stores
Airports	Legislative bodies in session
Railway station	Art galleries
Assembly plants	Fire station
Post office	Newspaper printing facilities
Television or radio station	Bakery
Courthouse	Observatory
Factories	Canal locks
Farms	Harbor
Urban planning commission	Police station
Docks	Cannery
Dairy	University
Shopping center management office	Water purification plant

Computer Resources

Let's turn from actual field trips to virtual or electronic field trips using computers and the Internet. Then we will examine other computer resources: museums, newsgroups, civic discussions, biography material, and simulations. But first, some general comments about computers in social studies education are necessary.

PLANNING A FIELD TRIP

Preparing for the Field Trip

1. Clearly establish the purposes of the trip and make certain that the children understand the purposes, too. The excursion should provide opportunities for learnings that are not possible in the classroom.

2. Obtain administrative permission for the field trip and make arrangements for transportation. As a matter of policy, it is better to use a public conveyance or a school bus than it is to use private automobiles. In using private cars, the teacher is never sure if the driver is properly insured, is competent behind the wheel, or even has a valid operator's license.

3. Make all necessary preliminary arrangements at the place of the visit. This should include the time for the group to arrive, where the children are to go, who will guide them, and so forth. It is recommended that the teacher make the excursion prior to the time the children are taken. This will alert the teacher to circumstances and situations that should be discussed with the children before leaving the classroom. Make sure that the field trip guide is aware of the purposes of the field trip.

4. Delve into informative resources on the subject. No teacher should approach a field trip unprepared. This knowledge will later be valuable in helping prepare children for the field trip and in initiating follow-up and study activities.

5. Obtain written permission from each parent or guardian for the child to go on the trip. Do not take children who cannot or do not return signed permission slips. Although this action does not in itself absolve the teacher of responsibility or liability in the event of an accident, it indicates to the teacher that the parent or guardian knows of the field trip and approves of the child's going. Most schools have forms for this purpose that are filled out by the teacher and sent home with each child for the parent's signature.

6. Prepare the class for the field trip. The easiest way is to conduct a KWL activity: "What do you already **K**now about this? What do you **W**ant to find out?" And, afterward comes "What did you **L**earn?" A more ambitious preparation is desirable, however, something that will help children observe more keenly, question more knowledgably, and absorb more thoroughly the whole experience. *It is helpful, therefore, if the field trip fits into an inquiry the class is conducting or provides a rich example for concept formation.* A trip to the airport, rather than merely a sight-seeing visit, becomes an example to be studied thoroughly in a unit centered on the concept *transportation.* A trip to the dairy farm or to a grocery store becomes a "data chunk" (as in the *Titanic*

inquiry example) in an inquiry on the question, Where does our food come from, and who and what are involved? Accordingly, in place of or in addition to KWL's "What do you want to find out?" we have "What hypotheses are we testing?" and "What questions do we want to be sure to ask the guide?"

Through careful planning and preparation the teacher helps children to be more observant and makes a genuine research activity out of the field trip. The children probably will be taken to places to which many of them have been before. Depending on the economic class of the students you are teaching, most of them have been to the airport, some have been to the harbor, and all have been to a filling station. Why, then, should the school take children to such places on field trips? The answer is that different purposes exist for the field trip than for incidental visits. The children are prepared to look for things they would not otherwise see. Discuss with the children how they will record the information obtained on their trip. If they are to take notes, teach the needed note-taking skills. Will each of them need a clipboard? (A class set of clipboards, which are brought out only for such occasions, are aids to note-taking and question-asking, and they have a symbolic value as well: They symbolize that field trips are a special way to learn.)

The class should set up standards of conduct for the trip before leaving the school. Children are quick to accept the challenge that the responsibility for a good trip rests personally with each member of the group. Time spent on this part of the preparation for the excursion will pay dividends when the trip is underway. Nothing is more embarrassing for the teacher, more damaging to school-community relations, or more devastating to the educational purpose of the field trip than a group of rude and unruly children. This often happens when the children have been inadequately prepared for the trip.

7. If the trip is to be long, make arrangements for lunchroom and restroom facilities. Take along a first-aid kit.

8. Have an alternate plan in case the weather turns bad or something interferes with your plans.

Conducting the Trip

9. Take roll before leaving the school grounds and "count noses" frequently during the trip to make sure that some of the children have not become lost or left in some restroom along the way. With young children it is a good idea to place them in pairs because a child will know and report immediately the absence of a partner. To assist with supervision of the children and to help ensure a safe trip, the teacher should arrange for other adults to

continued

accompany the group. Teachers can usually count on parents to assist in this way but should plan to meet with them prior to the trip and explain the purposes, standards of behavior, the route to be followed, and other important details. The adults accompanying the children must be prepared for the excursion also.

10. Arrive at the designated place on time, and have children ready for the guide. Be sure to introduce the guide to the class. Supervise children closely during the tour to prevent accidents or injury. Before leaving, check again to make sure all children are with the group.

11. Make sure that time is allowed for answering children's questions.

12. Make sure that each child can see and hear adequately. Be sure to summarize the experience before the trip is concluded.

Evaluating the Trip

13. Engage the class in appropriate follow-up activities. This should include writing a thank-you note to the firm and to the adults who accompanied the class. In the primary grades, the children should dictate such a letter to the teacher who writes it on the chalkboard or chart. Individual children then copy the letter, and one may be selected to be sent, or in some cases, they may all be sent. If the host has an e-mail address, the children's letter also can be sent using this medium.

    The teacher and children will also want to evaluate carefully the extent to which the purposes of the trip have been achieved. "Did we accomplish what we set out to do? Did we get the answers to our questions? What did we learn that we didn't know before? What are some other things we will want to find out?" Finally, the teacher and children will want to evaluate the conduct of the class in terms of the standards set up before the trip was made. This evaluation should always include some favorable reactions as well as ways in which the group might improve on subsequent trips. A list of these suggestions for improvement may be saved for review just before the next trip is undertaken.

14. Discuss enrichment projects in which children may engage for further study, such as construction activities, original stories, reports, dramatic plays, and diaries. Survey other resources available in the community for study.

15. Use opportunities to draw on information and experiences from the field trip in other subjects taught in the classroom.

The use of computer technology in education has been promoted vigorously, to say the least. Nowadays, the absence of computers in a classroom or school is thought by many to symbolize poor education. In the eyes of the community, computers in the classroom have come to symbolize a school curriculum that is up-to-date and instruction that is benefiting from "the latest technology." This is, of course, a silly leap of faith. Both curriculum and instruction can be very good indeed without "the latest technology" and, conversely, the presence of computers in no way symbolizes good curriculum or good instruction. The quality of the intellectual work students are helped to accomplish, the importance of the subject matter they are asked to study, and the power and reach of the understandings they are helped to construct are far more important criteria than the presence or absence of this or that hardware or software. In brief, the presence of computers in the classroom is widely misunderstood as an *end,* when in truth computers are *means.*

> The quality of the intellectual work students are helped to accomplish, the importance of the subject matter they are asked to study, and the power and reach of the understandings they are helped to construct are far more important criteria than the presence or absence of this or that hardware or software.

In the social studies, as in other curricular areas, the challenge to the teacher is to adapt the use of this technology to the ongoing instructional goals of the classroom. The emphasis should be on using computers to assist teaching and learning of social studies subject matter—democratic citizenship, ideas, facts, issues, and skills drawn from history and the social sciences, and the inquiry process.

In the social studies, the contribution of computer-assisted instruction (CAI) falls into the following three categories: knowledge construction, skills application, and communication (see Figure 9–2).

1. *Using the Computer to Build Knowledge—to Gather* Examples *Needed in Concept Formation and* Evidence *Needed for Inquiry.* There is a growing number of electronic databases, many of which are relevant to social studies. Databases can be purchased on laser videodisks and the smaller CD-ROMs (compact disk–read only memory). Also, databases can be accessed through various online services on the Internet, which are accessed through computers connected by modems and phone lines.

   Here is a brief example related to concept learning: A fourth-grade class has been studying the geography of the United States. The central concepts organizing their study are *landforms, farm products, manufactured products,* and *cities.* Now they are ready to extend their knowledge of these concepts with examples from far-away places: Asia, Africa, Oceana, Europe, and South America. "Search teams" for each continent take turns going to the library to use the school's two CD-ROMs: a database called *Grolier Multimedia Encyclopedia* and a computer simulation called *Where in the World Is Carmen Sandiego?* Each team searches for information related to the four concepts. The librarian notices that each team is coming up with very little about the *cities* on each continent, so she helps them find the website at *http://www.city.net/.* There, each team clicks on its continent and then goes to cities.

FIGURE 9–2   CAI in social studies: Three approaches.

Here is a brief example related to inquiry: The "search teams" now are taking turns going to the library to use the same three databases as above, only now they are engaged in an inquiry. Accordingly, *before* going to the library, they generated hypotheses on a question. Now in the library, they are searching for evidence to confirm or reject the hypotheses. For example, "Does Africa have distinct geographical regions or is the whole continent one big region?" (*Note:* This example applies nicely to the study of each continent.)

Electronic databases rapidly are including much of what is now found in libraries, government document centers, archives, museums, encyclopedias, and other information collections. They place enormous stacks of information at students' fingertips, so enormous that another problem is raised: How do we equip children with the background knowledge they need to sort and sift intelligently through the stacks. (The irony! In order to gain knowledge, students need to have knowledge already.) The teacher, therefore, needs to provide assistance, helping to bridge the knowledge gap so that Internet searches are educative.

2. *Using the Computer to Practice and Apply Social Studies Skills.* This contribution is closely related to the first one on knowledge construction because it focuses on the skills needed to build that knowledge: map reading, interpreting graphs and charts, creating data-retrieval charts, gathering information from multiple resources, comparing and contrasting examples, summarizing, classifying, distinguishing between primary and secondary documents, forming and testing hypotheses, drawing conclusions, and making decisions all along the way. These skills are best taught and learned as part of knowledge construction, for this is the place where they are applied.

3. *Using the Computer to Communicate.* Children in many schools have been using word processing programs for some time to help them revise and edit reports and essays for the classroom newspaper. They can scan photographs into the newspaper file with little trouble if they have the equipment. And in an increasing number of classrooms, they are communicating by electronic mail (e-mail), in online "chat rooms," newsgroups, and so forth. E-mail allows children to have cyberpals or keypals in another community in the state or a sister city across the sea. Using e-mail, children can inform the president of the United States (and probably your state's governor and city's mayor) of decisions they have reached on public problems.

Now let's turn to virtual field trips and other computer resources for social studies teaching and learning.

VIRTUAL FIELD TRIPS

Thanks to the Internet, children can visit places "virtually." In other words, they can venture far from home electronically and capture some aspects of a distant place. While obviously not as richly textured as an actual field trip to this place, an electronic visit nonetheless may help to set imaginations afire and provoke additional research.

With virtual field trips as with actual ones, the recommended approach is to plan the three phases of the trip: before, during, and after. Here are several terrific trips.

- The White House
- China and Egypt
- Holiday Celebrations in Other Lands
- The Seven Wonders of the World
- Plymouth
- Abraham Lincoln's Home
- U.S. Capitol
- The Declaration and Constitution
- United Nations
- Philadelphia

Bon voyage!

But first, a caution: *Websites change.* We have reviewed these sites for accuracy and appropriateness, but teachers must do so themselves before sending students off.

A Virtual Field Trip to the White House

To set the context, let's say that this field trip takes place in a third-grade unit called "Countries and their Capitals." Its aim is to help students develop the concepts *nation* and *national capital*.

Before. Students use their textbooks and other reference material to learn how Washington, DC, became the capital of the United States. The teacher helps them distinguish between state (or in Canada, provincial) capitals and national capitals and then reads them a story about Benjamin Banneker who drew up the plans for the new capitol and another about Abigail and John Adams, the first occupants of the new White House in 1800. (Children's literature can be found on each.)

During. Students set off for the White House. They begin at *http://www.whitehouse.gov/*, the White House home page, where they click on "White House History" and "Tours" and then proceed with their virtual tour, clicking as follows:

- A floor plan of the White House
- The artworks in the White House
- First Families at Home: A glimpse into the lives of families who have lived in the White House.

From there, students can go to "The White House for Kids" home page at *http://www.white-house.gov/WH/kids/html/kidshome.html*. Here, students look behind the scenes at the White House by clicking on various "newsletters." Each deals with a different behind-the-scenes activity. The first newsletter introduces visitors to the three branches of government. Students learn that the White House and the President belong to the executive branch. If they aren't exhausted yet, they might go on to *http://www.pbs.org/weta/whitehouse/whhome.htm*. This is one of the sites of the National Geographic Society. Students can visit the Oval Office and pretend to be the president.

After. With this background knowledge, students are ready to compare Washington, DC, and the White House to a capital city and "first residence" in another nation. Perhaps London, England, and 10 Downing Street. Or Dakar, Senegal, and its Presidential Palace.

A Virtual Field Trip to China, Then Egypt

This is a cooperative field trip for older students. First, the teacher provides an overview of the activities that take place in each of the three phases to the entire class.

Before. Students are assigned first to home teams and then to "expert groups" (see "Jigsaw Groups" in Chapter 11), one expert per team for each of five topics: (1) political system, (2) history, (3) art, (4) customs, and (5) current events of China. Expert groups search their social studies textbook chapter on China as their initial data source, gathering whatever information is there about their topic. Note-taking procedures need to be established. Then they set off on a virtual field trip to China to gather *additional* information on their assigned topic. (Why? Because the Internet is very difficult to search intelligently when students have no background knowledge of the topic they are searching.) Numerous web addresses could provide useful text and images (maps, artifacts, etc.). One website we like is *http://www.ihep.ac.cn/tour/china_tour.html*.[2]

FIGURE 9–3 Sample data-retrieval chart.

	Political System	History	Art	Customs	Current Events
China					
Egypt					

During. Assuming there are not enough computers for each student, expert group members take turns exploring this site for information related to their assigned topic, each recording notes. Then they compile notes, discuss their "visit," and prepare together an oral report (see Chapter 11). One expert group's oral report is called "Art of China"; another's is "Political System of China," and so on through the five topics. Each expert group member will give the report to members of his or her home team. The team will compile a data-retrieval chart like the one shown in Figure 9–3.

After. (a) Group members make oral reports to the class. (b) The teacher reassigns teams and expert groups (see Chapter 2 on "flexible grouping"), and the class now goes to Egypt (e.g., begin with *http://www.memphis.edu/egypt/artifact.html* and *http://www.memphis.edu/egypt/egypt.html*). Students are helped to seek information on the same five topics. After the visit to Egypt, the teacher leads the class in comparing and contrasting China and Egypt across the five categories. A challenging follow-up would be to add the United States to the list.

A Virtual Field Trip to a Holiday Celebration

The idea here is to visit other countries during their holiday celebrations. By visiting many holiday examples, students will construct a vigorous concept of *holiday* and will be introduced to cultural diversity around the world.

Before. Ask students to list all the holidays they can think of that are celebrated in their community. Remind them of holidays not on their list (e.g., other religious holidays such as Good Friday, Hanukkah, and Buddha's birthday; Chinese New Year; Veterans' Day; Kwanzaa; Cinco de Mayo; etc.). Then use the list-group-and-label strategy (see Chapter 8) to help them think about the similarities and differences among the holidays on their list (some are religious, some are governmental, some are local only). Ask students if they think any of these are celebrated in other nations, too. Ask if any holidays celebrated in other nations are not celebrated in the United States. Take a straw poll: "How many say yes? No? Not sure?" Then, "Let's find out. . . ."

During. Since 1994, students from all over the world have been contributing to a website called KIDPROJ Multi-Cultural Calendar at *http://www.kidlink.org:80/KIDPROJ/MCC/*. Here, children can click on a month or a country and find a long list of holidays to explore.

Clicking on "month" and then "March," we see many entries for "girls' day" in Japan and "women's day" in China and Italy. Sometimes there is more than one entry for a single holiday, meaning that more than one child has written a description.

Help children browse and then select a holiday to investigate further. Begin by having students locate on the classroom map where their holidays are celebrated and place index cards with brief descriptions, written by your students, of each. For further investigation, students can visit *http://www.dkonline.com/epals/*, where students can click "calendar" and, again, read about many holidays as described by the children who celebrate them. Also, ask a student to check the school library for the book, *Celebrations: Festivals, Carnivals, and Feast Days Around the World* by Barnabas and Anabel Kindersley (DK, 1997), or something similar.

After. Create a classroom calendar depicting the holidays selected by students. Ask students to choose a good name for the calendar: "International Holidays"? "Our Multicultural Calendar"? "Holidays of the World"? Finally, the class can select one or two of the holidays to celebrate in their own classroom, making decorations and holiday snacks.

ADDITIONAL FIELD TRIP SUGGESTIONS

The Ultimate Field Trip: The Seven Wonders of the World

Children are typically introduced to world history in a systematic way in grade 6. Our favorite way to kick off this mind-expanding subject is with the ultimate field trip to the Seven Wonders of the World. *Who* chose them? *What* kinds of places are they? *Where* are they? *When* were they built? and *Why?* Buckle your seatbelt and go to *http://pharos.bu.edu/Egypt/Wonders/*.

A Virtual Field Trip to Plymouth

At website *http://pilgrims.net/plymouth/,* students can visit what is today Plymouth, Massachusetts, which was the "Plimouth Plantation" in 1627 (site of the famed Plymouth Rock and the first permanent European settlement in southern New England). Several houses can be seen, a defensive bastion, and an outdoor oven. At the Hobbamock home, click on "meal being cooked" and "food storage containers." As children see how Pilgrims cooked meat on a spit, ask them to compare cooking methods then and now and to identify cooking technology that has changed from how modern Americans cook (e.g., indoor ovens, refrigerators, and freezers).

A Virtual Field Trip to Abraham Lincoln's Springfield Home

At website *http://www.netins.net/showcase/creative/lincoln/gallery/pict.htm*, students visit the Abraham Lincoln home in Springfield, Illinois. This is not the famous log cabin where Lincoln was born, but the house where he lived with his family just before he became President. From his home, the field trip can continue at *http://www.netins.net/showcase/creative/lincoln/sites/sites.htm,* which connects to the courthouse where he worked as a lawyer, the site of the Lincoln-Douglas debates, and his tomb.

A Virtual Field Trip to the U.S. Capitol and the Woman Suffrage Sculpture

At website *http://www.aoc.gov/art/suffrage.htm* is a group sculpture honoring the Woman Suffrage Movement, which won women the right to vote in 1920. Three leaders are portrayed: Elizabeth Cady Stanton (1815–1902), Susan B. Anthony (1820–1906), and Lucretia Mott (1792–1880). Students will see the 14,000-pound sculpture itself; then have them click on "rotunda" to see where it is located in the Capitol building.

A Virtual Field Trip to See the U.S. Constitution, the Declaration of Independence, and the Bill of Rights

At website *http://www.nara.gov/exhall/charters/charters.html*, students can visit the National Archives in Washington, DC, and "see" these three founding documents of the United States.

A Virtual Field Trip to the United Nations

At website *http://www.un.org*, students can visit the United Nations in New York City. This large, information-intensive site will be helpful for students in grades 6 through 8 who want to investigate, for example, the U.N.'s land mine "demining" program (Princess Diana of England publicized this cause), famine-relief programs, or current crisis spots around the globe.

A Virtual Field Trip to Philadelphia

At website *http://www.libertynet.org/iha/index.html*, students can visit the Liberty Bell, Independence Hall, Betsy Ross's home, the First Bank of the United States, the burial ground at Christ Church (a "who's who" of early U.S. history), the First Quaker Meeting House, and other places on what is called the "Historic Mile." There are also excellent links here to other sites (e.g., tour Betsy Ross's website for flag history).

EXPLORING MUSEUMS ONLINE

Museums around the world are rapidly putting their collections (databases) online. You can help your students become museum-wise by arranging field trips to local museums and teaching them to access museum databases online. Here are some favorites:

- A list of web pages for many museums in the United States (*http://www.museumca.org/usa/*). Each student can choose a state and report back to the class on the number and kinds of history museums he or she found. The teacher can lead a list, group, and label activity, helping students perceive the similarities and differences among the museums. Then the class can select a few for virtual field trips.
- The Smithsonian Institution (*http://www.si.edu/organiza/museums/nmah/start.htm*). Teachers will find helpful the Smithsonian's Resource Guide for teachers (*http://educate.si.edu/resources/resource/sslist2.html#start*).
- The National Civil Rights Museum, with virtual tour at *http://www.mecca.org/~crights/cyber.html*.
- The Mariner's Museum (*http://www.mariner.org/*).

RESOURCE GUIDE

Arts

Language Arts

Science

Social Studies

Help

EDUCATION Home Page

Welcome to the "social studies and history" section of the *Smithsonian Resource Guide for Teachers*! The Acrobat file above is twenty-four pages long and lists materials organized under the following subsections: African American studies; American cultural and social history; American political history; history of industry, aviation, and technology; Native American studies; and world history and cultures. At the end of the file you will find a list of the museums and programs that offer materials listed in this section, as well as the forms and instructions that tell you exactly how to order these products.

**LESSON PLANS || RESOURCE GUIDE
VISITING THE SMITHSONIAN**

Teachers can help sutdents become museum-wise by arranging museum field trips, both actual and virtual.

- The Pacific Rim Museum (*http://wwwkms.bham.wednet.edu/lobby.htm*).
- The Diego Rivera Museum (*http://www.diegorivera.com/diego_home_eng.html*).

NEWSGROUPS

The third-grade teachers at Cascade Elementary School participate in "kidsphere," a newsgroup for K–12 teachers. (To subscribe, send an e-mail request to *joinkids@vms.cis.pitt.edu* or search the Internet for "kidsphere.") Today, an Alaskan teacher is requesting keypals for village children, and a Detroit student teacher is looking for a conversation with peers in

The LIBRARY of CONGRESS

SEARCH THE CATALOG | SEARCH OUR WEB SITE | WEB SITE MAP

USING the LIBRARY
Catalogs, Collections
& Research
Services

AMERICAN MEMORY
America's Story in
Words, Sounds
& Pictures

THOMAS
Congress
At Work

BICENTENNIAL
1800-2000
Libraries • Creativity • Liberty

EXHIBITIONS
An On-Line
Gallery

COPYRIGHT
OFFICE
Forms &
Information

HELP & FAQs
General Information

THE LIBRARY
TODAY
News, Events
& More

AMERICAN
PRESIDENTS
Life Portraits

Above, the interior of the dome of the Main Reading Room of the Library of Congress

101 INDEPENDENCE AVE. S.E.
WASHINGTON, D.C. 20540
(202) 707-5000

Comments: lcweb@loc.gov
NOTICE

Visit the Library of Congress website at *http://www.loc.gov.*

other urban elementary schools. They join two ongoing discussion groups: one on the curriculum standards from the National Council for the Social Studies, another on the issue of multigrade classrooms. Also, they browse the list of descriptions of classroom projects.

JOINING CIVIC DISCUSSIONS

Sixth-grade children learn in the local newspaper about the city council's debate over establishing curfews for children and teenagers. They locate Kidlink online (at *http://www.kidlink.org/*), which is a newsgroup for older children. They strike up a conversation with students at other sites about the issue. Then, they e-mail the council members a report of their discussions and recommendations.

BIOGRAPHY WRITING

In Chapter 13 we provide a detailed explanation of a wonderful, integrated social studies/language arts unit that can be done in grades 3 and up. In cooperative teams, students write an original biography of an important historical figure. Aside from the writing hurdles that must be jumped in a project such as this, a tremendous amount of information must be gathered about the subject of the biography. Fortunately, the school library has loads of information, and so do online databases. For example,

- Thomas Jefferson at *http://www.monticello.org/Day/A_Day_in_the_Life.html*.
- Diego Rivera at *http://www.diegorivera.com/diego_home_eng.html*.
- Susan B. Anthony at *http://www.lkwdpl.org/wihohio/anth-sus.htm*.
- Ben Franklin at *http://sln.fi.edu/*.
- Chief Joseph-Nez Perce at
  http://www.powersource.com/powersource/gallery/people/default.html.
- Voting: Biographies of people who struggled for the right to vote at
  http://educate.si.edu/spotlight/elect.html.
- Civil Rights: Biographies of civil rights leaders from Rosa Parks to Malcolm X at
  *http://infoseek.go.com/WebDir/People/Famous_people/U_S_history/Civil_rights_
  leaders?sv=M6&svx=related*

COMPUTER SIMULATIONS

The fifth-grade teachers at Mapleton School are great fans of *The Oregon Trail,* produced by the Minnesota Educational Computing Consortium (MECC). This popular simulation is available in computer stores, and some of your students may have it at home. The story line is that of a wagon train party moving westward in the mid-1800s. Along the way the wagon train has to deal with a number of contingencies such as foul weather and sickness, and they encounter the native peoples who already inhabit the area. Decisions have to be made, and the stakes are high: A poor decision can have disastrous consequences for the entire party. Most critics praise this simulation. But some, such as Bill Bigelow,[3] have pointed to its cultural biases. African Americans are present, but only in the most superficial way, for example. Indians are not portrayed as the "enemy," but they are definitely not "us" either.

Popular simulations involving citizenship decision making are *Decisions, Decisions* (for grades 5 and above), *Choices, Choices* (K–6), and *Our Town Meeting* (5–8), all from Tom Snyder productions. The first two can be used with an entire classroom and only one computer; the third is designed for use with up to 15 students and one computer. All promote group interaction and community decision making. In *And If Reelected,* a presidential simulation for grades 7 and up, students grapple with numerous public policy controversies, such as nuclear waste and budget deficits.

Emphasizing geography is the very popular *Where in the World Is Carmen Sandiego?* Produced by Broderbund Software, this exciting game has students play detective as they use geography clues and a reference book (*The World Almanac and Book of Facts*) to solve a crime. Also available are *Where in the U.S.A. Is Carmen Sandiego?* And *Where in Europe Is Carmen Sandiego?*[4]

Other commercially prepared simulations that have been used with success in elementary and middle school grades are

1. *The Market Place* (grades 3–6) produced by MECC is designed to develop economic concepts and relationships as the player is placed in the role of an entrepreneur.
2. *President-Elect* (grades 8 and above), produced by Learning Arts, P.O. Box 179,

Wichita, KS 67201, focuses on variables associated with the election of a president of the United States.

3. *Stock Market* (grades 4–6) and *Millionaire, the Stock Market Simulation,* both produced by Learning Arts, are designed to teach principles of the stock market.

Newspapers

Newspapers are ideal resources for teaching current events and reading instruction. Many teachers in grades 3 and up find daily and weekly newspapers valuable resources to support the goals of current events instruction. Not only are newspapers authentic and readily available resources for teaching *current events,* but they are also authentic and readily available resources for teaching *reading.* Newspaper articles contain the kind of text commonly called "news reports" or journalism. This is nonfiction text material, and it can help children bridge the gap from the easier-to-read children's fiction narratives to the more difficult expository writing found in much of the historical and social science writing that older students—and citizens—are expected to comprehend.

Most communities have more than one newspaper. This is especially true of metropolitan areas where there will be one or two daily newspapers and several or perhaps many weekly or monthly periodicals. The suburbs around the city probably each have a weekly newspaper. And, because American cities are all multiethnic, there will usually be small newspapers published by various ethnic organizations. There will also be neighborhood newspapers within the city. These suburban, ethnic, and neighborhood newspapers are especially useful in the classroom for geographic study of the metropolitan area. The smaller, focused newspapers give children an anthropologist's view of local cultural variations within metropolitan life. Each newspaper will have editorials and letters to the editor that children can use to search for local controversial issues and multiple perspectives. "Eyewitness accounts" can be placed under the "primary documents" section of the history bulletin board. And news articles can be read with an eye to the writing process: How are they written? What is the "lead" of an article? And the "byline"?

A guest speaker from a newspaper will help bring all this to life. He or she can be asked to teach children about the "lead" and the "byline" and share personal experiences as a reporter, editor, or staff writer. The division of labor at the newspaper can be described and artifacts (e.g., an edited draft of an article or a piece from an old printing press) can be passed around to the students. After such work in the classroom, building as it does background knowledge and enthusiasm for learning still more, a field trip to a newspaper should be a rich and memorable experience for each child.

The local newspaper most likely has a special program for teachers and their students, or it will connect you to the Newspapers in Education (NIE) program. A class set of the newspaper probably can be made available at a nominal cost (this is a good project to assign a parent volunteer). When students have in front of them an entire newspaper, this is an opportunity to learn the skills of using a newspaper (see Lesson Plan 11 in Chapter 8 on using a newspaper's directory). If the entire newspaper is not available, the teacher may select an especially appropriate article from his or her personal copy, one that relates to the social studies unit underway. This is then copied for students and a lesson built around it.

Let us now very briefly review from Chapter 6 (the "current events" chapter) the basic plan for using the newspaper to teach a current event. For a more complete review, please turn back to Chapter 6.

USING THE NEWSPAPER TO TEACH A CURRENT EVENT

1. Help students read and comprehend a newspaper article about a current event they can productively study.

2. Have students identify the *facts* of the case.

3. Have students identify the *issues* in the case.

4. Select with students one of the issues—one requiring a *decision.*
    a. Identify alternatives.
    b. Predict consequences of choosing each alternatives.
    c. Discuss.
    d. Decide.

5. Publish the decision in a report to the classroom, the school newsletter, or in a letter to the city council.

Map and Globe Collections

It is absolutely essential that students have access to maps of all kinds and globes. A great variety of maps will be found in the textbook program, but globes, desk maps, wall maps, and a large floor map are also needed. There are online map collections, too, but these can be quite unhelpful to younger or older students who haven't had actual (versus virtual) experiences with maps and globes.

Textbook Program. Contemporary maps are collected in contemporary social studies textbooks. A first-grade textbook program will have 20 to 30 maps, a third-grade program around 50, and a fifth-grade program over 100. These will be of all types, from simple child-friendly maps of the school and neighborhood to political and geographical maps of regions, nations, and the world.

Globes. You will need one globe for every two students, minimally, though an entire class set is ideal for the sorts of globe exploration recommended in Chapter 5.

Desk Maps. These often are included with textbook programs, and they can be purchased from several publishing companies. The map should fit well on the desktop, and the surface should permit students to draw directly on the map and then wash it off.

Wall Maps. These can be purchased from numerous companies and should be provided by the school district for each classroom. It is best if they roll up and down, allowing the space to be used for other things. Minimally, a map of the United States, a map of the world, and a map of the state or region are needed. Use them often and encourage students to study and play with them.

Floor Maps. These sometimes accompany textbook programs, but can be purchased separately or made by older students, teachers, or parents. They must be made of material that can be walked on and folded up and stored when not in use.

Maps Online. There are several online map collections, but these should not replace the maps described above. Rather, they should supplement them. One plentiful website is the National Geographic Society (*http://www.nationalgeographic.com/maps/political.html*), where you will find physical and political maps of the world and individual nations along with links to resources for students and teachers. See also *http://www.atlapedia.com/* and *http://www-atlas.usgs.gov/*. Margaret Hill, who is the social studies curriculum coordinator in San Bernadino County, California, also recommends historical map sites (e.g., *http://www.ac.wwu.edu/~stephan/48states.html*) that show the boundary changes in the 48 contiguous states since 1650. She also urges us to teach children the various map search capabilities that accompany the different Internet search engines (e.g., Yahoo, InfoSeek). Students can, for example, learn to enter an address and up comes a map. Then they can zoom into the neighborhood or out to the region.[5]

Multiple Resources: Grappling with Competing Viewpoints

Beginning in grades 2 and 3, children should be exposed to and helped to grapple with multiple viewpoints. This way, they learn (a) that there are different perspectives—different ways of seeing and judging—on the same topic; (b) that even well-informed people (whether average citizens or specialists on the topic) often disagree about what happened, why something happened, or what will happen next; (c) that there may be discrepancies or inaccuracies or omissions that go undetected when we rely on a single viewpoint; and (d) that we have no choice but to learn to negotiate and weigh these competing viewpoints and draw defensible conclusions.

These are important objectives for two reasons. First, today's children are tomorrow's jurors, voters, representatives, judges, mayors, governors, and presidents. Only one of these citizen roles is required by law (jury duty), yet every citizen is expected to vote regularly and many citizens take up the other roles at one time or another as well. Each role assumes the individual is capable of dealing with conflicting accounts, discrepancies, and disagreements—in brief, the ability to handle competing viewpoints in a way that is fair and competent. The second reason is that one cannot learn history, geography, civics, economics, anthropology, or the other social sciences without exposure to multiple viewpoints and the need to make sense of them.

As we saw in the case of the *Titanic* inquiry in Chapter 8, inquiry is a teaching/learning strategy that helps children develop this ability. As they test their hypotheses, they must grapple with conflicting evidence and perspectives: Was it the captain's pride that sank the *Titanic,* not an iceberg? Was it cutthroat competition between the shipping companies? Was it simply an accident? Evidence can be found to support each conclusion.

There are strategies in addition to inquiry that help students grapple with competing viewpoints, but let's stay with inquiry for the moment and look at an activity in which students are asked to grapple with competing viewpoints contained in multiple primary documents. After this, we turn to historical fiction.

Assume that you are planning a unit on the American Revolution that will integrate the history, reading, and writing curricula. Within that unit, you are about to lead fifth-grade students on a historical inquiry on this question: Did the American colonists *want* independence from England? You know that many of them did but that many did not, and that the conflict between "Loyalists" (to England) and "Patriots" (the rebels) was intense. The Patriots eventually prevailed, writing the Declaration of Independence and fighting a war for independence. Figure 9–4 presents three different resources on this question. Each is a letter, which is the most common kind of primary source document.

The children will need help reading and comprehending the three letters, to be sure. Then they will need help grappling with the competing viewpoints. You might lead them through each letter with the question, "What was the position of each person? And how did each support his or her position?" These questions help students distinguish between one's *position* on a question and one's *reasons* offered in support of that position. This should be followed with comparing and contrasting the viewpoints:

> In what ways are the viewpoints alike?
>
> In what ways are they different?

Now you can lift up your students' reasoning with a more challenging question:

> What other viewpoints can you imagine that others might have on this question?

Surely these three viewpoints do not cover the entire spectrum. This question helps the class gather a wider range of positions and reasons and may require additional research: interviewing parents, for example.

Students might now be ready to practice the skill you taught them earlier, how to take and defend a position. This would be a writing assignment preceded by classroom discussions in which students "try out" their own viewpoints and deal with challenges from other students.

Teachers face two difficulties when planning such instruction: they need to develop a plan for helping students grapple productively with multiple viewpoints, and they need to locate the multiple resources. Because we have just dealt with the first of these, let us turn to the second.

FIGURE 9–4   Inquiry: Did American colonists *want* independence from England?

Viewpoint #1 **William Franklin** Governor of the New Jersey Colony Excerpt from a letter to the New Jersey Legislature, 1776	Viewpoint #2 **Sarah Morris Mifflin** Wife of General Thomas Mifflin of the Continental Army Excerpt from a letter to a friend in Boston, 1776	Viewpoint #3 **"A Son of Africa"** Excerpt from a letter written anonymously by an (enslaved? free?) African American published in *Massachusetts Spy*, February 10, 1774
. . . Depend upon it, you can never place yourselves in a happier situation than in your dependence on Great Britain. Independence has not even a chance of being gained without the loss of the lives and properties of many thousands of the honest people of this country—yet these, it seems, are as nothing in the eyes of the patriots! But remember, Gentlemen, that I now tell you, that should they by chance achieve their purpose, yet their government will not be lasting.	. . . I know this, that as free I can die but once; but as a slave (to British rule) I shall not be worthy of life. I have the pleasure to assure you that these are the (feelings) of my sister Americans. They have sacrificed parties (gatherings) of pleasure . . . and finery to that great spirit of patriotism which moves people throughout this country.	. . . You are taxed without your consent . . . and have petitioned for relief, and cannot get any. Are not your hearts also hard, when you hold men in slavery who are entitled to liberty by the law of nature, equal as yourselves? When the eyes of your understanding are opened, then will you see clearly between your case and Great Britain, and that of the Africans. If so, is it lawful for one nation to enslave another?

Source: A New Nation (McGraw-Hill), a fifth-grade social studies textbook program.

Much help can be found in modern textbooks, which are, as we saw above, *collections* of resources. The school library is bound to have multiple resources on numerous topics, and students can be taught the skill of skimming through them, searching for competing viewpoints.

The Internet, too, is a rich source of multiple viewpoints. It is not as well organized, however, as the textbook and the school library. Accordingly, teachers and students need to become familiar with a few reliable websites and then branch out from there. An experienced teacher who is planning to lead an inquiry on the American Revolution might begin by searching the following two websites:

http://rs6.loc.gov/amhome.html

http://www.mmhschool.com/teach/socialstud/socstu1.html

The first is produced by the U.S. Library of Congress and is a collection of collections called "The American Memory." Navigating your way through this site, you'll come upon *http://lcweb.loc.gov/exhibits/,* where you'll find a collection called "Declaring Independence:

Drafting the Documents." What we particularly appreciate at this site is how it can help students study the conflict between the Patriots and the Loyalists through the persuasive writing of Thomas Jefferson. Students will find the first "rough draft" of the Declaration of Independence, for example; the final draft lists over 20 specific reasons the colonists should declare independence.

The second (*http://www.mmhschool.com/teach/socialstud/socstu1.html*) is a website operated by McGraw-Hill, the publishing company from whose textbook program the three "viewpoints" were excerpted in Figure 9–4. At this site, the teacher will find lesson plans for conducting this online activity. There are three objectives listed:

- To investigate how the Declaration of Independence was drafted
- To view original documents relating to the Declaration of Independence
- To create a storyboard illustrating the sequence of events in the creation of the Declaration of Independence.

And there are suggestions at this site for what to do before the online activity, during it, and afterward. Each of the major textbook publishing companies operates an Internet website that helps teachers conduct online activities tied to the units in the textbook.

HISTORICAL FICTION

Assuming that "grappling with competing viewpoints" is a major objective of this integrated American Revolution unit, then children's historical fiction might be brought in at this point. These stories should be combined with the lessons just described (the three letters; the Internet search)—that is, with data gathered from the textbook, maps, the Internet, and other information sources—so that students are not left only with narrative, fictionalized treatments of the War for Independence. Lesson Plan 13 shows how to use two popular pieces of historical fiction on the American Revolution. Both, rather than only one, are used so that students have the opportunity to grapple with the cultural and gender viewpoints contained in the two stories.

Curriculum Guides

As we did in Chapters 1 and 7, we again urge you to use local, state, and national curriculum guides to help you plan social studies lessons and units. When you are asked to teach a topic such as "Egypt," "Civic Ideals," or "The American Revolution," you do not need to start from scratch or work in isolation. Ample advice is available from colleagues, curriculum coordinators in the school district, and numerous printed curriculum guides.

- *Sampler.* Excerpts from the social studies curriculum guidelines published by National Council for the Social Studies accompany this text in the *Sampler.* If you want to find more classroom teaching examples using these standards, search for them at the NCSS website, *http://www.socialstudies.org/.*

THE AMERICAN REVOLUTION: TWO PERSPECTIVES FROM LITERATURE

Lesson Plan 13

Grade	5
Time	Two weeks
Objectives	Children will understand that descriptions of events depend to some extent on who is describing them and that people can interpret events differently. Also, they will enrich their knowledge of the American Revolution with the personal narratives of a fictional boy and girl; one black, one white; one free, one enslaved. Also, they will form an initial concept of *historical fiction.*
Literature	*Historical fiction:* James Lincoln Collier and Christopher Collier, *My Brother Sam Is Dead* (Scholastic, 1974) and *War Comes to Willy Freeman* (Dell, 1983).
Viewpoints	These two pieces of historical fiction present very different perspectives on the American Revolution. His brother Tim tells Sam's story. Both Sam and Tim are European-American males. Their father is against Sam joining with the American Patriots to drive out the British. Younger Tim is torn between his father and Sam. Willy, on the other hand, is a young female who has to disguise herself as a male because she is alone and separated from her family. Soldiers are everywhere. Also, she is African American. It doesn't make much difference to her which side wins. Her father, unlike Tim's, joins the Patriots and, before many pages are turned, is killed defending a Patriot fort.
Interest Building	Engage students' interest in the idea that *perspective* makes a difference. Use Lesson Plan 4 in Chapter 4 on "Primary and Secondary Sources" in which students themselves are eyewitnesses to a surprise event.
Lesson Development	1. Teach the two books as you normally would, using your favorite literature circle (or other) techniques. Students should write in their response journals and participate in numerous interpretive discussions while reading these books. 2. The culminating activity is to have students themselves write a new piece of historical fiction in which Tim and Willy meet and learn of one another's experiences and perspectives on this war. Before they begin this work, however, use the two texts they have read as the examples in a concept-formation or concept-attainment lesson on the concept *historical fiction* (see Chapter 8).
Summary and Assessment	Have several students share their original stories and help the audience evaluate each story on two criteria: the story itself (as taught in literature) and the degree to which Tim's and Willy's perspectives were effectively represented. After revision, have the original stories placed in students' social studies portfolios.
Integration	*Literature:* Children's literature is infused here to help children achieve important social studies objectives. Thanks to the concept lesson on *historical fiction,* they learn about a particular literary genre. *Writing:* Writing in response journals builds literacy skills. Writing a new story in which Tim and Willy meet gives students the opportunity to apply their concept of historical fiction.

■   ■   ■   ■   ■

- *Voluntary National Standards for History, Civics, Geography, and Economics.* See summaries, website, and ordering information in Chapter 1.
- *States' Guidelines.* Most states have social studies curriculum guidelines posted online. Search for yours through the website of your state department of education. See Chapter 1 for samples.
- *Districts.* Most districts have social studies curriculum guidelines. A cooperating teacher or principal will be able to give you a copy, or call the curriculum coordinator at the school district's central office.

Conclusion

A variety of resources for teaching social studies were presented, beginning with the school library or resource center. We began there for a reason. The late Hilda Taba, an educator whom we greatly admired, insisted that expensive excursions away from the school were too often lost on children who hadn't actually learned yet to *observe* the environments and *use* the resources that are *near* at hand—namely, the school. The children will need the resources located there, both print and electronic, and the maps, filmstrips, photo sets, and almanacs for the multimedia approach to teaching and learning that is encouraged here. They need to "break the ice" with the library and the librarian, to become comfortable there, and learn well the resources there that they will need for their social studies projects.

Teachers and students alike were encouraged in this chapter to use a wide range of instructional resources because inquiry and concept formation require extensive information searches and because not all children learn in the same way. Also, different resources—both fiction and nonfiction, both primary and secondary accounts—will surely provide competing viewpoints on the same subject. Discrepancies or inaccuracies will go undetected when a single source is used. Accordingly, field trips and guest speakers, textbooks and newspapers, map and globe collections, eyewitness accounts and children's historical fiction, online museums, and games and simulations—are all part of the mix called social studies teaching and learning.

Discussion Questions and Suggested Activities

1. Ten kinds of resources were addressed: the school library, textbook programs, guest speakers, field trips (both real and virtual), computer resources, newspapers, map and globe collections, primary documents, children's historical fiction, and curriculum guides. Assume that you are going to teach a class of teacher interns about these resources. Create a data-retrieval chart, such as the one shown in Figure 9–3 for the virtual field trip to China and Egypt, that will help them compare and contrast these resources. You'll list the resources down the left and, across the top, place the dimensions on which you believe these should be compared.

2. Choose one of the virtual field trips for which the before-during-after plan was *not* given and sketch a before-during-after plan for it.

3. Find out which libraries and museums in your state have Internet sites. Choose one dealing with social studies subject matter and create a plan to help your students explore it online.

4. Find two *current* social studies textbook programs for a grade that interests you and compare the way multiple viewpoints are presented to students and how students are guided through them. Are primary documents used? How are readers asked to make sense of them?

5. According to a new study of gender differences in education, "girls have narrowed some significant gender gaps, but technology is now the new 'boys' club' in our nation's public schools" (Janice Weinman, citing *Gender Gaps: Where Schools Still Fail Our Children,* by the American Association of University Women, online at *http://www.aauw.org/2000/ggpr.html*). Do your own education and experience support this finding?

Selected References

American Association of University Women. (1999). *Gender gaps: Where schools still fail our children.* Washington, DC: Author.

Braun, Joseph A., Fernlund, Phyllis F., & White, Charles S. (Eds.). (1998). *Teaching social studies with technology.* Wilsonville, OR: Franklin, Beedle & Associates.

Ehman, Lee H., & Glenn, Allen D. (1991). Interactive technology in social studies. In James P. Shaver (Ed.), *Handbook of Research on Social Studies Teaching and Learning* (pp. 513–522). New York: Macmillan.

Social Education. (1999, April). Theme issue on technology and social studies.

Social Studies and the Young Learner. (1995, Jan./Feb.). Theme issue on technology and social studies.

Notes

1. Barbara M. Taylor & S. Jay Samuels, Children's use of text structure in the recall of expository material, *American Educational Research Journal, 20* (Winter 1983): 517–28.

2. We found this website at the website for the national curriculum standards for geography, *http://www.nationalgeographic.com/education/Standards.html.*

3. On the road to cultural bias: A critique of the Oregon Trail CD-ROM, *Rethinking Schools 10,* no. 1, pp. 10–18, 27.

4. A very helpful resource for teachers who want to get the most out of the Carmen Sandiego simulation is Carmen Sandiego: Crime can pay when it comes to learning, by Terry Carroll, Cheryl Knight, and Ed Hutchinson. In *Technology tools in the social studies classroom,* edited by Joseph A. Braun, Jr., Phyllis Fernlund, and Charles S. White (Wilsonville, OR: Franklin, Beedle & Associates, 1998).

5. Margaret Hill, Geography on the Net, *Sunburst, 24* (May 1999): 14.

Websites

http://www.loc.gov
http://www.ourworld.compuserve.com/homepages/james_baker/
http://www.williams.edu:803/Biology/orienteering/o~index.html
http://www.abanet.org/publiced

http://www.city.net

http://www.whitehouse.gov

http://www.whitehouse.gov/WH/kids/html/kidshome.html

http://www.pbs.org/weta/whitehouse/whhome.htm

http://www.ihep.ac.cn/tour/China_tour.html

http://www.memphis.edu/egypt/artifact.html

http://www.memphis.edu/egypt/egypt.html

http://www.diegorivera.com/diego_home_eng.html

http://www.kidlink.org/

http://www.monticello.org/Day/A_Day_in_the_Life.html

http://www.lkwdpl.org/wihohio/anth-sus.htm

http://www.sln.fi.edu/

http://www.powersource.com/powersource/gallery/people/default.html

http://www.educate.si.edu/spotlight/elect.html

http://www.infoseek.go.com/WebDir/People/Famous_people/
   U_S_history/Civil_rights_leaders?sv=M6&svx=related

http://www.nationalgeographic.com/maps/political.html

http://www.altapedia.com/

http://www.atlas.usgs.gov/

http://www.ac.wwu.edu/~stephan/48states.html

http://www.rs6.loc.gov/amhome.html

http://www.mmhschool.com/teach/socialstud/socstu1.html

http://www.lcweb.loc.gov/exhibits/

http://www.mmhschool.com/teach/socialstud/socstu1.html

http://www.kidlink.org:80/KIDPROJ/MCC/

http://www.dkonline.com/epals/

http://www.pharos.bu.edu/Egypt/Wonders

http://www.pilgrims.net/plymouth

http://www.netins.net/showcase/creative/lincoln/gallery/pict.htm

http://www.netins.net/showcase/creative/lincoln/sites/sites.htm

http://www.aoc.gov/art/suffrage.htm

http://www.nara.gov/exhall/charters/charters.html

http://www.un.org

http://www.libertynet.org/iha/index.html

http://www.museumca.org/usa

http://www.si.edu/organiza/museums/nmah/start.htm

http://www.educate.si.edu/resources/resource/sslist2.html#start

http://www.mecca.org/~crights/cyber.html

http://www.mariner.org

http://www.kms.bham.wednet.edu/lobby.htm
http://www.socialstudies.org/
http://www.aauw.org/2000/ggpr.html
http://www.tapr.org/%7Eird/Nordick/Standards.html

10
Assessing Student Learning

Main Idea

Assessment goes on continually in the classroom and is a natural part of the learning environment. The primary purpose of assessment is not to sort children or to compare schools; it is to improve teaching and learning.

Key Concepts

purposes, principles, and methods of assessment; formal and informal assessment; performance standards (criteria) and scoring guides

Chapter Outline

- Assessment Is Natural
- Purposes of Assessment
- Principles of Assessment
- Methods of Assessment
- Conclusion
- Discussion Questions and Suggested Activities
- Selected References
- Notes

Chapter Snapshot

Mr. Bailey usually introduces his students to the concept *democracy* as part of the fourth-grade social studies-language arts curriculum. But there's so much on TV news now about dictatorships and democracies that he figured he should find out what this new group of students already knows about it. He proceeds by asking a few questions: "Are our weekly classroom meetings democratic? Thumbs up if you think so, down if you think not, sideways if you're not sure." He counts thumbs and cajoles a few nonparticipants into the exercise, reminding them of the "not sure" option. "Thank you. Now let's hear your reasons." Their three-options decision tells him little about their understanding of democracy, but listening to their *reasoning* he learns a great deal—mainly that they have very little understanding, only something vague about "elections." The next week, he launches the unit on democracy. At the end of it, he will revisit this question and listen again to their reasons.

 A favorite website http://nces.ed.gov/nationsreportcard/site/home.asp Click on history, geography, or civics and then examine sample questions for grades 4 and 8 on the assessment called the "Nation's Report Card" from the National Assessment of Educational Progress (NAEP).

Mrs. Rivera is a new fourth-grade teacher who plans to teach children to read and make maps of their state and the United States. The school district curriculum guide states that fourth-grade teachers should achieve the following objectives. The first specifies understandings, the second skills:

> *Knowledge:* At the end of the fourth grade, pupils should understand (1) the difference between state and national maps and (2) the differences and similarities among different kinds of maps: political, landform, and shaded relief maps.
>
> *Skills:* Pupils at the end of fourth grade should be able to (1) use map symbols and directions, (2) make different kinds of maps of the school grounds, and (3) locate places on the U.S. map using longitude and latitude.

Before she begins planning a unit of instruction, she decides to find out what these children presently know about maps. She considers asking the whole class several questions: "What is a map? Have you ever used a map? What kinds of information do maps give us? What things make a map a really good map? Who knows what a map legend is?" She also considers listing key map terms on the board and asking students to define each of them on a sheet of paper. These are fine ideas. After considering these alternatives, Mrs. Rivera decides to create a brief pencil-and-paper test so she can maximize the amount of information she obtains from each child. Using ideas from her college methods course, she finds a map skills practice exercise in the students' social studies workbook (Figure 10–1) and makes a copy for each child.

The next day, Mrs. Rivera informs the children that she wants to find out what they know about maps so she can plan instruction accordingly. She warms them up to the task by asking them about their experiences using and making maps. Then, she directs them to take 15 minutes or so to answer the 10 questions below the map. After they finish, to find out their immediate reactions, she asks the class which items were the most and least difficult for them. She jots down a few notes on what they say.

Later that day, she looks over her notes and scores the assessment. She notes that two-thirds of her students marked 4 or 5 of the 10 items correctly. Two students answered none correctly, and two answered 9 of the 10 items correctly. No one got all 10. Examining responses item by item, she observes that no students correctly answered the question about "due north," and nearly all the children identified the railroad. This is good information, and she figures it will help her plan instruction on maps.

She goes back to school the next day eager to gather more information. She decides to lead a class discussion of the same 10 items. She makes a transparency of the map and questions and displays it on the overhead projector. This time, she asks the class to respond to each question out loud. Her questioning procedure goes something like this: She directs her students' attention to the first question and asks the children which responses they selected yesterday. She uses the "fingers" technique to maximize participation: "Hold up one finger if you said it was a swamp, two if you said it was a desert, and three fingers if you said it was mountainous." Then she calls on a student to give reasons for his or her choice. After listening, she asks another child for his or her reasoning, then another child. This way, she is able to hear their reasoning—something that yesterday's exercise did not allow. As she moves through the 10 items, she is able to hear each student reason aloud at least once. Children are able to hear one another's reasoning, too. Mrs. Rivera is careful to call on as many girls as boys.

FIGURE 10–1 Assessing map skills.

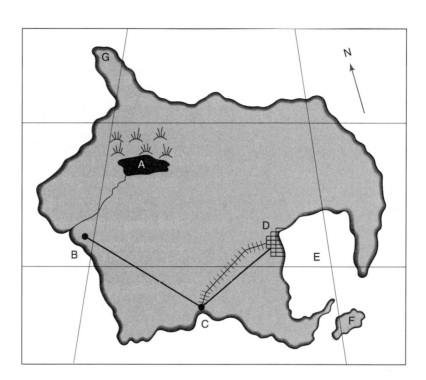

Use the map above to decide the correct answers. Then underline the correct answers.

1. The land north of A is (a swamp), (a desert), (mountainous).
2. The mouth of a river is located near letter (A), (B), (C).
3. The city at D is perhaps a (capital), (seaport), (mining town).
4. The river flows (from southwest to northeast), (from northeast to southwest), (from east to west).
5. An island is marked by the letter (A), (B), (F).
6. A railroad runs between (B and C), (D and B), (D and C).
7. The letter E marks (a bay), (a peninsula), (an island).
8. A peninsula is shown on this map at (B), (G), (C).
9. A delta might be found just north of (C), (A), (B).
10. The letter G is due north of (C), (A), (B).

Hungry for still more information, she turns to a different kind of assessment procedure on the following day. She places a blank sheet of paper in front of each student and asks them individually to try to draw from memory a map of the United States. She tells them to sketch very roughly the nation's general outline, add the Rocky Mountains and the Mississippi River, and draw in their own state, locating it as best they can. She asks them to indicate compass directions as well and to create a legend/key to explain any symbols used. Her students are nervous and a little embarrassed at the prospect of drawing. Mrs. Rivera calms them with a little humor and impresses upon them how important it is for her to find out what they now can do so she can plan the very best instruction for them.

She has a hunch, based on the prior assessment, that several children will do very well on this map-drawing exercise, but mainly she is genuinely curious to see what they will draw, where they will draw the Mississippi, whether they will use symbols, and where they will say north is.

After mulling over all the information she has gathered, Mrs. Rivera plans a unit. The learning activities begin with conversations about road maps found in automobile glove compartments, which several students bring from home, and she displays well-worn trail maps that she has used on summer hikes. During the unit, pairs of children learn to make maps of the classroom and playground, and they search for explorers' routes on CD-ROM programs. Assigned to cooperative teams, the class develops expertise on different regions of the United States, making political and landform maps of each region. Each day, they practice drawing an outline map of the United States from memory, after studying once more the map hanging in the front of the room. Global comparisons are made between each region and a geographically similar region on another continent; for example, the Rockies are compared to the Swiss Alps, Death Valley to the Sahara, the Great Plains to the Steppes of Russia, and so forth.

When introducing the unit, Mrs. Rivera (with great flourish) informs the class that "by winter vacation this year, each of you will be able to place in your portfolio a landform map of the United States drawn from memory, and it will include our own state mapped in correctly."

Assessment Is Natural

Assessment means finding out what students know and are able to do. Like a detective trying to get the facts, assessment's emphasis is on observation of what is happening *now*. *Evaluation*, by contrast, involves value judgment: comparing what is—the facts about the child's present understanding—with what *ought* to be—the desired outcome of instruction. This distinction is often blurred. When teachers assess children's present understanding of *landform map* or *map legend* (or *citizenship* or *immigration*), they usually do so with a desired level of understanding—a standard—in mind. Indeed, assessment and evaluation often occur in one breath. In this chapter, we will follow common practice and use the terms *assessment* and *evaluation* almost interchangeably, making the distinction where necessary for clarity.

MRS. RIVERA'S ASSESSMENTS

Mrs. Rivera was assessing her students' map knowledge and skills. For what purpose? To help her plan an effective unit of instruction. Was she doing anything out of the ordinary? Not really. Teachers assess their students almost continually, observing them at their desks, checking their homework, and looking over their shoulders as they make models, paint lakes and mountains, read about deserts of the world, and write stories about historical events. They notice when children raise their hands higher and higher, hoping to be called on, and when they slump down in their chair, avoiding the teacher's gaze. They notice when children are rejected from one another's play and observe how they negotiate tasks in small cooperative groups. Teachers are constantly assessing.

Mrs. Rivera is a model of curiosity. She loves to learn what her children already know and can do. She is able to make them feel comfortable as she gathers information. They know she has much to teach them and that she diagnoses their present knowledge and skills so she can properly plan instruction.

Note the variety of assessment procedures she used. First, there was the paper-and-pencil assessment. She pulled an activity from the workbook and adapted it to her assessment purpose. This paper-and-pencil assessment was of the *selection,* or multiple-choice, type because students were asked to choose the best response from several given. After that, she asked the whole class which items they found difficult and easy. Informal questioning of this sort is probably the most common kind of assessment conducted by teachers. Mrs. Rivera then placed the same map and questions on the overhead projector and conducted a sort of group interview—using a planned sequence of questions and the "fingers" technique to get all of her students involved—so she could gather information about how they puzzled their way through these items. She did not provide correction or instruction; these would come later, during the unit. She was only trying to find out how they thought about these things. Finally, she used a *production* (also called *supply*) assessment when she had students sketch the U.S. map. When Mrs. Rivera introduced the unit to students, she informed them of a key performance expectation or *target.*

These are only a few of the kinds of assessment commonly carried on in classrooms, and Mrs. Rivera's purpose—to plan instruction—is only one purpose. We will explore these and other kinds and purposes of assessment in this chapter. For now, let us emphasize that assessment goes on continually in classrooms. And it *ought* to. Assessment "ought to become part of the natural learning environment," writes Howard Gardner. "As much as possible it should occur 'on the fly,' " as part of a teacher's or learner's "natural engagement in a learning situation."[1] What is to be avoided is a view of assessment as a formal procedure that occurs only at the end of an instructional unit for the purpose of reporting a score or grade. That is one purpose of assessment, and a necessary one. But it is a narrow purpose and not one that helps teachers plan or children learn.

Purposes of Assessment

In this section and the next, we invite you to think about purposes and principles of assessment. Following this, we explain the main kinds of assessment techniques, from simple observation to self-assessment checklists, scoring guides, and portfolios. First, though, consider three general purposes of assessment (Figure 10–2).

FIGURE 10–2 Purposes of assessing student learning.

Instructional Planning

Assess in order to
- diagnose students' understanding of maps before developing a map unit
- provide feedback to students on their progress and problems
- decide how to modify a unit plan
- identify cultural differences
- identify ability strengths and weaknesses
- provide evidence of success to students; therefore, motivate them to persevere

Public Accountability

Assess in order to
- report student progress to the community
- compare students across schools, school districts, states, and nations
- discuss with parents students' progress and problems

Student Placement

Assess in order to
- assign students to pairs and cooperative groups or ability groups
- decide which students require an IEP
- place profoundly retarded and extraordinarily gifted children in special programs

Mrs. Rivera's assessments were serving the purpose of diagnosing her students' knowledge and skills, which in turn served the purpose of planning effective instruction. This—*instructional planning*—is the primary purpose of assessment as far as the teacher is concerned. Instructional decision making without assessment data would be subject to considerable error. Not only does assessment information allow teachers to tailor instruction to individual students, it also helps them decide on the instructional objectives themselves and monitor students' progress. If Mrs. Rivera knows, for example, that her children's oral reports on the geographical regions of the United States will be graded on organization, accuracy, voice clarity, and use of visual aids, then these become major performance objectives of the unit. We will discuss this in detail in the next section.

Public accountability and program evaluation is a second purpose of assessment. Most states in the United States have developed social studies assessments that will be administered to students statewide, and the U.S. Congress funds assessments of students' knowledge in history, geography, and civics.[2] Assessments such as these are administered typically to students in grades 4, 8, and 12, and the results are used by parents and public officials to compare education programs and student achievement within districts, across states, and among nations. Assessments designed for this purpose are usually standardized and norm-referenced. *Standardized* means that the test is designed to be administered and scored in the same way wherever it is given. *Norm-referenced* means that the results will be used to compare one group of students (e.g., those in your school or state) to another (students in the nation as a whole).

A third purpose of assessment is the *selection of students for particular schools and programs* or, simply, *placement.* IQ tests and the Scholastic Aptitude Test (SAT), introduced in 1926, are perhaps the best-known tests used for this purpose. IQ and other similar tests are often used to determine placements of exceptional children. The SAT has determined college and university admission for millions of high school students. In the elementary grades, standardized reading and math tests are often used to determine ability-group placement, and other assessments of social competence, intelligence, and language proficiency are used to place students in special programs.

Critics of testing for this purpose have called attention to some of its abuses, one of which is to sort children into categories from which there may be no escape. As was pointed out in Chapter 2, once a child is labeled, the label often "sticks" long after its supposed benefits to the child have worn off. It may generate negative effects as a *self-fulfilling prophecy:* Teachers' expectations of the child may be lowered in a way that is not warranted, the child's self-perceptions may be lowered accordingly, and, making matters worse, he or she may be permanently (rather than only temporarily) separated from other children. As a result of the separation, the child may experience a less challenging and less empowering curriculum. As a consequence, he or she will know and be able to do less than his or her peers. Labels have been misused especially with racial-, ethnic-, and language-minority children. For these reasons, teachers are urged to use extreme caution when using test results for placement purposes.

Principles of Assessment

When teachers plan to assess their students' learning, they should also be thinking about curriculum objectives and alternative ways to provide instruction. The reverse is also true: When teachers plan curriculum objectives and think about how they will teach to them, they need also to consider how they will assess student achievement of these objectives. They are, in effect, thinking about three things at once. For this reason, it has become popular to say that the boundaries between assessment, curriculum, and instruction are "blurred."[3] This brings us to the first principle of good assessment practice.

PRINCIPLE 1: ASSESSMENT IS AN INTEGRAL PART OF CURRICULUM AND INSTRUCTION

Assessment planning should not be tagged onto the *end* of a unit, *after* curriculum has been planned and instruction delivered. Good assessment is not an add-on or an afterthought. If assessment is to facilitate student learning, it must be woven into the fabric of curriculum and instruction. It must be done before, during, and after instruction.

Assessments conducted before instruction are *diagnostic assessments*. Mrs. Rivera developed her unit to address the geographic knowledge and skills she found wanting in the assessments she conducted *before* planning the unit. Assessments conducted *during* instruction are *formative* assessments. These assessments help teachers decide what to do next in a lesson or unit. They are called formative because they help teachers "form" or modify instruction to help children achieve the objectives. This is certainly the most common kind of assessment. Often they are nothing more than observations made of students while they are engaged in project or committee work or while they are working independently at their desks, but they may also be brief paper-and-pencil tests given periodically through a unit of instruction. Teachers do this to check students' understanding of the topic at hand and then to alter the lesson as needed. They also do it to give students knowledge of the results of their work and a sense of making progress, which can be of tremendous help in motivating learners of all ages to carry on with the task at hand. Frequent formative assessment provides both teachers and students with the feedback they need to teach and learn better.

Assessments conducted *after* instruction are *summative* assessments. These are used to judge students' overall achievement at the end of instruction. They sum up the learning that has taken place and may incorporate many quizzes, work samples, performances, and other evidence of learning. Chapter and unit tests are the most common kinds of summative assessments, along with the grade given at the end of the school term.

PRINCIPLE 2: DEVOTE TIME TO ESSENTIAL LEARNINGS

Teachers should spend their assessment time on a relatively small number of *essential* subject matters or skills. Key themes of citizenship, history, and geography were discussed in Chapters 3 through 6, and the teacher should direct assessment in social studies primarily to these. It is more important, for example, to develop assessments related to ideas such as democracy, cultural pluralism, and human-environment interaction than it is to spend time listing crops produced in Latin America, Civil War battlefields, and hometowns of U.S. presidents. Of course, these latter subjects may have their place in a well-conceived curriculum, but *school time is precious*. Skillful teachers spend most of their instruction and assessment energies on the learnings that matter the most.

PRINCIPLE 3: SET HIGH STANDARDS FOR TEACHING AND LEARNING

The minimum competency movement of the 1970s and 1980s was an attempt by the educational community to restore public confidence in American education. Test data indicated a downward trend in scores on tests of basic school subjects over a period of several years. It was widely believed by the public—rightly or wrongly—that the achievement of American school children was falling behind that of their counterparts in other industrialized nations. Out of this concern came the idea that schools should identify minimum levels of competency for basic school subjects that presumably all students would be expected to master. Teaching for these minimum competencies would be followed by minimum competency tests. This movement had great appeal and received strong support from public officials. Several states developed programs to implement minimum competency testing. What was not anticipated in this process was the detrimental effects of foreshortening achievement by focusing on *minimum* requirements. Minimum expectations gave no hint of the kinds of targets toward which students and teachers should put forth their best effort.[4]

"Social studies teaching and learning are powerful when they are challenging," according to the vision statement developed by the National Council for the Social Studies.[5] Assessments, like the curriculum objectives to which they are connected, need to capture the richness and depth of social studies subject matter. Teaching children whether Geronimo was a hero to the Cherokee or Apache people is a far cry from helping them to write and dramatize a biography of his life. Knowing the names of those who signed the U.S. Constitution is important, but it falls short of knowing why the Constitution has the content it does, grasping the principles on which it relies, and knowing what democracy requires of citizens.

To set high standards for children's learning and to assess their attainment in relation to these standards, teachers need to be familiar with the several sets of curriculum standards developed in recent years. These were addressed in Chapters 1, 3, 4, and 5. Consider the two following curriculum standards for social studies learning developed for children in the early grades.

> By the end of the fourth grade, students should be able to:
> - Identify key ideals of the United States' democratic form of government, such as individual human dignity, liberty, justice, equality, and the rule of law, and discuss their application in specific situations.[6]
> - Demonstrate understanding of events that exemplify fundamental values and principles of American democracy.[7]

Teachers who teach to these standards in the early grades are "aiming high." But there is more. To assess student achievement of these standards, it is necessary to envision the levels of achievement that students must reach to receive particular scores, awards, or certificates. These levels are called *performance standards* or *performance criteria*. They define levels of achievement—that is to say, degrees of mastery or proficiency—from high to low. Teachers often define three levels: good, fair, and poor. When a fourth level is added, it usually specifies a higher level still: excellent, superior, commendable, highly proficient, distinguished, and so forth. Sometimes five or six levels are specified. Below is a set of performance criteria developed for use in the fifth grade. They spell out three levels of achievement related to the second of the two curriculum standards given above: Students will show understanding of events that exemplify fundamental values and principles of American democracy. These performance criteria were developed to assess the quality of short essays that students write about important events in American history, such as the signing of the Declaration of Independence or the Emancipation Proclamation.

> - *Level 3—Proficient:* Response shows considerable knowledge of the time period and geographic factors, as appropriate, and frequently demonstrates insight. It usually supports ideas and conclusions with specific historical examples. Response is well reasoned and organized and is largely historically accurate.
> - *Level 2—Adequate:* Response contains adequate information about the event. It demonstrates some knowledge of the time period and geographic factors, as appropriate. Response demonstrates some understanding, but reasons and evidence are in limited depth.

- *Level 1—Minimal:* Response addresses the question, but shows minimal understanding. It may lack historical and geographical context. It may contain numerous historical errors. It may simply rephrase the question but includes at least a word or phrase showing historical knowledge.[8]

PRINCIPLE 4: CLARIFY TARGETS EARLY

Teachers need to clarify for students early in the instructional unit the targeted level of performance. In other words, they should "let students in on" the objectives of instruction and try to describe those objectives as clearly as possible, specifying what students will know and be able to do if they achieve the objective. If teachers want children to develop their skills and knowledge to a high degree of proficiency—if they want children to hit the target—then the children must know the target well in advance. Just as an archer cannot shoot an arrow to the bull's-eye if she cannot see the target, children cannot become proficient if they have no idea of the level of performance they are striving for. Skillful teachers, therefore, clarify the goals of instruction at the beginning of the year and state specific objectives/performance criteria at the beginning of the unit.

For example, Ms. Paley's kindergartners know in advance that their dramatizations of historical events must be *rich in detail.* Consequently, each time she repeats to them the story of Rosa Parks' bus ride or of Squanto, the Pilgrims' friend, it is with the expectation that their retellings of the story will evolve. And they do.[9] Likewise, Mr. Smith tells his seventh-grade class in September that by June they *will draw a world map beautifully from memory on a blank piece of tag board.* "When they arrive here, I tell them they'll end up with 150 countries, and they tell me, 'No way.'" But they do, confidently. "I used to hear about countries on television and think they were over there somewhere," admitted one student. "I hadn't heard of half of them. Now I can figure out better what's going on in the world. I'll always know that Angola is in Africa and not just over there somewhere."[10]

Teachers like Ms. Paley and Mr. Smith make clear for children the "destinations" of their efforts. Ms. Paley's specification that dramatizations are to be "rich in detail," and Mr. Smith's that their world maps will be "drawn"—more than that, drawn "beautifully" and "from memory," both let children in on the performance criteria by which their work will be judged and toward which their work should be aimed. This can be called "backward design"[11] because the end point (the arrow hitting the target) is envisioned first, then specified ("in rich detail"; "drawn beautifully from memory"), and only then are learning activities planned (see Figure 10–3).

Teachers then assess continuously, in large and small ways, formally and informally, within learning activities and between them. Such teachers can provide additional instruction and experiences as needed, calibrating them to student progress toward the desired results. In this way the first principle of assessment is realized: improving teaching and learning.

PRINCIPLE 5: AIM FOR MORE AUTHENTIC ASSESSMENTS

Assessments should be geared to finding out students' ability to apply knowledge and skills successfully in meaningful or *authentic* tasks. These tasks are exhibitions of children's ability to *use* what they have learned. Such tasks are meaningful because they are goal directed,

FIGURE 10–3
From target to learning activity.

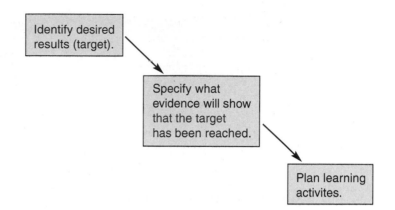

and these goals have a real-world quality; hence, they are not "school-bound" tasks that have no bearing on what people do in their lives as citizens, workers, family members, and neighbors. Rather than focusing only on what children have memorized, they require children to use information—to analyze, manipulate, or interpret it in some way; consequently, higher-order thinking is incorporated into the assessment.

Examples of authentic tasks in social studies are plentiful. Teachers can assess students' ability to:

- Participate in discussions of classroom/community problems as part of maintaining a healthy civic life.
- Use reference books as part of social studies inquiry projects.
- Work cooperatively as part of a team accomplishing a challenging task.
- Display historical reasoning by writing a biography of a grandparent, president, explorer, or social reformer.
- Create a museum exhibit of a geographic region (the Southwest), a landform (Salt Lake), or a historical event, era, or person.
- Interpret primary documents, such as speeches, newspaper accounts, photos, and songs.
- Read and make charts and graphs showing food supply, election results, census data, and economic data.
- Explain supply and demand or the relationship between savings accounts and economic growth.
- Take and defend a position on a controversial issue in the school or community.
- Write and illustrate a travel brochure of the community.

PRINCIPLE 6:
COLLECT MULTIPLE INDICATORS OF LEARNING—AN ARRAY OF EVIDENCE

Teachers should collect multiple indicators of student achievement. A score on a lone chapter test or a summative performance assessment does not go far enough to tell us what a child knows and is able to do, and it gives no indication of progress. Teachers can have students

One way students can display the depth of their understanding of the U.S. Constitution is to create, democratically, a classroom constitution. Lots of deliberation should precede voting on rules.

collect numerous work samples into a *portfolio* that documents their work over the course of a unit. The portfolio might contain a chapter test from the social studies textbook program along with two or three other paper-and-pencil tests and quizzes. There might also be a team-written biography to which the student contributed a chapter, letters to the editor on current events, self-assessments of the student's reading and thinking skills, and several drawings and maps. In this way, students have much to show for their work, and teachers can justify the grades they give by pointing to an array of evidence.

PRINCIPLE 7: PROVIDE AMPLE OPPORTUNITIES TO LEARN

Students should not be held accountable for learning subject matter on which they have not been provided adequate instruction. This is why schools should not provide only targets for learning, but also the *means* of achieving them—teachers, curriculum materials, classrooms, wall maps, libraries, stimulating environments. Children must be provided *support* or *assistance* if they are to reach the targets. School buildings in poor physical condition, outdated curriculum materials, school administrators who deny teachers the assistance of knowledgeable curriculum coordinators, unsupportive citizens, and teachers who have little professional competence or are not themselves readers and learners all combine

FIGURE 10–4 Principles of good assessment.

Principle 1: Treat assessment as an integral part of curriculum and instruction.

Principle 2: Direct assessments toward essential learnings.

Principle 3: Set high standards for teaching and learning.

Principle 4: Clarify targets early.

Principle 5: Assess student performance in authentic tasks.

Principle 6: Collect multiple indicators of learning.

Principle 7: Provide ample opportunities for students to learn.

to deny children sufficient opportunities to learn. Clearly, some of these problems are larger than what individual teachers can deal with in their own classrooms. Nonetheless what teachers *can* do is assess what is taught, teach what will be assessed, and assure the community that what is taught and assessed are essential learnings. Figure 10–4 summarizes the seven principles.

Methods of Assessment

We turn now to a variety of methods of assessment. We begin with informal techniques and then turn to more formal methods of paper-and-pencil tests, performance assessment, and portfolios. The latter are more formal because they are done less "on the fly," require more planning, and necessitate the development of materials, such as scoring guides.

INFORMAL ASSESSMENT TECHNIQUES

Much of the evaluation of learning in social studies is done informally by the teacher. Many times each day the teacher observes learners and judges the quality of their work. The teacher notices what problems individual children are encountering or what kind of help they need to progress. The teacher then decides what deficiencies are apparent in children's work, whether the instruction is proceeding too rapidly or too slowly, what materials are required, how well concepts have been understood, or how proficient children are in their use of skills. Of course, formal tests have a place in this process, but most of the assessing a teacher does involves informal methods and simple observation. This means that careful records must be kept if the progress of each child is to be reported accurately. Some of the more commonly used informal assessment techniques are described on the pages that follow.

Group Discussion

The teacher should reserve some time near the end of every social studies period for the class to discuss its progress and to make plans for the next day's work. This helps children identify concepts needing further study and reminds them of all the things they are learning in social studies.

Observation

Observation is among the best techniques the teacher can use to learn about children, appraise their progress, and determine their needs for improvement. Although all teachers use this method of learner appraisal, not all teachers are skillful in its application. The teacher who makes the most of observation knows what to look for, systematizes observations, and tries to objectify the information so obtained. To this end, we suggest that the teacher:

1. Spell out what is to be evaluated in terms of child behavior. For example, if the teacher is looking for progress in *historical reasoning,* it would be important to determine whether the student asks where a primary document came from and wants to know who wrote it rather just reading it and believing it without question. Or, if the teacher wants to observe progress in *consideration for others,* the following would be appropriate:

   Does the child
   a. Show respect for the ideas and feelings of classmates?
   b. Abstain from causing disturbances that make it impossible for others to do their best work?
   c. Carry a fair share of the work load in a small group?
   d. Enjoy helping a classmate when needed?
   e. Display sensitivity to injustices that may occur in the course of life in and out of the classroom?
   f. Return borrowed materials? Obtain permission to use materials that belong to others?
   g. Observe group rules?
   h. Fulfill responsibilities on time?

2. Select certain children for intensive observation and study rather than observing "in general." This intensive observation might be limited to certain specific situations. For example, just what happens to David when he is placed on a committee to accomplish some task in connection with a social studies unit? The purpose of observations of this type is to gain insight into the child's behavior in the context of a specific set of circumstances.

3. Record observations in writing and do not depend on memory. Keep a written record of information obtained through observation and maintain this record over a period of time. Here now are six entries in one teacher's anecdotal record on a child:

   Sara Larsen
   9/24   Difficulty in getting going in independent choice work; ignored all suggestions of activities. . . . "It's boring."

9/26   Found a fiction book related to unit for Sara. Read during work time. Took it home today.

9/27   Finished book . . . took suggestion to make a poster showing main characters.

10/1   Asked for time to show class the poster and to tell about the story.

10/2   Showed work. Talented artist. Received lots of compliments/support from classmates.

10/3   Sara asked for another book; suggested biography to her; also suggested she draw a map showing the area in which the person lived.

Asking Classifying Questions

Asking questions is perhaps the most widely used assessment technique of all time. The Socratic method relies on questioning; parents could not get along without it, and skillful teachers turn it into an art form. The journalist's standard set of questions form the basic assessment questions: who, what, where, when, how, and why? But the *classifying* questions discussed in Chapter 8 may be the most widely useful for purposes of assessment. Recall, they are geared to assessing understanding of a concept, and there are four types of classifying questions. Take a moment to review the four types of classifying in Chapter 8 (page 262) so that you can follow what this teacher is doing:

- "Children, I want to ask a few questions about what you think *transportation* (or *immigration* or *citizen*) is."
- "Hold up one finger if you think walking from the cafeteria to the playground is an example of transportation. Hold up two fingers if you think it is not an example. Hold up a closed fist if you aren't sure."
- "Good. Now let's hear some of your reasons. Rosa? Tom?"
- "Let's get lots of examples of *transportation* on the board. Who will give us the first example. Okay, Sara? Rick?"
- "Good. We have 15 suggestions on the board. Now let's hear the thinking behind them. Nicole, you suggested covered wagons. What makes you think covered wagons are an example of transportation?"
- "Thank you. No one mentioned the space shuttle. Is it an example of transportation? Think about it for a minute and then jot down your decision and your reasons. In a minute I'll ask several of you to share your response with the class."

Note that this teacher is not providing instruction on the critical attributes of *transportation*. She is not using concept formation or any other concept teaching strategy. Rather, she is using classifying questions to *find out* what her students already know about this concept. Their decisions and the reasons they give will provide this teacher with ample information to decide what sort of instruction the students need on this concept. Do they think transportation means simply movement? If so, a cloud and a worm are both examples of transportation. Or do they think one thing is being moved by another? The teacher will find out as she listens to their decisions and justifications.

Readers may wish to read again the opening vignette of this chapter. Mrs. Rivera uses classifying questions as she diagnoses her students' knowledge of the concept *map*.

Conferences

Conferences with children should teach them how to assess their own work, thereby leading to increased self-direction. The teacher-learner conference can help identify particular learning problems and difficulties that children may be having, provide insight into students' feelings about schoolwork, and help the teacher become aware of special personal-social problems the children may be having. The conference is a method of assisting every child individually in a personal way. Teachers need to budget their time to allow regular 10-minute conferences with individual children. Children need the personal contact with their teacher that a conference can give.

A conference will be of little value if the teacher does all the talking and the child all the listening. A friendly, helpful approach is needed, one that results in greater feelings of personal worth on the part of the child along with some constructive and concrete help for improvement. This close working relationship with children is critical to good education, especially in the social studies.

PAPER-AND-PENCIL TESTS

Paper-and-pencil tests in the classroom usually are constructed by the teacher or selected from the collection of tests that accompany textbook programs. Even though they can be used successfully with primary grade children (assuming they are designed accordingly), their value increases as the child moves into the third and fourth grades and beyond. Such tests can help teachers gather data about how well students understand the concepts they are learning, their ability to write and to reason, their ability to recall key information, and their ability to use skills.

Mrs. Rivera's diagnostic exercise relied on a paper-and-pencil test of map symbols and directions (Figure 10–1). It assessed both knowledge and skill. The classifying test shown in Figure 10–5 is a straightforward way to assess students' understanding of economic concepts concerning the theme of *production*. Note that it is a variation of classifying type 3, in which children are asked to produce an example. In this case, the test provides one example and then asks the student to produce another. Students' understanding of any concept, from climate to culture, government to market, ecosystem to rain shadow, can be assessed in this simple way.

Even a complicated skill such as using the encyclopedia can be assessed, at least somewhat, using a paper-and-pencil format. Figure 10–6 suggests a test in which students find topics in one encyclopedia and then locate the same topics in another. A benefit of this particular test is that children find their way around not one but two encyclopedias. From the standpoint of concept formation, the teaching strategy discussed in Chapter 8, two examples are always better than one.

Paper-and-pencil tests lend themselves to both formative and summative assessment. Short matching and true-false quizzes can be written and scored quickly, and these can help students feel successful if they are made purposefully to be somewhat easy. A favorite way of ours to give these formative tests is to put children in teams of four. Hand the team *two* sheets of paper. One has the questions only; the other has the answers filled in. Of course, the material on the test has been taught to students over the previous one or two days. Ex-

FIGURE 10–5 Understanding concepts.

UNDERSTANDING CONCEPTS

One example is given for each of the terms listed. Your job is to write down *another* example.

1. Raw material   *Wood* is a raw material for making furniture; another raw
material is _____

used in making _____

2. Fuel   *Oil* is a fuel used for heating; another fuel is _____

used for _____

3. Grain   *Corn* is a grain used for feed; another example of a grain is _____

used for _____

4. Industry   *Dressmaking* is an industry; another example of industry is _____

that makes _____

5. Natural resource   *Water* is a natural resource necessary for life; another natural
resource is _____

used for _____

6. Manufactured product   A *rocket booster* is a manufactured product used for space exploration; another
example of a manufactured product is _____

used for _____

---

plain that the reason you have given students both the questions and the answers is that the team's job is to make sure that each person on the team understands *why* these are the answers. Inform them that they will have 20 minutes for this review. Appoint a timekeeper and chairperson for each team. Explain that this review will be followed by a quiz on the same material and that the teams who do well will earn a certificate. After the time has expired, administer the same test to each individual. Robert Slavin, who conducts research on cooperative learning, has shown that this assessment technique has many positive benefits, which we will examine in Chapter 11, Cooperative Learning. Not the least of these benefits is that children learn the material on the test.[12] This is good news, reflecting the primary purpose of assessment: to *improve* teaching and learning.

Of course, more challenging and authentic assessments are needed as well. Two kinds of paper-and-pencil test items are becoming increasingly popular. Both challenge students. Both require higher-order thinking. One uses multiple-choice items; the other requires short essay responses. Remember that multiple-choice tests require students to select the best response of those given. The major shortcoming of such tests is that too often they are not *authentic* tasks; that is, people rarely engage in multiple-choice tasks outside of school settings. But this shortcoming can be offset when the questions (1) deal with essential social

FIGURE 10–6 Using the encyclopedia.

Directions: Using the ten-volume *Our Own Encyclopedia* shown in this diagram, select the number of the volume in which you would find information about each of the items listed below. Write the number of the volume you select in the spaces on the left side of the sheet. Then list the volume number of *World Book* in which the same items are found in the spaces on the right side of the sheet.

Our Own		*World Book*
1. _____	1. Earthquakes in Japan	1. _____
2. _____	2. The Mexican leader Zapata	2. _____
3. _____	3. The history of rocketry	3. _____
4. _____	4. The People's Republic of China	4. _____
5. _____	5. The U.S. Constitution	5. _____
6. _____	6. Apple-growing in Washington State	6. _____
7. _____	7. The Pony Express	7. _____
8. _____	8. Countries that are members of the United Nations	8. _____
9. _____	9. Confucius	9. _____
10. _____	10. The history of computers	10. _____

studies learnings and (2) require higher-order thinking: analysis, interpretation, application, or manipulation of information. The multiple-choice test items shown in Figure 10–7 accomplish both. How?

Note that these are multiple-choice *with justification* items. Such items present students with more than one reasonably correct answer. The student's task is to choose the response that can best be supported with reasons based on knowledge. In other words, the child has to justify his or her selection. The emphasis, therefore, is on the reasoning children bring to

FIGURE 10–7 Multiple-choice with justification.

Example #1	Example #2
I. Which of these was a cause of the Declaration of Independence?	I. Which of these is an example of the idea *culture*?
a. The Intolerable Acts.	a. The life of the people living in a Lakota Sioux village.
b. The King sent troops to force the colonists to obey.	b. The rules of cooperation and interaction in our classroom.
c. Americans wanted to keep their wealth rather than sharing it with England.	c. The way kittens in a litter are raised by cats.
d. The way the English treated the colonists.	d. The animals and plants living together in a forest.
II. Give your reasons.	II. Give your reasons.

Source: See Steven L. McCollum, *Performance Assessment in the Social Studies Classroom: A How-To Book for Teachers* (Joplin, MO: Chalk Dust Press, 1994), 26, for additional examples.

the choices they make. "By justifying their answers, students must go beyond mere rote learning. The answers they give provide teachers with greater insight into the knowledge and thinking patterns of individual students."[13]

Turning now to short essay assessments, Figure 10–8 shows a short essay item used to assess fifth-grade students' understanding of historical events. There are several impressive features here. First, it deals with essential learning, events leading to the American Revolution. Second, it presents students with something for them to examine—a stimulus—in this case, a time line. Other possibilities are a map, photo or painting, or a *brief* quote from a primary document, such as the Declaration of Independence or an eyewitness account of the Boston Tea Party.[14] Third, the directions for student writing are given in one very clear sentence. Fourth, assistance or scaffolding is provided in the form of several "be sure to" prompts. These are intended to help students to reason with facts (in this case, explain the relationship between two events) rather than only to recall facts. Applying these four attributes, teachers can construct similar items for other historical events. Try this now with one of the following events: the Cherokee "Trail of Tears," Columbus's first voyage, the first women's rights convention at Seneca Falls.

PERFORMANCE ASSESSMENT

Figures 10–7 and 10–8 actually are performance assessments. Why? Performance assessments are assessments that help teachers find out how well students can *translate knowledge into action.* In the multiple-choice justification assessment (Figure 10–7), children are required to use the knowledge they have acquired to defend the choice they make. In the short essay assessment using the time line (Figure 10–8), students are required to use their knowledge of cause and effect to explain the relationship between two events on the time line.

The construction of time lines can be used to assess students' knowledge of symbols and chronology and their ability to display graphically the amount of time between events.

Both are *authentic* tasks, too. Using one's knowledge to defend a position or explain a choice one has made is a valuable and necessary life skill; being able to determine what caused what, and how, is another.

Performance Criteria

If students are to aim high in their responses, performance criteria are needed. *These performance criteria serve also as instructional objectives,* and this is why performance assessment truly "blurs the boundary" between instruction and assessment. The criteria are the behaviors we want students to learn. On a scoring *guide* (also called a scoring *rubric* or rating scale), these criteria are identified and sequenced from high to low proficiency.

As we said in the discussion of the third principle of good assessment, these criteria can be arranged on a three-level rating scale with descriptors such as *proficient, adequate,* and *minimal.* Doing so helps students to aim high, toward "proficiency," and to want to know just what a proficient performance will look like. Look again at the short historical essay item (Figure 10–8). A rating scale needs to be created that spells out for students and teachers the criteria that will help them distinguish between a proficient short essay and one that is merely adequate or only minimally competent. Suggested criteria were given earlier in the chapter in the explanation of Principle 3. That was a three-point scale, and while it certainly will be more helpful to students and teachers than a simple "yes/no" checklist, a five- or six-point scale can make for a still more powerful instructional tool and scoring guide.

A six-point scoring guide for teaching and assessing short-essay historical writing is found in Table 10–1. California teachers have field-tested this rubric with fourth- and fifth-grade students. Its advantage over the three-point scale is that is has greater explanatory power: More distinctions are made and, thus, the quality of students' performances can be refined. Just as pianists at a recital or divers at a tournament are not judged merely "good," "fair," and "poor," historical reasoning—even in the elementary grades—can be advanced beyond the three-point scale. Of course, the six-point scale is more difficult than the three-

FIGURE 10–8 Short essay item.

EVENTS LEADING TO THE AMERICAN REVOLUTION

(Suggested time: 30 minutes)

In history, important things happen that cause other things to happen. This is very plain when we talk about the events leading to the American Revolution.

Study the timeline below.

1773	1774	1775	1776
Boston Tea Party	Intolerable Acts	Battles of Lexington and Concord	Declaration of Independence

Circle two events on the timeline and write a short essay about them, using your knowledge of history.

Be sure to:

• Describe each event.
• Explain how the two events are related to each other.
• Explain how the events are related to the American Revolution.

Source: California Department of Education, *A Sampler of History—Social Science Assessment, Elementary* (Sacramento: California Learning Assessment System, Department of Education, January 1994), 35. Used by permission.

point scale—difficult both to comprehend and to use. Teachers can start students out on the simpler scale and graduate them, as they become able, to the more complex one. (Different scales can be used with students of different ability.) A good illustration of this difference can be found in Table 3–1 and Figure 3–3 in Chapter 3. In that chapter the point was made that discussion competence is one of the most important of all citizenship behaviors. Two rating scales were presented for assessing students' discussion abilities: one that might be more appropriate for children in the primary grades, the other for students in the fourth grade and higher (or students with greater discussion ability in the primary grades). The latter was field-tested in the Oakland County, Michigan, schools with sixth-grade students.

How to Create a Scoring Guide

Remember, the three-point scoring guide is a terrific place to begin. It is easy to develop because children's work so easily falls into three categories: the good, the bad, and the in-between. Creating a scoring guide, whether three-point or more, is a fairly direct procedure with five steps.

Step 1. Objectives/curriculum standards. Determine what students are to learn. Refer to state and school district curriculum guidelines, the curriculum standards published by professional organizations (e.g., the NCSS curriculum standards; the History, Geography, and Civics standards), and to Chapters 3 through 7 in this book. Be sure to think in terms of processes (intellectual and social skills) as well as knowledge (concepts and information). Also consider democratic values and attitudes. Here, for example, is an illustrative list of social studies objectives: By the end of the fifth grade, children should:

- Know the history, government, and geography of their home town/state.
- Know why the American colonists declared independence from England.
- Know the parts and principles of the U.S. Constitution.
- Understand how and why so many different ethnic groups have come to the United States.
- Be able to distinguish between goods and services, production and distribution.
- Be able to compare and contrast the geographic regions of the United States.
- Be able to develop different kinds of maps to represent the same physical space.
- Be able to participate competently in discussions of classroom problems.

Step 2. Performances. Determine how children might exhibit or demonstrate what they have learned. That is, what *evidence* could they give to show that they have learned and how could they show (exhibit; perform) it for all to see? Brainstorm performances with colleagues and ask your students for their ideas. Pianists usually have recitals, artists exhibit their work in galleries, athletes perform in tournaments. What about your students? Above, we discussed two kinds of performances, both using paper-and-pencil formats. Below we will suggest others that do not rely on writing.

Step 3. Criteria/performance standards. Create a relevant scoring rubric. It should provide students, teachers, and parents with indicators, or actual descriptions, of the behaviors at different levels of mastery.

TABLE 10–1 Short essay scoring guide for elementary–middle school historical writing.

Development of Historical Ideas	Historical Accuracy	Organization and Communication
A "6" short essay Always stays on the historical topic. Uses many important historical facts and reasons to support ideas, and makes detailed conclusions. Shows understanding of the historical time period by • comparing and contrasting ideas, events, and people, or • showing cause and effect between events, or how past and present connect.	**A "6" short essay** Has no historical mistakes.	**A "6" short essay** Is very well organized. Has very clear beginning, middle, and end. Makes excellent sense. Responds to all parts of prompt.
A "5" short essay Same as a "6," but doesn't use as many important historical facts and reasons to support ideas.	**A "5" short essay** Has minor historical mistakes.	**A "5" short essay** Is well organized. Has clear beginning, middle, and end. Makes good sense. Responds to all parts of prompt.
A "4" short essay Mostly stays on the historical topic. Uses some important historical facts and reasons to support ideas, and makes conclusions. Shows some understanding of the historical time period and tries to: • compare and contrast ideas, events, or people, or • show cause and effect between events, or how past and present connect.	**A "4" short essay** May have a big historical mistake, but most information is correct.	**A "4" short essay** Is organized. Has beginning, middle, and end. Makes sense. Sometimes responds very well to part of prompt, and not very well to other part of the prompt.
A "3" short essay Sometimes stays on the historical topic. Shows some knowledge of the historical time period with a few facts and reasons. Makes a few connections between events or people. Describes an event but doesn't analyze it.	**A "3" short essay** Has some correct and some incorrect information about history.	**A "3" short essay** Does not have beginning, middle, and end. May respond only to parts of prompt. Makes some sense, but sometimes writing and grammar make it hard to read and understand.
A "2" short essay Often goes off the historical topic and describes events or people that are not correct for the prompt. Lists historical facts with little description.	**A "2" short essay** Has serious historical mistakes.	**A "2" short essay** Has very little organization. Doesn't make much sense, and often writing and grammar make it very hard to read and understand.
A "1" short essay Mentions historical topic with very few facts. Describes mostly events or people that are not correct for the prompt.	**A "1" short essay** Has very little knowledge of history and may have many serious mistakes.	**A "1" short essay** Doesn't make any sense.

Source: California Department of Education, *A Sampler of History-Social Science Assessment, Elementary* (Sacramento: California Learning Assessment System, Department of Education, January 1994), p. 31.

Step 4. Share. After creating the rubric, discuss it with students. Listen carefully to the questions they raise about these performance criteria and watch for confusion. Typically, teachers will learn enough from this experience to revise the rubric somewhat before trying it. Naturally students will not understand these criteria very well, for they have not yet received instruction on them. The point is to provide students a reasonably clear idea of the target, so they will be able to marshal their efforts accordingly.

Step 5. Revise the rubric. Explain the performance criteria and provide the instruction that should help children develop proficiency. Use what you learn to revise the rubric before using it again.

Checklists

Scoring guides come in all sizes and shapes. The simplest are *checklists* that specify how often a desired behavior (the learning target or objective) occurs. A four-point scale might read: "Always," "Usually," "Rarely," "Never." Figures 10–9 and 10–10 present two checklists. The first lists the behaviors called *consideration for others* that were given above under the informal technique "observation." Using a checklist, teachers can assess each student periodically and record the observations directly on the checklist. This is much preferred to relying on memory. At conference time, checklists can be shared with parents.

Children also can be taught to assess their *own* behavior using the same four-point scale. Figure 10–10 shows a self-assessment checklist that can be used during the unit (formatively) as well as at the end (summatively). Both formative and summative assessments can be gathered into students' portfolios.

PORTFOLIOS

The practice of saving samples of children's work in a portfolio has become increasingly popular in recent years.[15] In some schools, it has become the primary means of assessing children's progress both through a single school year and across several years. This practice is similar to that of the parent who cuts notches on the inside of a closet door recording the height of a child at various ages. Both the parent and the teacher know that changes are occurring, but, because of their continuous, day-to-day contact with the child, changes are sometimes imperceptible. They need, therefore, a specific sample of the child's status at one point to compare with his or her status at a subsequent time.

Work samples saved for this purpose are usually written material and may include a biography, a story, a classroom test, an explanation, a booklet, and a conclusion drawn after a research project. The teacher will also want to save a child's map work, artwork done in connection with the social studies, and photos of a construction project such as the "museum exhibit" the children created for parents' night. A tape recorder can be used to obtain a sample of the child's public speaking. For example, children find it profitable to hear reports privately that they have made to the class at various times during the school year. The entire class can use the recorder to evaluate their progress in discussions, dramatizations, and similar public-speaking situations. Care must be taken that the work samples saved are closely related to essential learnings and desired social studies outcomes. There is no need to clutter the portfolio with relatively unimportant work when so many learning outcomes are critically important and in need of continuous assessment.

FIGURE 10–9 Checklist: Consideration for others.

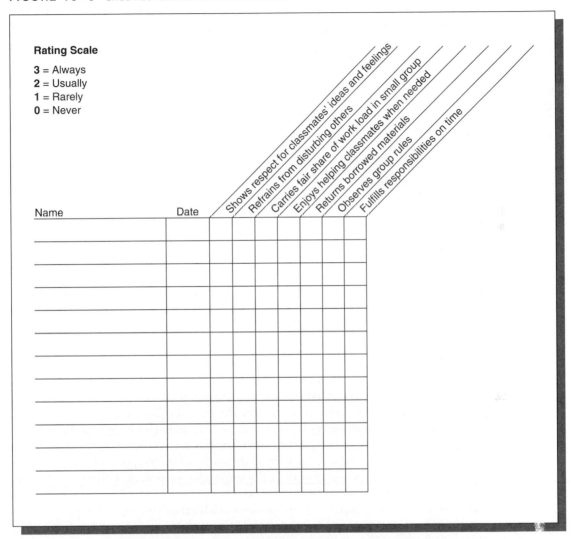

The portfolio of the child's work can be useful during parent conferences at the regular reporting periods during the school year. Additionally, some teachers send samples of the child's work home from time to time simply to keep the parents informed of the child's progress in school. To make sure the parent has received the material, teachers may want to use a message sheet that asks the parent to comment, sign, and return.

We conclude the chapter with two sample portfolios. Figure 10–11 shows the contents of a collection of maps the children have made. The collection is tailored to the fourth-grade mapping objective that Mrs. Rivera was working with in our chapter-opening vignette. Mrs.

FIGURE 10–10   Checklist: Student self-assessment.

SELF-ASSESSMENT CHECKLIST

DATE _____   NAME _____

In this unit I was able to:	Always	Usually	Rarely	Never
Choose appropriate activities				
Use my work time efficiently				
Work cooperatively with another person				
Use materials from the Resource Center				
Keep my work area clean				
Use suggestions that others gave me				

Comments:

Rivera's students, after much instruction and practice, eventually became proficient at creating three different kinds of maps, and six different places were mapped, ranging from the playground to the North American continent. The second collection (Figure 10–12) contains children's written responses to social studies literature. This collection displays students' ability to integrate literacy skills and social studies subject matter. Note the categories of responsive writing (paraphrasing, composing a new verse, interpreting) and the variety of social studies literature—from trade books and textbooks to songs. Other portfolios can capture students' sustained work over time on other important social studies objectives. A teacher who takes seriously the objective to teach children to *do* history rather than only *absorb* the history written or told by others (see Chapter 4's Figure 4–2) can begin this portfolio with the "snapshot autobiographies" her students composed at the beginning of the school year. Next might come their "oral histories" based on interviews with old-timers in the community and then the "oral histories" conducted with students who had moved from one neighborhood, state, or nation to another. Next might come their first brief biography written about a U.S. president, followed by a more extensive "cooperative biography" written with a team of classmates. In this way, a body of work is collected that displays, first, that historical reasoning is being attempted (itself an ambitious endeavor) and, second, that progress is being made.

Finally, we provide an assessment glossary (Figure 10–13) that should assist readers as they try to make sense of the specialized vocabulary that is used to describe assessment procedures in social studies.

FIGURE 10–11   A map portfolio.

Contents of my Map Portfolio		Name _____
Type of Map	**Place**	**Date/My Comments**
landform	our community	_____/_____
landform	North America	_____/_____
political	United States	_____/_____
political	counties in our state	_____/_____
shaded relief	playground	_____/_____
shaded relief	state	_____/_____

Conclusion

Assessment means, simply, to find out what students know and can do. It goes on continually in the classroom and is a natural part of the learning environment. Sometimes it is used
to place children in this or that group (in the "gifted" class or a "special education" program,

FIGURE 10–12 A response to literature portfolio.

**Contents of my Social Studies
Literature Response Portfolio**

Name _____

Response Type	Selection (genre)	Date/My Comments
paraphrase	Paul Revere's Ride (poem)	_____/_____
compose new verse	"Oh Freedom" (song)	_____/_____
memorize	"I Have a Dream" (speech)	_____/_____
book review	*Aekyung's Dream* (book)	_____/_____
explain	The Pledge of Allegiance (oath)	_____/_____
short story	climate of Sahara (textbook)	_____/_____

in this or that reading group, in this or that college). And sometimes it is used to compare schools, school districts, states, and nations. But the overwhelming purpose *for classroom teachers and students* is to improve teaching and learning.

Like all of teaching, assessment is a principled activity: one has to know what one is doing and for what purposes. Then, the various methods can be implemented judiciously. Mrs. Rivera used a paper-and-pencil test and informal questioning, conducted a group interview,

FIGURE 10–13 Assessment glossary.

Assessment
The process of gathering and interpreting information about students in order to plan instruction and evaluate achievement.

Authentic Assessment
Assessing students' ability to succeed in meaningful (goal-directed, "real-world") tasks. For example, observing students' participation in a discussion of a classroom problem or their use of reference books while drawing maps.

Criteria
The aspects of a performance task that are most important to its successful completion and are used by judges to evaluate the quality of the performance.

Curriculum (or Content) Standards
Statements that describe what students are supposed to learn; they specify the knowledge, skills, and values that students should learn.

Evaluation
The process of making judgments about the quality of a performance.

Grade
A symbol (usually a letter, word, or number) that represents a student's level of achievement of one or more curriculum standards.

Formative Assessment
Assessment conducted during a unit of instruction for the purpose of improving student learning; providing feedback to students to help them improve their performance (see *Summative Assessment*).

Objective
A statement that describes what students are expected to learn; in performance assessment, the behaviors they will learn to perform (see *Criteria*).

and watched while students sketched a map of the United States—all this to find out what they already knew about maps and map reading. This is often called *diagnosis,* and its purpose is to help the teacher plan instruction: what *this* group of children needs *now.* There are other purposes and other methods, not the least of which is performance assessment and the development of scoring guides. The popularity of performance criteria and scoring guides in the past 10 years has helped countless teachers and students clarify the targets of learning— helping everyone know exactly what target they are aiming at. Portfolios in social studies have been of tremendous help, too. They can be used to encourage students to develop a body of map work, a body of literature, a body of historical interpretation, a body of persuasive writing to legislators and newspaper editors, and so forth, making these efforts not mere hit-or-miss occasions but *sustained, continuous work* at objectives worth achieving.

FIGURE 10–13 *continued.*

Performance Assessment
Assessing students' ability to translate knowledge into action—that is, to *demonstrate* their knowledge and skills.

Performance Standards
Levels of attainment that students must reach to receive particular grades, awards, or certificates. They are based on criteria and define what degree of mastery is "good enough."

Portfolio
A collection of a student's school work that can be used to document achievement over time.

Reliability
The extent to which an assessment procedure will produce the same information about a student each time it is used.

Scoring Rubric
A rating scale that describes levels of attainment in relation to an assessment task. Used to score performances and to focus curriculum and instruction.

Summative Assessment
Assessment conducted at the end of a unit of instruction for the purpose of determining a grade (see *Formative Assessment*).

Task
An *authentic* assessment activity within which a student is asked to demonstrate his/her knowledge and skills.

Validity
The extent to which an assessment procedure measures what it claims to measure and is appropriate for making decisions.

Fortunately, teachers teach for more than one school year! This means that the assessments they develop in one year can be revised and used again the following year. In this way, teachers, too, develop a "body of work" consisting of well-honed assessments, scoring guides, teaching strategies, and resources. This teacher portfolio represents the development of expertise over time.

Discussion Questions and Suggested Activities

1. Determine whether your state has developed a social studies assessment and the grade levels at which it is administered. Find out whether and when individual school districts participate in this assessment and for which of the purposes discussed in this chapter. Also determine whether the school district in which you live or work has developed a social studies assessment.

2. List each of the assessment samples provided in this chapter. Then discuss how each could be used formatively or summatively.

3. Item construction: (a) Construct two multiple-choice-with-justification items similar to the ones given in Figure 10–7. Focus the first item on an important *event* in American history; focus the second on an important *concept*. (b) Then, construct a short-essay item with the same four attributes as you see in the item in Figure 10–8.

4. Plan collections of student work (portfolios) similar to those shown in Figures 10–11 and 10–12. Focus one on an important curriculum objective (e.g., valuing diversity or knowing how to use reference books and computer software). Develop another for an entire grade level, for example, "My Second-Grade Portfolio." Try to integrate literacy and social studies; that is, help children display their reading and writing *through* social studies subject matter, and vice versa.

5. Do you think it is fair to evaluate teacher effectiveness on the basis of student achievement? What is the relationship between the two?

Selected References

Airasian, Peter W. (1996). *Classroom assessment.* 3rd ed. New York: McGraw-Hill.

Baron, Joan Boykoff. (1990). Performance assessment: Blurring the edges among assessment, curriculum, and instruction. In Audrey B. Champagne, Barbara E. Lovitts, & Betty J. Calinger (Eds.), *Assessment in the service of instruction* (pp. 127–148). Washington, DC: American Association for the Advancement of Science.

California Department of Education. (1994, Jan.). *A sampler of history-social science assessment, elementary.* Sacramento: California Learning Assessment System, Department of Education.

Gardner, Howard. (1993). *Multiple intelligences: The theory in practice.* New York: Basic Books.

Nickell, Pat. (1997). Performance assessment in principle and practice. In Mary E. Haas & Margaret A. Laughlin (Eds.), *Meeting the standards: Social studies readings for K-6 educators* (pp. 378–381). Washington, DC: National Council for the Social Studies.

Social Education. (1999, October). Guest editor Pat Nickell created a wonderful issue called "Authentic Assessment in Social Studies."

Valencia, Sheila. (1998). *Literacy portfolios in action.* Fort Worth: Harcourt Brace.

Wiggins, Grant, & McTighe, Jay. (1998). *Understanding by design.* Alexandria, VA: Association for Supervision and Curriculum Development.

Notes

1. Howard Gardner, *Multiple intelligences: The theory in practice* (New York: Basic Books, 1993), 174–175.

2. National assessments are developed and administered by the National Assessment of Educational Progress (NAEP). Information can be obtained by writing to the National Assessment Governing Board, 800 N. Capitol St. NW, Washington, DC 20002 (or, online at *http://nces.ed.gov/nationsreportcard/site/home.asp*).

3. Joan Boykoff Baron, Performance assessment: Blurring the edges among assessment, curriculum, and instruction, in *Assessment in the service of instruction,* ed. Audrey B. Champagne, Barbara E. Lovitts, & Betty J. Calinger (Washington, DC: American Association for the Advancement of Science, 1990), 127–48.

4. Grant Wiggins, *Assessing student performance: Exploring the purpose and limits of testing* (San Francisco: Jossey-Bass, 1993).

5. National Council for the Social Studies, A vision of powerful teaching and learning in the social studies: Building social understanding and civic efficacy. In *Curriculum standards for social studies* (Washington, DC: Author, 1994), 167.

6. *National standards for history for grades K–4: Expanding children's world in time and space* (Los Angeles: National Center for History in the Schools, 1994), 52.

7. Adapted from California Department of Education, *A sampler of history-social science assessment, elementary* (Sacramento: California Learning Assessment System, Department of Education, January 1994), 30.

8. Ibid.

9. Vivian Paley, *Wally's stories* (Cambridge, MA: Harvard University Press, 1981).

10. Sam Allis, Quick! Name Togo's Capital, *Time* (July 16, 1990): 53.

11. Grant Wiggins & Jay McTighe, *Understanding by design* (Alexandria, VA: Association for Supervision and Curriculum Development, 1998), 7.

12. Robert E. Slavin, *Student team learning: An overview and practical guide* (Washington, DC: National Education Association, 1986).

13. Steven L. McCollum, *Performance assessment in the social studies classroom: A how-to book for teachers* (Joplin, MO: Chalk Dust Press, 1994), 24.

14. Kristin Palmquist, Involving teachers in elementary history and social science test development: The California experiment, *Social Education, 56,* (February 1992): 99–101.

15. Dennie Palmer Wolf, Portfolio assessment: Sampling student work, *Educational Leadership, 46,* (April 1989): 4–10; Valencia, Sheila, A portfolio approach to classroom reading assessment: The whys, whats, and hows, *The Reading Teacher, 44,* (January 1990): 338–340.

Website

http://www.nces.ed.gov/nationsreportcard/site/home.asp

11

Cooperative Learning in Social Studies

Main Idea

Cooperative groupwork is more than placing students in groups and giving them a task. Teachers who orchestrate groupwork effectively create a positive class-room climate, and they work up to groupwork gradually. They use different small-group frameworks for different purposes. Most important, they teach groupwork skills directly rather than only wishing students had already formed them.

Key Concepts

cooperative learning, positive interdependence, individual accountability, hidden curriculum, Jigsaw, Structured Academic Controversy

Chapter Outline

- Creating a Positive Climate for Human Relations
- Getting Started with Cooperative Groups
- Managing Cooperative Groupwork
- Identifying and Teaching Groupwork Skills
- Teaching and Using Discussion Techniques
- Conclusion
- Discussion Questions and Suggested Activities
- Selected References
- Notes

Chapter Snapshot

Mr. Kira expects the children to get lots of work done in their small groups. The task, therefore, is always challenging and definitely requires "more heads than one." "The task has to *require* a group," he always says. "That's the key. And it has to be difficult enough." He makes it a point to become so familiar with each student's talents that, by November, he can purposefully mix them in small groups. A student who likes to draw is placed in each group as well as someone who can help the others search through databases or other reference materials. He also tries to place a strong mediator in each group—someone with good interpersonal skills.

 A favorite website http://www.giraffe.org/tall.html The Giraffe program for kids teaches character by example, featuring everyday heroes who stick their necks out for the benefit of others.

The process of group interaction is "enormously interesting" to children, observes Elizabeth Cohen. Professor Cohen has learned a great deal about groupwork. She is an acclaimed sociologist and teacher, and her research projects in schools have centered on managing groupwork in diverse classrooms. There's something about group interaction, she observes, that is almost magical. Yet it is not magic; children can learn procedures that enable them to learn *and* to cooperate successfully. They act as a team, caring for one another while accomplishing an engaging task. [handwritten: Work together] [handwritten: Coop. learning.]

> Students who usually do anything but what they are asked to do become actively involved with their work and are held there by the action of the group.[1]

What causes this dynamic? First, face-to-face interaction helps children pay attention, because it requires a response and other forms of interaction. Second, children care deeply about the judgments of their peers, and this only increases as children move into adolescence. Third, children get assistance from one another in their groups; the teacher, therefore, is not the only "coach" in the classroom. The importance of this last point cannot be overestimated: students who do not understand the task at hand become quickly disengaged from it, and disengagement from school work is precisely what teachers and parents want very much to avoid. And for good reason: It can be the proverbial straw that breaks the camel's back for a child who is a member of a language or ethnic minority or for any other child who is at risk of school failure.

Groupwork is important for other reasons, as we shall see in this chapter. Democratic citizenship is certainly one of them. As we saw in Chapter 3, societies that are organized under democratic ideals place special demands on their school systems. Children in these societies need to be educated to be the kind of citizens who can and will share in popular sovereignty. It is not easy work, and it does not appear to come to us naturally. Indeed, our "primary nature" is egocentric.[2] For this reason, all of us to some degree are tempted to let others look after the common good while we tend to our private affairs—to our friends, families, jobs, hobbies, religions, shopping, entertainment, and so on. But the democratic ideal requires people to extend their caring beyond private life to public life—to share in decision making, join in efforts to reduce crime and poverty, fight injustice and work for peace, help prevent delinquency and substance abuse, create public parks and museums, reduce and repair damage to the natural environment, improve public health, and so on. The list is long. Everyone's help is needed. This is the democratic vision.

Most basically, the work of democracy requires citizens who can work well together in task-oriented groups. These may be study groups, decision-making groups, or both. These are different from play groups, where there is no task *per se,* and they are different from other group settings, such as a baseball game or a service at a church or temple, where people may be physically near one another and may even share materials. Task-oriented groups have work to do, often problem solving, *and their members are mutually dependent on one another for planning the work and getting it done successfully.*

Can a classroom be such a group? It can and it should. Classroom life is a social apprenticeship, and the character of that apprenticeship most likely will be carried with the children into later years, especially the work habits that are formed there, the skills and norms of interaction that are fostered, and the attitude toward learning and cooperating that takes shape there. Put differently, children learn by doing, and the kind of doing shapes the kind of learning that will take place. Teachers play the central role in determining the kind of apprenticeship it will be, and they can do much to help fashion it into an apprenticeship for cooperation and democracy.

Consider two additional reasons people need to learn to work well together. First, the business community in the United States increasingly is demanding employees who can function on teams—together identifying problems worth solving, setting priorities for them, planning, integrating diverse ideas, dividing the work load, and building on one another's contributions. Second, the population of North America is becoming rapidly more diverse racially, ethnically, and linguistically. All of this requires students to overcome initial prejudices rapidly, to learn to appreciate people who are culturally different, and to build healthy, working relationships.

Creating a Positive Climate for Human Relations

An emotionally supportive atmosphere is one characterized by trust and by evidence that individuals care about each other. When a child volunteers, "Robin's group had more to do than the rest of us. They should have more time to finish," the observer senses that he or she is in a caring environment. Or when a minor classroom accident results in damage to material or broken equipment and the teacher treats the incident as an accident, one concludes that the teacher values human beings more than things. Teachers who develop comfortable classroom environments are concerned with a broad range of educational outcomes, including those that relate to the emotional and social development of children, in addition to attending to subject matter and skills goals. The classroom conditions that establish the *setting* in which children learn the basics of human relations is sometimes referred to as the *hidden curriculum*.

A CARING ENVIRONMENT

The most significant characteristic of a desirable classroom climate is the absence of hostility between children and the teacher and among the children themselves. Put positively, a desirable classroom atmosphere is one in which caring, kindness, encouragement, and support are fully present. This means many things, of course, but it includes modeling for children what it looks and sounds like to care for others, children and adults and pets alike. It means helping children to see the origin of classroom rules in caring. As well, it means "attributing the best motive" to children—assuming that a child's intentions were good even when she or he has done something bad. Making this assumption is a basic act of kindness on the teacher's part, and generally it should be communicated to the child directly. For example, the teacher might take aside a student who has cheated, beginning not with a reprimand or punishment, though these may well come, but with caring, saying, "I know you want to do well." Likewise, a student who has called another student a cruel name can be taken aside, and the conversation can begin with, "I know you mean to treat others as you want to be treated yourself."[3]

To clarify these ideas further, consider the eight sets of contrasting teacher behaviors in Figure 11–1.

FIGURE 11–1 Dimensions of the hidden curriculum.

Practices and Procedures That Tend to Increase Hostility in a Classroom

1. *Excessively competitive situations* Fair competition in classrooms is highly desirable. It can stimulate good work, motivate children to do their best, and help children learn the graces associated with winning and losing. It becomes undesirable when it is of the "dog-eat-dog" variety where each child is pitted against every other child whether the competitive situation is fair or unfair.

2. *Negative statements by the teacher* Ridicule, sarcasm, criticism, and negative and tension-producing statements made by a teacher to children invariably lead to hostility, emotional disturbance, selfishness, fear, and criticism of others. Examples:

"I wish you would start acting like fourth-graders instead of kindergartners."

"Someone is whispering again, and I guess you all know who it is."

"Most fifth-grade classes could understand this, but I am not sure about you."

"Why don't you listen when I give directions? None of you seems to know how to listen."

3. *Disregard for individual differences* Classrooms where some children are made to feel "this place is not for me" contribute much toward breeding hostility in children. Such rooms are characterized by one level of acceptable performance applied to all, uniform assignments, one system of reward, and great emphasis on verbal, intellectual performance.

4. *Rigid schedule and pressure* A rigid time schedule and constant pressure associated with "hurry up," "finish your work," "you will be late," or stopping lessons exactly on time whether completed or not can create insecurity in children that leads to hostility. A class that is always "one jump behind the teacher" is likely to be one in which children blame others for their failure to finish, invent excuses for themselves, and seek scapegoats.

Practices and Procedures That Tend to Decrease Hostility in a Classroom

1. *Positive interdependence* The teacher often structures learning activities so that "students perceive that they can reach their learning goals if and only if the other students in the learning group also reach their goals"*. This is the most basic element of cooperative learning, and it helps children learn to care about and support one another's progress.

2. *Positive statements by the teacher* Friendly, constructive statements by the teacher tend to reduce tension and hostility in the classroom. Examples:

"We will all want to listen carefully in order not to miss anything Sue is going to tell us."

"All of us did our work so well yesterday during our work period. Do you suppose we can do as well today?"

"It is really fun for all of us when you bring such interesting things for sharing."

"It's nice to have Jason and Kendra back with us again. The boys and girls were hoping you would come back today."

3. *Recognition of and response to individual differences* In such classrooms, all children are challenged at a level commensurate with their abilities and in ways that are mindful of cultural and linguistic differences. The teacher strives to see *all* children's gifts and talents.

4. *Relaxed, comfortable pace* Good teachers working with young children maintain a flexible schedule and will not place undue pressures on children. They will have a plan and a schedule, yet will not be compulsive in adhering to it. They will deviate from their plan now and then in the interests of the needs of the boys and girls they teach.

---

* David W. Johnson, Roger T. Johnson, Edythe J. Holubec, and Patricia Roy, *Circles of Learning: Cooperation in the Classroom*, (Alexandria, VA: Association for Supervisions and Curriculum Development, 1984), 2.

Practices and Procedures That Tend to Increase Hostility in a Classroom

5. *Highly directive teaching practices* Teachers who must make every decision themselves, give all the assignments, and allow for very little participation on the part of children in the life of the classroom may encourage feelings of hostility. Such practices usually mean that teachers refer to the class as "my children," or in addressing them, say, "I want you to . . . ," or more subtly, "Miss So-and-so wasn't very proud of her class this morning."

6. *Lack of closeness between teacher and children* Some teachers feel they must "keep children in their places," meaning they must remain socially distant from them. This leads to a cold relationship between the children and the teacher, causing the children to feel that the teacher lacks affection and warmth for them.

7. *Lack of satisfying emotional experiences* Some classrooms do not provide opportunities to express positive affect. Everything is deadly serious business—work, work, work. Even the music, art, story time, or dramatic activities are made to seem like work. Little time is spent on teaching children to enjoy one another, feel the inner joy that comes from a good poem or music selection, or express their feelings in some art medium.

8. *Rules are about obeying*   Some teachers have elaborate systems for dealing with violations of classroom rules, but fail to capitalize on them to teach children about caring. Obedience becomes the sole aim, rather than understanding the purpose of the rule.

Practices and Procedures That Tend to Decrease Hostility in a Classroom

5. *Student involvement in planning and managing the class*   Giving children some opportunity to plan and manage the affairs of the classroom does much to develop feelings of "we-ness" of a democratic community. Children under such circumstances are less inclined to want to think of ways to disrupt the teacher's orderly room but will work hard to make "our" room a good place to work.

6. *Warm and friendly relationship between teacher and children*   One of the basic needs of children is that of love and affection. They need it in their homes, in their playgroups, and in their schools. The feeling that children will not respect the teacher who is friendly with them is incorrect. They are likely to respect the teacher more who they feel is a "human being" capable of warm personal relationships with others. This is a professional relationship, however, and teachers are advised *against* trying to develop a peer relationship with the children they teach.

7. *Many opportunities for pleasurable emotional experiences*   Teachers can reduce tensions that build up in children during the course of classroom life by providing opportunities for the release of these tensions through various emotional experiences. Children have the opportunity to express their feelings orally, in writing, or through art forms. They talk together and enjoy one another's company. They prepare skits, do creative dramatics, and role play situations to help get the feelings of others. All these activities tend to reduce feelings of hostility.

8. *Rules are about caring*   Teachers can use rule violations to help children appreciate that we have rules because we care for one another. We do not call other children names because it hurts their feelings; we don't write on desks and tables out of respect for others who use them; we tell the truth because others deserve sincerity, not lies; we try to be punctual because we care for those who are waiting.

Getting Started with Cooperative Groups

Committee work or small-group enterprises are effective instructional procedures in the social studies and have many values for children. In the small group children get experience with and develop skills in group processes. These experiences should begin in a limited way even as early as the kindergarten. In block play, for example, the teacher can let some children choose the things they wish to build with blocks. Some will want to build an airport; some, a house; others, a post office; others, a supermarket; and so on. The teacher can let each child choose two other children to help build the project. The children proceed with the building and, when it is completed, tell the class or their teacher a story about their building. Early experiences in such block play will consist mainly of parallel play—three children may be building an airport but each is working independently of the other two. As the year progresses, there will be more evidence of cooperative endeavor. Children become more conscious of what others in their group are doing and will plan their own contribution in terms of the other children and the group goal.

A good way to familiarize primary-grade children with small-group work is to have committees responsible for various housekeeping duties in the classroom. José's committee has the responsibility of keeping the library table neat, Paul's committee is in charge of the game shelf, Long's committee is responsible for the care of the aquarium, and Denisha's committee keeps the coat corner orderly. Membership on these committees can be changed from time to time to include all the children in the class. Such experiences will help prepare children for the committee work that is done as a part of the instructional program.

Small-group enterprises in the primary grades need careful supervision and direction. The goals or purposes of the group should be well defined, concrete, and easily understood. Materials needed for the group to do its work must be immediately at hand. Rules and responsibilities of working on committees should be discussed, explained, and posted conspicuously in the room. Groupwork skills develop slowly and gradually and require practice, as do any other skills. The skills of groupwork can be learned only by working in groups.

In the intermediate grades (4–6), small-group work becomes an increasingly greater part of the social studies instructional program. At these grade levels, each group member can be given an assigned task to help the group achieve its goal. Small groups are used to prepare reports; discuss issues; plan activities; do construction, art, or dramatic activities; write plays, biographies, and short stories, gather resources for the class; interview community resource persons; and so on. Through instruction and experience, children will learn that the success of the group depends on the initiative and cooperation of individuals within the group.

The class will be divided into small work groups on many occasions. These groups are task oriented; they are formed to do things that really need doing. In this way, groupwork can avoid artificiality. Groups are not formed merely to have children practice cooperative groupwork; *they are formed to get some sort of work done.* Groupwork therefore can be relatively short lived. A committee may be assigned to find out how bridges are built or to create a map of a nearby river system. When the committee has completed its task and reported to the larger group, it can be dissolved.

When attempting for the first time to organize small-group work, the teacher may find the guidelines in the box, "Forming Academic Committees," helpful. Note that it is not necessary to place all students in small groups at the same time, at least not when the teacher is just learning to manage small-group instruction. Instead, we recommend a gradual, diagnostic approach. This permits the teacher and students to "get their feet wet" little by little, all the while observing group dynamics and strengths and weaknesses in the children's cooperative behaviors.

How might these guidelines look in action? In the following example, a teacher appoints a committee to help introduce and question a classroom guest.

> The children in Mr. Shigaki's fourth-grade class have been involved in a career awareness study and are going to have resource persons visit their classroom. The children have indicated careers they would like to have included. Mr. Shigaki has asked four children to meet him in the rear of the classroom and is now speaking to them.
>
> "Because the four of you are particularly interested in learning about computer science careers, I am asking that you take responsibility for introducing Ms. Timms tomorrow. You will have to select one person to do the introducing. The others can help by suggesting things that should be said about her in the introduction. Also, all of you should help develop some questions to ask her after her presentation. Remember one of our objectives is to find out what kind of training and skills computer scientists need and what opportunities there are in that field. Is there anything else you think you will need to prepare to be the host group tomorrow?"
>
> One member of the group asks if they were to thank the visitor for coming.
>
> "Yes. Good point! I'm glad you thought of that, Mark. You will need to select someone to thank Ms. Timms. Anything else?" (No further suggestions are offered.)
>
> "I guess you are ready to begin your work then," says Mr. Shigaki. "Lisa, would you act as the group leader and report to me when your group is finished planning?"
>
> Mr. Shigaki then leaves the group to its task and supervises the remainder of the class who have been working on individual assignments.

Managing Cooperative Groupwork

Let us turn from forming the occasional committee that accomplishes one or more tasks to simultaneous involvement of all children in small-group instruction. First, we consider goals, then group size, group composition, and alternative small-group structures.

GOALS

It would be reasonable to assume that if children are given instruction and have several guided experiences in cooperative groups, they are likely to develop group interaction skills and the disposition to be cooperative. But do cooperative learning strategies also affect a child's overall academic achievement? The answer is a confident "Yes!" "Results indicate that cooperative learning experiences tend to promote higher achievement than do competitive and individualistic learning experiences."[5] These results apply to all age

FORMING ACADEMIC COMMITTEES

1. Defer small-group work until the management of the class has been well established and until the work habits, interpersonal skills, and special needs of individual children are known.

2. Select children who already have good interpersonal skills for your first academic committee. Keep the group small—never more than five children.

3. Assign the committee an academic task that is simple and well defined, one that the group is certain to accomplish successfully.

4. Have the remainder of the class engage in individual assignments while the teacher is giving guidance and direction to the smaller group. Either designate a leader for the small group or have the children choose a leader. Explain the nature of their assigned task and begin to discuss some of their special responsibilities when working in a small group.

5. Have resource materials available for the children. Later on, as they become accustomed to working in groups, they will be able to secure needed materials themselves.

6. Meet with the small group every day for a few minutes before they begin work and again at the end of their work period to make sure things are moving along as planned. If possible, have them make a progress report to the other, larger group during the summary and evaluation that should come at the close of each social studies period.

7. Give students specific help and suggestions in how to organize their work and how to report what they are doing.

8. Have their report to the class be short, concise, and interesting. Have members of the group explain to the class how they did their work as a group. Begin calling attention to some of the responsibilities of persons working collaboratively in small groups.

9. Follow the same procedure with another group of children as soon as possible. Gradually include other children, selecting some who have had previous experience in groupwork and some who have not. Observe carefully the children who need close supervision and those who are responsible and work well in groups.

10. After all the children have had an opportunity to work in a small group under close supervision, more than one group can work at a time. Eventually, the entire class should be able to work in small groups simultaneously. When this is attempted, precede the work with a review of the standards of groupwork and a clear definition of objectives. A careful evaluation should follow.

Positive interdependence means that each member of the team does his or her part.

levels and subject areas and for all sorts of academic tasks, from simple retention to concept learning and problem solving. Kristin Gruber, a third-grade teacher in Minnesota, tells this success story:

> Andy, a low-achieving student who received LD (learning disability) services, was failing social studies, health, and language early in the year. He needed constant supervision just to stay on task, paid little attention to classroom discussions, and seldom completed assignments. With a cooperative group to support and encourage him, however, Andy completed many assignments during class and brought back homework consistently. . . . By mid-February, he was passing every subject; and he was able to maintain his grades for the rest of the year.[6]

Why is this so? Researchers look to the main ingredients of cooperative learning: positive interdependence and individual student accountability. Positive interdependence means that group goals cannot be attained unless each member of the group does his or her part; individual accountability means that the group's success depends not only on group members doing their parts but also on *learning*. Indeed, they will be held accountable for learning: Grades go to individual students, not groups. Add to these another attribute of cooperative learning—discussion. Discussion is a rich stew of face-to-face talking, listening, responding, paraphrasing, and questioning. Positive interdependence makes all this necessary. Putting thoughts into words requires students to think about the task at hand and to clarify what they mean; trying to understand what others mean involves still more talking, thinking, and clarifying. Further, discussion often produces disagreements—healthy social and academic conflicts—which, when managed skillfully by the teacher and students, promote deeper levels of both academic learning and interpersonal development.[7] Controversies and disagreements flourish in democratic civic life; students must learn to deal with them productively.

Closely related to discussion and controversy is still another reason cooperative learning improves academic achievement—it promotes what researchers call *engaged time* or *time on task*. Cooperative groupwork generally helps children to be more engaged in the task (more attentive and involved) than does seatwork. The main drawback of seatwork is that children are working on their own with little or no guidance, which allows them to drift far from the assigned task or to attempt it without understanding its purpose and without using helpful strategies. This is especially unfortunate when we consider that seatwork often consumes over half the available instructional time in both primary and intermediate grades and, ironically, is prescribed most often to children who already are doing poorly in school! Elizabeth Cohen sums up this problem:

> Choosing a method of classroom organization that leaves the student who rarely succeeds in schoolwork quite alone may indeed be the root cause of the observed disengagement on the part of low-achieving students in seatwork settings. These students are receiving very little information on the purpose of their assignment, on how to complete it successfully, on how they are doing, or on how they could be more successful. The tasks themselves are rarely sufficiently interesting to hold the students' attention.[8]

Cooperative learning promotes active student involvement in learning and therefore helps teachers to spend wisely the most valuable aid they have—time.

GROUP SIZE AND COMPOSITION

The size of a small group affects its achievement both of academic knowledge and cooperative skills. If groups are too large, there may be duplication of responsibilities, less opportunity for individuals to carry their share of the group effort, difficulty achieving face-to-face interaction, and a tendency for some members to fade out of the group activity. Also, the larger the group, the more skillful group members must be with cooperative behaviors. On the other hand, if groups are too small, there may be insufficient division of labor to warrant groupwork and too few opportunities to cooperate. In general, however, groups should be kept small—from two to five children, with four or five as the optimal size. When teaching groupwork skills, teachers often begin by placing children in pairs to practice particular skills, such as using names, making eye contact with the speaker, and asking for help. Pairs can then be combined into groups of four.

Group size influences the sort of academic work that can be accomplished. Structured Academic Controversy, discussed later in this chapter, requires two pairs of children in groups of four; meanwhile, STAD (also discussed later) has no required group size. The number of students in a Jigsaw group determines the number of topics that can be studied or, when writing original biographies, the number of chapters in the book students produce (see Chapter 13).

Just now, our discussion of goals emphasized learning cooperative behaviors and academic achievement. Let us consider a third goal, which bears particularly on group composition: positive intergroup relations among students of different ethnic and racial backgrounds in integrated classrooms. Anyone who has visited a desegregated school knows that friendships across ethnic groups did not automatically follow the placement of diverse children together in the same school or classroom. To the contrary, especially in the upper grades, children of the same ethnic group, whatever it is, often stay together, playing together at recess and eating together in the cafeteria.[9]

A good deal of research shows that when diverse groups of youngsters work together to attain a group goal, positive feelings are generated: they begin to like and trust one another, more often choose to be with one another during free time, and in general grow in their respect for one another. Of course, a teacher cannot expect these results as a consequence only of placing diverse students together in a small group and structuring a cooperative task for them; rather, students must be prepared for groupwork. They must learn the skills and norms of cooperation. But placing them in diverse groups is a precondition—it at least provides the *opportunity* to tackle the goal of positive intergroup understanding.

Thus, the cardinal principle of group composition is to achieve the greatest mix possible given the student population. A teacher should achieve this mix using whatever student variables are available—academic record, interpersonal skill, gender, ethnicity, disability, language, race, and social class. In this way, small groups are as heterogeneous as the whole class. Ability grouping is ruled out (as far as this third goal is concerned) because it minimizes rather than maximizes the mix.[10]

The teacher may use one or more of several methods to form heterogeneous student groups:

1. *Work, not play.* Do not allow friends to choose one another for small-group work. Friends tend to play rather than work when placed in the same group, and groupwork should be thought of in terms of work rather than play.[11]

2. *Random assignment.* With a brand-new class, a teacher might randomly assign students to small groups of four to five students each. Forming groups alphabetically is a good way, and it should result in mixed groups. Look over the resulting lists of group members and make any adjustments needed to achieve a greater mix of gender and ethnicity.

3. *Purposeful mixing.* Once a teacher is more familiar with students' work habits, interpersonal skills, and past academic achievement, groups can be purposefully mixed. Some teachers have good success simply by mixing within each group students who are strong and weak on each of these characteristics. Students with poor interpersonal skills and/or poor academic records should not be placed together any more than friends or highly successful students.

4. *Special helper.* A variation on purposeful mixing is to select one or more students for each group who will serve as a special helper. The help needed will depend on the kind of work the teacher has structured for the groups. For example, if groups are to construct a papier-mâché map of the United States, each working on a different region, the teacher might identify students who are good with paper products (mixing, gluing, painting) or at creating map legends. One of these helpers is placed in each small group. If the teacher has decided that groups of four children each are to write historical fiction about Harriet Tubman or James Madison, with each student working on a different "chapter," it will help to have someone who likes to sketch in each group. It will also help to have a strong planner in each group—someone who can help the group decide on four different chapter topics.

In general, social and academic skills that can come in handy are reading, writing, planning, decision making (comparing alternatives), note-taking, brainstorming, operating tape recorders or cameras, observing detail, using the library, creating time lines, using reference books, finding websites on the Internet, loading software on the computer, using creative dramatics, assisting students with disabilities, interviewing, building with cardboard, drawing, taking surveys, and so on.

5. *Index cards.* Write the name of each student on an index card, strip of construction paper, or popsicle stick. Decide on the task each group will tackle and identify the special help that will be needed. Identify the special helpers, putting at least one in each group, and sort the other students into each group. Aim for the greatest mix possible with regard to interpersonal skills, ethnicity, language, academic achievement, gender, and so on. (The teacher can use a random method, such as shuffling the deck of name cards, once special helpers have been selected.)

6. *Duration.* A cooperative group exists until the cooperative task is completed. Rather than reforming groups for the next group task, the same group usually remains together for the purpose of further developing its cooperative skills. Groups should stay together long enough to make progress on the interpersonal problems that inevitably arise. While the group remains the same, the task, of course, changes (e.g., from making maps to writing a biography). A new task is an opportunity for the teacher to select a different set of special helpers. The teacher should keep searching for everyone's special talents so that different helpers can be used on each new task.

ALTERNATIVE FRAMEWORKS FOR COOPERATIVE TASKS

There are many different ways to structure groupwork, all with positive interdependence, individual accountability, face-to-face interaction, and discussion. Teachers often invent their own ways and share them with one another. Teachers just beginning to experiment with cooperative learning may prefer *STAD* (Student Teams Achievement Division). When teacher and students are ready, they may want to experiment with *Jigsaw* or *Structured Academic Controversy.* We discuss each in turn.

STAD

STAD has the students listening to the teacher present information—except that a cooperative task is tagged onto the end, thus adding the advantages of cooperative learning to the disadvantages of the teacher talking *at* students.[12] Students are placed in groups before the lesson begins. First, the teacher explains the purpose and rationale of the lesson and then presents needed information. (In a lesson on map legends, for example, the teacher takes 20 minutes or so to display three different maps, explaining the design and function of the legend on each.) Second, the teacher gives the groups one handout with questions *and* another handout with responses. Each group receives only one copy of each so that group members must share materials. Each group is given 20 minutes to accomplish their task: to understand *why* the answers are correct. Third, students are given a short quiz over the questions and answers, and the group with the highest average score (or that shows the greatest improvement over the last quiz average) is rewarded with special certificates and honorable mention in the class newsletter. This constitutes one round of STAD.

Jigsaw

We encountered Jigsaw in Chapter 8 as a method for incorporating cooperative learning into the teaching strategy called *concept formation.* In that example, students were members of two groups—the usual group of four or five students, which in Jigsaw serves as the students'

FIGURE 11–2
Jigsaw group assignments.

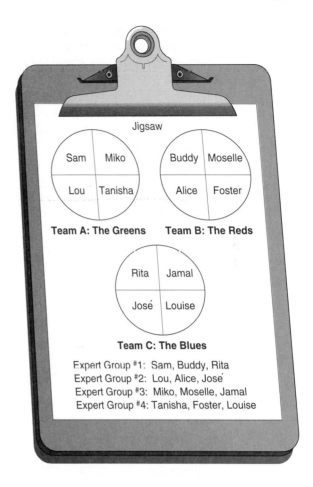

Jigsaw

Team A: The Greens

Sam | Miko
Lou | Tanisha

Team B: The Reds

Buddy | Moselle
Alice | Foster

Team C: The Blues

Rita | Jamal
José | Louise

Expert Group #1: Sam, Buddy, Rita
Expert Group #2: Lou, Alice, José
Expert Group #3: Miko, Moselle, Jamal
Expert Group #4: Tanisha, Foster, Louise

home team, plus an additional "expert group."[13] Typically, the teacher divides the task—whatever it is—into four or five parts. In concept formation, each part is one example of the concept children are to form. Or the task might be to prepare a report on the geography of a continent, say Asia, and that task is divided into four or five parts: perhaps five geographic regions on that continent or the five themes of geography (Chapter 4). Or the task might simply be to comprehend a difficult chapter on Native Americans in the textbook, and the parts are the chapter's four or five lessons. Whatever the task, each member of the home team is assigned to work on one of the four or five parts, but he or she is not alone (Figure 11–2). All students from the different home teams who are assigned to the same part join together to work in "expert groups" (called this because, relative to their teammates, they become "experts" on this one part). The goal of working together in expert groups is very simple: to learn their part of the task better than they would working alone. This may require anywhere from 30 minutes to a week or more, depending on the task. Eventually, experts return to their home teams, where they serve as the teacher for their teammates, helping them learn all about that part they studied in the expert groups. Following this, student understanding of the *whole* task (all the parts) is assessed. The teacher rewards the home team that has the highest average score, or that has improved the most, or the one that demonstrated the best use of cooperative skills. This is one round of Jigsaw.

Structured Academic Controversy

We would not want to let the opportunities afforded by cooperative learning to restructure the *ways* we teach social studies or cause us to ignore the chance it provides to reconsider *what* we teach in social studies.[14] Structured Academic Controversy, developed by Roger and David Johnson, provides just this opportunity.[15] It asks teachers to perceive the academic controversy in whatever social studies knowledge they want students to learn and to engage students in that controversy. Rather than teaching about the protection of endangered species, for example, as though the topic were devoid of debate, teachers can help their children to participate in that debate. Other examples are the American Revolution (the colonists had to decide whether to declare their independence), deciding whether a Bill of Rights was necessary, developing cafeteria rules, deciding who is responsible for making new students feel welcome, and current events issues involving public health (such as placing nutritional information on food labels) and advertising on children's television programs. The study of each of these topics can be designed so that the disagreements at their core are made the object of study. *Doing so boosts both the intellectual rigor and the excitement of social studies lessons.* Structured Academic Controversy makes such study manageable, even for the beginning teacher and for very young students, and it relies on groupwork.

First, the teacher assigns students to four-person teams. Second, the teacher helps students gather background information on the topic; for example, the American Revolution. The textbook will provide perhaps ample background, and supplementary resources, such as primary documents and children's literature, can also be assembled. In the third phase, each four-person team is divided into two pairs, and each pair studies one side of the debate. On the American Revolution, one pair would study the arguments that eventually led to the colonies declaring their independence, and the other would learn loyalist arguments. Fourth, pairs present their perspectives to one another. Fifth, as a test of their listening and questioning, the pairs reverse perspectives, giving now the argument of the *other* pair until that pair is satisfied that its perspective has been heard and understood. In the final phase, genuine discussion begins as the two pairs join together for the purpose of striving for a team consensus. A spokesperson for each team reports on his or her team's progress toward consensus.

Identifying and Teaching Groupwork Skills

Teachers who have experimented with small-group instruction and found it frustrating commonly feel that groupwork breaks down either because some children within the groups do most of the work or because the children waste time and accomplish little or nothing. Such responses indicate that the children have not yet developed the prerequisite skills for successful cooperative endeavors. If children are only given the *opportunity* to work in groups without being *prepared* to do so, there is little reason to expect them to function effectively in these groups.

Children need to be taught how to behave during cooperative groupwork so that they can function reasonably well without the teacher's direct supervision. Of course, this is not only a matter of teaching the needed interpersonal skills; group members also need the appropriate academic skills for completing the assigned task. If group members are expected to write a report together, they will require instruction on report writing and have some general writing experience. This instruction does not need to occur in advance; providing it *during* the action, when it is needed, can be more effective. In summary, the nature of the task assigned to a small group should be consistent with the preparation they have received.

> If children are only given the *opportunity* to work in groups without being *prepared* to do so, there is little reason to expect them to function effectively in these groups.

In this section, we offer suggestions on which skills need to be taught and we suggest strategies for teaching them. Two kinds of skills are highlighted—skills for getting started as a cooperative group and skills for functioning in a cooperative group.

SKILLS FOR GETTING STARTED

Tell children both the purpose and rationale for having them learn to work cooperatively in small groups. Teachers have found it helpful to provide examples of real-world situations, both civic and job related, where people need to function well in groups with others who not only are not their friends but may even be strangers (town meetings, fire departments, fast-food restaurants, hospital emergency rooms, and so on), and, whether strangers or not, disagreements are common.

Children typically need to be taught behaviors that help them to do the following:

- Move into groups efficiently.
- Stay with the group during group time.
- Use quiet voices.
- Make everyone feel welcome.
- State and restate the assignment.
- Set or call attention to time frame.

SKILLS FOR FUNCTIONING IN SMALL GROUPS

When groups are practicing the skills of getting started, it is especially important that the task be short and simple. Once some progress is made in these skills areas, the teacher should instruct the class on some of the behaviors crucial to a group working well together when the task is more complex. These should be posted in the room and referred to often. Examples include:

- Plan how best to proceed.
- Encourage everyone to participate.
- Use one another's names.

FIGURE 11–3

A sample T-chart used to help children understand a cooperative skill.

SKILL: Encouraging Participation	
Looks Like	*Sounds Like*
smiles	"What is your idea?"
eye contact	"Excellent!"
thumbs up	"That's a good idea!"
pat on the back	"I'd like to hear what you think."

- Face the speaker and make eye contact.
- Avoid putdowns.
- Ask for help when you need it.
- Ask questions.
- Be a good sport.
- Offer to explain, clarify, or summarize.
- Listen carefully when others are speaking.
- Paraphrase another's statements.
- Talk openly about disagreements.
- Criticize ideas, not people.
- Cheerfully take the jobs the group wants you to do.
- Suggest new ideas when the group's motivation is low.

TEACHING COOPERATIVE SKILLS

Practicing any cooperative skill requires that learners *understand* the skill. Otherwise, they are not really *practicing* anything. One effective skill-teaching procedure was given in Chapter 8. The T-chart (Figure 11–3) is another popular method for helping children understand a cooperative skill.[16] The teacher writes the name of a skill on the chalkboard and creates two columns beneath it, one for a group of adjectives describing what the skill *looks* like, another for phrases that exemplify what the skill *sounds* like. Children are then asked to generate a list for each.

Once a skill is understood well enough to make practice worthwhile, practice should begin in earnest. Some teachers find role playing to be a valuable technique in teaching the skills needed in small-group work. By selecting four to five children to serve as group members, the teacher can demonstrate to the class what it means to "help everyone become a part of the group" or any of the skills that have been discussed. When the role playing is completed, the remainder of the class can analyze the situation to determine why the group was functioning well or poorly. It is helpful to have children observe certain specific elements in the situation to be presented. For example, they might try to answer such questions as these:

1. What did individual members do to help the group do its job? What did members do that did not help the group?
2. What did the leader do to help the group get its job done?
3. How did the group find out exactly what it was to do?
4. Did the group use good resources in solving its problems?
5. Did the group seem to be working together as a team? Why or why not?
6. How can we help the group do its job better?

Following the role playing, the class can discuss the situation in terms of the specific points being observed. It may then be helpful to replay all or a portion of the situation to help children appreciate the forces at work in group situations. With young children it may be desirable to have an older group demonstrate such things as a domineering leader, an uncooperative group member, a member who wants only the fun tasks, the noncontributor, the irresponsible leader, the member who must always have his or her own way, the member who talks too much, and so on. In teaching groupwork skills, the teacher will want to do more than talk about what should or should not be done. Children really need an opportunity to see and experience how it works as well as an opportunity to experiment and try their hand at doing productive groupwork. Role playing can do much to sensitize them to the various subtleties and forces that come into play in small-group situations.

Videocassette recorders can be useful in teaching cooperative skills. The teacher can videotape a group role playing certain skills needed for productive small-group work. The tape can then be used for analysis. The videotape provides a way to demonstrate over and over again the essential characteristics of groupwork. This teaching procedure is widely used in teaching athletes, and greater use could be made of it in classrooms today.

REWARDING GROUPWORK APPROPRIATELY

Part of the reason that groupwork is at times ineffective is because it is not rewarded as generously as are the academic aspects of the classroom work. This stems from the teacher's attitude toward the value of group activities. If the rewards (recognition, praise, value statements, reports to parents, grades) go only to those who do well in paper-and-pencil activities, children rightly conclude that group activities do not count much in the entire scheme of things. Groupwork will be enhanced if the teacher regards it as an important part of the instructional program and rewards appropriately the children who have done commendable work in group endeavors.

DEBRIEFING

While rewarding good skill use is necessary, it is just as important to talk in detail with students about the progress they are making. All groupwork should involve the deliberate practice of one or more cooperative skills; therefore, all groupwork sessions should be followed by a debriefing in which students are asked to reflect on how often cooperative skills were used, how well they were used, and what skills especially need attention. This is both important but surprisingly rare. A quite common mistake in cooperative group-work is, first, not helping students identify and clarify just which cooperative skills need to be practiced during a particular groupwork session, and second, forgetting to debrief the session.

GIVING ORAL REPORTS

Teams and expert groups will be giving oral reports to the entire class from time to time in the normal course of groupwork. Structured Academic Controversy, recall, ends when a spokesperson for each team reports to the class on the team's attempt to reach a consensus on the issue at hand. Oral reports also are commonly used to share information obtained through individual research and study. Whether the report represents work done as part of a group or inquiry conducted individually, it serves the purpose of bringing to the group the information and ideas that were acquired, as well as teaching children how to organize, plan, and present a report.

It is the teacher's responsibility to take an active part in helping the child prepare the report. This includes suggesting suitable topics, suggesting references, helping with its organization, and suggesting visual devices to use. The teacher should find a few minutes a day or two before the presentation to sit down with the youngster and review what is to be included in the report. Once prepared, the child should be left alone while the report is being given unless help is specifically requested.

Only a few reports should be scheduled on the same day. It is impossible for children to sustain any degree of interest if they must listen to 5 or 10 reports consecutively. A better procedure is to have two or three reports given at a time and to spread the reporting over a period of several days.

The following are suggested as alternatives to the traditional oral and written reports.

1. Dramatize an incident, sequence, or situation relating to the topic and incorporate essential data to be communicated in the dramatization.
2. Use children's own drawn illustrations, charts, and graphs as the basis for a presentation or use illustrations found in newspapers, magazines, or other sources.
3. Pretend to be a tour guide taking the class through the area studied. Different children report on different "stops" on the tour.
4. Use the overhead projector for visual aids in a presentation.
5. Role-play the part of a newscaster making an on-the-spot report.
6. Interview a classmate who is role-playing the part of an expert on the topic under study.
7. Collect pictures, arrange them in sequence, and use them as the basis for a report.
8. Write a diary or letter that might have been written by someone in an earlier period.
9. Use artifacts as the basis for a report.
10. Prepare and explain a bulletin board display or diorama.
11. Prepare a narration for a filmstrip.
12. Do an original narration for a film or videotape with sound turned off.

13. Write news stories that might have been appropriate to a particular period or prepare and publish a single issue of a newspaper that might have appeared in some historical period.

14. Tape-record a presentation for playback to the class, which frees the speaker to point to parts of a chart or model or to show photos or slides. In this way the child is accompanying him- or herself.

Teaching and Using Discussion Techniques

We saw in Chapter 3 that discussion generally and deliberation (which is discussion aimed at making a decision on a controversial issue) particularly are fundamental democratic processes. We have seen in this chapter that discussion is a key ingredient in cooperative learning. Its value lies chiefly in the fact that it represents a type of intellectual teamwork, resting on the principle that the pooled knowledge, ideas, and feelings of several persons have greater merit than those of a single individual. Without discussion a student may never grasp the fact, for example, that there are multiple points of view and opinions on a problem, not just his or her own. Furthermore, this student may never have the opportunity to practice the most fundamental work of popular sovereignty—talking with others about common problems and reaching a decision about what to do. In this section, we look more closely at discussion, concentrating on large-group, roundtable, panel discussions, and buzz groups.

INVOLVING EVERY CHILD

Because the strength of discussion is obtained from the information and viewpoint of many members of the group, it is necessary that most members of the class participate. It is a thinking-together process that breaks down if one member or group dominates it. It is the teacher's responsibility to encourage the more reluctant children to participate. Although there cannot be a single answer to the question of what to do with the child who dominates the discussion, skillful teachers usually take care of the matter with a statement such as "Jack, you have given us so many good ideas today, and I know you have many more good suggestions, but we want to find out what some of the others think would be a good way to. . . ."

Another strategy for dealing with students who dominate discussions is to use student observers. One or two children are asked to observe the day's discussion. Their task is straightforward—to keep track of who talks and how much. Because student observers learn a good deal about discussion, the domineering student can purposefully be placed in this role. One first-grade teacher placed such a student in the role of student observer, instructing him to gather data without talking. He gathered data on who talked and did a good job, noting that one student had done quite a bit of talking in the group while another had talked very little. The next day when he was back in the group and no longer the observer, he started to talk, clamped his hand over his mouth, and glanced at the new observer. He knew what behavior was being observed, and he didn't want to be the only one with marks for talking. The teacher said he may have listened for the first time all year.[17]

ROUNDTABLE DISCUSSIONS

A *roundtable discussion* usually involves a small number of persons, perhaps no fewer than three and no more than eight. It requires someone to serve as a moderator to introduce the members of the discussion group, present the problem to be discussed, and keep the discussion moving. The leader's role is to guide the group rather than to dominate it. A relaxed atmosphere needs to prevail, and the presentations are conversational rather than oratorical.

Roundtable discussions are difficult for young children (and many adults!) because they are, essentially, a conversation held in front of an audience. They can be used in the intermediate and middle grades (4–8) by having a group of children discuss a problem in front of the rest of the class or by dividing the class into several small discussion groups that function without an audience. It is perhaps best to use this procedure with one group at a time, either with or without an audience, until the children have learned how to participate in discussions of this type. It will be necessary for the teacher to introduce the procedure to the class and to explain and demonstrate its purposes and the way it works. Such points as the following need to be emphasized:

1. *Responsibilities of the moderator*—to be informed on the topic to be discussed, introduce the topic, keep the discussion moving, avoid having the group become sidetracked, ask members to explain more fully what they mean, avoid having members argue and quibble over irrelevancies, and summarize and state conclusions.

2. *Responsibilities of members of the discussion group*—to be well informed on the topic to be discussed, especially some phase of it; speak informally while avoiding arguing and quibbling; stay with the topic under discussion; have sources of information available; back up statements with facts; and help the group summarize its conclusions.

3. *Responsibilities of the audience*—to listen attentively, withhold questions until presentation is completed, ask for clarification of ideas, ask for evidence on questionable statements, confine remarks to the topic under discussion, and extend customary audience courtesies to members of the roundtable.

Roundtable discussions may be used for any of the following purposes:

1. Discuss plans for a major class activity.
2. Evaluate the results of a class activity, the merits of a film, school assembly, or a decision of the student council.
3. Make specific plans, such as the best way to present the work of the class to the parents on Parents Night.
4. Discuss a current event.
5. Present differing views on a community issue or a school problem.
6. Make decisions and recommendations to the class. (The student council, for example, wants to know how the class feels about a new play schedule. A committee of five children discusses this matter and presents its findings and recommendations to the class.)

PANEL DISCUSSIONS

A *panel discussion* is similar to a roundtable discussion in many respects, but there are some important differences. The responsibilities of the moderator are approximately the same as they are for the moderator of the roundtable, as are those of the participants. The procedure, however, is more formal than that of the roundtable. It usually begins with a short statement or presentation by each discussant before the panel is opened for free discussion by members. Panels are usually more audience oriented than roundtables, and frequently some provision is made for audience questions or participation at the end of the panel's presentation. A greater responsibility is placed on participants to prepare themselves well for their particular part on the panel, for each panelist is considered to be more or less an "expert."

One sixth-grade teacher used a panel discussion format in the following way.

The topic for the panel to discuss was a community problem involving the conversion of a military base into a community resource. Various special-interest groups were competing for the use of the newly acquired property. In class the teacher asked children to volunteer to represent one of the following special-interest groups:

1. City planner
2. Golf enthusiast
3. Representative of the local community club
4. Condominium builder
5. Representative of a local Native American tribe
6. Moderator

The children were provided planning time in which to prepare a three- to five-minute statement explaining their point of view regarding the future of this property. Time was allowed for questions to clarify points made in the presentations or to raise other issues.

BUZZ GROUPS FOR BRAINSTORMING

The following is an example of a "buzz" group in operation. The members of Ms. Kryzinski's class viewed in class a CNN television special dealing with homelessness in the United States. They were eager to discuss the program and even more anxious to do something about the problem it portrayed.

"What can we do, Ms. K, to help other kids in our school know about some ways they can help the homeless?" a child asked.

"Why don't you decide?" Ms. Kryzinski responded. "You are already arranged in small groups, so why don't you take the next 10 minutes and come up with some ideas? Be prepared to give us two or three good ideas that would be possible for us to carry out in our school."

After about 10 to 15 minutes, the children's attention was refocused, and each group presented some ideas. There was no attempt to evaluate suggestions at that time.

All the suggestions were listed on the board and discussed. The class then voted on the list to determine which one they would implement.

We have here a brief description of a *buzz-group* or *brainstorming* technique. It is an informal consideration of ideas or problems where the chief purpose is to solicit the suggestions, feelings, ideas, or consensus of the members participating. In brainstorming for ideas and suggested solutions to problems, it is important *not* to evaluate each one at the time it is offered. If each is discussed, the list will not be very long. *The objective of brainstorming is to get as many ideas to the surface as possible, no matter how outlandish they may seem.* After the complete list has been generated, time can be taken to evaluate each one and select the best ones by consensus. It is usually best for the group to have a designated leader and recorder.

Talking things over in a buzz session can be helpful in clarifying ideas, getting a wide sampling of opinion and feeling, obtaining suggestions and ideas, and getting children to participate who might be reluctant or fearful in a more structured discussion situation. Likewise, it has some limitations. Buzz sessions can easily get out of hand and become noisy and boisterous where nothing is accomplished except the creation of confusion. There is need, therefore, for the teacher to have firm control of the class before such a procedure is attempted and to establish standards that are clearly understood beforehand. Lesson Plan 14 incorporates buzz groups, individual work, oral reports, and whole-class discussion.

Conclusion

Many of us remember numerous small-group experiences in our K–12 and college years. Unfortunately, these were not always planned in such a way that *learning*—both social learning and academic learning—would be increased because of our participation in them. This chapter has stressed that more goes into planning small-group experiences than placing students in groups and giving them a task. Teachers who orchestrate cooperative groupwork successfully create a positive classroom climate and they work up to groupwork gradually. They plan work tasks that *require a group*—that require more heads than one (a superb example of this is found in the cooperative biography unit explained in Chapter 13). Teachers also teach the skills of groupwork rather than only wishing students had already formed them. Moreover, they use different small group frameworks—Jigsaw, committees, panels, buzz groups, etc.—for different purposes. In all, positive interdependence and individual student accountability are the guiding principles. Managing cooperative groupwork requires a good deal of thought and planning, not to mention observation of skilled colleagues and reading about the experiences of others. Fortunately, you have years of teaching, and learning to teach, ahead of you. We highly recommend the readings on cooperative learning that appear under "Selected References."

Discussion Questions and Suggested Activities

1. Define cooperative learning. Then brainstorm different ways a teacher can build readiness for cooperative groupwork with a class that has always worked on a whole-class basis.
2. Develop a role-playing exercise designed to teach groupwork skills.
3. Examine the dimensions of the hidden curriculum given in Figure 11–1 and add examples from your own experience that tend to increase the level of care and community in a classroom or decrease the level of hostility.

| Lesson Plan 14 | CHARACTER TRAITS OF PROMINENT PEOPLE |

Grade 4–5

Time Three to five class periods

Objectives Children will practice the skills of working cooperatively in "buzz groups," develop an awareness of the character traits of prominent people, and learn what a biography is.

Interest Building Place children in buzz groups of three or four and ask them to review the following rating scale. Ask different students to clarify the meaning of each point. Introduce today's lesson and indicate that you will ask each of them to assess their own participation in the small-group work using this rating scale:

	Always	Sometimes	Very rare
1. Focuses on the task	☐	☐	☐
2. Listens to what is said	☐	☐	☐
3. Considers what others say	☐	☐	☐
4. Gives own ideas	☐	☐	☐
5. Takes turns	☐	☐	☐

Ask the buzz groups to brainstorm as many names of "famous people"—living or dead—as they can think of in 5 to 10 minutes. Have the recorder from each group list the names. Ask the groups next to examine their lists and categorize the people on it based on what they did that made them famous (possible categories: musicians, sports figures, politicians, business persons, scientists, artists, social activists, television stars). Ask the children to try to think of missing categories and to generate names for them. Have the recorders list their groups' categories on the board. Ask the whole class to eliminate duplicates and then try to think of categories still missing (e.g., painters, religious leaders, soldiers, inventors). Ask the children to discuss why the individuals listed on the chalkboard became well known, whereas most of their contemporaries did not. Tell the class that over the next few days they will study the qualities and character traits of famous people more carefully.

Lesson Development Have a wide selection of biographies of prominent people available for children. (Prominent means well-known, but not necessarily for good or ill.) Ask each child to choose one biography to read. Tell them what a biography is. The books are to be read in the next week, and children are to write in their response journals answers to the following three questions:

1. What, if anything, do you admire about the person?
2. What qualities (character traits, dispositions) did the person have that made him/her come to the attention of others?
3. What did the person *do* that made him/her famous?

At the completion of the assignment, have children return to their small groups and share their responses. Help each group create a data-retrieval chart with the names of their prominent persons listed down the left side and the three questions across the top. This serves as a guide and organizer for their sharing. After each child has shared, ask the groups if any character traits were common to each of the persons about whom they read (there may be none). Have each group choose a representative to give a brief oral report on its findings to the entire class.

Summary   Have the class generate a list of character traits that (1) applied to all; (2) applied to some; (3) applied to a few; and (4) applied to none. Ask the children if prominent persons necessarily have admirable character traits and why it might be that they do or do not. Ask them if *famous* people are necessarily *good* people and work to clarify this distinction.

Assessment

1. Have students assess their own participation in the small groups using the rating scale shown in "Interest Building" and to share their assessment with you. (You may want them to do this in writing or in private conferences.)

2. Following the summary, ask the class to take out their response journals. Each child is to identify his/her favorite prominent person and state the qualities they believe make this individual prominent. Collect and read the journals.

3. Ask the class, "What is a biography?" and listen to as many responses as time allows. Provide feedback and correction as needed.

Materials   Biographies of prominent persons at suitable reading levels for the class, to be secured from the school library. Get ideas from

- *http://www.giraffe.org/tall.html,* the Giraffe Heroes program with a storybank of over 800 real-life heroes
- *http://www.myhero.com/home.asp,* where the expansive directory broadens the concept of hero to include family members, teachers, and artists

Integration   *Literature:* Biography is a genre in its own right and plays a crucial role in historical understanding. Because many biography examples are present in this lesson, students can be helped to build the *concept* of biography—what it is, its role in literature and history, and how it differs from autobiography.

Other subjects: Biographies of musicians, scientists, writers, politicians, leaders, artists, mathematicians, philosophers, educators, and architects are all appropriate for this lesson.

■   ■   ■   ■   ■

4. Make a T-chart (Figure 11–3) for several of the skills mentioned in this chapter.

5. Discuss similarities and differences between traditional small-group instruction as used in teaching reading and cooperative learning groups as used in social studies and other content areas.

Selected References

Cohen, Elizabeth G. (1994). *Designing groupwork* (2nd ed.). New York: Teachers College Press.

Johnson, David W., Johnson, Roger T., & Holubec, Edythe J. (1993). *Circles of learning: Cooperation in the classroom* (4th ed.). Edina, MN: Interaction Book Co.

Mosher, Ralph, Kenny, Jr., Robert A., & Garrod, Andrew. (1994). *Preparing for citizenship: Teaching youth to live democratically.* Westport: Praeger.

Noddings, Nel. (1992). *The challenge to care in schools.* New York: Teachers College Press.

Stahl, Robert J. (Ed.). (1994). *Cooperative learning in social studies: A handbook for teachers.* Menlo Park, CA: Addison-Wesley.

Tatum, Beverly Daniel. (1999). *Why are all the black kids sitting together in the cafeteria?* New York: HarperCollins.

Notes

1. Elizabeth G. Cohen, *Designing groupwork,* 2nd ed. (New York: Teachers College Press, 1994), 3.

2. Richard Paul, *Critical thinking* (Rohnert Park, CA: Sonoma State University, 1991).

3. Nel Noddings, *Caring: A feminine approach to ethics and moral education* (Berkeley: University of California Press, 1984).

4. David W. Johnson, Roger T. Johnson, & Edythe J. Holubec, *Circles of learning: Cooperation in the classroom,* 4th ed. (Edena, MN: Interaction Book Co., 1993), 15.

5. Ibid., 15.

6. Dianne K. Augustine, Kristin D. Gruber, & Lynda R. Hanson, Cooperation works! *Educational Leadership 47:* 4 (December 1989/January 1990): 4–7.

7. David W. Johnson & Roger T. Johnson, Conflict in the classroom: Controversy and learning, *Review of Educational Research, 49* (Spring 1979): 51–70.

8. Cohen, *Designing groupwork,* 21.

9. Beverly Daniel Tatum, *Why are all the black kids sitting together in the cafeteria?* (New York, HarperCollins, 1999).

10. There is a time and place for ability grouping, of course (see Chapter 2), but not when the goal is positive intergroup relations.

11. Cohen, *Designing groupwork,* 71.

12. Robert E. Slavin, *Using student team learning* (Baltimore, MD: Johns Hopkins University, 1986).

13. Elliot Aronson, *The Jigsaw classroom* (Beverly Hills, CA: Sage, 1978).

14. Mara Sapon-Shevin & Nancy Schniedewind, Selling cooperative learning without selling it short, *Educational Leadership, 47:* 4 (December 1989/January 1990): 63–65.

15. David W. Johnson & Roger T. Johnson, Critical thinking through structured controversy, *Educational Leadership, 45:* 8 (May 1988): 58–64.

16. David W. Johnson & Roger T. Johnson, Social skills for successful group work, *Educational Leadership, 47:* 4 (December 1989/January 1990): 29–33.

17. Johnson et al., *Circles of Learning,* 35.

Websites

http://www.giraffe.org/tall.html
http://www.myhero.com/home.asp

12

The Literacy–Social Studies Connection

Main Idea

The idea that children *learn to read* in the basic reading program and then *read to learn* in the social studies program is not quite right. Actually, the two are interdependent: Children improve their reading ability—expanding and deepening it—as they read to learn social studies material: primary documents, charts and graphs, maps and globes, narratives and exposition. In social studies units, with good coaching, children's reading ability will develop in ways that will rouse their minds and empower them (and their society) for the rest of their lives.

Key Concepts

literacy apprenticeship, practical literacy, informational literacy, pleasurable literacy

Chapter Outline

- Literacy and Content-Area Learning
- Reading Skills Essential to Social Studies Learning
- Using Textbooks as Study Aids
- Locating and Using Reference Materials
- Building Social Studies Vocabulary
- Improving Reading Comprehension: Making Sense
- Using Children's Trade Books for Multiple Perspectives
- Conclusion
- Discussion Questions and Selected Activities
- Selected References
- Notes

Chapter Snapshot

Ms. McKean was determined that her fourth-graders read *lots* of social studies material. This was, therefore, the subject area in which she would provide most of her language arts instruction. She didn't want them reading only narrative writing, whether fiction or nonfiction. That was "too limiting," she said. "I am educating future judges and senators, and they have to know how to read more than stories." She taught them to preview and skim as a way of giving them a leg up on complex nonnarrative material. "I want you to read and understand the Constitution, the Declaration of Independence, and Lincoln's Gettysburg Address. I want you to know your way around the atlas, the almanac, and public records. For that, you'll need to learn to take a helicopter ride *first*—get above the material. This is called 'previewing.'"

 A favorite website http://www.ncss.org/resources/notable/home.html We return to the National Council for the Social Studies website, this time to find an eagerly awaited annotated bibliography, "Notable Social Studies Trade Books for Young People."

Schools can become "sites for true literacy apprenticeships," writes Lauren Resnick,[1] but this requires ample school activities in which students *use* and *develop* reading and writing skills as they pursue practical and informational goals, as well as pleasure. Among other things, this means that reading and writing skills must be taught and used in the content areas. This is the main idea of Chapter 12.

This chapter also focuses on two additional ideas. First, reading and writing are best thought of as a common enterprise rather than as distinct endeavors. Readers make meaning when they comprehend text in much the same way that writers make meaning when they compose text.[2] Skillful teachers attend to this similarity by paying special attention to the *meaning-making* process itself, whether situated in reading or writing. Briefly, children construct meanings in relation to what they already know. Children will do this in rigorous and empowering ways or in mediocre ways depending on the presence of a stimulating environment and skillful coaching and guidance. That's where the teacher and the curriculum come in.

Second, children do not make meaning in a vacuum; children read and write to accomplish goals. In social studies, for example, they read and write to investigate the disappearance of the American buffalo, to follow rivers to the sea, to grasp how the Aztecs could possibly have been conquered, and to figure out why there are homeless people and what can be done about it. They read and write, then, to build and express social studies understandings.

Literacy and Content-Area Learning

If teachers regard the teaching of reading as something that is done in three small groups during the reading period and ignore the reading needs of children during the remainder of the school day, they may expect children to have many disappointing experiences reading social studies material. The feeling that children *learn to read* in the basic reading program and then *read to learn* in the social studies, for example, is not an entirely correct understanding of the relationship between these two processes. Actually, the two occur simultaneously; children improve their reading ability as they read to learn. Children can extend and improve their reading skills and abilities far beyond the basic reading program as they use reading for a variety of purposes.

This view of literacy education and content learning sees each situated in the other—mutually dependent. It sees the central work of the skillful teacher as creating *apprenticeships* for children in which they are gradually helped to achieve expertise in both. By apprenticeship we mean a learning situation with at least three characteristics: (1) Learners learn as a consequence of being coached into higher levels of capability by adults or more capable peers; (2) practice occurs as learners work to accomplish all or part of a worthwhile task with the guidance and support of the coach or coaches; and (3) the coaching gradually decreases as the learner's capability increases.[3]

In the classroom, the "head coach" is the teacher. Sometimes, the teacher orchestrates situations in which peers who are more capable at a particular task will guide and support students who are less capable on that task. In the cooperative group work strategy called Jigsaw

TABLE 12–1   Literacy apprenticeships in social studies.

Practical Literacy	Informational Literacy	Pleasurable Literacy
Reading the ballot	Studying the candidates' positions	Enjoying a biography of the pharaoh, Ramses
Reading directions to the polls	Reading a political analysis	Reading an absorbing book of historical fiction
Reading the election returns	Reading a news article about a political campaign	Enjoying Milton Meltzer's *Ten Queens: Portraits of Women of Power* (Dutton, 1998)

(Chapter 11), learning is fashioned so that every student serves as a more capable coach to other students and is in the same way helped by other students. This should be familiar to every parent who has had an older child teach a younger one to wash dishes.

Three literacy practices deserve the attention of elementary school teachers, and each requires its own form of apprenticeship.[4] The first is the practice of reading or writing written texts in order to function in everyday life. This is *practical literacy*. Examples include reading food labels and bus schedules, following instructions for videotaping a television program or assembling a bookshelf, completing job applications, and writing letters. Most of this apprenticeship occurs within families with the guidance and modeling of parents and older siblings. The second literacy practice is reading or writing to gather data about the world. This is *informational literacy*. Typical examples are reading newspapers and weekly news magazines, studying campaign literature, reading and writing letters to the editor, getting bus or plane schedule information from the Internet, taking notes at lectures, looking up the location of Tibet in an almanac, and reading about Gandhi in a history textbook or on a CD-ROM. For much of this information-driven learning, we depend on the school curriculum. The third form of apprenticeship concerns reading for pleasure. *Pleasurable literacy* is the one form of literacy practice that is not a means to an end. It is an end in itself: One picks up and puts down the book or article at will. This apprenticeship often occurs at home when children are read to by parents, but also at school when literature is read aloud to children and then dramatized, or when children read engaging stories themselves and then discuss them with other children or use them as a springboard for writing an original story. Table 12–1 shows these three practices, or apprenticeships, in relation to one another.

Reading Skills Essential to Social Studies Learning

Most elementary schools provide time during the school day when a major effort is made to teach basic reading skills. In this developmental reading program, children acquire a basic reading vocabulary and learn to use various word recognition techniques along with other skills and abilities that characterize the flexible, independent reader. For example, they learn to identify words, create hypotheses about the meaning of a selection, and revise their

FIGURE 12–1

Social studies reading skills.

In social studies, the capable reader:
- Reads flexibly
- Uses chapter and section headings as aids to reading
- Uses context clues to suggest meanings
- Talks with classmates about possible meanings
- Adjusts reading speed to purpose
- Hypothesizes cause-effect relationships
- Uses reference material freely to understand vocabulary
- Investigates the author of primary documents (who, when, why, where?)
- Seeks data in maps, charts, pictures, and illustrations and interprets data and symbols found there
- Uses various parts of a book (index, table of contents, introduction, etc.) as aids to reading
- Previews the selection to become familiar with text structure and to hypothesize general meaning
- Skims to locate facts and hypothesize main ideas
- Compares one account with another
- Recognizes and seeks topic sentences
- Uses library and Internet skills to find needed material
- Uses the newspaper directory to locate articles, letters, arts, comics, and editorials

hypotheses as they read, write, and reread. But even a strong basic reading program will not meet all the reading needs of children because each area of the school curriculum requires reading tasks that are somewhat unique to that special area.

The special reading skills needed to make sense of social studies material may be identified by examining the sorts of reading tasks children will confront in a genuine social studies program. The most important point to be made is that this material is neither all fiction nor all narrative. Much of it is expository, where a story is not being told but, instead, an explanation is being given. It may be a cause-effect explanation (history), or a "thick description" of cultural life in east Asia (anthropology) or of human-environment interaction on the Horn of Africa (geography). In many primary documents, we find neither narrative nor exposition. It may be a letter home from a Civil War soldier on the eve of the battle at Gettysburg or a diary entry of a midwife in the American colonies. It may be a speech, a map, a chart, or a graph. An examination of this material will suggest reading skills such as those given in Figure 12–1.

Some of the skills on this list may never be used if children are reading only fiction narratives. Skimming is a good example. If you skim a fiction story, you may find out "what happened," which would spoil the story. Nobody wants that! But skimming a nonfiction essay or chapter in a biography or textbook is an extremely intelligent thing to do—not so that you can avoid reading it, but so that you can comprehend it better once you *do* read it. (Please take a minute to skim ahead in this chapter now. Find the sections on previewing and skimming.)

The teacher's responsibility regarding reading instruction in the social studies is twofold. First, those special reading skills unique to social studies must be taught in relation to the subject matter under study. These include the skills listed in Figure 12–1. The teacher's second responsibility is to help children learn how to use reading as a tool to gain needed information. Of course, reading should not be the only means through which children encounter new social studies information. Throughout this text, the idea is stressed repeatedly that a multimedia approach (what Howard Gardner calls multiple "entry points"[5]) is vital to inspired teaching of social studies. But in the broad spectrum of media and activities potentially available to children today, reading remains undoubtedly the most important and, in the long run, the most critical to their success in learning social studies.

Using Textbooks as Study Aids

In contrast to reading a storybook simply for enjoyment, much of the reading in social studies involves a search for information in sources that bear no resemblance to storybooks. Social studies textbooks are written to be used as information sourcebooks and are not intended to become the social studies curriculum. They can be used in a variety of ways, and individual children may make different uses of the same book. Similarly, different teachers may choose to make different uses of the same book, depending on their skill, experience, and method of teaching. One may mine it for primary documents, another may use it all as the basis for reading and writing instruction, and another may rely on its maps and other visuals. We encourage teachers to make differential use of textbooks rather than to "cover" the content uniformly and require children to master all the material they contain.

Recall from our discussion of textbooks in the Resources chapter of this book (Chapter 9) that social studies textbooks are textbook *programs*. They contain an *array* of resources that teachers otherwise must gather on their own. There are primary documents, artwork, explanations of all sorts, narrative histories, maps, map skill lessons, vocabulary lessons, thinking skill lessons, and questions and activities. Ancillaries are common as well: CD-ROMs, videotapes and videodisks, giant maps that can be spread out on the classroom floor, smaller maps with washable surfaces that are placed on each student's desk, and anthologies of speeches, plays, and short stories. The *Teacher's Edition* also contains a wealth of resources: lesson and unit plans, overviews and summaries, additional background information on the subject of the lesson, website suggestions for online activities, links to the literature curriculum and other curriculum integration ideas, student projects, guest speaker and field trip suggestions, role-playing suggestions, discussion topics, classroom museum ideas, and both formal and informal student assessments.

Social studies print materials almost always present problems of reading difficulty. This is true of textbooks, too, even though they are written at a level that is suitable for the average reader. The reason for this inherent reading difficulty is that these books are designed to deal with substantive content, and this means that the terms and concepts relating to that subject matter must be used in explaining the ideas presented or explained in and of themselves. For example, a book may be attempting to help children understand something they may have memorized but do not understand: the Pledge of Allegiance.

Social studies textbooks can be used in many ways, and individual children can make different uses of the same book—as a source for primary documents, as a basis for reading and writing instruction, or for its maps and visuals.

I pledge allegiance to the flag of the United States of America
and to the republic for which it stands,
one nation, under God, indivisible,
with liberty and justice for all.[6]

What is the central idea, the central concept in this text other than allegiance? *Republic*. This is the concept that the flag is symbolizing—"for which it stands"—and to which one is pledging allegiance. There's just no way of getting around *republic* if one is to understand the meaning of the pledge. What is unique about this pledge is that citizens are pledging their allegiance not to a person (e.g., in a dictatorship, to the dictator himself) or to a land, but to a way of living together.

To take another example, let us assume that teacher and students are immersed in a unit on Canada (or any other place). A *place* cannot be meaningfully presented without using core geographical terms such as *land form, climate, culture, region, longitude,* and *latitude.* If such terms are eliminated from a reading selection to simplify the reading task, it is no longer a reading about the geography of Canada. The complexity and frequency of concepts often make reading social studies textbooks difficult, and there is no way to overcome this problem entirely. (The same is true in science textbooks.) An easy-to-read text is probably not a good social studies text because its purpose should be to provide information, charts, documents, and challenging ideas rather than be a simple storybook.

It is important *not* to try to overcome this inherent difficulty of reading content-oriented textbooks by changing the content. As we saw in Chapter 2, this happens again and again to children who are already at risk of school failure, and it causes some Hispanic and African-American children and children whose home language is not English to fall behind their same-age peers. It is a *lowering* of expectations. The answer to the problem is not changing from Canada, or Our Nation's Government, or whatever the topic is, to What I Did Over Summer Vacation, Sports Heroes, Circuses, Kite-flying, or some other content that is easier to read about because the terms and content are already familiar to children. Doing so would be miseducative and disabling. *The answer instead is to apprentice children into social studies reading—make it a goal of the classroom community and help them do it successfully.*

Complementing this reading work (and it is work) should be ample nonreading work: dramatizations, music, simulations, and construction activities—i.e., other entry points to the subject at hand. These will build comprehension through other channels and resonate with a classroom's multiple intelligences.[7]

Good news: The design of a social studies textbook provides many aids to make the job of reading easier. The teacher cannot assume, however, that children will use such aids unless they are taught to do so. The skills associated with the use of study aids must be taught, reviewed, and retaught each year throughout the elementary school grades. Here are the most basic teaching suggestions, each of which is discussed in turn:

1. Using the parts of a book
2. Using the organization of the book
3. Using pictures to aid comprehension

USING THE PARTS OF A BOOK

The parts of a book should be taught as aids to getting information. Sara, for example, was studying famous women in American history. She had heard that a native woman assisted Lewis and Clark, and she wanted to know more. How would she find it? She had learned that the Table of Contents was usually very general, so she turned instead to the Index. She couldn't look under the woman's name, though, since she didn't know it; so she looked under Lewis and Clark and found the following:

Legislative branch, 345, 356–357
Leirich, Julie, 253, 571
Lewis, Meriwether, 371–372
Lexington, Massachusetts, 300
Liberator, The, 420

She turns to page 371 and notes a boldfaced section heading near the bottom of the page that reads, "The Lewis and Clark Expedition." She skims the sentences that follow it. Nothing. She turns the page, skimming quickly, and finds it. In the second column on page 372 she reads:

> The expedition spent the winter with the Mandan Indians beside the great bend of the Missouri River. There Lewis and Clark hired a French-Canadian fur trapper as their guide. They also invited the trapper's wife, Sacajawea, a Shoshone, and her newborn son to accompany them. Lewis and Clark believed that if they traveled with this woman and her baby, the Indians whom they met would understand that the explorers were a peaceful group.[8]

Thus, in a matter of moments, Sara is able to find precisely the information she seeks. Contrast this with the boy sitting next to her who needs the same information, but, lacking an efficient way of finding it, goes through the book page by page looking for a picture or a clue that will reveal the name of that famous Shoshone woman. Without an index lesson from the teacher or Sara, he may never find what he is looking for.

Rather than teaching parts of a book in a didactic way, the teacher should use exercises that require children to apply these skills. Often such exercises are included in the book itself. Here is one example:

LEARNING THE PARTS OF A BOOK

Directions: In the right column are listed the parts of your book. In the left column are listed some things you might want to find out. For each item in the left column, tell what part of the book you would turn to *first* to get the information.

You Want to Know:	Parts of Your Book:
the number of chapters in the book	title page
the meaning of *treaty*	copyright page
how to say the word *Iroquois*	preface
when the book was published	table of contents
the population of various states	list of maps
the date Geronimo was captured	list of illustrations
what a sod house looks like	glossary
the route of Marco Polo	atlas
whether the book tells anything about Canada	index

Variations of this exercise are possible. For example, the right column can be omitted, and students can be asked to find and supply the information. Or the child can be asked to indicate the specific page on which the information appears.

Naturally, the complexity of activities of this type should be appropriate to the age and maturity of the learners. Even in the first grade, children learn that books have titles and authors and that pages are numbered. They also learn that sections of their "chapter books" have titles. In the second and third grades, they can begin to use the table of contents to find a particular story. In the third and fourth grades they can learn simple variations of alphabetical arrangements that assist them in using an index.

USING THE ORGANIZATION OF THE BOOK

Units, chapters, section heads, and subheads; study aids at the end of sections, chapters, and units; maps, charts, or picture captions; introductory questions—all of these make sense to the mature reader who uses them as valuable aids to understanding the organization of a book. But left unguided, a child is not likely to make good use of them. In fact, a child is likely to lose sight of the forest for all the trees. Knowledge of how a text is organized is a significant factor in children being able to negotiate the text and comprehend and recall what they have read.

Please look back now to Figure 9–1 on pages 290–291. It shows a very typical "Using Your Textbook" feature that can be found in the front of most student texts. Students whose teachers help them master this structural information about the book—how it is put together, its parts and features—have the advantage of viewing the "forest" from above.

USING PICTURES TO AID COMPREHENSION

The most widely used of all visual aids are paintings, photographs, and illustrations. These are used to obtain realism, to clarify ideas, to recall the real object, and, in short, to give meaning to learning. It is well known that words cannot convey meanings as vividly or quickly as pictures.

Publishers invest huge sums of money to provide instructive illustrations for social studies textbooks. Unfortunately, the full value of these aids to reading is not realized unless children are taught how to make good use of them. Illustrations are not simply cosmetic touches to make the book more appealing. They are, or should be, an integral part of the message of the text.

Paintings, photos, and illustrations elaborate concepts presented in the narrative but usually do not repeat exactly what is said in the text. Neither do picture captions simply tell what would be obvious to the reader only by looking at the picture. Thus, captions should call attention to some element or relationship in the picture or illustration that might be missed by the casual viewer. Often this is done by using a question or series of questions. In this way a photo or illustration can provide the reader with a wealth of information. In teaching children how to use pictures and illustrations, teachers will find questions such as these appropriate:

- What is being shown in the picture?
- What kind of picture is it? a photo? painting? illustration?
- When was this picture made?

- Does the picture illustrate something we discussed in class?
- What causes or effects can be detected in the picture?
- What does the picture show that illustrates the roles of men, women, and children in that society?
- What can you say about the geography of the area shown by the picture?
- What conversation might be going on between the persons in the picture?

Locating and Using Reference Materials

Children should use a wide variety of reference material in studying social studies topics. The value of such references depends not only on their availability but also on the ability of the children to make use of them. The teacher's responsibility in this respect is, therefore, twofold: teaching children (1) which references to use for various purposes and (2) how to use the reference efficiently once it is found. These are continuing responsibilities of the social studies program and cannot be completely taught in any one grade or any one year. A beginning will be made in the primary grades, but the child will continue to extend and refine the ability to use references throughout high school, college, and in later life. Instruction usually begins as soon as the child develops a degree of independence in reading. The reference materials used in the social studies may be grouped as shown in Figure 12–2.

Much of the instruction given on the use of references will have to be specific to the particular resource used. For example, one uses the Internet and the *World Almanac* differently than one uses an atlas or an encyclopedia. Moreover, the references may be used at varying levels of sophistication. The library may be used by primary grade children under teacher guidance to check out books and CD-ROMs, to look at magazines, or to have stories read to them, whereas upper-grade children should be able to use the library independently, making use of the card catalog and locating references themselves. The use of the various references should be taught as the need for them arises in the social studies.

The skills students need for using references can be practiced and learned on an individual basis or by children in pairs using *task cards,* as is illustrated in Figure 12–3.

Building Social Studies Vocabulary

The vocabulary density of social studies reading material is one of the major causes of poor comprehension in social studies. Even with the careful attention that contemporary authors give to word difficulties and text structure, the social studies vocabulary remains a stumbling block for many children. Although a degree of simplification is possible, some specialized vocabulary cannot be avoided. This is not altogether undesirable if the teacher accepts vocabulary development as one of the goals of the total social studies program. The same situation exists in other areas of the curriculum; the child must learn the language associated with mathematics, science, art, music—all of which have their own peculiar words, terms, or phrases. Figure 12–4 shows some of the types of words that are peculiar to social studies.

FIGURE 12–2 Types of social studies reference materials.

Books
Textbooks
Supplementary reading books
Picture books
Biographies
Historical fiction

Primary Documents
Letters
Diaries
Journals
Recordings
Speeches
Photos
Posters
Newspapers
Police records
Funeral records
Editorials
Essays (anything created at the time)

Special References (paper and electronic)
Encyclopedias
Maps and globes
Online museums (the Smithsonian)
   and libraries (the Library of Congress)
Atlases
Dictionaries
World Almanac
Charts and graphs
Constitution of the United States
Yearbooks
Legislative manuals
Internet
C-SPAN
Channel One
CNN

Reference Aids (paper and electronic)
Card catalog
The Reader's Guide
Bibliographies
COMCATS

Miscellaneous Materials
Advertisements
Magazines and periodicals
City and telephone directories
Labels
Guidebooks and tour books
Letters, diaries, and journals
Travel folders
Postcards
Newspapers and news clippings
Comic books
Pictures
Schedules and timetables
Pamphlets and booklets (such as
   those from the information services
   of foreign countries, superintendent
   of documents, conservation
   departments, historical societies, art
   galleries)
Weather reports
Manufacturers' guarantees and
   warranties
Money, checks, coupons for premiums,
   receipts
Reviews
Government documents

The teacher should anticipate likely word difficulties *before* asking children to read a social studies selection. Two types of word problems must be expected. One is the inability to recognize the word in print; the other is not knowing the meaning of the word once it is recognized. Therefore, new words and terms should be presented and developed in the context of a phrase or a sentence rather than in isolation.

FIGURE 12–3 An example of teacher-prepared task cards.

SIDE ONE

Find Out for Yourself

(If you cannot do any one of these, look for a clue on SIDE TWO of this card.)

1. Find the article on "Safety" in the *World Book*.

2. Into how many sections is the article divided? _____

3. Skim through the article to find these two facts:

    a. Where do most accidents happen? _____

    b. What do the letters *UL* on electrical wiring and appliances stand for?

    _____

4. Suppose you heard that someone had been killed in an accident in his or her home but you did not know what kind of an accident it was. You would be right most of the time if you guessed that the accident was a
_____ or _____ or _____

5. Suppose you questioned the accuracy of this article. What is there about the article that might renew your confidence in its authority?

    _____

SIDE TWO

CLUES

1. Select volume *S–Sn.* Look for the article according to the alphabet.

2. See the "Outline" at the end of the article.

3. a. Look under the section "Safety/Home."

    b. Look under "Safety with Electricity."

4. What does the article say about the major causes of accidental deaths in the home?

    _____
    _____
    _____

5. What group critically reviewed the article?

    _____
    _____
    _____
    _____
    _____

FIGURE 12–4 Terms needing special attention in social studies.

Technical terms—Words, terms, and expressions peculiar to social studies and usually not encountered when reading selections from other fields of knowledge. *Examples: veto, meridian, frontier, latitude, longitude, legislature, polls, franchise, temperate, plateau, hemisphere, mountainous, balance of power, capitalism, democracy, nationalism, civilization, century, ancient, decade, pueblo, fjord, iceberg.*

Figurative terms—Expressions that are metaphorical; having a different connotation from the literal meaning usually associated with the word. *Examples: political platform, cold war, closed shop, Iron Curtain, pork barrel, open door, hat in the ring, domino theory, Sunbelt.*

Words with multiple meanings—Words that have identical spelling but whose meaning is derived from context. *Examples: cabinet, belt, bill, chamber, mouth, bank, revolution, fork, court, assembly, range.*

Terms peculiar to a locality—Expressions peculiar to a specific part of the country that are not commonly used elsewhere. *Examples: truck, meeting, borough, gandy, draw, coulee, right, prairie, section, run, butte, arroyo, geoduck, goobers, grits, potlatch, bayou, haul cane road.*

Words easily confused with other words—Words that are closely similar in general configuration. *Examples: continent for country, alien for allies, principal for principle, longitude for latitude, executive for execution, conversation for conservation.*

Acronyms—Words that are abbreviated expressions. ***Examples:*** *NATO, NASA, OPEC, SALT, NOW, UNICEF, AIDS, MADD.*

Quantitative terms—Words and terms signifying amounts of time, space or objects. ***Examples:*** *shortly after, century, fortnight, several years later, score, 150 tons.*

Vocabulary development should be conducted in relatively short, fun settings. Having children look up a long list of terms in the dictionary prior to reading a selection is not productive. No expert reader does this. A better strategy is to write the key terms in a sentence on the chalkboard and discuss their meanings. These should be the few terms that, in the teacher's judgment, are critical to student comprehension of the selection. Better still, the sentence in the text in which the word or term appears can be selected for directed study.

It is essential for the teacher to model a curiosity about new words. Curiosity about words and a genuine interest in good communication, after all, are central features of a successful apprenticeship in reading and writing. Teachers should encourage children to use the specialized social studies vocabulary in their discussions and writing. They should also, from time to time, encourage children to create new words or nicknames for old ideas. During a concept-formation lesson (Chapter 8) on *culture*, the children may be encouraged to think of a term other than *culture* that might more powerfully convey the meaning of the concept—*lifeway,* for example. Creating new words puts children at the inventing end of language, rather than the receiving end, which can be an enlightening change of vantage point.[9]

Moreover, the teacher may want to involve students in word games. Devising riddles, providing synonyms or antonyms, making or completing crossword puzzles, or participating in spelling bees can increase students' interest in wordplay. Bulletin board displays and other classroom exhibits can feature new words encountered in social studies. Students who enjoy vocabulary may elect to author a "cool words" column in the class newsletter.

Teaching how known words can be used to construct new words can help students recognize new words and understand their meanings. Among the simplest variations are compound words or the addition of prefixes or suffixes. Some examples are these: construct, construct*ed*, construct*ing*, construct*ion*; consume, consum*er*, consum*ed*, consum*ing*; loyal, *dis*loyal, loyal*ist*; dictate, dictat*or*, dictator*ship*.

Improving Reading Comprehension: Making Sense

Reading with comprehension means that readers are able to make sense of what they are reading and come away from the selection with mental pictures of essential facts and understandings. Through discussion with the teacher and classmates, writing, dramatizations, discussions, and returning to the selection perhaps numerous times, children can check the sense they made with the sense made by others, perhaps revise their interpretation, and, in this trial-and-error way, come to some negotiated understanding about what the author meant to say.

It is obvious that the child who brings the most to a reading situation—whether practical, informational, or strictly for pleasure—will receive the most in return. Researchers call this the Matthew Effect (Chapter 1). What the child brings that will enhance social studies reading the most are intellectual aptitude, a storehouse of experience and ideas (prior knowledge), knowledge about reading, and motivation. A teacher cannot do much to increase children's intellectual aptitude, but a great deal can be done about the other three: Teachers can capitalize on the knowledge and cultural experience children bring to the reading situation, they can build children's knowledge of important components of the reading process itself, and they can establish clear purposes for reading tasks. To help children *want* to comprehend, teachers can make connections to students' interests and goals, and they can make sure that the reading tasks they give students to accomplish are authentic—that is, they are not mere "busywork," nor are they the sort of thing that has no larger purpose. ("Drill-and-practice" activities are often off the mark on both counts.) Rather, tasks should be related to a worthy challenge. Children are not just practicing writing sentences, for example, but they are writing sentences in the biographies they are producing about people who work to protect the environment from polluters. In these ways, children can be helped to perform nearer to their full potential.

Perhaps the most important general rule of thumb used by good readers is the one that seems so mundane: *Read flexibly.* This means that readers vary their speed and the skills they use depending on the selection at hand. Expert readers do this routinely; poor readers do it rarely; mediocre readers do it unevenly. Apprenticing children into the routine practice of flexible reading should be a daily goal in social studies teaching and learning.

Because reading comprehension varies according to the particular topic and selection at hand, *previewing* may be the most important single comprehension strategy. It means, essentially, looking before you leap. Good readers use it because it tells them what lies ahead, providing a general picture of the terrain. Looking ahead indicates whether familiar or strange material is at hand and, consequently, which additional strategies, such as skimming, may be required. Previewing in this way builds prior knowledge "on the spot."

A simple narrative account of an African-American girl who must survive on her own during the American Revolution, for example, may be relatively easy to understand for many children. They can read accounts of this type without difficulty because they rely on motivating storylines, familiar story structures (e.g., problem-solution), and well-known words. On the other hand, the child may encounter in the textbook an expository selection called "Democracy, not Monarchy." This is a complex idea that may be difficult for many young children. Not only is its vocabulary specialized (separation of powers, civil rights, limited government, and so on), its place in children's experience will be marginal. Yet, it is easily one of the most important topics in the social studies curriculum.

What's to be done? Several strategies have been shown to be effective in improving reading comprehension. We briefly consider four:

1. Activate prior knowledge.
2. Preview.
3. Skim for ideas and related details.
4. Summarize.

ACTIVATE PRIOR KNOWLEDGE

Just as the rich get richer, the knowledgeable get more knowledgeable. What we know before coming to a learning task influences, often greatly, the kind and amount of learning we will accomplish once we get there. Learners who have more background knowledge about the topic of the text selection they are about to read, all things being equal, will better comprehend that chapter than learners who know little or nothing about it. Minimally, they will comprehend it differently, making better sense of it than their less knowledgeable counterparts. Such is the influence of prior knowledge on comprehending text. Over the long term, therefore, schools should do everything possible to contribute to the prior knowledge of students. Extensive use of field trips to construction sites and factories, study trips to museums, exposure to films of historical events and far away places, assemblies, plays and pageants, projects, pictures, guest speakers, displays, artifacts—all will assist the child in comprehending the ideas encountered in reading.

But there is a problem. When the next learning task is here, staring them in the face, learners will not necessarily use the prior knowledge they have. Ask any teacher! The knowledge they have built up over the years, even in last week's lesson, may lie dormant and untapped in today's lesson. How can a teacher "activate" this prior knowledge so that students can use it to make sense of the reading selection? A popular strategy is helping children make a visually vivid image called a *semantic map*.

Semantic mapping provides a graphic representation of a key concept that the teacher (or student) has chosen from the reading selection. Consider a teacher who has chosen Exploring North America as the central theme for a fourth-grade social studies/language arts

This class creates a *semantic map* to activate prior knowledge about immigrants.

curriculum. Developing in-depth knowledge of each region of the United States is the content focus, and the Lewis and Clark expedition has been selected as the first unit. Before having students read a selection from the textbook on Lewis and Clark, the teacher decides to activate the whole array of ideas and information students associate with the concept *exploration*. The procedure follows.[10]

1. The teacher places the term *exploration* on the chalkboard and asks students to jot down individually any words they can think of related to this theme. They may think of words such as *Columbus, Marco Polo, past, future, time machine, explorers, ships, astronauts, underwater exploration,* and so on.

2. Next the teacher identifies or elicits from students major category labels related to the theme, prompting students to think of categories they may overlook. These are arrayed graphically around the concept term, which serves as a hub (see Figure 12–5).

3. Now the teacher asks students to generate additional ideas under each category. The teacher can also suggest items and ask students to decide under which category label they belong. Figure 12–6 shows two sample categorization exercises.

PREVIEW

Good readers have a general idea of what the material is about *before* starting to read it. How do they get it? By previewing. Comprehension is significantly increased because previewing sheds some light on the subject; consequently, the reader does not have to proceed totally in the dark. It is a method for acquiring prior knowledge "on the spot."

FIGURE 12–5

A simple semantic map on the theme "exploration."

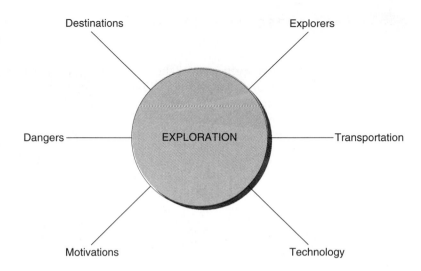

FIGURE 12–6 Expanded semantic maps on the themes "exploration" and "water."

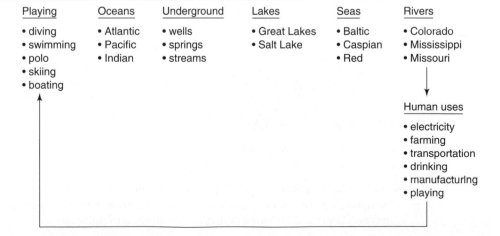

Previewing generally will be directed by the teacher, who typically introduces this strategy to children and helps them initially learn it. But children should develop the habit of previewing material themselves; if instruction goes as planned, the teacher's coaching gradually should diminish as students begin to assume responsibility for previewing. Let us say that a class is about to read *part* of a new chapter entitled "The World of Carmelita and José."

Teacher: Boys and girls, for the next few days we will be reading from our social studies books. I would like to introduce you to two children we will visit in this unit whose names are Carmelita and José. Please open your books to page 86. (The children take time to find the page.) Notice that the large print says "The World of Carmelita and José." Just looking at this page, what do you think this unit is about?

Frieda: Mexico.

Teacher: Why did you say Mexico, Frieda?

Frieda: Because Carmelita and José are Mexican names. Besides, it shows their pictures, and they are dressed in Mexican clothes. . . . We learned that when we studied the community in Texas. . . .

David: That doesn't mean they are from Mexico. They could be from *New* Mexico, even Iowa or Vermont, and have names like that.

Teacher: Those are both good ideas. Perhaps if we page through this unit, we can discover the country it talks about. Turn to the map on page 88. . . .

It is established that the unit is, indeed, about Mexico, and the teacher continues:

Teacher: As you look at these pages, what do you suppose you will be reading about in the world of Carmelita and José?

Eric: Well, it looks like . . . uh . . . it tells like . . . what they do every day . . . in school . . . at home.

Lisa: It shows how they do many of the same things we do.

Teacher: What do you mean?

Lisa: Well, we have homes and families, we go to school, we go shopping, and things like that, and they do, too.

The discussion concludes after the teacher is satisfied that the children are oriented to the material to be read. Previews should accomplish the following:

1. Help the reader get the general idea of the selection.
2. Help the reader understand how the material is organized.
3. Help the reader understand how pictures relate to the subject matter to be read.

SKIM FOR IDEAS AND RELATED DETAILS

Once children have previewed the selection they intend to read, it is a good idea to skim it for ideas and related details. The teacher begins:

Teacher: Now that you have some general ideas about what you will be reading, let's take some time to become still more familiar with it. We will be using a strategy good readers use called *skimming*. What do you think skimming means?

Mei: It means taking something off the top, like skimming off the bugs at the swimming pool. I see them do it because we go early.

Eddy: Yeah, and it means going really fast.

The teacher helps the children define *skimming* and then directs them as follows:

1. Students are given 30 seconds to thumb through the selection, noticing as best they can what is on every page.
2. The teacher asks what they noticed and takes responses.
3. The teacher directs students to read the questions under the last heading, *Review.* Students are asked if, based on those questions, they want to revise what they earlier said the selection was about. The teacher elicits revisions. For example, a student responds:

Lisa: Well, it must not be only about Carmelita and José. I mean, it's also about the country because the second question asks about the climate.

4. The teacher directs students' attention to the other section headings and asks students to skim again to find the number of sections and the topic of each.
5. Next, students are directed to quickly read the first few sentences under each section head. After just one minute or so, the teacher asks them what they found.

Teaching students to preview and skim nonfiction material, whether a primary document or a textbook chapter, should improve their comprehension. Lesson Plan 15 approaches this goal in a somewhat different way than above, employing a powerful analogy.

SUMMARIZE

As we indicated in Chapter 7, "Planning Units, Lessons, and Activities," summarizing what has been read is both powerful and difficult. The skill of summarizing takes a lifetime to learn because it is so intimately dependent on prior knowledge and judgment. "While good summarizers are invariably older, poor summarizers may be found at any age."[11] The key skill in summarizing is deciding what is important in a text. Summarizing requires readers to sift through the material to determine what will be included and excluded. The writer must also decide how to reword and whether to reorganize the information. This is challenging work.

What to do? Teachers who are serious about summarizing work at it slowly and continually. One way they do this is simply to build summarization practice into nearly every lesson as part of the closing phase: "Now, let's summarize what we learned today. What information that you gathered today might be most important to our objective?" In the case of the Constitution: "Who will summarize for us how the Constitution is organized?" In the case of the Canada: "What information have you found that best helps you predict whether or not Canada will remain unified?" About the American Revolution: "Who can summarize the reasons the colonists decided to declare their independence from England?"

A second, more formal way to teach summarizing is to follow the two guidelines below, which are derived from the research on teaching summarization.

PREVIEWING AND SKIMMING THE U.S. CONSTITUTION (OR OTHER NONFICTION TEXT)

Grade 4 or 5

Time One class period

Objectives To become familiar with the structure and, very generally, the contents of the U.S. Constitution. To practice previewing and skimming a primary document to build background knowledge before reading.

Interest Building Ask students to imagine they are about to go on a cross-country hike together to explore a forest that none of them has even seen before. Everyone packs a "day pack" for the trip with the usual supplies: lunch, poncho, emergency supplies. A bus picks them up at school and takes them on a two-hour trip across the plain to the forest. It stops at the edge of the forest where helicopters are waiting. Groups of students climb into them and are flown high above the forest. From this perspective, they can see the land below them. The forest appears to be ring-shaped and in the middle are two lakes and marshland. The helicopters return our explorers to the ground where the children see motor scooters awaiting them. Their teacher instructs them to use the scooters to "get a feel for this territory. See it all but don't linger in any one place. Keep moving. The purpose is to decide where you want to hike. Set your watches. Return in no more than 30 minutes." Two by two, the kids jump on the scooters and off they go. Thirty minutes later they return bursting with information about the two lakes, the marsh (which turned out to be not so marshy after all), the forest pines, a few deer sightings, and a ton of rabbits and mockingbirds. After this, they set out on foot in pairs with instructions to return in two hours. Some head straight for the northernmost lake for a swim, others for the pine forest, and others for the not-so-marshy marsh for a game of soccer. When they return, they gather in a circle and excitedly share their experiences.

Lesson Development

1. Explain the analogy. Exploring a complicated reading selection is like the imaginary adventure they just had: They don't know where to go until they have familiarized themselves with the territory. Knowing the territory gives hikers and readers a huge advantage. Once familiar with the lay of the land, they can get on their scooters and quickly visit the places they saw from the air, getting a close-up view but not so close that they stop to linger. Their purpose then is to move quickly through the whole territory so they will know where to linger later. Reading something complicated has the same phases: before, during, and after. The "before" has two parts: the helicopter view from above, called *previewing,* and the quick scooter trip on the ground, called *skimming.* What we learn from quickly previewing and skimming lets us know where we are during reading. They keep us from getting lost. Later, after reading, like after hiking, we share to find out what experiences each of us had.

2. Have students examine the U.S. Constitution. Explain the document's importance to all of us as the rulebook for our society. Read aloud and discuss an excerpt from Jean Fritz, *Shh! We're Writing the Constitution* (Putnam, 1987).

3. *Previewing.* Demonstrate how to flip back and forth through the pages, also known as "thumbing through" the pages. (This is important for both previewing and skimming, and it is something we almost never do when reading a story.) Guide the students through a preview of the Constitution. For example, "Let's get into the helicopter. You'll have to flip the pages back and forth, because I'll give you just two minutes and I don't want you lingering anywhere. Find out how long it is, how many parts it has,

the names of those parts, and whether there are any pictures of any sort." Call time in two minutes and ask students to share what they found. (There are three parts: a preamble, seven articles, and 27 amendments, in that order.)

4. *Skimming.* Now guide the students through skimming the Constitution. For example, "Now hop on your scooters to get a close-up view of each of these three main parts. There'll be lots of new words, but just speed on past them. In 10 minutes, I'll ask you to describe very generally what each part seems to be about. Remember to keep moving; don't get stuck." Call time in 10 minutes and ask students what each part seems to be about. Help students treat every response as a hypothesis that can be checked in the next phase.

5. *Reading.* "Now let's go through the Constitution on foot." Ask students to choose which of the three parts they want to find out more about. Have the three groups cluster in different corners of the classroom to read silently then talk with one another about the contents of that part. "Change your purpose from getting to know the overall territory to really getting to know one area—the area you chose."

6. *Sharing.* Ask members of each group to share with the whole class what their part is about. Keep track on the chalkboard of the new vocabulary. Encourage different interpretations of the same part (e.g., "Who thought this part was about something different?")

Summary and Assessment

Review the analogy. Then, ask for a definition of *previewing* and *skimming*. Provide correction as needed. Ask students to jot down a summary of the three parts of the Constitution and then ask several to read theirs aloud. Use what you find out as you plan the follow-up study of the Constitution.

Materials

1. A copy of the U.S. Constitution for each student (such as the one provided in Chapter 3 of this text and typically included in fifth-grade social studies texts).

2. Artwork: a painting of the signing of the Constitution (e.g., by Howard Chandler Christy or Junius B. Stearns).

3. *Shh! We're Writing the Constitution* by Jean Fritz (Putnam, 1987).

Integration

Reading. Obviously, this lesson teaches two powerful reading skills needed to comprehend social studies material.

Literature. Following this lesson, use the textbook and Jean Fritz's book to help students learn the story of the U.S. Constitution: what it is, why it is important, who wrote it, and where, when, and why its predecessor (the Articles of Confederation) failed. In many cities, the American Bar Association will provide an attorney to come to your class as a guest speaker on law and the Constitution.

■   ■   ■   ■   ■

- *Choose a short text excerpt.* Even grown-ups will have difficulty summarizing the entire Constitution. Summarization practice should be geared, therefore, to short excerpts. Students might try summarizing just the Preamble. It is important that they hear one another's attempts at summarization (e.g., "It gives six reasons *why* these people felt they needed a constitution"). A good follow-up question is, "What do the rest of you think? Does that capture what is important in the Preamble?" After this work, students can try summarizing the seven articles.

Teacher: Gina, what do you think this section is about?

Gina: I think it tells how our country is organized.

Teacher: Thanks, Gina. Let's work with that. What do you others think?

Lorraine: I'd say government, not country.

Brad: Doesn't our summary need to include something about the branches?

Teacher: Let's try those revisions.

- *Choose an easy kind of text.* The U.S. Constitution is not an easy kind of text, so it is a very difficult place to begin. Better to begin summarization work with narrative writing that students can readily understand. Jean Fritz's story about the Constitution used in Lesson Plan 15 will serve well. But don't leave your students on this lower rung on the ladder; be sure to scaffold them up to more difficult kinds of text.[12]

Remember that summarizing is a set of skills and that the first step in any skills teaching is modeling (Chapter 8). This means that the teacher needs to demonstrate summarizing for the children often. The most common way to do this is to "think aloud" as you summarize a short excerpt of text. For example:

Teacher: When I look at the third part of the Constitution, where all those things called "amendments" are, I think to myself: Self, these are really 27 of the same kind of thing, and that thing is called an amendment. Then, I remember from our discussion that *amendment* means change. So, my summary might be this: "The third part of the Constitution is a long list of the changes that have been made to the Constitution."

Using Children's Trade Books for Multiple Perspectives

Children's trade books have always been popular curriculum resources in elementary social studies education. For 25 years, one of the most interesting and active committees of the National Council for the Social Studies has been a joint committee of the NCSS and the Children's Book Council, called the NCSS-CBC Joint Committee. One project of the committee is the annual production of an annotated bibliography, "Notable Social Studies Trade Books for Young People." The list is eagerly awaited, appearing each spring in an issue of the NCSS journal, *Social Education.* (See also the website at *http://www.ncss.org.*)

The Joint Committee has always been clear about one very important point: If teachers are to teach social studies effectively, they need to "be familiar with children's books *and* know how to use them purposefully."[13] The books selected for these bibliographies "(1) are written for children in grades K–8, (2) emphasize human relations, (3) represent a diversity of groups and are sensitive to a broad range of cultural experiences, (4) present an original theme or a fresh slant on a traditional topic, (5) are easily readable and of high literary quality, and (6) have a pleasing format and, when appropriate, illustrations that enrich the text."[14]

But what is the unique contribution of children's trade books in social studies? Perhaps their most important purpose *in social studies* is (a) helping to launch a unit and, (b) once in the unit, helping children gather information from multiple perspectives.

LAUNCHING

You may recall from Chapter 7 that much hinges on how a new unit begins. Effectively launching a new unit means arousing the curiosity of students, assessing their present understandings, exploring with them some of the possibilities for study presented by the topic, and, in general, setting the stage for learning to take place. Children's trade books can help, especially when used in combination with dramatization. According to one of the most accomplished teachers we have witnessed, Paula Fraser in Bellevue, Washington, "Literature is a way to entice and engage students initially so they are motivated to discover the substance and the facts."[15] Another master, Tarry Lindquist, uses Scott O'Dell's *Sarah Bishop* (Houghton Mifflin, 1980) to launch a study with her fifth-graders of colonial life and the American Revolution. Tarry writes:

> I like this book because both boys and girls find it engaging. It does a good job of bringing out multiple perspectives about the Revolutionary War and provides a setting for the more historically driven information the students will need later to understand the Constitution and the Bill of Rights.[16]

Tarry integrates good literature instruction here, having students create a "storyboard" about the novel. Each student divides a 12″ × 18″ piece of white construction paper into 8 rectangles. She directs them to express their interpretation of the story by writing and drawing in each box, working in pairs, talking as they go:

- Title and student's name
- Main character
- Setting (time and place)
- Conditions before the problem
- The problem/antagonist
- Conflict
- Resolution
- Denouement, wrapping up loose ends.[17]

As pairs share their work, interpretations are juxtaposed; consequently, students' understandings are challenged and deepened. Tarry writes, "The hook is in, the kids care. Ready now to gather more factual information, we move to the textbook and other resources. . . ."[18]

PROVIDING MULTIPLE PERSPECTIVES

Sometimes, a single children's novel will contain multiple historical or cultural perspectives. Better still, however, if time permits, is to bring together two children's stories on the same topic. In this way, multiple perspectives are strengthened by multiple authors. By perspectives we mean viewpoints or interpretations: Children are helped to see events, both historical and current, from more than one angle, more than one vantage point. When multiple perspectives are examined routinely, as part of studying any event, a compare-and-contrast method of teaching and learning becomes a common classroom experience. Encouraged in this way—immersed in this literary apprenticeship—children will form the habit of looking at events from more than one angle. Our aim is that they become students who regularly ask, without prompting, "Have we examined all the relevant viewpoints? Is there someone we are ignoring? Are we imagining all the possibilities?"

This strategy has at least two important advantages over the single-perspective approach. First, any one perspective is prevented from being put forward, uncritically, as "neutral." When the English colonists' perspective on the American West is the only viewpoint that is studied, for example, then it does not seem to children like a perspective at all; rather, it seems to them to be simply the truth—the way it happened. Actually, different things happened, depending on who we talk with. If we were to talk to a conquered Apache Indian or the conquering U. S. cavalry general, we would get quite a different interpretation of what the English might call the "discovery of the New World." This is true of *any* event, from the Pilgrim landing at Plymouth to a fight on the playground, from the assassination of President Kennedy to the "surprise event" we staged as part of Lesson Plan 4 in Chapter 4.

This takes us to the second advantage of teaching with multiple perspectives, which is that children are brought into the actual work of historians: making sense of competing accounts. When children are apprenticed into this form of historical inquiry, they "begin to understand and appreciate differences in historical perspectives, recognizing that interpretations are influenced by individual experiences, societal values, and cultural traditions."[19] This is a valued form of higher-order thinking generally, and historical reasoning in particular. All our children should be helped to do it and to excel at it.

One children's trade book often represents one perspective quite well, sometimes brilliantly, going into considerable detail and providing rich contextual detail. When teachers use two (or even three) of these books, in combination with background information, primary sources, and maps, multiple perspectives can easily be brought to bear on the event. Using a data-retrieval chart (see Chapter 8), the perspectives can be organized for careful study and comparison. Through creative activities such as role playing, readers' theater, construction activities, simulation games, and the cooperative learning technique called Structured Academic Controversy (Chapter 11), children will deepen their understanding of the perspectives.

A teacher who wishes to use trade books in this way might implement the following procedure.

- Select a historical or current event that is related to curriculum goals.
- Browse trade books and other resources (film, artwork) to assemble two or three perspectives on the event.
- Read aloud or assist students in reading and discussing the resources.
- Incorporate dramatizations and other activities to help children comprehend the perspectives.
- Use a data-retrieval chart or other scheme to help children compare and contrast the perspectives on the event.
- Use roundtables, panel discussions, multiple storyboards, or other techniques to help children come to a conclusion, based on evidence, as to what happened, its meaning, and its consequences.

Here now are two brief examples of the multiple-perspectives approach using children's trade books. The first concerns immigration, now and long ago; the second involves European- and Native-American perspectives. A third example can be found in Lesson Plan 13 in Chapter 9, which uses the Collier brothers' *My Brother Sam Is Dead* and *War Comes to Willy Freeman*.

IMMIGRATION: THEN AND NOW, GRADE 3

Materials

Social studies text:	*Communities* (McGraw-Hill, 1999)
Trade books:	Laurence Yep's *Dragonwings* (Harper Trophy, 1989), Ann Morris's *Dancing to America* (Dutton, 1994)
Primary document:	U.S. Constitution

Cultural Perspectives

Immigration is a popular and important social studies topic. Since immigrants come from all over the world to the United States, and for diverse reasons, it is not difficult to help children study this phenomenon from multiple perspectives. The children's own family history should provide still another perspective.

Activity

This teacher spends an entire year on the theme "Immigration: Then and Now" with her third-grade class. The children learn from the textbook program about European and Asian immigrant communities. They build replicas of the Plymouth and Jamestown colonies and also Santa Fe, New Mexico. They compare and contrast the New York Harbor to the San Francisco Bay, to which Europeans and Asians, respectively, have come for entry to the United States. They read the citizenship rules in the Constitution. They focus especially on the Chinese men who immigrated to work on the railroads, listening to their teacher read *Dragonwings*, and on a family that recently came to American from the Soviet Union, listening to *Dancing to America*. They create a data-retrieval chart to compare Ellis Island and Angel Island immigrants' stories.

Note

Local immigrant communities may have organized speakers' bureaus. In any event, people who have immigrated are often quite pleased to be invited to share their stories, foods, and photos with the class. One of the children's parents might be willing to help.

EUROPEAN/NATIVE AMERICAN ENCOUNTERS, GRADE 1

Materials

Trade books: Speare's *Sign of the Beaver* (Yearling, 1994) and Bulla's *Squanto: Friend of the Pilgrims* (Scholastic, 1990).

Cultural Perspectives

European colonists arriving on the east coast of North America encountered not a new world but a very old one inhabited by millions of people belonging to many different cultures. Children's tendency to stereotype Native Americans—that is, to gloss over the differences among them—can be countered by presenting the differences straightforwardly using historical fiction. In this activity, the class contrasts two native men: the legendary *Squanto: Friend of the Pilgrims,* and the Native American at the center of Elizabeth George Speare's *Sign of the Beaver.* The latter is neither "savage" nor "friendly," and children learn something of his culture.

Activity

The teacher reads these stories aloud, stopping occasionally to have the children retell what they have heard so far. This lets the teacher assess their understanding and watch for what catches their interest. Eventually, students dramatize imaginary meetings between the two men in which they share stories of their respective cultures.

Note

Consider using both books as springboards for in-depth study on the two native cultures presented. Where exactly did they live? What kind of a place was it? How did they interact with the natural environment? Were they different from other Native American groups in the same geographical regions? What was their language? religion? law? medicine? family structure? shelter? food? education? economy?

Conclusion

We will turn our attention more directly to writing in the next chapter, where we present a rich and engaging way to integrate reading and writing instruction with social studies subject matter: Working in teams, children create an original, multichapter biography of a pivotal historical figure.

In the present chapter, we emphasized that reading and writing are best thought of as a common enterprise. Readers make meaning when they comprehend text in much the same way that writers make meaning when they compose text. The skills involved in summarizing probably make this point most clearly, for to write a summary of a reading selection has as much to do with reading carefully as it has to do with writing carefully. And both are about thinking. Meanings are constructed by the child's own intellectual labor—his or her own construction activity. The quality of this labor will depend on the child's own intellectual resources working in combination with a skillful coach—a teacher—and a well-planned curriculum.

Our second emphasis was that children do not make meaning in a vacuum; children read and write to accomplish goals. That's where the social studies curriculum comes in. Here they read and write to build and express social studies understandings and to improve their ability to read and write. It sounds circular because it is. The two are interdependent.

Discussion Questions and Suggested Activities

1. If social studies textbooks are written for the average reader, why do all good social studies textbooks tend to be difficult for the average reader?
2. Select a children's social studies textbook and examine it to find examples of instruction on the reading skills listed in Figure 12–1. On what other skills is instruction provided in the textbook?
3. Choose one of the reference materials listed in Figure 12–2. What skills should a child have to use that reference effectively? List them and select one. Then, use the skill-teaching strategy provided in Chapter 8 (Lesson Plan 11) to plan a lesson on that skill.
4. What does the following statement mean: Previewing is a method for acquiring prior knowledge "on the spot."
5. Select an era of United States history and identify two or three trade books that bring different perspectives to bear on that era.

Selected References

Au, Kathryn H. (1993). *Literacy instruction in multicultural settings.* Fort Worth: Harcourt Brace.

Campbell, Kay, & Knight, Richard S. (1991). Reading research and social studies. In James P. Shaver (Ed.), *Handbook of research on social studies teaching and learning* (pp. 578–588). New York: Macmillan.

Kozol, Jonathan. (1986). *Illiterate America.* New York, Penguin.

Lipson, Marjorie Y., & Wixson, Karen K. (1991). *Assessment and instruction of reading disability.* New York: HarperCollins.

Notable social studies trade books for young people. (1999, May/June). *Social Education, 63,* 1–16.

Resnick, Lauren B. (1990, Spring). Literacy in school and out. *Daedalus, 119,* 169–85.

Wineburg, Samuel S. (1999). Historical thinking and other unnatural acts. *Phi Delta Kappan, 80,* 488–499.

Zarnowski, Myra, & Gallagher, Arlene F. (Eds.). (1993). *Children's literature and social studies: Selecting and using notable books in the classroom.* Washington, DC: National Council for the Social Studies.

Notes

1. Lauren B. Resnick, Literacy in school and out, *Daedalus, 119* (Spring 1990): 183.
2. Marjorie Y. Lipson & Karen K. Wixson, *Assessment and instruction of reading disability* (New York: HarperCollins, 1991).

3. See the influential study of coached practice, also known as "scaffolding," by Annemarie Sullivan Palinscar & Ann L. Brown, Reciprocal teaching of comprehension fostering and monitoring activities, *Cognition and Instruction* 1: 2 (1984): 117–175.

4. Resnick, Literacy in school and out, 169–185.

5. Howard Gardner, *The disciplined mind* (New York: Simon & Schuster, 1999).

6. The pledge was recognized by the federal government during World War II, in 1942. In 1954, during President Eisenhower's administration, the words "under God" were added by Congress.

7. Gardner, *The disciplined mind.*

8. *The United States and its neighbors* (New York: McGraw-Hill, 1995), 372.

9. Walter C. Parker & Samuel A. Perez, Beyond the rattle of empty wagons, *Social Education, 51* (March 1987): 164–66.

10. William E. Nagy, *Teaching vocabulary to improve reading comprehension* (Urbana, IL: ERIC Clearinghouse on Reading and Communication Skills, National Council of Teachers of English, and International Reading Association, 1988).

11. Valerie Anderson & Suzanne Hiki, Teaching students to summarize. *Education Leadership* (January, 1989): 26–28.

12. Ibid. See also Anne Brown & Jeanne D. Day, Macrorules for summarizing texts: The development of expertise. *Journal of Verbal Learning and Verbal Behavior* (1983), 22(1): 1–14.

13. Myra Zarnowski & Arlene F. Gallagher (Eds.), *Children's literature and social studies: Selecting and using notable books in the classroom* (Washington, DC: National Council for the Social Studies, 1993), vii.

14. Notable children's trade books, *Social Education, 59* (April/May 1995): 212.

15. Quoted in Tarry Lindquist, *Seeing the whole through social studies* (Portsmouth, NH: Heinemann, 1995), 89.

16. Ibid, 88.

17. Ibid, 172.

18. Ibid, 89.

19. National Council for the Social Studies, *Curriculum standards for social studies* (Washington, DC: Author, 1994), 22.

Websites

http://www.ncss.org/resources/notable/home.html

http://www.ncss.org

13

Social Studies as the Integrating Core

Main Idea

Integrated education is a strategy (a means or tool), not a goal. Used as a strategy, it can enrich a lesson or unit, deepen students' understanding, and help students construct a powerful kind of idea called a unifying generalization. Two approaches to curriculum integration are presented—*infusion* and *fusion*—and each is exemplified in detail.

Key Concepts

strategy, goal, integrated education, infusion, fusion, unifying generalization

Chapter Outline

- Making Sense of Curricular Integration
- Two Approaches: Infusion and Fusion
- An Infusion Example: Composing Cooperative Biographies
- A Fusion Example: Understanding Living Things
- Conclusion
- Discussion Questions and Suggested Activities
- Selected References
- Notes

Chapter Snapshot

Ms. Trafford wanted her third-grade students to understand something very important: *Decisions made by human beings influence the survival of other living things.* This idea was so big and complex that it would require the integration of two of the third-grade subjects at her school: science and social studies. This was the only large idea-construction project she would attempt before the winter vacation, so she pulled out all the stops and developed a unit using her most powerful teaching strategies: concept formation, inquiry, and decision making.

 A favorite website http://educate.si.edu/spotlight/ The Smithsonian Institution's expansive website contains this gem where brief biographies can be found on inventors (Ben Franklin), Native Americans (Pocahantas), and social reformers (Lucretia Mott).

This is the second unit-planning chapter in this book and an extension of Chapter 7. We would have placed it directly after that one, but it would have been incomprehensible; for this chapter on integrated units utilizes the intervening chapters on teaching strategies (8), resources (9), assessment (10), cooperative learning (11), and literacy (12). Integrated education, done well, is difficult. As one colleague said to us, "It's like deep-frying foods at home: easy to do badly, hard to do well." This is, then, a culminating chapter. Its contents integrate much of the material presented in the preceding chapters.

Making Sense of Curricular Integration

In Part One of this book, social studies education was defined as the integrated study of the social sciences to promote civic competence. Helping children construct powerful social understandings and take seriously the responsibilities of democratic citizenship are the basic goals of social studies education. A vision this important to society and this basic to the well-being of our students can easily serve as an *integrating core* for much of the teaching and learning that goes on in elementary and middle schools.

We must begin by clarifying the concept *integrated* education or, as it is often called, *interdisciplinary* education. These terms mean many different things to different teachers. Compare the following meanings.

- By integration, some teachers mean that their reading and writing, literature, and art and music instruction are focused on social studies subject matter. When they teach students to use "context clues" as aids to comprehension, for example, they are using a primary document, such as the journals of Lewis and Clark or the Declaration of Independence; or they are using the social studies textbook or a selection of historical fiction. When they teach literary concepts such as plot, theme, character, narrative, fiction, poem, and biography, they are using social studies materials. When they teach composition (persuasive writing, journaling, report and letter writing), the subject matter is drawn from the social studies curriculum. They teach color, value, and shape in paintings that represent the historical era or geographic place under study. The same goes for the rhythm, melody, and lyrics of songs. In this way, social studies objectives are the horses pulling the wagon (so to speak); they are the curricular center of gravity pulling all the other objectives toward the same integrating core.

- Others mean that a powerful theme—a *concept* really—such as exploration, has been selected as the centerpiece of the curriculum, whether for a unit or the entire year. The teacher then orients social studies, science, language arts, and math toward this concept. Explorers of new places (Marco Polo, Meriwether Lewis, Sally Ride) are studied alongside explorers of new ideas (Confucius, Galileo, Jefferson) and perspectives (Leonardo, Mozart, Picasso). Reading and writing instruction, art and music, and drama are infused into these studies. Mathematics may be included as well.

- For still others, integration means that a different kind of theme—not a concept but a generalization—has been selected as the centerpiece. Generalizations, as we will see, are larger than concepts for they *combine* and *synthesize* concepts. For example, *animals adapt to their environments* (from biology) or *the family is the fundamental social environment in most cultures and the source of the most basic socialization* (from sociology), or *the decisions of human beings influence the survival of other living things* (from both social studies and science). Needless to say, generalizations are abstract. Therefore, a large amount of subject matter, often drawn from more than one school curriculum area, and a tremendous amount of intellectual labor and guidance are needed to construct them.

These three meanings do not exhaust all the possibilities of "curriculum integration," "interdisciplinary education," or "integrated education," but they help display the variety of examples within this concept.

DEFINITIONS

To understand integrated or interdisciplinary education, one must first understand the idea of the scholarly "disciplines," which are fairly distinct bodies of knowledge and methods of constructing that knowledge. Anthropology, for example, is the discipline concerned with accumulating a body of knowledge (facts, concepts, generalizations, and issues) about people's culture and customs. Anthropologists' preferred method of building this knowledge is ethnographic fieldwork. Biology, sociology, political science, literature, history, and archeology are other distinct bodies of knowledge and methods.

The disciplines, according to psychologist Howard Gardner, "represent the formidable achievements of talented human beings, toiling over the centuries, to approach and explain issues of enduring importance. . . ."[1] The disciplines are, he stresses, "indispensable in any quality education," and he urges educators not to abandon disciplinary education in the name of integrated education. "The disciplines represent our best efforts to think systematically about the world, and they are prerequisite to competent interdisciplinary work," he continues.[2] Integrated education is not "better," therefore, than nonintegrated education any more than a shovel is better than a hammer. It all depends on the goal to which these tools are put. Compare now these definitions:[3]

> *Discipline:* An integrated body of teachable knowledge with its own key concepts and generalizations, issues, and methods of inquiry. Quoting Howard Gardner again, "The scholarly disciplines represent concerted efforts by individuals (and groups) over time to address essential questions and answer them. . . ."[4]
>
> *Interdisciplinary or Integrated:* A curriculum approach that purposefully draws together knowledge, perspectives, and methods of inquiry from more than one discipline to develop a more powerful understanding of a central idea, issue, person, or event. Note that the purpose is not to eliminate the individual disciplines but to *use* them in combination. Wise teachers do not hide the disciplines from students any more than farmers hide their seeds, shovels, and plows from their apprentices. Quite the opposite, they call the disciplines by their proper names and teach children about them—their ideas and methods of inquiry.

PITFALLS

Integrated education has numerous shortcomings that must be understood if they are to be avoided. These range from causing confusion (rather than providing clarity and power) to trivializing learning (turning teachers' attention to unimportant topics). Watching out for these pitfalls, teachers can steer integrated education clear of the extremes and toward high standards of quality.

Ends and Means

The greatest pitfall regarding curriculum integration is to treat it as a goal. Curriculum integration is a strategy, not a goal. Like a pencil, it is a tool that has little value in itself; what matters is how, when, and where it is used. In other words, curriculum integration is not an end in itself; it is neither good nor bad on its own. It *may* be good, but this depends on the worthiness of the goal toward which it is directed. It may be a skill or process goal, such as learning and applying the inquiry method. It may be a content goal, such as learning why American colonists rebelled against England or understanding that the decisions made by human beings influence the survival of other living things. "The most basic of all principles is goal relevance," write two scholars who have closely examined social studies learning activities. "Each activity should have at least one primary goal that, if achieved, will represent progress toward one of the major social education goals that underlie and justify the social studies curriculum."[5]

Either/Or Thinking ("Putting All the Eggs in One Basket")

This error involves the assumption that either a discipline-based curriculum or an interdisciplinary curriculum is the right thing to do. Neither is true. Both are needed, but at different times and for different purposes. It is important to exercise professional judgment, using each when appropriate. This is the eclectic approach—the middle way—and it is often the best course.

Trivializing Learning

While discipline-based education compartmentalizes knowledge for the purpose of studying it, thoughtful teachers know that interdisciplinary education can create its own problems. It is particularly susceptible to trivializing the curriculum. This occurs when unimportant content is selected for instruction simply because it can be integrated easily with other content. Meanwhile, important content that may not lend itself to integration goes untaught and, soon, integrated education is associated in the public's mind with low-quality education. *The point to remember is that a learning activity that crosses disciplinary boundaries is not necessarily worthwhile.* What makes an activity worthwhile is that students are forming or extending a powerful understanding or skill. As psychologist Jerome Bruner put it years ago, "The first object of any act of learning, over and beyond the pleasure it may give, is that it should serve us in the future. Learning should not only take us somewhere; it should allow us later to go further more easily."[6]

Confusion

Interdisciplinary education needlessly confuses learners when teachers require them to study simultaneously topics that more fruitfully could be examined separately. Imagine students trying to study three cultures' customs, literature, art, and scientific achievements all at the same time. The loss in analytic clarity and the increased difficulty would not justify the gains hoped for by integrating social studies, literature, art, and science. Experts in a field—craftspersons and connoisseurs and scholars and gifted readers, etc.—do not attempt to tackle a problem by focusing their attention on all its parts at once! That would make the problem a tangled knot. John Dewey advised, wisely, that we limit a topic for study in such a way as to avoid what he called "the great bad." This is "the mixing of things which need to be kept distinct."[7] Experts limit the problem they are working on; they analyze it and break it into its component parts. They do this to understand the big picture better and, therefore, to know where they most profitably might begin chipping away at the problem.

> Disintegration, then, can be helpful. It can also be needlessly fragmenting. Knowing how and when to separate topics to clarify them and knowing, on the other hand, when to integrate them is a major achievement of skillful teaching.

We should not train students to study a topic by making a jumbled mess of it. Readers may remember the clear plastic overlay illustrations often found in biology textbooks. These made it possible to achieve a sort of layered understanding of the human body. Readers are permitted to focus only on the skeletal system, or only on muscle tissue or major organs, and then to lay these systems on top of one another to examine the whole picture and the interaction of parts. Similar transparent overlays are found in some student atlases. The child can look at the African continent with only the national boundaries marked in or overlay this with a physical map showing the deserts, savannas, and mountain ranges. Then they can add another overlay showing major cities. *Dis*integration, then, can be helpful. It can also be needlessly fragmenting. Knowing how and when to separate topics to clarify them and knowing, on the other hand, when to integrate them is a major achievement of skillful teaching.

A Little Bit of This, a Little Bit of That

Closely related to the pitfalls of trivializing the curriculum and confusing the learners is what one expert calls "the potpourri problem,"[8] which occurs when a unit is composed of bits of information from each discipline. If the subject is the Mayan civilization, for example, we could find a bit of history, a bit of art, a bit of science, a bit of math, but not the proper depth in any of these to make the study meaningful and coherent. Better to help children dig into Mayan history in depth than to "superficialize" learning in the name of integrated education.

Two Approaches: Infusion and Fusion

If the pitfalls are to be avoided, then what is to be done? We divide the various approaches to curriculum integration into two groups, which we call *infusion* (helping) and *fusion* (synthesizing). Both can be useful tools for achieving important curriculum objectives. Let us spend some time distinguishing between the two, and then we will provide in depth a powerful example of each.

INFUSION

The first approach to curriculum integration is the *infusion* approach. Aspects of one subject area, such as language arts, are inserted or infused into a second to enhance the learner's grasp of the second. One subject area is in the role of helper, and the other is being enriched. This is by far the most common kind of curriculum integration. One or more objectives in one subject area are being achieved thanks to material borrowed from another.

In social studies, the most common use of the infusion model is, appropriately enough, when reading and writing skills are brought to the service of social studies goals. Children cannot read *reading* or write *writing,* after all; these are means, not ends. Skillful teachers of social studies link literacy instruction to social studies goals and, in this way, give literacy skills purpose and meaning while helping to achieve social studies goals. This means that children are using reading and writing, which are among the most powerful of learning tools, to achieve social studies curriculum objectives. Two things are accomplished: Skills are used to help achieve valued content goals, and the skills themselves are strengthened by being engaged with content. The "helper" is being strengthened in the course of helping.[9]

Examples of infusion can be found throughout this text. Turn back, please, to the Table of Contents and find, at its end, the list of Lesson Plans. Turn to Plans 1–15 and locate the "Integration" heading at the end of the plan. There you will find an example of infusion. Most often, literature (children's trade books) is used to enrich one or more social studies objectives. Sometimes it is art or music that is helping; other times it is science or mathematics. But *helping* is the role. When you look to the top of the lesson plan at the objectives, they are social studies objectives. Here now are additional examples of infusion.

- Use the concepts *plot* and *character* from children's literature to analyze a social event such as the American Revolution, the Underground Railroad, the Civil Rights Movement, or a current event in the children's hometown.

- Use historical paintings along with concepts drawn from the fine arts to study major events in American history, such as Howard Chandler Christy's depiction of the signing of the U.S. Constitution; Marcia Sewall's illustrations of the native people, the Wampanoag, whom the Pilgrims encountered at Plymouth, in her book *People of the Breaking Day* (Antheneum, 1990); and Jacob Lawrence's paintings of the migration of African Americans from the South to the North after World War I in *The Great Migration* (HarperCollins, 1995).

- Use ideas and skills from mathematics, such as estimation and figuring proportions, to project population trends at the time when the children in the class will graduate from high school.

- Use acting techniques from theater arts to help children dramatize the Underground Railroad, Paul Revere's ride, or the journey of Lewis and Clark.

FUSION

An alternative approach to curriculum integration is the *fusion* model. Now, two or more subject matters are joined together—synthesized—*in such a way that a new, unified idea is formed.* There is no sense, as in the infusion model, that subject matter A is helping subject matter B, or vice versa; rather A and B are fused to produce something new: C. C is a powerful idea (sometimes a *concept,* but more often a *generalization*) that requires for its proper development in children's minds information from more than one subject area. Consider, for example, the concept *living things.* This idea is made more powerful when it includes *human beings* as well as what the science curriculum will call *flora* and *fauna* (plants and animals). Similarly, the concept *communities* is strengthened when comprised not only of human communities around the world but plant and animal communities as well (such as old growth forests, ant colonies, and schools of fish), even the communities of planets called solar systems.

Generalizations are bigger and more complex ideas than concepts. Generalizations are two or more concepts combined into a meaningful statement. The generalization *The decisions of human beings influence the survival of other living things* links several concepts together: decisions, human beings, influence, survival, and living things. Because generalizations are relationships between two or more concepts, they are summarizing statements that have wide applicability. Generalizations are *generally* true: Scientific investigation has proven that in most cases the statement is not contradicted by the facts.

To learn a generalization, teachers and students sometimes have to draw information and concepts from more than one subject—from science and social studies, for example. That is clearly the case with the generalization we are working with: *The decisions of human beings influence the survival of other living things.* This is the fusion type of integration: Bring subjects together so that a big, complex idea (that is worth learning!) can be built. Below are additional examples of fusion:

> This is the fusion type of integration: Bring subjects together so that a big, complex idea (that is worth learning!) can be built.

- Fusing social studies and science subject matter should help children learn the procedures and dispositions of the *scientific method*—that is to say, the *inquiry process.* Two powerful concepts included in the scientific method are *hypothesis-testing* and *evidence.* To form either concept thoroughly and to learn the inquiry process, children will require examples from the social sciences (e.g., geography, history, anthropology) as well as the natural sciences (e.g., biology, geology, chemistry).

- A unified understanding of the voyages of Columbus can help children understand this as a turning point in human history that is far more complex and important than the story of a single explorer and his conquests. The exchange of plant life, animal life, and disease between the Eastern and Western Hemispheres that resulted from these voyages changed the world forever. Cultures and customs were exchanged, to be sure, but so were seed packages (called *biota* by biologists). Smallpox and horses were brought from Europe to America; corn and sugar were taken from America to Europe. "Seeds of Change" is what the Smithsonian Institution called the event, and to appreciate that title one has to crawl inside both the social studies and the science of the event.

As these examples show, the objective of the fusion approach is to help children build big, complex ideas that cannot be built adequately without joining together two or more subject areas. In other words, the idea children are helped to construct is a *unifying whole* that has a character and significance different from the sum of its parts.[10]

Still, the fusion approach is not superior to the infusion approach. More is not better. Some ideas, whether concepts such as *prejudice* or *community helpers* or generalizations such as "scarcity limits people's ability to have all they want and need," may not be strengthened and may only be confused by fusion. Just because subject areas *can* be integrated on a topic or idea is not in itself a reason to do so.

OVERVIEW

Now we provide two powerful examples in considerable depth, one of infusion and one of fusion. Neither are lessons; both are units.

The example of *infusion* is a popular one that is used successfully by teachers across the United States and Canada to help children write, with teammates, original biographies of major historical figures: great citizens, social activists, heroes, villains, scientists, writers, inventors, kings and queens, explorers, labor leaders, and presidents. The essence of this approach is that reading and writing skills are applied (infused) into social studies teaching and learning.

The *fusion* example provided next is a unit that joins (fuses together) social studies and science curricula to help children build a deep understanding of a particular generalization. The generalization in the sample unit is *The decisions of human beings influence the survival of other living things.* The unit is taught today by third-grade teachers in Northglenn, Colorado.

An Infusion Example: Composing Cooperative Biographies

Reading and composing biographies is an elegant and authentic way to infuse language arts and literature instruction into the history curriculum. The reading of biographies is what we called "absorbing" history or "learning about" history in Chapter 4. (Recall the two wings of the airplane: absorbing treasured historical stories is one wing of the history learning airplane, and creating such stories oneself, from primary and secondary sources and artifacts—*doing* history—is the other wing. Neither wing alone will suffice in history learning.) In this cooperative biography unit students will both absorb biographies of the selected historical figure and then *compose,* with teammates, an original biography of this same figure.[11] In this way, they are using historical reasoning, interpreting sources, wrestling with competing eyewitness accounts, and deciding what story to tell about this person's life and times. They are *being* historians.

Our example will feature Sojourner Truth, the 19th-century social activist who fought against the institution of slavery and then for women's rights. Ample biographical material about Ms. Truth can be found in most school libraries and social studies textbooks, making it feasible for teachers to teach children about her and help them to write original, brief narratives of her life and times.

Sojourner Truth was first "sold" when she was nine years old, probably in the year 1807. She had been born into slavery in New York to a Dutch man named Hardenbergh, so that became her name, too—Belle Hardenbergh. When she was nine, John Neely became Belle's new owner. He paid $50 and got both the Dutch-speaking African girl and 100 sheep. Two years later, after learning some English and suffering beatings at the hands of the Neely family, she was sold again, this time for $105 to Martin Schryver, who had a farm near the Hudson River. In 1810, Belle was sold yet again. Her new master, Mr. Dumont, wrote in his ledger, "For $300, Belle, about 13 years old, six feet tall." Years later, with the help of Quakers, Belle won her freedom and chose the name Sojourner Truth. It was a good handle for the life she was about to live: a seeker and speaker of truth.

Her speeches attracted great crowds and are today among school children's favorites. For example, in May of 1851, she attended a women's rights convention in Akron, Ohio. Before she or any of the other women could speak, Protestant ministers—all male—dominated the proceedings. They derided the women who wanted social reform. Francis Gage later wrote this eyewitness account of what happened after the ministers were finally through:

Then, slowly from her seat in the corner rose Sojourner Truth, who, till now, had scarcely lifted her head. She moved solemnly to the front, laid her old bonnet at her feet, and turned her great speaking eyes on me.

There was a hissing sound of disapprobation above and below. I rose and announced, "Sojourner Truth," and begged the audience keep silence for a few moments.

The tumult subsided at once, and every eye was fixed on this almost Amazon form, which stood nearly six feet high, head erect and eyes piercing the upper air like one in a dream. At her first word there was a profound hush. She spoke in deep tones, which, though not loud, reached every ear in the house and away through the doors and windows:

"Well, children, where there is so much racket, there must be something out of kilter. That man over there says women need to be helped into carriages and lifted over ditches—and to have the best place everywhere. Nobody ever helps me into carriages or over mud-puddles—or gives me the best place at the table!"

Raising herself to her full height, and lifting her voice to a pitch like rolling thunder, Sojourner asked, "And ain't I a woman? Look at me! Look at my arm!" She bared her right arm to the shoulder, showing her tremendous muscular power. "I have ploughed and planted and gathered into barns, and no man could get ahead of me! And ain't I a woman?

"I could work as much and eat as much as a man—when I could get it—and bear the lash as well! And ain't I a woman?

"My mother bore ten children and saw them sold off to slavery, and when I cried with my mother's grief, none but Jesus heard me! And ain't I a woman?

"Then that little man in black says women can't have as many rights as men. If the first woman God ever made was strong enough to turn the world upside down all alone, these women together" (and she glanced over the platform) "ought to be able to turn it back and get it right side up again! And now that the women are asking to do it, the men better let 'em."

Long cheering greeted this. "I'm obliged to you for hearing me," she concluded, "and now old Sojourner hasn't got nothing more to say."[12]

Sojourner had much more to say. When she wasn't speaking for women's rights, she was speaking against slavery. And after President Lincoln ended slavery, Sojourner worked in Washington, DC—"Mr. Lincoln's city"—to overcome the remnants of slavery: virulent racism and deeply entrenched prejudice. She tried to help freed Africans find work and homes, and she worked for a time as a nurse in Freedman's Hospital. These were chaotic, heartbreaking times. The Civil War, in which her son fought in the famous 54th Massachusetts Regiment, became a slaughter on both sides. And just as it ended, Lincoln, whom she had met and much admired, was killed by an assassin.

Still, she was not defeated. One of our favorite biographers for children, Jeri Ferris, writes of yet another of Sojourner's efforts to right wrongs:

> One afternoon as Sojourner walked back to the hospital with an armful of blankets, she was so tired she just couldn't walk any more. Horsedrawn streetcars clanged up and down the road, filled with white folks. Sojourner waited for a car to stop, but none did. Finally, as yet another car passed her, she called out, "I want to ride!" People crowded around, the horses stopped, and Sojourner got on. The conductor was furious and demanded she get off. Sojourner settled back in her seat. "I'm not from the South," she said firmly. "I'm from the Empire State of New York, and I know the law as well as you do."
>
> The next day she tried to ride another streetcar. Again the conductor would not stop. Sojourner ran after the car and caught up with it. When the horses stopped, she jumped on. "What a shame," she panted, "to make a lady run so." The conductor threatened to throw her off. "If you try," she said, "it will cost you more than your car and horses are worth." He didn't.
>
> The third time Sojourner tried to ride a streetcar, she was with a white friend. "Stand back," shouted the conductor to Sojourner, "and let that lady on."
>
> "*I* am a lady too," said Sojourner, and she stepped aboard with her friend.[13]

WRITING ABOUT HISTORICAL FIGURES

We provide this brief sketch of the life and times of Sojourner Truth so that readers can better follow the procedure we now outline for guiding children to produce biographies themselves. The creation of an original biography is a splendid way to invite children to read, write, and discuss their way into an in-depth understanding of a historical figure. Not only are their horizons expanded and their historical reasoning encouraged by this exposure to lives different from their own, but their skills in reading, writing, revising, planning, and co-operating are developed along the way.

The names of the historical figures on the list that follows are a small sample of the persons whose lives and times warrant in-depth study by elementary and middle school children. Readers might notice that the persons listed could all serve as examples of *democratic citizens.* In the spirit of the teaching strategy called concept formation (Chapter 8), teachers can select three or four persons who together would help children to form the concept of *democratic citizen.* The class could write three or four biographies during the school year, keeping track of the similarities among these citizens—similarities that make them all examples of democratic citizens:

- They knew that popular sovereignty is the bedrock of democracy and that this means taking personal responsibility for the common good.
- They took time from their private lives to be active in civic life.
- They understood the difference between complaining and proposing solutions.
- They understood, within the constraints of their times, that democracy means majority rule *and* minority rights.
- They exhibited courage on behalf of these principles.

Biographies of Democratic Citizens

James Madison	Abraham Lincoln
Susan B. Anthony	Jane Adams
Thomas Jefferson	Mary McLeod Bethune
Benjamin Franklin	Gordon Hirabayashi
Eleanor Roosevelt	Patrick Henry
George Washington	Martin Luther King, Jr.

Democratic citizen is not the only concept around which subjects can be selected for biographies, though it is one of the most important. Other central ideas are *explorers, inventors and scientists, champions of the poor, friends of nature, leaders, dictators, revolutionaries,* and *heroes.* Recall that the discussion of concept learning in Chapter 8 emphasized multiple examples. Here this means that a teacher might orchestrate children's biographical studies around one of these themes, having them produce over the year three or four biographies on that theme rather than one each on different themes. This approach should help children to build an in-depth understanding of that theme. On the other hand, teachers might, to cover more ground, mix the kinds of subjects about whom their students write, for example, choosing a hero (Crazy Horse or Harriet Tubman), an inventor (Benjamin Franklin or Eli Whitney), a scientist (Galileo or Newton), and a great citizen (Sojourner Truth or James Madison). Figure 13–1 suggests several themes and related subjects.

PROCEDURE FOR PRODUCING BIOGRAPHIES

The teacher will need to plan the several phases of the biography project:

1. Decide on the learning objectives.
2. Select the person about whom children will write their biographies.
3. Introduce the project to students, clarifying the objectives, rationale, and audience.
4. Help the children learn about the person and keep track of what they are learning.
5. Help children reflect on the person's life and times and identify key events in the person's life.
6. Orchestrate the cooperative production of biographies in small groups.
7. Conclude the project.

OBJECTIVES

The learning objectives or targets for this project will vary with the curriculum, the teacher, the students, the local community, and the person about whom the children will write. Generally, however, the following objectives are pertinent. Note that skills, knowledge, and habits of mind are targeted.

FIGURE 13–1   Examples of thematic clusters of persons suitable for cooperative biographies.

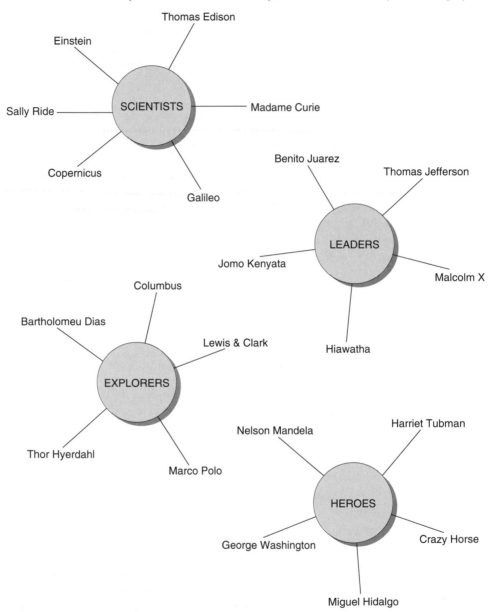

As a result of producing a historical biography with teammates, the students will learn to:

1. Understand that people's lives are shaped by history and that the way they lead them shapes the history into which the next generation is born.

2. Use the writing process to compose and publish a biography.

3. Recognize the genre of literature called *biography* and organize and present biographies they compose.

4. Work cooperatively in small groups to which they have been assigned.

5. Understand that a variety of reference sources are needed to assemble an understanding of the life and times of a person because different sources—both "primary" and "secondary" (see Chapter 4)—provide different information and perspectives.

6. Make sense of competing accounts of an event that they find in diverse resources and compose a fair-minded account of that event.

7. Construct time lines of a person's life.

Not all of these objectives need to be addressed to the same extent. The class may have achieved some before the project begins; others may come in a subsequent biography project. Teachers should select objectives that are developmentally appropriate for the children in the class and that can feasibly be achieved given the constraints of time and available materials. Still, this list displays the impressive array of objectives for which the biography project is suitable. Teachers may wish to include the following objectives as well:

8. Determine which events in a person's life are turning points (milestones, pivotal events).

9. Understand how a person's geographical setting(s) may have influenced his or her life.

10. Examine character traits in a historical figure's life and draw lessons for one's own life.

11. Empathize with others' dilemmas and struggles.

12. Make books.

13. Illustrate a section of narrative using charcoal pencil.

SELECTING A SUBJECT

Several criteria guide the selection of subjects for children's biographies. Most important is that the person chosen brings children into contact with powerful ideas of history, government, geography, economics, and other social studies disciplines. This study can not only help children build understandings but also bring them to the heart of social studies and build firm foundations for further learning.

Another criterion for subject selection is the likelihood that children will be captivated by this life. It may help some children become more interested in the person if information is available on his or her childhood. Ben Franklin's early troubles with his brother James, for example, James Madison's illnesses as a child, and Sojourner Truth's harrowing childhood all seem to fascinate children, broadening their experiences by giving them access to *other* children's lives—lives that are different but reassuringly similar, too. Learning a great deal about a person can itself make that person captivating to the young biographer. As this third-grade student quite wisely reported, one cannot know for certain what makes a subject interesting. He seems to conclude, however, that familiarity breeds interest, not contempt:

> Everyone else was real interested in Hiawatha but I wasn't because, well, the things I knew about him just were boring. But the more I found out, the way they learned to hunt and stuff in the long house, and all the magic, well it got real interesting. Now I know him a lot.

A third criterion is the availability of materials. The "snapshot biography" method we outline here requires students to learn a great deal about the subject.[14] If the subject is obscure, chances are good that neither the textbook nor the school library will have ample books, primary documents, narrative biographies, or other materials.

Consider how Ms. Brem, a fourth-grade teacher, selects biographical subjects. She has decided to weave a yearlong study of *leadership* through the state history curriculum her school district requires in that grade. She wants her pupils to study and eventually write biographies of three state leaders. She wants the leaders to be culturally diverse, and she wants them to expose students to different historical periods and geographical areas of the state. Now Ms. Brem begins her materials search. A booklet she received last year from the state arm of the League of Women Voters provides information on several civic leaders, and she asks a committee of students to select one for the class to study. The social studies education office at the state capital publishes material on the state's governors; Ms. Brem selects the state's first governor. Now she has selected two of the three subjects she needs. Since they are both European Americans, Ms. Brem wants the third leader to belong to an ethnic minority.

Unaware of who this might be or where materials can be obtained, she appoints another student committee to go to the school librarian for help. The librarian refers them to information on a civic leader who helped to organize the early Chinese-American community in the state. Now the class has a set of three leaders and is ready for the reading-and-writing approach to biographical study.

INTRODUCING THE PROJECT

On the day the biography project is introduced to students, the teacher should have in mind five purposes: assess, activate prior knowledge, provide purpose, provide rationale, and identify the audience. First, the teacher will need to diagnose what the children already know about biographies and what sense they make of the notion of a person's "life and times." A few informal assessment questions should accomplish this task (see Chapter 10's opening example with Mrs. Rivera). It is assumed here that the teacher has assessed previously the children's reading and writing ability and knows something of their home cultures, special needs, and prior experiences. Second, based on this brief diagnostic assessment, the teacher can further draw out the children's knowledge and experience. A semantic map might be created on the chalkboard (see Chapter 12), and the school librarian can be invited to discuss biographies with the children.

Third, the teacher should reveal clearly the objectives or targets of the project. These may be posted on the bulletin board and explained. Fourth, the teacher should help the children understand *why* these targets need to be reached—why they are important. For example, it is important to study historical biographies because they can introduce us to amazing new worlds and help us avoid mistakes made in the past. It is important to learn to cooperate in small groups to which one has been assigned because this mirrors realities in the workplace and civic life. Finally, the teacher should help the children identify an audience for their biographies. For example, if they have recently visited the residents of a rehabilitation center, they may wish to write the biographies for this audience and take them personally to the center. Or they may wish to write them to members of the city council, encouraging them to be wise and fair-minded leaders.

LEARNING ABOUT THE SUBJECT OF A BIOGRAPHY

Before children can begin to write about a biographical subject, they need to learn something about that person's life. Let us be clear, however, that the learning sequence is not read, then write. Rather, it is write a little drawing on prior experience and then find out a little by reading, viewing a film, or listening to taped speeches. Write some, learn a little more, write some more, and so on. One of the major advances in the science of instruction in the past 10 years is that teachers do not have to provide all of the facts *before* asking students to think. The advice instead is to integrate data gathering and reflection; the revision process is used to correct prior errors as the writing and learning proceed. The teacher should concentrate student attention on the higher-order task, in this case production of the biography, which in turn motivates gathering facts about the subject and interpreting his or her life.

Accordingly, students begin learning about the subject, such as Sojourner Truth, by finding out a little something about her. Perhaps the teacher begins by reading aloud for just 20 minutes from Jeri Ferris's book, concentrating on the beginning of the story when Sojourner is taken from her mother and sold to Mr. Neely at the age of nine. Then the teacher asks the children to discuss this passage—the idea of buying and selling persons, in this case a child. She asks them to imagine the feelings of Belle on the auction block and the feelings of her mother and father. She may ask them what they have learned elsewhere about the enslavement of people. Perhaps some of them will talk about the Jews in Egypt in biblical times. Some may have seen the old movie about Spartacus; perhaps some will talk about the Holocaust. Some children may know quite a bit about the capture and subsequent ownership of Africans through books they have read or lessons they have had in prior grades or in church. The discussion will provide the teacher with diagnostic information about children's current knowledge of slavery while activating the students' prior knowledge.

Now the teacher can ask students to bring out their journals and begin to write. She may ask them to write about the same things she previously asked them to talk about, which should be the easiest for them. Then she might ask them to predict what will happen to Sojourner in her new master's home. This should make them want to gather more information. Where will they get it?

The teacher knows that Sojourner's life with Mr. Neely is documented in the textbook. So, the next day she has children take out their journals to remind themselves of the predictions they wrote yesterday. Then, they are given 20 minutes to read the pertinent section in the text and return to their journal to write what really happened. Next, the teacher turns student attention to the map of the Northeast in the textbook and, based on clues given in the passage read aloud yesterday and the text passage today, helps them to find the state where Sojourner first was bought and sold (New York). In their journals, she has them enter the date and sketch a map of New York under the title, Where Sojourner Truth's Story Begins.

Now that they know where the story began (the geographic theme *location*), students are helped to get a feel for New York (the geographic theme *place*). Their teacher has them go to their cooperative teams and, working with the textbook, answer these questions:

1. What states, countries, and bodies of water border New York?
2. Is the geography of New York all the same, or are there different landforms? If so, what are they?

3. If Sojourner were able to fly away from the Neely farm, which route would have the fewest mountains to fly over?

The teacher then tells students to sketch all of this on a blank handout map of New York, including a legend so readers can understand their symbols.

The next day, the teacher reads aloud Virginia Hamilton's retelling of the folktale, *The People Could Fly.* A wonderfully hopeful tale, though at the same time tragic, it tells of enslaved people literally flying from bondage to freedom:

> They say the people could fly. Say that long ago in Africa, some of the people knew magic. And they would walk up on the air like climbin' up on a gate. And they flew like blackbirds over the fields.[15]

But when the people were captured for slavery, we learn in the tale, they shed their wings. The slave ships were too crowded for wings. A few, however, kept the power. "Toby" did, and he used it to help the others to escape. One day Sarah was hoeing and chopping as fast as she could, a hungry baby on her back, but the baby "started up bawling too loud." The Overseer hollered at Sarah to keep the baby quiet, but Sarah fell under the babe's weight and her own weakness. The Overseer began to whip her. "Get up, you black cow," he called. Sarah looked to Toby: "Now, before it's too late," she panted. "Now." Toby raised his arms and whispered the magic words to her. "Kum . . . yali, kum buba tambe."

> Sarah lifted one foot on the air. Then the other. She flew clumsily at first, with the child now held tightly in her arms. Then she felt the magic, the African mystery. Say she rose just as free as a bird. As light as a feather.[16]

Afterward, students return to their journals to reflect on this new material. The teacher continues over the next two or three weeks to read aloud from biographies and other accounts of Sojourner Truth, as well as from related stories and reference material. Student committees are sent to the library to gather data on people, places, events, and issues raised in the teacher's readings that students want to find out more about. The teacher also assembles some material for the students to read themselves—material in the textbook on Lincoln's decision to free the slaves and material on influential abolitionists: Frederick Douglass, who escaped from slavery in the South; William Lloyd Garrison, who published *The Liberator,* an abolitionist newspaper; and the Grimké sisters, Angelina and Sarah, who moved north after having been raised with captive Africans on a South Carolina plantation. This information helps to elaborate the children's understanding of Sojourner's life, as well as her civic missions, and should lead to their producing much stronger, richer biographies.

For this reason, information on the women's movement of the 1800s also needs to be gathered, such as the Seneca Falls Convention convened by Lucretia Mott and Elizabeth Cady Stanton in 1848. This is the same movement Sojourner jolted with her "Ain't I a Woman?" speech, delivered three years later at a second women's rights convention.

The setting for all this information needs also to be grasped; consequently, students should study the geography of New York, Ohio, and Michigan—the three states where Sojourner spent much time working, speaking, and living. In this way, students learn about the subject of their biography and gradually piece together in their minds a model of Sojourner's life and times.

REFLECTION AND SETTING PRIORITIES

After several weeks of reading, writing, and mapping their biographical subject's life, children are ready to reflect on this life and its times and places and to select key events. A few of these events will become the focal points of the chapters in the book students will write together. The following procedure is recommended.[17]

1. *Opening.* The teacher announces that today the class begins to pull together all they have learned about the subject and informs students of what is to come.

2. *Brainstorming.* The teacher asks students to brainstorm all the events in the subject's life that they found interesting, all the events they believe were pivotal in the subject's life, all the events they figure made the subject the most and least proud, and so on. The point here is to get a long list of varied events in the subject's life. Here are just a few of the events in Sojourner's life that students have suggested.

   - The time she was separated from her mother
   - The second time she was sold
   - The third time she was sold
   - Confronting Mr. Dumont
   - Rescued by Quakers
   - Names herself Sojourner Truth
   - "Ain't I a Woman?" speech
   - Meeting President Lincoln
   - Working as a nurse in Washington, DC
   - Confronting the trolley conductor
   - Meetings with Garrison and Douglass

   When the brainstorming slows, the teacher has students take a break—go to recess, clean the room, do something physically active. When they return, they open their journals and search for other events to add to the list. They come up with more:

   - Being born in captivity
   - Speaking out for women's rights
   - Becoming an abolitionist
   - Living in New York
   - Traveling by buggy in Ohio

3. *Selecting.* The class is now asked to select four or five of the key events brainstormed earlier. These might be the four events that interested students the most, or the teacher might direct them to use other criteria. For example, if the teacher previously has worked with children on constructing and interpreting time lines, she or he might have them divide Sojourner's life into four equal segments and choose one event from each segment. Or, the teacher might have them choose one event in each of several categories that make particular sense with the person being studied. In the case of Sojourner Truth, these categories might be life in slavery, meetings with remarkable people, and life as an abolitionist. Still another criterion would have

students select events that are turning points—pivotal events. The point is that they must make selections and set priorities. This is what every historian has to do. "No historian tries to write a 'complete' account and no one would have time to read one."[18] Children, who are beginning historians and beginning writers, definitely should not try to do more than an experienced writer-historian would attempt.

Once the key events have been selected, the children are placed in cooperative groups of four or five members. Each group is directed to divide the events among themselves, each choosing one event. Dividing the events—and thus the labor—is crucial to the coming task: producing an original biography.

WRITING AND ILLUSTRATING

The students are now ready to write and illustrate a biography of their subject. Each cooperative group will produce a biography on the same subject, in this case Sojourner Truth. Some teachers have each group use the same biography title, *The Life and Times of (Sojourner Truth)*. Others let each group create its own variation on this title.

Each person on the team is responsible for one chapter. The chapter's topic is the key event selected before. If the teacher wishes, he or she can use the cooperative groupwork technique called Jigsaw (see Chapter 11). One member of each small group is working on the same key event as one child on each of the other groups; consequently, these children can meet together to work on their chapter, discussing, sharing, and revising one another's drafts. Thus, the book may shape up like this:

Title: *The Courage and Conviction of Sojourner Truth*

Chapter 1: "Sold for 50 Dollars!"

Chapter 2: "New Name, New Life"

Chapter 3: "Ain't I a Woman?"

Chapter 4: "The Trolley Incident"

The child on each team who is responsible for Chapter 1 joins with other children from other teams also working on "Sold for 50 Dollars!" Meanwhile, the child on each team responsible for Chapter 2 joins with the other "2s," and so on. These are *expert groups*. Together they discuss what they will write and draw, read one another's drafts, and provide feedback. This is advisable with younger children who are just beginning to write early versions of paragraphs; the group support is helpful, and the teacher can more easily monitor and coach the four expert groups than if every child in the room were writing on a different topic.

Whether the teacher uses the Jigsaw technique or not, the children's work has two parts: They write a description of the key event for which they are responsible, and they draw an accompanying illustration. The least experienced writers may produce only a one- or two-paragraph description and may fit their illustration on the same page. The teacher may press more experienced writers, however, to produce a two- or three-page description. The illustration is embedded in the text somewhere as in "real" biographies. Skillful teachers are able to boost their children's confidence about both writing and drawing by encouraging them

FIGURE 13–2
An example of a cooperative
biography final product.

to "just get started, get something on paper, pull something together from your journal, whatever; we'll go back and polish it later." (Teachers and children who play the board game *Pictionary* understand that illustrating is very different from producing realistic drawings. Virtually anyone can illustrate.)

Each team thus produces the rudiments of a biography: a title page and four chapters. But real biographies have more, and so should these. The following parts of a book make a more complete biography, and even the youngest children generally can do them all:

Title Page

Title plus complete publication information, for example: *The Life and Times of Sojourner Truth* (see Figure 13–2).

Foreword

Written by someone other than the four authors; for example, a parent, another teacher, the mayor, a school board member, a bus driver. Instruct the Foreword writer to write no more than one page and to address two matters:

1. Tell readers some ways you feel you can relate personally to the person about whom the biography was written.
2. Tell readers something about the book.

Introduction with Time Line and Map

The introduction should contain a brief message to readers telling them the subject of the book: Who is its subject? Where and when did he or she live? What, in a nutshell, did he or she do? Why? It is also considerate to tell readers the topic of each chapter. A helpful way to portray the *when* is to sketch a time line of the subject's life. The *where* statement should be illustrated with a map, either physical or political, or both, with a legend to help readers understand the symbols.

Chapters 1–4

Each chapter needs a title and author name. Its body is a written description of a key event in the subject's life with an illustration that captures the key event.

About the Authors' Page

Ask each child to write a sentence or paragraph about her- or himself. The teacher might ask each group to decide how long the author statement should be. Children can be prompted to tell readers their full name, the name of the city or town where they live, their age, and something they like to do:

> Wing Luke lives in Denver, Colorado, with his family. He is 9 years old and loves to play soccer. He wrote Chapter 4, "The Trolley Incident."

CONCLUDING THE PROJECT

Time should be set aside for drawing the biography project to a close after the books have been completed. The biographies need to be copied so that one can be placed in each child's portfolio. A self-assessment checklist, similar to the one shown in Figure 10–10, might be completed by each child and clipped to his or her copy. Details concerning the delivery of the books to the audience identified at the beginning of the project need to be discussed. A committee could be appointed for this purpose. A concluding discussion focusing on the objectives of the project should follow. Focus questions such as the following, each matched to an objective, will be helpful:

1. What have you learned about how history shaped Sojourner Truth's (or name of other person studied) life, and about how her life shaped the history into which the next generation was born?

FIGURE 13–3   Literacy research emphases, then and now.

Early Research Emphasis:	Current Research Emphasis:
Reading and writing instruction are separated.	Reading and writing instruction are integrated.
Both are separated from content learning.	Both are developed within content learning.
Reading and writing are fixed abilities that, like muscles, are the same everywhere.	Reading and writing ability evolves like a craft and mirrors the local literacy community.
Reading and writing are finished products.	Reading and writing are complex processes.

2. What have you learned about writing?

3. What is a biography? Who would you like to read about next?

4. At which cooperative skill do you excel?

5. What have you learned about locating resources in the library?

6. What was difficult about writing a fair-minded account?

7. How would you describe a time line to a younger student?

SUMMING UP: THE CHANGING CONCEPT OF LITERACY

Biography writing infuses literacy instruction and practice into the social studies curriculum. By embedding literacy instruction in social studies content *and* cooperative group-work, the teacher creates the kind of social context that can support in-depth learning. Reading comprehension and writing instruction become much more than plodding through new vocabulary and learning sentences and paragraphs in a vacuum; literacy comes to mean problem solving, interpretation, competing interpretations, conversation, provocation, writing, and rewriting to find out what one thinks is true and what one believes ought to be done, and experimenting with new possibilities that exist now only in the imagination. This is "high" literacy.

Reading and writing are processes—more precisely, *crafts*—that evolve through trial, error, and support from those more accomplished. This process-oriented notion of literacy learning is different from what research told us only 20 years ago.[19] Then, it was quite common to define literacy as a finished product: You either had it or you didn't; you were "literate" or "illiterate" (see Figure 13–3).

This emphasis on process is changing the way highly skilled teachers orchestrate literacy instruction. They understand that an individual's reading and writing skills grow and change over time. One's literacy is not static; it evolves, and its evolution depends on the individual's social context—his or her "literacy community." All of us belong to one sort of discourse community or another, and that membership socializes us into one or more patterns of using our minds—of reading, writing, and talking.

The biographical approach is, of course, only one way to enrich literacy instruction, but it is a powerful and feasible one. The noted biographer Milton Meltzer observed that the biography approach is a vehicle for developing children's natural curiosity about people and the world around them to the point where they themselves investigate a particular life and, through the artful use of language, tell that human story to others.[20]

A Fusion Example: Understanding Living Things

We turn to an example of another approach to curriculum integration, the fusion model. Now two subject areas are tapped because the construction *of a particular idea* requires it. The idea in the following example is that living things are interdependent. Put differently, *the decisions made by human beings influence the survival of other living things.* Recall that this idea is a generalization: a statement that meaningfully links two or more concepts. The main concepts we address in the unit are decision making, living things, and what they need to survive. Both the generalization and the concepts that compose it are made stronger by reference to subject matter that is conventionally found in the science curriculum and other subject matter found typically in the social studies curriculum. These subject matters are fused in this unit so that the big idea can be developed.

This unit is part of an integrated social studies/science curriculum called *Explore.*[21] It is a K–6 program; accordingly, there are many units like the one featured here—similar, that is, in the way that subject matters are fused to help children build a powerful idea. *Explore* was developed by curriculum specialists and teachers working in Northglenn, Colorado, along with the late Sydelle Seiger-Ehrenberg, a renowned curriculum planner in the Hilda Taba tradition[22] and specialist in higher-order thinking, particularly concept formation. Working with Seiger-Ehrenberg was elementary school principal, Dr. Pat Willsey. The two believe that integrated units of this kind (fusion) can help children form complex ideas *by* engaging them in higher-order thinking. Without this higher-order thinking, the children will not be able to form or integrate the concepts, thereby constructing the big idea.

The general goal statement for the entire K–6 *Explore* program makes explicit this relationship between curriculum integration and higher-order thinking:

Explore Curriculum Goal

As a result of using thinking strategies and other relevant skills, K–6 students will develop an understanding of the orderliness, diversity, relationships, and changes that exist and are created in the natural world and in human experience. Further, they will learn to make intelligent, responsible decisions and plans in light of each understanding.

PLANNING A FUSION UNIT: INGREDIENTS AND PROCEDURE

Teachers who wish to plan a fusion unit should find this unit from *Explore* a helpful model. Its ingredients include many of the most important material in the prior chapters of this book:

- Sets high expectations for achievement.
- Engages children in inquiry and concept formation so that subject matter and higher order thinking are blended.
- Provides assessments that are challenging and geared to what was taught.
- Incorporates citizenship education—decision making, values, and community action.
- Expects children to use the textbook as a data source.
- Includes carefully planned focus and follow-up questions.
- Fuses important material from two subject areas to help children construct a powerful and unifying idea.

The procedure for planning a fusion unit is not etched in stone. What follows is a very basic procedure that should help teachers get started. The planning form shown in Figure 7–2 may be helpful.

1. *Identify a unifying concept or generalization that is also important and powerful.* "Kites are colorful and ride the wind" is a unifying generalization that could potentially integrate science (aerodynamics) and social studies (production, consumption, and distribution), but it is not important or powerful enough to warrant much school time. The prior chapters of this book, the work of curriculum standards committees, and teachers' own subject matter expertise will suggest generalizations that are critically important for children to develop: For example, *in the following unit example, the unifying generalization is: The decisions made by human beings influence the survival of other living things.*

2. *Identify the component concepts.* The teacher needs to examine the unifying generalization and identify the concepts that compose it. For example, *In the following unit, the key concepts are decision making, living things, and survival. Another key concept is the scientific method (inquiry process), because this is how children will build the unifying idea.*

3. *Plan a sequence of learning activities that will help children construct the unifying generalization.* Each lesson plan should have an objective and a focus question that anchor the activity to the overall unit goal, which is to help children build the generalization. For example, *In the following unit, the objective and focus question are given at the beginning of each of the four lessons.*

4. *Select teaching strategies that will help children achieve lesson objectives.* Concepts are sure to be the focus of one or more lessons, because generalizations are composed of concepts. Therefore, one or more concept teaching strategies will be relevant (see Chapter 8). Likewise, because the scientific method is featured, strategies for teaching children to inquire scientifically will be relevant (again, Chapter 8). For example, *In the following unit, the concept-formation and inquiry strategies are the chief, though not the sole, teaching strategies.*

What follows are the four lesson plans in Unit 1 of the third-grade *Explore* curriculum.

When a field trip, such as this one to a park, is placed inside an inquiry unit, such as *Explore*, then students are not merely visiting the park, they are gathering data and testing hypotheses.

1. The first lesson introduces children to "the scientific way of learning"—that is, the inquiry method. Note that the assessment asks children to classify a number of activities, selecting the ones that represent the scientific method.

2. The second lesson helps children form the concept *living things*. Note the use of the data-retrieval chart, the concept formation procedure, and classifying.

3. The third lesson helps children form the concept *survival needs* of living things.

4. The fourth develops the decision making and social action component of the unit: Students become aware of and committed to individual and group actions that help living things meet their needs and reach their potential. The result should be that children have constructed an initial understanding of the unifying idea, *The decisions made by human beings influence the survival of other living things.*

Lesson Plan 16

EXPLORE: UNIT 1, LESSON 1: WHAT IS THE SCIENTIFIC WAY OF LEARNING?

Objective

Students will become aware of the general inquiry procedure they will be following this year to study science and social studies topics.

Focus Question

What is the scientific way of learning?

Learning Activities

Students are told that this year they will be studying science and social studies "as if all of you were scientists." They are then placed in pairs to discuss the question, "From what you know, what does it mean to be a 'scientist'? What does a scientist do?"

As students share their responses, the teacher often asks *verification* questions, especially the central question of science, *How do you know that's true?* This becomes a common question in *Explore* classrooms. Eventually, the teacher presents the following four-step procedure on a chart.

The Scientific Way of Learning

Step 1—Question

Step 2—Hypothesize, Predict

Step 3—Investigate

Step 4—Analyze/Evaluate Data, Conclude

The teacher then puts the following list on the board:

Some Things Scientists Investigate

What plants need to grow

What the stars and planets are made of

How people in communities get along with each other

What the dinosaurs looked like

How people lived long ago

How people live now

What happens when you mix certain chemicals

How we know about weather and climate

After making sure that the class understands each item on the list, the teacher asks students what they know about each topic *as a result of scientists investigating it.*

The teacher then asks the students to go back over the list and name the kind of scientist that investigates some of these things. For example, "What do people call a scientist who investigates stars and planets? life in human communities? how people lived long ago? dinosaurs?" It is not important that students learn all the names of scientists, but that they realize, first, that there are different types of scientists and, second, that social studies stems from the work of *social* scientists.

To review, the teacher then says, "As you study science and social studies this year, you will be working just like the scientists we have been talking about. What does that mean? What will you be doing? What are the four things we said all scientists do?"

Assessment 1

The teacher displays a list of activities related to airplanes and says to students: "Suppose we were going to study airplanes and how they fly, and I told you that you would be working like real scientists. Which of the things on this list would you expect to be doing?"

1. Make up a story about airplanes.
2. Find some facts about airplanes and how they fly.
3. Ask questions about airplanes and how they fly.
4. Draw a picture of an airplane.
5. Describe a trip you took on an airplane.
6. Try to think of possible answers to your questions about airplanes and how they fly.
7. Build a model of an airport.
8. Keep looking for more facts about airplanes to see if the answers to your questions are right.

Assessment 2/ Homework

The teacher reviews the four-step procedure and then shows students a rock, leaf, shell, or similar item, giving them this task: "Suppose you were a scientist and had never seen anything like this before. What would you do to investigate it? Be prepared to tell us what you would do, how, and why."

■　　■　　■　　■　　■

Lesson Plan 17

EXPLORE: UNIT 1, LESSON 2: WHAT IS TRUE OF ALL LIVING THINGS?

Objective

Students will develop the concept *living things* in terms of both the characteristics common to all living things and those that distinguish living things from nonliving things.

Focus Question

What is true of all living things that distinguishes them from nonliving things?

Learning Activities
Step 1: Question

The teacher introduces the lesson: "First we are going to study living things and how they are *alike*. Since we're going to work as *scientists*, what is the first thing we need to do to study living things?" The teacher then reviews the chart, "The Scientific Way of Learning," now focusing on the topic, Living Things and How They Are Alike.

Step 2: Hypothesize

Student attention is focused on the question, "How do we know whether something is or is not alive?" The teacher points to the second step in the four-step procedure and asks students what they need to do after they have asked a question: Come up with possible answers. Then the teacher repeats the question, and students hypothesize. The teacher elicits responses, helping students to explain what they mean and writes them on a chart:

We *think* something is alive if it has these characteristics:

_____

_____

_____

_____

_____

_____

The teacher emphasizes that students should give the information they *think* is true. Later they will investigate to find out which of their present ideas are correct. After a few characteristics are placed on the chart, students work in pairs to come up with additional responses.

Step 3: Investigate   The teacher helps children move to Step 3 of the scientific procedure: "As scientists, what is our next step?" Students should respond that they need to *investigate*, that is, find new information to check the accuracy of what they have put on the chart and find out what else belongs on it. They may ask, "How can we find the kind of information we need?" At this point *Explore* takes students through a detailed introduction to their textbooks and other references where relevant information might be found. This amounts to teaching students how to *use* their textbooks as an information source (see Chapter 12).

Once students are familiar with information sources, they are ready to investigate, to test the characteristics they have listed on their charts. *Explore* uses the concept formation strategy, discussed in Chapter 8. The teacher says, "To test our ideas, let's investigate several living things and find out whether the things we have listed are true of all of them." Each child is given a data-retrieval chart (see Figure 13–4).

In pairs, using the reference books they just studied, students gather the information each question requires for each living thing on the chart. Pairs then report their work to the whole class, and the teacher uses a class-size retrieval chart to record their work. A transparency of the student chart placed on an overhead projector works well.

Step 4: Analyze Data/Conclude   The teacher guides students through the concept-formation strategy as a way of making sense of all the data by drawing it together into a concept. "Let's see what all this information tells us about all living things. First, what do you see is true of some living things but not

FIGURE 13–4 Data-retrieval chart.

LIVING THINGS					
List from chart	Bird	Tree	Fish	Cactus	Person
Moves? How?					
Grows? For how long?					
Changes? In what ways?					
Reproduces others like self?					
Needs food? What kind? From where?					
Needs air?					
Needs water?					

of others?" Here the teacher is eliciting *differences* among the examples. Then students are directed to focus on *similarities*. "What do you find is true of *all* living things, regardless of what kind?" After this, students are asked to compose a conclusion, or *summary:*

We know something is a living thing if it:

_____

_____

Writing a Conclusion

Students write a paragraph explaining what living things are, giving examples and telling how they differ from nonliving things.

Classifying

Continuing the fourth step in The Scientific Way of Learning, students are helped to push their understanding of the concept still further. The teacher has them test their conclusion and at the same time identify the characteristics that distinguish living from nonliving things by having students inspect a nonliving thing—a cloud, an airplane, popcorn, fire, or a balloon.

The teacher says, "Let's consider something nonliving, like a cloud. What answers do we get to each question on our chart when we ask it about a cloud?" Later, "Based on the information we now have about a cloud, what about it could make it *seem* like a living thing?" and, "What is true of all living things that is not true of a cloud and proves it is not a living thing even if it moves?" This classifying activity is repeated with airplane, popcorn, fire, and balloon.

Labeling

Students should be introduced to the term scientists use as a synonym for a living thing: *organism.*

Review

Students are helped to review *how* they learned what distinguishes living from nonliving things.

Assessment

The teacher prepares a bulletin board with two sections, one marked LIVING THINGS, the other NONLIVING THINGS. Students are directed to bring in a magazine picture or drawing of something that belongs in each section. Each student should be prepared to tell the class the characteristics that make each item belong in one category or another.

■   ■   ■   ■   ■

Lesson Plan 18

EXPLORE: UNIT 1, LESSON 3: WHAT DO ALL LIVING THINGS NEED TO SURVIVE?

Objective

Students will develop a concept of the needs of all organisms.

Focus Question

What do all living things need to survive and develop as they should?

Learning Activities

Now that the children have developed the concept *living things,* Lesson Plan 18 is designed to help them build another idea at the heart of the unit generalization: the *needs* of living things. Again, the concept-formation strategy and a data-retrieval chart are used. The same living things are listed across the top of the chart as in the prior lesson (see Figure 13–5), but point out to students that the questions running down the left side of the chart have changed.

FIGURE 13–5 Data-retrieval chart.

			NEEDS OF LIVING THINGS			
Question	Bird	Tree	Fish	Cactus	Person
1. Does the organism need *food* to live? What kind? Where and how does it get its food?					
2. Does the organism need *water* to live? What has to be true of the water? Where and how does it get water?					
3. Does the organism need *air* to live? What has to be true of the air? Where does it get air?					
4. Where does the organism usually *live?* What other organisms live there? How do the organisms live together?					
5. What can *harm* the organism? How does the organism stay safe from harm and disease?					
6. What is the organism *able to do?* What sometimes prevents the organism from doing this? What helps the organism do all that it is able to do?					

Numerous library resources and the science and social studies textbooks are used by children to gather this information. Using the concept-formation strategy, the teacher helps them draw all the data together into a concept. "Let's see what all this information tells us about the *needs of* all living things. First, what do some living things need but others do not?" Here the teacher is eliciting *differences* among the examples. Then students are directed to focus on *similarities.* "What do you find that *all* living things need, regardless of what kind?" After this, students are asked to compose a conclusion, or *summary.*

"We know that all living things need:

_____ .

The teacher helps them conclude that the needs of living things include:

    Proper nutrition

    Clean air and water

    Sufficient light and warmth

    Protection from enemies and disease

    Opportunity for the organisms to reach its potential

Writing a Conclusion

Assessment

Students write a paragraph explaining what the needs of living things are, giving examples.

The teacher and class listen as several students read their conclusions aloud. The teacher clarifies and asks for revisions as needed.

■   ■   ■   ■   ■

Lesson Plan 19

EXPLORE: UNIT 1, LESSON 4: WHAT DECISIONS DO PEOPLE HAVE TO MAKE?

Objective

Students will develop an awareness of and commitment to individual and group action that ensures that living things can meet their needs for survival and development.

Focus Question

What decisions and plans do people have to make to see to it that living things have what they need to survive and develop?

This lesson moves children from conceptualizing the attributes of living things (Lesson Plan 17) and what they need to thrive (Lesson Plan 18) to human action on their behalf.

    Attributes of living things → Needs of living things → Human action

There are two learning activities in this lesson.

Learning Activities

The first learning activity in Lesson Plan 19 has students consider cases where threatening conditions are putting living things at risk by making it difficult or impossible for them to get what they need. Students are then helped to suggest courses of action that might improve the situation.

Sample situations:

    1. There has been a very heavy snowfall. All the food and water for birds and deer have been covered with snow for several days, and the animals can't get to any.

2. It has not rained for weeks. The farmers are worried because their crops are not getting enough water.

3. People who picnic near the lake have been throwing junk into it for years. Much of this junk is harmful to the fish, insects, birds, and plants that live in or near the lake.

Students discuss these situations in small groups of three and recommend courses of action. Two focus questions guide their work on each case:

1. Which living things would have trouble surviving if no one did anything to change the situation? Explain why they would have trouble surviving.

2. What could people like you and me do so that the living things in this situation could survive? Explain how each suggestion would help the living things survive.

The second learning activity has children gather data on situations in which the needs of living things are threatened *and* in which people took specific actions that helped living things meet their needs. The teacher assembles reading materials about such people and invites them to class from the community. After gathering and recording data about them, students use the concept-formation strategy to compare and contrast these people and their specific actions. Finally, they return to the courses of action they suggested in the first part of the lesson, revising and adding ideas for action based on the information they gathered about real situations.

Assessment   The children make posters summing up what they have learned. Each poster addresses three questions, and children are encouraged to address them however they want:

1. What are living things?

2. What do living things need?

3. What have humans done to help other living things meet their needs?

■   ■   ■   ■   ■

Conclusion

The fusion model of curricular integration does not have one curriculum area help another achieve its objectives, as in the infusion model, nor does it simply join two or more subject matters, taking "a little bit of this and a little bit of that." *The joining of subject matters is not even the goal.* (Remember, curriculum integration is a strategy, not a goal.) Rather, as *Explore* illustrates, the goal of the fusion model is to help children build a powerful and unifying *idea.* This idea cannot be constructed without joining material that is traditionally assigned to separate school subject areas, and it requires higher-order thinking to form and integrate the constituent concepts. In this way, curricular integration is made goal-relevant, and that goal concerns something vitally important and empowering for children: the development of a powerful idea that they can then carry with them "in their heads" into new experiences, both in school and out. In the *Explore* unit here, that big idea was the generalization, *The decisions made by human beings influence the survival of other living things.* By the third lesson, the children had constructed a rudimentary notion of two of the constituent concepts (*living things* and *survival needs*), and they were ready to explore what actions humans can and are taking to help other living things thrive.

With the two approaches to curricular integration presented in this chapter, infusion and fusion, teachers have two promising tools with which they can launch integrated units of their own. One is not better than the other, in our judgment. Infusion, as we saw it in the cooperative biography unit presented in this chapter and as suggested in Lesson Plans 1–15 in this book, is frequently the more appropriate of the two models. It all depends on the goal at hand.

Discussion Questions and Suggested Activities

1. Compare and contrast the infusion and fusion approaches to curriculum integration. Infusion, recall, is by far the most common model, and it is possible that readers have never seen a fusion unit. Is one better than the other? Of what other approaches are you aware? Three meanings of integrated education were given at the beginning of this chapter. Which of them is an example of infusion? Of fusion? (We judge the first to be infusion, the third to be fusion, and the second to be unclassifiable on the basis of the information given.)

2. Design an array of biography "book" formats. What form could first-graders' books take? How about fifth-graders'? See the accordion-style "autobiography" book in Chapter 4.

3. In the infusion example—the biography writing project—which literacy skills will need to be taught explicitly to children? Will they already be familiar enough, for example, with *writing process* techniques such as *revision*? Should instruction on *revision* be planned? It is important in the infusion approach that children know how to use the skills they are expected to apply. One way to think through this problem is to develop a scoring guide for use with the cooperative biographies (see Chapter 10). Once you have identified the performance criteria, you can *diagnose* your students' knowledge and ability prior to beginning the unit and thereby determine which subject matter needs direct instruction and which subject matter is ready to be applied. Our experience suggests that the concepts *biography* and *primary source* will need direct instruction along with the skills of revision, illustration, and cooperative groupwork.

4. Review the *Explore* curriculum. Then, add a fifth lesson to the four-lesson unit that was described. Select one of the following topics as its focus, then write an *objective* and a *focus question* and sketch the needed learning activities. Remember that fusion units help children form big ideas *by* engaging them in higher-order thinking; accordingly, your activities will need to engage children's minds.

   • Careers involving the study or protection of living things
   • International comparison of living things and their needs
   • An organism's "potential"
   • Biographies of one or more people studied in Lesson Plan 19
   • Community service related to actions suggested in Lesson Plan 19

5. With a classmate, sketch a fusion unit using the four-part planning guide given in the chapter. Make it appropriate to a specific grade level and its conventional subject matters. (*Explore* does this by marrying the third-grade social studies emphasis on communities with the third-grade science emphasis on living things.) You'll need to identify a unifying generalization and its component concepts. Then plan the sequence of learning activities and determine the teaching strategies.

Selected References

Alleman, Janet, & Brophy, Jere. (1993, Oct.). Is curriculum integration a boon or a threat to social studies? *Social Education, 57,* 287–291.

Calkins, Lucy McCormick. (1994). *The art of teaching writing.* Portsmouth, NH: Heinemann.

Case, Roland. (1994, Winter). Our crude handling of educational reforms: The case of curricular Integration. *Canadian Journal of Education, 19,* 80–93.

Gardner, Howard. (1999). *The disciplined mind.* New York: Simon & Schuster.

Jacobs, Heidi Hayes. (1989). *Interdisciplinary curriculum: Design and development.* Alexandria, VA: Association for Supervision and Curriculum Development.

Lindquist, Tarry. (1995). *Seeing the whole through social studies.* Portsmouth, NH: Heinemann.

Lockledge, Ann, Porter, Pricilla, & others. (1993, Sept./Oct.). Articles on the integration of mathematics and social studies in *Social Studies and the Young Learner, 6.*

Rutherford, F. James, & Ahlgren, Andrew. (1990). *Science for all Americans.* New York: Oxford University Press.

Valencia, Sheila V., & Lipson, Marjorie. (1998). Thematic instruction: A quest for challenging ideas and meaningful learning. In Tafy E. Raphael & Kathryn H. Au (Eds.), *Literature-based instruction: Reshaping the curriculum* (pp. 95–122). Norwood, NJ: Christopher Gordon.

Zarnowski, Myra. (1990). *Learning with biographies: A reading and writing approach.* Washington, DC: National Council for the Social Studies/National Council of Teachers of English.

Notes

1. Howard Gardner & Veronica Boix-Mansilla, Teaching for understanding in the disciplines—and beyond, *Teachers College Record,* 96 (Winter 1994): 199.

2. Howard Gardner *The disciplined mind* (New York: Simon & Schuster, 1999), 54. See also Sam Wineburg & Pam Grossman's *Interdisciplinary curriculum: A second look* (New York: Teachers College Press, in press)

3. Adapted from Heidi Hayes Jacobs, The growing need for interdisciplinary curriculum content, in *Interdisciplinary curriculum: Design and implementation,* ed. Heidi Hayes Jacobs (Alexandria, VA: Association for Supervision and Curriculum Development, 1989), 1–12. See also Nathalie J. Gehrke, Explorations of teachers' development of integrative curriculums, *Journal of Curriculum and Supervision,* 6 (Winter 1991): 107–117.

4. Gardner, *The disciplined mind,* p. 217.

5. Janet Alleman & Jere Brophy, Is curriculum integration a boon or a threat to social studies? *Social Education,* 57 (October 1993): 290.

6. Jerome Bruner, *The process of education* (Cambridge, MA: Harvard University Press, 1960), 17.

7. John Dewey, *The public and its problems* (Chicago: Swallow, 1927), 83.

8. Jacobs, The growing need, 2.

9. Judith A. Langer & Arthur N. Applebee, Reading and writing instruction: Toward a theory of teaching and learning, in *Review of Research in Education,* vol. 13, ed. Ernest Z. Rothkopf (Washington, DC: American Educational Research Association, 1986), 173.

10. Jerrold Coombs, *Thinking seriously about curriculum integration* (Simon Fraser University, Burnaby, British Columbia: Tri-University Integration Project, 1991), 2.

11. Myra Zarnowski, *Learning with biographies: A reading and writing approach* (Washington, DC: National Council for the Social Studies/National Council of Teachers of English, 1990).

12. Francis Gage's account was published in an antislavery journal and is reproduced in many biographies. (e.g., Edward Beecher Claflin, *Sojourner Truth and the struggle for freedom* (New York: Barron, 1987), 81–82).

13. Jeri Ferris, *Walking the road to freedom: A story about Sojourner Truth* (Minneapolis: Carolrhoda Books, 1988), 53, 55.

14. Zarnowski, *Learning with biographies,* Chapter 4.

15. From *The people could fly,* retold by Virginia Hamilton. In *Cricket, 15* (February 1988): 21–26.

16. Ibid.

17. Adapted from Zarnowski, *Learning with biographies,* Chapter 4.

18. Linda S. Levstik & Keith C. Barton, *Doing history: Investigating with children in elementary and middle schools* (Mahwah, NJ, Lawrence Erlbaum Associates, 1997), 5.

19. Glynda Ann Hull, Building an understanding of composing, in *Toward the thinking curriculum: Current cognitive research,* ed. Lauren B. Resnick & Leopold E. Klopfer, 1989 ASCD Yearbook (Alexandria, VA: Association for Supervision and Curriculum Development, 1989), 104–28.

20. Milton Meltzer, Foreword to Zarnowski, *Learning about biographies,* x.

21. *Explore curriculum,* developed and written jointly by Sydelle Seiger-Ehrenberg and School District no. 12, Adams County, Northglenn, Colorado, 1990. The material in this section is quoted or adapted from *Explore* curriculum documents.

22. Hilda Taba's work on concept development at San Francisco State University and in the Contra Costa school district is featured in Hilda Taba et al., *A teacher's handbook to elementary social studies: An inductive approach* (Reading, MA, Addison-Wesley, 1971).

Website

http://www.educate.si.edu/spotlight/

INDEX